CRUCIBLE OF REASON

Intentional Action, Practical Rationality, and Weakness of Will

KEITH D. WYMA

ROWMAN & LITTLEFIELD PUBLISHERS, INC.
Lanham • Boulder • New York • Toronto • Oxford

ROWMAN & LITTLEFIELD PUBLISHERS, INC.

Published in the United States of America
by Rowman & Littlefield Publishers, Inc.
A Member of the Rowman & Littlefield Publishing Group
4501 Forbes Boulevard, Suite 200, Lanham, Maryland 20706
www.rowmanlittlefield.com

PO Box 317
Oxford
OX2 9RU, UK

British Library Cataloging in Publication Information Available

Library of Congress Cataloging-in-Publication Data

Wyma, Keith David.
  Crucible of reason : intentional action, practical rationality, and weakness of will
/ Keith D. Wyma.
      p. cm.
  Includes bibliographical references and index.
  ISBN 0-7425-3537-1 (alk. paper) — ISBN 0-7425-3538-X (pbk. : alk. paper)
1. Act (Philosophy) 2. Hare, R. M. (Richard Mervyn) 3. Davidson, Donald,
1917– 4. Thomas, Aquinas, Saint, 1225?–1274. I. Title.
  B105.A35W96 2004
  128'.4—dc22   2004003842

Printed in the United States of America

♾™ The paper used in this publication meets the minimum requirements of
American National Standard for Information Sciences—Permanence of Paper for
Printed Library Materials, ANSI/NISO Z39.48-1992.

CRUCIBLE OF REASON

For R. M. Hare and Alasdair MacIntyre,
two masters who showed patience in
dealing with a troublesome journeyman

CONTENTS

ACKNOWLEDGMENTS

I wish to thank Alasdair MacIntyre for invaluable advice and criticism in helping me to conceive and produce this manuscript. Thanks also to W. David Solomon and the philosophy department at the University of Notre Dame for their valuable help and input. And to my parents, Richard and Janice Wyma, for their unflagging support from the very beginning. Lastly, my most heartfelt gratitude and admiration go to my wife, Tanya Hillier Wyma, for all her patience with me during the unbelievably long writing process, and for doggedly reading through the murk of drafts and revisions in her work as "the Inspector General of Clarity."

INTRODUCTION

It pains me to admit it, but the truth is that I have never been particularly good at being good. It is not that I have not realized what I ought to do, I have; I just characteristically have had difficulty following through and *doing* the things I have identified as what I ought to do. I have often found myself in the predicament of wanting to do, and doing, deeds that I did *not* want to do, in the sense that I judged them to be wrong.

Given my experience with this kind of predicament, then, I find myself quite struck by this story told by Socrates in Plato's *Republic*:

> Leontius, the son of Aglaion, was going up from the Piraeus along the outside of the North Wall [of Athens] when he saw some corpses lying at the executioner's feet. He had an appetite to look at them but at the same time he was disgusted and turned away. For a time he struggled with himself and covered his face, but, finally, overpowered by the appetite, he pushed his eyes wide open and rushed towards the corpses, saying, "Look for yourselves, you evil wretches, take your fill of the beautiful sight!" (439e–440a)

What hits me is the way Leontius did something that he both wanted to do—as expressed by his appetite—and judged that he ought not do—as shown by his disgust and resistance. Even as he looked his "fill of the beautiful sight," he angrily disapproved of that action. Leontius's experience resonates with me—I can recall many occasions when I felt similarly about my own actions—but it also has puzzled me. I can affirm that such things happen, yet I have had trouble understanding how. Would not Leontius's judgment that looking at the corpses was base and wrong imply that he intended not to look? But in that case, how is it that he seems to have intentionally

1

looked anyway? I have asked myself the same kinds of questions regarding my own actions.

Furthermore, this puzzling kind of action is not some aberration limited to Leontius and me. It seems to plague humanity generally; we even have a name for the problem. When someone acts in a manner similar to Leontius's or my actions, we say that she is exhibiting "weakness of will" or that she is experiencing "incontinence." Plato and his contemporaries called that experience *akrasia*, and Aristotle described the common perception of it as when a "person knows that his actions are base, but does them because of his feelings" (*Nicomachean Ethics* 1145b13). In what follows, then, I shall use all three terms synonymously.

Moreover, others also have shared my perplexity about weak-willed actions. Indeed, incontinent actions can pose a daunting riddle to systematic explanations of intentional action. I want to investigate the mystery surrounding weak-willed actions. So in this book, I shall put that riddle to three prominent intentional action theories—those of R. M. Hare, Donald Davidson, and Thomas Aquinas—and I shall weigh their answers for plausibility and explanatory sufficiency. But in order to do that, we must first set forth exactly what the riddle of akratic actions is. To that end, we need to start by clarifying which actions count as incontinent.

I.1 COMPONENTS OF INCONTINENT ACTION

The first required element in an incontinent action is that the person acting, the agent, must judge that what she does should *not* be done. Regarding that disapproval, it could be a judgment that the action is morally wrong, that it is evil or bad or base. Or the judgment could be that the action violates duty or is rationally inappropriate given the circumstances. In order to make this requirement adaptable to the different theories we shall investigate, I purposely keep the options open here so that what is needed is simply that, for whatever reason, the action is judged to be such as *ought not to be done*. Moreover, it seems not to matter whether this judgment is knowledge or merely belief. What does seem important is that the judgment be *sincerely* held and accepted by the agent, *as applying to herself*. If her judgment only expresses something like "Society or common morality tells me that I ought not to do *x*," rather than "*I* affirm that I ought not to do *x*," then an agent is not exhibiting weakness of will in doing *x* in spite of the judgment. However, given his resistance to looking and his anger at doing so, Leontius's action displays the kind of sincere, disapproving judgment that qualifies it as akratic.

Second, the agent needs to judge against her incontinent action even *while* she performs it. Leontius's action shows this trait well. It is not simply the case that Leontius acted while not knowing better, and *later* judged that his action had been wrong. He is disgusted and resistant as soon as he has the appetite to look. Nor does it seem that he only regarded the action as base *beforehand* and changed his mind when the opportunity and appetite to act arose. Given his angry words, Leontius apparently disapproves of his action *while* he performs it. That concurrence of the performance and disapproving judgment is crucial to the perplexity of Leontius's akratic action.

Third, in an incontinent action the agent must realize that the action that she is performing violates her judgment about what ought not to be done. For example, even if Oedipus judges that he ought not to kill his father, and kills his father, if he does not realize that the man he is killing *is* his father—that is, that this action violates his judgment—then, whatever kind of wrong Oedipus might be committing, it is not on this account an akratic action. However, it yet again appears that Leontius's action does count as incontinent, since he identifies his action as base and as conflicting with his judgment about what he ought to do.

Fourth, and related to the prior requirement, the incontinent action must be *intentionally* performed, and with the recognition that it is being done intentionally. If the agent acts contrary to her judgment about what she ought to do, but only, say, by accident or—as with Oedipus, above—by not identifying her action correctly, then her action is not truly akratic. An old *Mad* magazine cartoon illustrates why this point also involves *identifying* the action's intentionality: a mother welcomes home her son and rests her hand on his head. "Your hair is wet! You shouldn't have gone swimming today!" she exclaims.

"I know," he replies, "but I wasn't swimming; I *accidentally* fell in."

"Oh *really*," the accusation comes back, "then why are your *clothes* dry?"

"Well, I had the feeling that I was going to be clumsy."

For the illustration, we need to give the boy some credit and suppose, first, that he did not simply disagree that he ought not to swim, and second, that his *plunge* was accidental. In that case, the boy's action seems to me to be almost, but not quite, truly incontinent. He might have intentionally stripped and skipped at the edge of the pool, but he could maintain that he did not intentionally *swim*, which was the action specified as not to be done. Obviously, though, self-deception plays a large role, here, in the (mis)identification of what action was intentionally done. However, since self-deception may possibly be an akratic act in itself—a point we shall have to consider later—I think that in the interests of avoiding confusion, we should restrict incontinence proper so as to exclude acts done under the influence of self-deception, and, generally, to exclude both acts done unintentionally and acts done intentionally but not recognized to be so. Leontius's peeping seems to meet this intentionality requirement, also, though, because he goes so far as to run toward the corpses, in order to get a better view.

All these above traits combine to make weakness of will characteristically painful and puzzling to the agent; her own action confuses her, since in spite of her intentional performance of it, she agrees that it should *not* be performed. Now, I realize that "weakness of will" is commonly applied to a greater range of actions—including some that I specifically exclude—than is allowed by my stipulations. However, I think that the kind of action which I label as "incontinent" lies at the heart of our experience of weakness of will. In addition, the difficulty presented by incontinent actions to theories of intentional action is most pressing in light of this narrower construal of incontinence. For these reasons, when I use the terms "weakness of will," "incontinence," and *akrasia*, I will restrict my meaning to apply only to a person acting in the manner described above. That is, in exhibiting weakness of will or incontinence or *akrasia*, a person S must intentionally perform an action x, such that she judges that she ought not to do x, and such that she realizes that she *is* intentionally performing x.

I.2 PRACTICAL RATIONALITY AND INTENTIONAL ACTION IN RATIONAL-ACTION THEORIES

At this point, we have a clear picture of incontinent action and can begin to examine why this kind of intentional action proves so difficult to explain. Some action theories define intentional actions in such a way that practical rationality is part of the nature of those actions. That is, in order to be an intentional action, a given action must be informed by practical reason. According to these theories, the role of rationality in intentional action is more than that such action is done for a reason, that is, for a *purpose*. Rather, the action must be performed according to, and even because of, a practical directive of reason. Now, that rational directive is represented by the agent's judgment about what action, in her given circumstances, is right or good or rationally appropriate or, at least, such as ought to be done.

Moreover, these theories go further and link the *motivation* of intentional actions to the judgment that an action ought to be done. In other words, they claim that a desire or motivation to perform an action is generated by, or at least in conjunction with, reason's judgment that the action ought to be done. In Alasdair MacIntyre's words,

> For only if and insofar as good reasons are the *causes* of actions, and only if and insofar as those good reasons are *causally efficacious* just because and to the extent that they are *good* reasons, are there any rational agents. Any account of practical rationality which fails as a causal account fails altogether. [Emphasis added.] (*Whose Justice? Which Rationality?* 125)

Thus, the reasoned directive is held to be practical both in its subject matter—that is, in concerning what ought to be done—and in its effect—that is, in providing motivation for the directed action. As an illustration of this point, suppose that I, for a change, rose early from bed this morning. According to these theories, my early rising does not qualify as an *intentional* action, unless: first, I judged that I ought to rise early; and second, my act of rising was, in some sense, brought about by that judgment. In this way, then, these theories maintain that an intentional action's nature requires that it be performed according to, and because of, the reasoned judgment that the action ought to be done. On that account, I shall call such construals *rational-action* theories of intentional action.

We should, however, note that the grounds that make it appropriate to judge that an action is such that it ought to be done may vary from theory to theory. Perhaps the action is required to be conducive to human fulfillment; or perhaps it simply must be the best-reasoned option, and so on. Also, these grounds may or may not assume a distinctly moral cast. Despite these differences regarding its grounds, for all the theories in question this judgment expresses the rationality that an intentional action needs to have.

Therefore, I shall characterize as "rational" the actions which possess the grounds (however they are understood) that make it appropriate to judge that an action is such as ought to be done. I shall use "irrational" to describe any action whose performance is inconsistent with those grounds. So, using those terms, if an agent judges that an action is such as ought to be done, she is judging it to be a *rational* action. If she judges that an action ought *not* to be done, she is judging that action to be *irrational*. According to these theories, then, intentional action must be judged by the agent to be rational action, and thereby is at least action in which intentions are consistent with the agent's properly formed judgments as to what ought to be done.

I.3 INCONTINENT ACTIONS' PUZZLE

Now, we can see that the rational-action theories in question have a problem in explaining weak-willed actions because they are committed to this thesis: if an action is judged by someone to be irrational, then she cannot intentionally perform that action. That does not imply that irrational actions can never be intentionally performed at *all*. An irrational action can, of course, be so performed if the agent mistakenly identifies it as rational; then the agent judges, albeit incorrectly, that the action ought to be done, and it is intentionally performed accordingly. This case is one of "It seemed like a good idea at the time." But, as we noted above, that kind of action does not exemplify *incontinence*, in which the agent judges that her action is irrational. Indeed, in cases where an action *is* recognized, or judged, to be irrational, the action should not give rise, in a rational person, to the desire or motivation needed to bring about its performance. More importantly, though, an action judged by the agent to be irrational seems *unintelligible* when considered as intentional action. That is, it appears impossible for such an action to be intentionally performed, to *be* an intentional action, since it would contradict the *nature* of that kind of action. Yet weakness of will involves actions that are judged to be irrational, but which are intentionally done anyway. So according to the rational-action theories, weak-willed actions apparently contradict the nature of intentional action and therefore seem theoretically impossible.

However, empirically speaking, incontinent actions—as, for example, with Leontius's shameful gawking—obviously *do* occur. Therein lies the riddle posed to the rational-action theorist: how can this incontinent action happen? If you say it cannot, how can you justify yourself against the charge that you fail to account for the phenomenon of incontinence? The rational-action theorists may try to answer that riddle in divergent ways. They might argue either that the *impossibility* of weak-willed actions is only apparent and not actual, or that the *occurrence* of weakness of will is only apparent. In the first case, they would need to offer an explanation both of how akratic actions can occur, and of how the connection between intentional action and practical rationality could be preserved in spite of those occurrences. In the second instance, they would need to show how the appearance of *akrasia* is deceptive, so that "akratic" actions could be denied to actually violate the theoretical requirements for intentional action.

I.4 EVALUATION OF PROPOSED SOLUTIONS

The explanation of incontinent actions presents a *crucible*, a test by fire, for proposed theories of rational action. Whatever else they might have in their favor—and in a moment, we shall see several important, attractive factors—if these theories cannot satisfactorily account for (or plausibly explain away) weak-willed action, then they ultimately cannot offer satisfactory models of practical reason and intentional action. Therefore, in the course of this book's analysis, we shall place three promising theories into the fire, into this *crucible of reason*, to see if their accounts of practical rationality emerge as dross to be discarded or as refined gold to be treasured.

But what would constitute success for a rational-action theory's justifying explanation of weakness of will? In either case—accounting for, or explaining away—we should compare its theoretical pictures to our experience of incontinence, and ask ourselves: how plausibly does this construal represent and explain what we experience, the phenomenon of incontinence? Furthermore, we also should examine the theoretical aspects of any rational-action justifications. At that level, we might question whether the analysis given of akratic actions remains consistent with the theory's general account of intentional action. In other words, does the specific explanation of *akrasia* retain the theory's overall characterizations of the elements of intentional action? Or again, how well does it uphold that theory's construal of rational action? All these questions will be central to our appraisal of how successfully our rational-action theorists, Hare, Davidson, and Aquinas, explain what they variously take to be either the reality or the mere appearance of weakness of will.

I.5 ADVANTAGES OF RATIONAL-ACTION THEORIES

We also might ask, however, why we should bother examining their solutions to this seemingly internally created theoretical difficulty. That is, if this apparent impossibility of *akrasia* emerges from the conception of intentional action as necessarily judged by the agent to be rational, why not abandon that characterization of intentional action? Why not adopt a different view of intentional action, one that entirely *avoids* the theoretical problem about akratic action?

A full response to this challenge would require another book, but I can sketch my reasons for thinking rational-action theories deserve an attempted defense. First, theories of rational action offer us the most commonsensical conception for understanding and explaining intentional action. Models of intentional action normally characterize it as the result of an interaction between the agent's beliefs and desires. The desires provide reasons to act, and perceptually based beliefs allow the agent to identify when and how to act. As a basic example, suppose someone is walking through a buffet line. She enjoys the taste of potato salad, and that gives her a reason to eat it, if she can. She then notices that the buffet includes potato salad, realizes she can now get some, and so takes a scoop for her lunch. Rational-action theories enter this picture in our attempts to explain intentional action in which the agent is choosing among options. Suppose in the situation above that the person enjoys coleslaw as well as potato salad. She notices the buffet has both. But her tray has room for only one more item. Which to take? If she likes both about equally, neither option then seems obviously better on that account. However, she also realizes that she already has mashed potatoes on her tray. So she can eat a more interesting variety of foods if she takes the coleslaw. Which item would we expect her intentionally to choose? The coleslaw, of course, because we see that this option is the one she judges is better—the one she judges she has more reason to do.

We expect her to do intentionally what she thinks she has most reason to do. Our expectation is so common and obvious it has even been described as a "self-evident" aspect of action-explanation (Davidson, *Essays on Actions & Events* 23). Thus, this expectation shows that we normally view intentional action as rational action. Or in other words, "the concept of an intelligible action is a more fundamental concept than that of an action as such. Unintelligible actions are failed candidates for the status of intelligible action" (MacIntyre, *After Virtue* 209). Therefore, since rational-action theories fit best with our commonsense appraisal of intentional action, such theories deserve a chance to solve the problem presented by weak-willed actions. Indeed, the commonsense nature of rational-action theory makes the puzzle of weak-willed action that much more philosophically interesting. How could we not want to investigate a matter in which our commonsense philosophy of action seems so badly mistaken?

Second, rational-action conceptions can valuably contribute to the study of *moral* intentional actions. Ethicists continually strive to show that to act *morally* is to act *rationally*; showing the rationality of moral action is one of the principal tasks for any realist or objective moral theory. Moreover, characterizing moral actions as rational will be most effective if we are able to evaluate those actions in comparison with other, *non-* (or *im-*) moral options. But that only becomes possible in the context of a theory of rational action, a theory that provides an explanation of how reason operates in action, generally. So a working model of rational action would be of enormous philosophical interest to ethics.

Further, rational-action theories can shed light on an interesting problem area for objectivist ethics. For supposing an objective ground for moral judgments creates two possible gaps of philosophical import. The first is the gap between what we *think* we ought to do and what we *actually* ought to do. The second gap opens between what we accurately *believe* we ought to do and what we actually *do* (which brings us back to incontinent actions). The former presents a problem of *cognitive* failure, the latter a failure in *execution*. Rational-action theory bears directly on the second problem by investigating how our beliefs and desires affect (and effect) our actions. That faces head-on the question of whether we can know the truth of what we ought to do and still not act on it. In short, must there always be some cognitive fault to explain our moral inaction—our weakness of will—or can we fail to act, anyway? This question is a matter for rational-action theory (indeed, we shall see various answers to it in the theories presented in this book). So models of rational action can perhaps help with an important problem in objectivist ethics. In fact, depending on how the models characterize the rational standard of intentional action, those models may help bridge—or at least explain the presence of—the other gap, between what we think we ought to do and what we really ought to do. Again, that usefulness validates our investigation into the possibility of a successful theory of rational action.

Third, a working conception of rational action can help us better understand our own human agency; that is, it may show us more clearly what it means to be a human agent. The possibility of gaining such a fundamental piece of self-knowledge surely would make our investigation worthwhile. Indeed, I believe that the present examination does yield valuable results along just those lines. However, why and how it does so can only become clear as we proceed. Therefore, for now, I must simply lay out this claim as a further reason why rational-action theories are worth investigating, in spite of their difficulty in explaining incontinent actions.

I.6 THE SELECTION OF THEORISTS

That said, I hope it is sufficiently clear why I think this book's project is philosophically important. Yet my choice of theorists remains to be justified. I focus on Hare, Davidson, and Aquinas for several reasons. In the first place, all three have offered highly influential accounts of weakness of will. Much of contemporary theorizing on this matter takes its cues from Hare and/or Davidson. Whether being attacked or defended, their views lie at the center of the current debate. Of course, I need hardly mention the enormous, enduring impact Aquinas's views have had, both within Christian circles and without; also, for investigative purposes Aquinas's theory provides a radical alternative to Hare's and Davidson's.

Indeed, that opposition brings forth a second reason behind my choice of theorists. I think Aquinas's view (or at any rate, a modified version of it) does the best job of any rational-action theory in accounting for incontinence. As we shall see, Hare's and Davidson's theories fail in serious ways. Yet because of their differences from Aquinas, Hare's and Davidson's failures can be particularly instructive to us. That is, in seeing where they stumble, and why, we will be better able to identify just what aspects of Aquinas's view are critical to his explanatory success.

A third reason for the selection lies in the specific *kinds* of approaches the theorists take to the problem. Each one tackles incontinence from a particular "angle" that relates it to our general reasons for the project. Hare deals with weakness of will by focusing on its moral-theoretic implications; he is especially concerned with examining the apparent gap between what we believe we ought to do and what we actually do. Davidson, on the other hand, approaches incontinence from an action-theoretic focus; what concerns him is how a commonsensically obvious rational-action conception of intentional action can appear so spectacularly inconsistent with our experience. In addition to attempting to deal with both Hare's and Davidson's questions, Aquinas zeroes in on the implications akratic actions have for understanding human agency. Thus, between them the theorists canvass all of our primary reasons for undertaking this investigation.

I.7 DEFENSE OF A CHRISTIAN CONCEPTION OF PRACTICAL RATIONALITY

One additional reason justifies my choice of theorists; but since it only emerged in my own mind after the project was well under way, and since it constitutes an added theme to the investigation, I separate it from the other reasons. Hare, Davidson, and Aquinas do not merely have different foci in their approaches, each also has a distinct conception of *practical rationality* itself. They differ on the *measure* reason uses to assess actions' rationality, on the *scope of application* for that measure, and on the *grounds* that make that measure rational in the first place

That does not mean that we cannot evaluate their rival claims, though, for we can engage in two kinds of comparison: (1) We can elaborate each system to examine it for *internal consistency* according to its own standards, and (2) if we discover common ground in what the theories attempt to explain, we can examine whether one does a better job—whether one can *explain what its rivals fail to* (and especially whether it can *explain why the rivals falter*). If one system emerges as more internally consistent and/or deals with difficulties its rivals cannot, that may give us grounds for preferring it. I believe this book's investigation carries out just such analysis. Each view is examined alone, spelled out in its systematic implications, and checked for adequacy against our commonly agreed-upon experience of weak-willed action. Thus, the book's argument gives us the means to make a comparative evaluation regarding the proposed rival notions of practical rationality.

Moreover, I shall argue that the upshot of that evaluation is that Aquinas's conception is clearly superior *because of* features that derive from its Christian basis. This part is what I only began to see when I was well into the project. I had begun the work believing (or at least hoping—one never quite knows how the argument will turn) that Aquinas's view could deal with problems the others could not. However, I had not made the connection between the Thomistic view's strengths and its Christian foundations. But I believe the examination shows just that: the Thomistic model of practical rationality does not simply work best and happen to be Christian (as I first thought); it works best *through* and *because of* its Christian elements.

Therefore, what began as a comparative analysis of rational-action theories also becomes the start of an inductive defense of Christianity. I think this book's argument begins to make the case that, compared to some front-running theoretical rivals on practical rationality, Christianity possesses superior explanatory power. Given this emerging theme of the argument, Aquinas is an even more obvious choice of theorist, since no other comes close to his systematic comprehensiveness in spelling out the Christian worldview. But Hare and Davidson remain good choices for this purpose, too, because both theorists have consciously attempted to keep their models free from the kind of metaphysical and speculative commitments required for Aquinas's. That is, Hare and Davidson offer conceptions of rational action that do not depend on any particular religious background, that do not commit to speculative points of metaphysics. So again, they serve as good foils to Aquinas, not only because they provide prime candidates of plausible rational-action theories, but also because their religiously and metaphysically streamlined conceptions help to highlight just how important the Christian aspects are to Aquinas's view. However, since this argument requires a kind of overall consideration of the competing views, it will only become the focus once all the views have been examined—it will only be worked out at the end, in the conclusion.

But enough of this preview. I hope my rationale in choosing to examine Hare, Davidson, and Aquinas is now clear, and that my bold (and so far unsubstantiated) claims have piqued the reader's interest. So let us turn to the argument proper, beginning with Hare's view.

1

R. M. HARE'S THEORY

I want initially to look at R. M. Hare's theoretical explanation of weakness of will, for his account is problematic at important points. By examining Hare's view first, we can spot and mark some pitfalls that Davidson and Aquinas will need to avoid if their accounts are to explain *akrasia* more successfully.

1.1 CONNECTION TO RATIONAL-ACTION THEORY

To start our examination, we need to understand in just what sense Hare's account qualifies as a theory of the rational-action type. For Hare is primarily a theorist of *moral* intentional action, not of intentional action in general. As such he concentrates on explaining the nature of, and the rationality inherent in, moral actions; Hare connects moral action to a conception of rational action. But it is important to our investigation to see how and why he distinguishes moral actions from the rest of intentional action. For that reason, I shall briefly piece together Hare's view of intentional action as a whole; then we can better understand his distinct account of moral action, and its rationality, by placing it into that larger context.

1.1.1 Intentional Action, in General

In setting out Hare's position on intentional actions as a class, we need to start with the basics. For Hare, intentional action is rooted in an agent's interests; and an "interest" is essentially "something which one wants . . . or which is . . . a means, necessary or sufficient, for the attainment of something which one wants" (*Freedom and Reason* 157/9.1). As an example of the second part of this idea, suppose that someone is not particularly fond of eating, that she is picky and has poor digestion. In itself, then, eating would seem not to be an interest for her. However, she also very much wants to live and to avoid starvation. Given those wants, because she needs to eat in order to satisfy them, eating is thereby an interest of hers. Now, Hare uses the term "want" quite broadly here. Thus, bodily desires like hunger for food could count as the "want" in an interest, and so could widely differing "wants," like a longing for love, or even a sense of obligation to contribute to charity (170/9.4).

What happens is that an agent expresses these interests in certain judgments that she makes. Those judgments are evaluations, such as "The Sistine Chapel ceiling is incredibly beautiful," or "That yak cheese has a truly foul odor." The former evaluation expresses an interest to see and enjoy the frescoes; and the latter represents an interest to stay out of smelling distance of the particular dairy product. In general, then, Hare would say that such an evaluation

> incorporates the desire to have or do something rather than something else. The wide sense in which we are here using "desire" [and similar to the use of "want," above] is that in which *any* felt disposition to action counts as a desire. [Emphasis in original] (170/9.4)

That second sentence is crucial, because there Hare indicates why these interest-incorporating evaluations are important to intentional action: they give expression to a motivational force that can bring about action.

Hare calls that kind of evaluation an imperative, or *prescriptive*, judgment—or sometimes, simply, a *prescription*. He asserts that these prescriptive judgments, such as "Vacuuming is hateful and tedious drudgery and is bad to do," differ from merely fact-stating *descriptive* judgments, like "The vacuuming took well over an hour." The difference lies in the former judgment's—unlike the latter's—power to motivate action (Hare, "Weakness of Will" 1304). Hare writes that prescriptive judgments have "a commendatory or condemnatory or in general prescriptive force which ordinary descriptive [judgments] . . . lack" (*Moral Thinking* 71/4.2). What he means here is that a prescriptive judgment contains—either explicitly or implicitly—a *command*, an imperative. So when a person makes a prescriptive judgment about an action, part of what is involved is that she is giving herself a command about what action to take. She is prescribing a course of action to herself. The interest expressed in the judgment's evaluation is the wellspring of that command. Further, that same disposition to act provides the motivational force to carry out what is commanded or prescribed.

To illustrate this notion of how these interest-incorporating evaluations involve self-commands, suppose that a person judges that an action *x*—say, walking her dog—would be healthful and pleasant, and that *x* is therefore good to do. In making that prescriptive judgment, the evaluation that "*x* is good to do," she is, in effect, commanding herself to do *x*. Hare asserts, "if [she] assents to the judgment, [she] must also assent to the command 'Let me do *x*'" (*FR* 79/5.7). Further, her interest in the healthful pleasure of dog walking supplies motivation, so that she *will* act on the prescriptive judgment which is based in that interest. Hare writes,

> It is a tautology to say that we cannot sincerely assent to a command addressed to ourselves, and *at the same time* not perform it, if now is the occasion for performing it, and it is in our (physical and psychological) power to do so. [Emphasis in original] (79/5.7)

So our agent makes the prescriptive judgment, rooted in her interests, that "*x* is good to do," and when she has the opportunity—assuming she still accepts the judgment—she performs *x* in accord with, and because of, that self-commanding judgment.

For Hare, then, the nature of intentional action, generally, seems only to require that an intentional action must be brought about by, and performed in accordance with, a prescriptive judgment—a self-commanding evaluation incorporating her interests—that the agent makes. Hare calls his view "prescriptivism" and holds that it sets forth

> the close logical relations, on the one hand between wanting and thinking good, and on the other between wanting and doing something about getting what one wants . . . [and thereby shows the] link between thinking good and action. (71/5.3)

1.1.2 Moral Intentional Action

At this point we can see how intentional actions are motivated by, and performed according to, prescriptions—those imperative, evaluative judgments; and we can now begin to explore what makes *moral* intentional actions distinctive. Hare contends that moral, imperative judgments differ from others, because the moral ones *must* be *universalizable*. This necessary universalizability stems from the logical implications in using the word "ought," which expresses the command in moral judgments. When someone judges that she *ought* to do something, Hare says,

> [I]t logically commits [her] to making a similar judgement about anything which is either exactly like the subject of the original judgement or like it in the relevant respects. The relevant respects are those which formed the grounds of the original judgement. (139/8.2)

Or again, more simply, Hare writes, "if I think that I ought to do *A* in these circumstances, I am committed to thinking that anyone else similarly placed ought to do the same" (71/5.4).

As an example of this universalizability implied in using "ought," suppose that I judge that, since my friend borrowed five dollars from me, he ought to pay me back that money. I then must also judge that in similar cases of money borrowing, the borrower ought to repay the lender, and that includes cases in which I am not involved or even in which *I* am the borrower. So, for Hare, because moral judgments employ the imperative concept of "ought," those judgments must be universalizable, and on that account must "entail identical judgements about all cases identical in their [relevant] properties" (*MT* 108/6.1).

Again, that necessarily universalizable nature is what makes moral judgments distinct from other kinds of prescriptive judgment. Hare notes that while moral imperatives must have a universal scope, imperatives that come from nonmoral desires and wants—such as curiosity or fear or hunger—do *not* have to be universalizable; instead, this kind of

> wanting is like assenting to a singular imperative. . . . If I want to do *A* in these circumstances, I am not committed to wanting anyone else placed in exactly or relevantly similar circumstances to do likewise. (*FR* 71/5.4)

Hare admits that some such desires *could* be universalizable, but he points out that universality is neither necessary for, nor characteristic of, that kind of interest (157/9.1).

1.1.3 Conception of Rational Action

Now, having seen this difference between moral and other prescriptive judgments, we can distinguish the aspects of Hare's view which constitute a conception of rational action. First, we should note that intentional action, in general, does *not*, by nature, seem required to be judged rational by the agent. The prescriptions which express nonmoral interests may or may *not* be informed by reason. Hare asserts that rationality certainly *can* be directed to answering questions about what action to take, when those actions are brought about by thought—which, of course, includes all the actions generated by a person's prescriptive judgments (*MT* 214/12.4). However, the level of rationality *required* to make, and to act upon, nonmoral prescriptions is negligible. On the one hand, a person *can* incorporate rationality into these nonmoral intentional actions. Hare writes,

> It is irrational to prescribe anything without regard to what, concretely, we are prescribing; and this involves cognizance of what our prescription means, and of what its execution in this concrete situation would entail. Obviously we cannot be cognizant of this without attention to the facts of the situation. (89/5.1)

That is, a person can rationally check her prescription to discern exactly *what* it is directing her to do in this circumstance (Hare, *EET* 37). Suppose, for example, that she is hot and wants to be cooler; she could rationally determine that the way to cool down, given her situation, is to open all the windows in her apartment. She could even go farther, and expose this cool-preference to logical calculation to see whether to act on it at all. She might ask herself, "Is feeling a cool breeze worth the effort of opening all those windows—something which, in itself, I would prefer not to do?" That effort would allow her "to answer rationally the practical question 'What shall I do now?'" (Hare, *MT* 104/5.6).

On the other hand, however, in order to act on her prescription, in order to act intentionally, our agent *need not* make that rational effort. She might simply judge, "Being cooler is good; I want to be cooler," and then—heedless of others in the room—immediately proceed to take off her clothes, or to wave her arms vigorously like a human fan in order to feel some cooler air. Either of those actions, while not rational in the way that the thoughtful-window-opening would have been, is just as much of an *intentional* action as the window-opening. So for Hare, it is not a requirement of the nature of intentional action, generally, for such action to be judged by the agent to be rational. Hare sees a continuum of degrees of rationality which are possible in the prescriptions that bring about intentional action. At the bottom end of that continuum, a person can act intentionally without the judgment, according to which she is acting, having to be approved or informed by reason.

But that lax rational requirement does not apply to *moral* intentional actions; it is in those actions that we encounter the kind of necessary rationality which would imply that they must be judged, by the agent, to be rational. Hare writes, "When the prescription [for action] is universal or universalizable, however, the [rational] requirement in consequence becomes much stronger" (89/5.1). For, he contends,

> In making up my mind what I most want to do I have to consult only my own desires. But in making up my mind what I ought to do [that is, in prescribing universalizably] I have to consider more than this; I have to ask myself "What [prescription] . . . can I accept as of *universal* application in cases like this, whether or not *I* play the part in the situation which I am playing now?" (*FR* 71/5.4)

The way to determine if a prescription is universalizable is to subject it to a rational process of considering hypothetical situations and their consequences. Thus, a moral judgment about an action, because it needs to be universalizable in order to *be* a moral judgment, must be informed by reason.

Let me more fully explain this rational nature of moral judgments. In making a moral judgment that an action *ought* to be done, I must, in order to be using the word "ought" correctly, "rationally prefer that the [judgment] should be acted on whatever role I play in the resulting sequence of events" (Hare, *MT* 215/12.4). In making sure that I can prefer such, I must submit my prescription "to logic and the facts" (104/5.6). Further, since fact-checking my prescription includes examining

> its application were [I] in the other's [that is, anyone else affected by my action] position . . . the facts [I] need to be cognizant of will include facts about his position as it affects him with his preferences (89/5.1)

In plainer words, I must ask myself both how my action will affect others, and, given those effects, how I would regard this action if I were in the others' shoes. This hypothetical consideration may require some imagination and sympathy, but the main work has to be done by reason—rational calculation assessing consequences, and so on. The end result of this process—which Hare calls "critical thinking"—is that "no judgement will be acceptable to [me] which does not do the best, all in all, for all the parties [concerned in the action]" (42–3/2.6). By this rational procedure, then, I arrive at a prescription which I can endorse in the universal scope required for a moral judgment.

1.1.4 Moral Intentional Action Is Rational Action

Now, at last, we can see why Hare's account of *moral* intentional action does qualify as a theory of rational-action. For Hare, to judge that an action morally ought to be done is to judge that action to be rational, in the sense that it meets the rational requirements for being universalizable. A moral judgment is thus informed by reason; and a moral action is thereby brought about by, and in accord with, a judgment of reason.

1.2 APPARENT IMPOSSIBILITY OF WEAK-WILLED MORAL ACTION

Having reached this point, though, it is still incumbent upon us to show why, for Hare, incontinence in the face of a moral judgment seems impossible. To accomplish this further task, we must examine what happens when prescriptions come into conflict. For as Hare says, the problem of weakness of will comes into focus, when we examine it as a particular kind of prescription-conflict (60/3.7).

1.2.1 Prescription Conflict

As a general example of such a conflict, suppose that a person has a nonmoral interest (like a desire for fried chicken) which she sincerely prescribes to herself, and yet she acts, not on that, but on some other competing interest (such as a desire for beef roast). The agent makes prescriptive judgments about both foods for herself, but on the given occasion, since she can satisfy only one of the prescriptions, she eats beef roast, but not chicken. I think Hare would affirm that *this* kind of "contest" *does* occur; and he explains how the "winning" prescription is chosen:

> [W]e shall in any case do what the balance of our present preferences requires—in other words, [we shall] act on the prescription which results when the prescriptions we are now disposed to accept have been balanced against one another in proportion to the strengths with which we accept them" (104/5.6)

This "strength" is, I take it, a measure of how intensely the interest is wanted, that is, of how strong the preference is. A person acts, then, on her most strongly affirmed prescription. So someone could act against her sincere prescriptive judgment, if she simply accepted or affirmed an opposing prescription with greater strength. Our agent wanted beef roast more than she wanted chicken, and, accordingly, acted to eat the former.

Hare calls it "overriding," when one prescription takes precedence over another in this fashion. It is not the case that the "losing" prescription does not apply, or that it is not accepted, here. The prescription and its motivational force are not being qualified or excepted; they are "simply overridden in this case" by the stronger—the more intensely desired—prescription (55–6/3.6).

From the general account of prescription-conflict, then, it looks as if morally incontinent actions *should* be possible in Hare's view. Suppose an agent experiences competition between a *moral* interest (say, a sense of obligation to contribute money to charity) and a nonmoral interest (say, a craving to buy and eat pizza). If her moral interest should be overridden by the nonmoral, she would not be acting from, and according to, a judgment of reason; but she would still be acting intentionally, since intentional action need not proceed from such reasoned judgments. So why should this situation differ from the one above, and be impossible?

1.2.2 Moral Prescription Conflict

That difference, according to Hare, arises because *moral* judgments can never be overridden in this way, since it is part of their nature to *be* overriding. That is, a moral judgment is not only prescriptive and universalizable by nature, it is also *overriding* (55/3.6). Hare defines the new property thus,

> To treat a principle as overriding, then, is to let it always override other principles [e.g. rules of table etiquette, or aesthetic ideals] when they conflict with it and, in the same way, let it override all other prescriptions, including non-universalizable ones (e.g., plain desires). (56/3.6)

And he asserts that "overridingness" is the characteristic which definitively distinguishes moral judgments from other prescriptive judgments (53/3.5).

Further, since it will be important in understanding Hare's account of incontinence, we should now note that this crucial property of overridingness seems to stem from the *rationality required in the moral judgment*. First, the moral judgment's rational nature excludes any vulnerability—any possibility of exception—from the prescription. The hypothetical reasoning employed in critical thinking—in assessing whether prescriptions are universalizable—uses "cases exactly similar in their universal properties [that is, in *what* the action and its surrounding circumstances are], and differing only in the roles played by the individuals" (Hare, *MT* 63/3.9). The universal-scope prescriptions which are then yielded can be "so specific and so adapted to particular cases that they do not need to be overridden" (60/3.8). In other words, the rational procedure of universalizing can be so detailed and exact, as to make the resultant moral judgments both so specific and so clear in their application, that they would never conflict or lend themselves to misapplication. There could never be a reason to make exception to these judgments. Their rational nature allows them to be "as specific as [is] required" to make them explicitly applicable and exceptionless (63/3.9). That means that a moral judgment's prescriptive "armor" has no "chinks" for any opposed prescription to exploit, in order to override the moral judgment.

Second, the role-changing in the hypothetical reasoning seems to make the moral judgment a kind of rational *superinterest*, so that the judgment *must* be overriding. Basically, when a person hypothetically puts herself into the positions of others who would be affected by her action, she seems, in some sense, to acquire their interests as her own (Hare, *EET* 209). In Hare's words,

> I cannot know the extent and quality of others' sufferings and, in general, [their] motivations and preferences without having equal motivations with regard to what should happen to me, were I in their places, with their motivations and preferences. . . . [And that results from considering] what should happen to me in the hypothetical case in which I am to be, forthwith, put into the position of somebody else. (*MT* 99–100/5.4–5.5)

But the rational universalizing-process does more than simply produce these hypothetically based interests. Now, we have already noted—with our earlier illustration of the person wanting to be cooler—Hare's point that examining interests in the light of logic and facts can affect how strongly, or toward which action, a person prescribes those interests (104/5.6). The hypothetical role-changing also has that effect (Hare, *EET* 40). Under the combined weight of the rational considerations of consequences and the rationally acquired hypothetical interests, a person's present interests are *conformed* to the moral judgment, to the prescription that commands the action which—since it will "do the best, all in all, for all the parties"—would be the overall rational preference of everyone concerned (Hare, *MT* 42/2.6). The rational process shapes her interests so that she will "rationally prefer" to act on the moral judgment, regardless of her role in the events—that is, regardless of how her other interests are affected (215/12.4; "Comments" 249). If we think of the agent's initial interests like a tree's branches—with the various individual interests having differing sizes (strengths) and pointing every which way—the rational process of universalizing acts like a bonsai gardener. It prunes back unruly "branches"; it ties and pushes the others to point in one certain direction. In this case, the "sculpture" that is left is a single column, a rationally generated superinterest, ready to serve as a battering ram for the moral judgment. That seems to mean that the moral prescription, with its accumulated force of real and hypothetical interests, will be a preference strong enough to *override* any competing interests which might "sprout." To recap this important point, then: the rationality inherent in a moral judgment makes that judgment overriding, first, by making it exceptionless, so as to exclude any weakness, any loophole, any rationale for *its* ever being overridden; and second, by bringing such strength to the interest-preference it expresses, that it will always override competition.

1.2.3 Overridingness Yields Apparent Impossibility

Unfortunately, not only is the property of overridingness integral to Hare's account of the rational nature of moral judgments, it also generates his theoretical difficulty in explaining incontinence. For as Hare, himself, makes very clear, he has a problem accounting for weakness of will. Moreover, he construes *akrasia* in the same way that I have. He carefully distinguishes true incontinence from cases in which the agent views the moral judgment merely as what *society* demands (*FR* 83/5.9; "WW" 1306). He eliminates from consideration cases in which the agent less-than-solidly affirms, or is less than sincere about, the judgment (*FR* 82, 83/5.9; "WW" 1305, 1306). He also discounts instances in which the agent either does not realize that her moral judgment applies to *this* action, or does not hold the judgment at the time of the action in question (*FR* 83/5.9; "WW" 1305). The above kinds of actions, Hare maintains, do not present the explanatory problem that incontinent actions do ("WW" 1305). The difficulty immediately emerges, however, when we "confin[e] our attention to cases in which a man does not do what he thinks (now) that *he* ought *to be* doing" (Hare, *FR* 83/5.9).

For if a moral judgment is overriding, then, seemingly, a sincerely held moral judgment should never fail to guide a person's conduct, even if it is opposed by other prescriptions (Hare, *FR* 70/5.3). That apparently makes morally incontinent actions impossible, since they involve actions intentionally performed against genuinely sincere judgments about what ought to be done—that is, against an accepted moral judgment. Hare characterizes his difficulty this way:

> The account I have just sketched would make it impossible for a moral principle to be overridden . . . by any other prescription. But [that does] . . . occur. . . . Some cases of weakness of will are examples of this. (*MT* 53/3.6)

Hare even goes further and poses to himself the riddle of incontinent actions, as it applies to his theory: if moral judgments—which bring about moral actions—were rationally informed in the way that Hare describes, it would be impossible to knowingly act intentionally against an accepted moral judgment; yet people apparently do just that when they act incontinently; do not morally incontinent actions, therefore, present a counterexample against Hare's picture of moral action as being brought about by, and in accord with, these rational judgments (*FR* 67/5.1)? So Hare not only sees the difficulty his theory has in accounting for incontinent actions, he also recognizes what a failing it would be, if his theory could not explain that phenomenon.

1.3 SOLUTION: INTUITIVE VERSUS CRITICAL MORAL JUDGMENTS

At this point, having examined both the mechanics of Hares's view, and the nature of his difficulty in accounting for moral weakness of will, we can begin to explore the solution Hare proposes for his problem. Essentially, Hare attempts to account for moral incontinence by distinguishing between two levels of thought at which a person can make a moral judgment. At one level, which Hare calls "critical" thinking, morally *akratic* actions are still declared to be impossible. But at the other, the level of "intuitive" thinking, it *is* possible, Hare claims, to akratically act against a moral judgment.

1.3.1 Critical Moral Judgments

The first level, at which critical thinking is done, is in fact the level of thinking which we have already described in explaining moral judgments. Hare sometimes also calls the judgments which emerge from this thinking "decisions of principle," and he reiterates that critical thought consists in prescribing an action

> under the constraints imposed by the logical properties of the moral concepts [that is, of the universalizability implied in using "ought"] and by the non-moral facts [that is, by the action's circumstances and consequences, which are used in the universalizing], and by nothing else. (*MT* 40/2.5)

At the critical level, then, a person engages in the by-now-familiar rational process of examining hypothetical situations and their consequences, and so on, in order "to find a moral judgement which [she] is prepared to make about this . . . situation and is also prepared to make about all the other similar situations" (42–3/2.6).

So nothing about the level of critical thinking is new to us, except for these two things, which are pointed out by Hare: first, these decisions of principle are fully rational and independently freestanding. Critical thinking works according to the rules of logic and of language use, and it uses nothing but the facts about the proposed action's situation (40/2.5). That gives critical thinking its rationally informed character (Hare, *EET* 46). It further means that critical thinking does not require recourse to anything but its own rational method in order to reach—or to justify—a moral judgment (Hare, *MT* 46/3.2). Once critical thinking has verified that my prescription—say, to work honestly for my pay—is universalizable, then it will also, as a result of the universalizing process, be overriding; and nothing further is needed in order to characterize or justify that prescription as a moral judgment. For that reason, Hare seems to regard the critical level as "moral thinking" in the truest sense of the term, and as the ultimate means for making moral judgments.

Second, the practice of critical thinking is hard—so hard, in fact, that a human being could never be expected to use it in regard to every moral action taken. For one, critical thinking is too *time-consuming* to be of much on-the-spot use. If Fred Nietzebaum calls long distance to the parking lot where I am the attendant and asks if anyone has found his wallet, he does not have the time to wait for me to engage in a round of careful critical thinking before I decide whether to tell him that I have it. For another, the weaknesses of human character make the use of critical thinking *unreliable* under tension (46–7/3.2; *EET* 188). As I stare at the pictured faces of Fred and his many dead-president friends gazing up at me from the depths of the wallet held in my sweaty fingers, my critical thinking might well yield something like this comment from comedian Emo Phillips: "If *I* had lost *my* wallet, I would want to be taught a *lesson*." Indeed, Hare is forced to talk hypothetically about an "archangel . . . a being with superhuman powers of thought, superhuman knowledge, and no human weaknesses," in order to be able to describe what systematic use of critical thinking would be like (*MT* 44/3.1).

1.3.2 Intuitive Moral Judgments

Given, then, that people could not, in fact, make all their moral judgments by thinking at the critical level, Hare proposes his second level of moral thinking in order to take up the slack. This second level, intuitive thinking, is not a "rival procedure" to critical thinking, but rather is part of a "common structure" with it (44/3.1). Intuitive thinking plays an auxiliary role and yields moral judgments for situations in which a person does not have the time or ability to do critical thinking (46–7/3.2). At this level, then, moral *intuitions*, which Hare often calls "prima facie principles," are meant to quickly provide prescriptions for instances of moral action. So intuitive thinking is not really a process of reasoning, but rather is a much quicker appeal to "a set of dispositions, motivations, intuitions, prima facie principles (call them what we will) which will have this effect [of prescribing moral actions]" (46–7/3.2). What happens is that this set of moral intuitions is inculcated in a person, by her family and society and so on, during the course of her development, so that she will be ready to deliver on-the-spot moral prescriptions (46–7/3.2). So, in the example, when Fred calls, I consult my pertinent moral intuition—which, in this case, is that "lost objects ought to be returned to their owners"—and it specifies the moral judgment, "I ought to return Fred's lost wallet." This consultation occurs speedily and without any recourse to confusable reasoning processes. The intuitions "are sound ones, if they . . . yield acceptable precepts in common cases" (49/3.2). In short, while these implanted intuitions are not mere moral rules of thumb (in conversation with me, Hare vehemently opposed that characterization), they do resemble such rules at least insofar as they are intended to quickly provide moral judgments for the *common* or *ordinary* moral actions.

This intuitive moral thinking is crucial to Hare's account of incontinence, so let us examine its nature more thoroughly. We notice, first, that intuitive moral thought does not rationally verify its moral judgments. There is no reasoning process to make sure the judgment is correctly universalizable; when consulted about a certain instance, the moral intuition, or disposition, automatically produces the specific prescription. For that reason, "intuitive moral thinking cannot be [rationally] self-supporting"; it needs "outside" rational validation for its judgments (46/3.2). That is provided by critical thinking, which—since it is self-justifying—is thus "prior" to the intuitive (46/3.2). The moral intuitions, or prima facie principles, must, therefore, "be selected by critical thinking [so as to be rationally justified]; if not by our own critical thinking, by that of people whom we trust to be able to do it" (46–7/3.2). Critical thinking accomplishes that selection like this:

> [W]e have to look at the consequences of inculcating [the proposed moral intuitions] in ourselves and others; and, in examining these consequences, we have to balance the size of the good and bad effects in cases which we consider against the probability or improbability of such cases occurring in our actual experience. (48/3.2)

That is, we hypothetically consider whether these intuitions will guide us well in common instances of moral action; and we measure that good effect against how badly or how often the intuitions may lead us wrong. If the good consequences outweigh the bad, our critical thinking validates the intuitions. In this way, since critical thinking chooses what the moral intuitions will be, those intuitions' moral judgments—although not rationally generated or informed—are rationally *justified*, in a derivative or secondary sense.

A second important aspect of intuitive moral thinking is that it acquires its motivational force differently from critical thinking. As we saw earlier, critical moral judgments gain their overriding motivational force from the rational process of arriving at a universalizable judgment. But since, as we just noted, intuitive moral judgments are not formed in that rational way, the source of their motivational force must be something else. The motivational "lever" is, in fact, a *disposition* or *feeling*—presumably, of obligation—which is a component of the moral intuition. Hare says that these

> "prima facie principles" . . . are associated, owing to our upbringing, with very firm and deep dispositions and feelings. Any attempt to drive a wedge between the principles [that is, their *content*] and the feelings [would violate the nature of those principles]. . . . *Having* the principles, in the usual sense of the word, is having the disposition to experience the feelings. [Emphasis in original] (38–9/2.4)

So the interest that a moral intuition and its resultant moral judgments express is not a rational superpreference, such as the critical level utilizes, but rather is only a feeling or disposition, albeit a strong one. That is crucial, because such a motivation, unlike the rational superpreference, is *not* inherently strong enough to be *overriding*.

Following that thought, we arrive at a third point to carefully note about moral intuitions: these prima facie principles "are rather simple and unspecific . . . they have to be to a certain degree simple and general" (59/3.7). That is, these intuitions do not have the specificity and explicit applicability of critical moral judgments. A moral intuition only expresses something like, "I ought not to steal," rather than the critically specified "Given the circumstances, this wallet ought not to be stolen." Hare maintains that this unspecific nature is necessary for these intuitive dispositions, since they must be the kind of thing children could learn and widely use during their moral and character development (59/3.7). But this practical necessity has a grave implication. Because of their unspecified generality, prima facie principles may conflict in prescribing action in our morally complex world (59/3.7). If someone is traveling to meet her spouse—as she has promised—and the car in front of her crashes, her moral intuitions then tell her to stop and offer help, and also to continue on so as not to miss her promised appointment. In the face of such potential conflicts, the moral intuitions and their resultant judgments must "admit of exceptions, in the sense that it is possible to go on holding them while allowing that in particular cases one may break them" (59/3.7). Thus, our agent stops to help the accident victims, although it means breaking her promise, and even though she intuitively judges that she ought to keep her promise. She makes an exception to the promise-keeping intuition and acts on the other instead. The upshot of this point is the keystone of Hare's proposed account of weakness of will: not only are intuitive-level moral judgments *not* inherently necessarily overriding (as we saw above), they *are* necessarily inherently *overridable* (59/3.7). The exception-possibility, which for practical use must be part of the moral intuitions' nature, makes it the case that these broad intuitive-level moral judgments can be both sincerely held and, at the same time, not acted upon. That is, their exception "escape clause" makes them vulnerable to being overridden (59–60/3.7).

Now we have set out the components of Hares's explanation of *akrasia*; but before we put them to work, let us recap: we have seen that critical moral thinking yields judgments that are rationally informed, completely specific in their prescriptions, and inherently overriding. Intuitive moral thinking, on the other hand, is unspecific and general in what it prescribes; it produces moral judgments that are not rationally informed, but only secondarily rationally approved, and that *can* be overridden. As for the interconnected tasks of the critical and intuitive levels, Hare writes:

> To sum up, then, the relation between the two kinds of thinking is this. Critical thinking aims to select the best set of prima facie principles for use in intuitive thinking. It can also be employed when principles from the set conflict [in what they prescribe]. . . . The best set [of intuitions] is that whose acceptance yields actions, dispositions, etc. most nearly approximating to those which would be chosen if we were able to use critical thinking all the time. (49–50/3.3)

Lastly, here, given the distinctions made between the critical and intuitive levels, Hare's grounds for regarding critical judgments and thought as primarily or principally exemplifying the rational nature of moral thinking and judging should be evident.

Now we are ready to put Hare's distinction between the critical and intuitive levels of moral thinking to work in accounting for morally incontinent actions. Hare proposes two possible ways for a person to incontinently act against a moral judgment; both methods depend upon, and occur at, the intuitive level.

1.3.3 Special-Pleading Morally Weak-Willed Action

The first way in which moral *akrasia* can occur is, according to Hare, by utilizing "special pleading" (*FR* 76/5.6). Special pleading exploits the exception-possibility required in the intuitive level's prima facie principles because of their generality (Hare, *MT* 58–9/3.7). Indeed, as Hare says, although these principles "are universal [in *form*, that is, in their use of "ought"] . . . in another sense they are not universal (they are not universally binding; one may make exceptions to them)" (59/3.7). The idea, here, is that the prima facie principles, or moral intuitions, are already a kind of moral judgment, even without being specified to a particular prescription about a certain action. At this point, the moral judgment is not a *singular* prescription, about *this* action *x* (Hare, *FR* 72–3/5.4). Instead, it is only a *general* prescription about actions of the same *kind* as *x*. Moreover, Hare writes that this type of "moral weakness is the tendency not to do ourselves something which *in general* we commend, or to do something which *in general* we condemn" (72/5.4). So, in a case of special pleading, a person makes an exception for herself, on a certain instance, against the general rule of her moral intuition.

As an example of special pleading, let us refer back to the instance involving Fred Nietzebaum's lost wallet. My moral intuition there was the general moral judgment that lost objects ought to be returned to their owners. Now suppose that I have not specified the particular moral judgment about returning Fred's wallet. Instead, I backslide against the moral judgment by pleading that *this* case is special and does not fall under the judgment's rule. I concoct some reason—such as, "because of my credit card bills, I need this money more than Fred does, and after all, 'to each according to his need'"—that allows me to make an exception for myself, with regard to *this* action. I might, however, still *say* that I know that I ought to return Fred's wallet; but, Hare maintains, I am now only *describing* that specific obligation—as if I were noting what society demands—but am not really *accepting* or *prescribing* it for myself (76–7/5.6). It is the action that I *perform*—here, keeping the wallet—that reveals what I am truly prescribing to myself on this occasion (Hare, "WW" 1306). Further, I might even have a guilty conscience at keeping the wallet; that feeling is left over from the prescriptive force in the excepted intuition (*FR* 76–7/5.6; "WW" 1306). But the conscience's general feeling of compunction is overridden by my singular interest in the money in *this* lost wallet, and I tell Fred that I cannot help him. In this way, then, I akratically act against my moral judgment that I ought to return lost objects.

It might seem, though, that by making this exception for myself, I have become insincere in my moral judgment, so that my keeping the wallet is not an akratic act. Not so, says Hare; my use of "ought" has become "less robust than formerly ... but then from the start the expression [in its intuitive use] ... had the potentiality of such a decline" (*FR* 76–7/5.6). At the critical level, I could not use "ought" in this twisted fashion; but, as Hare claims, the intuitive-level use of "ought" "has, built into its logic, all manner of ways of evading the rigour of pure prescriptive universality" (74/5.5). Indeed, Hare calls the intuitive-level "ought" a "Janus-word"; that name implies that there is a two-faced shiftiness in meaning, which is part of "ought's" nature, at this level (75–6/5.6). Not only, then, does the moral *intuition* have the possibility of exception built in, so does the moral *language* at the intuitive level. Thus, intuitive-level moral language accommodates the weakness that intuitive moral judgments allow (73/5.5; *MT* 58/3.7). For that reason, Hare writes that

> at the intuitive level ... sometimes the believer in [moral principles] can affirm their truth although [she] is not absolutely set on obeying them, and does not. This is what gives rise to [special-pleading weakness of will]. ("WW" 1306)

On that basis, Hare can maintain both that my intuitive moral judgment was sincere, even if I made exception to it, and that my not acting upon that judgment is indeed akratic.

1.3.4 Ought-but-Cannot Morally Weak-Willed Action

Moving on, the second way in which weakness of will can occur at the intuitive level exemplifies the case of "ought but can't" (Hare, *FR* 80/5.8). We need to be clear from the start, though, that Hare does not mean just any instance of inability to be grounds for labeling an action as weak-willed. If someone were to say, "I know I ought to have telephoned the police about the kidnapping, but I could not, since I was left tied up in the bathtub," Hare would not regard her failure to call as an incontinent action. Hare is not talking about cases where an action is a *physical* impossibility for the agent. Obviously, then, Hare must have in mind a particular sense of "can't" here—one that requires "very careful examination, since in other senses [an agent exhibiting weakness of will] . . . very well can do what [she] ought" (68/5.1).

In cases of weakness of will, the "can't"—the inability that is present— is *psychological.* What happens is that the temptation, or interest opposed to the moral judgment, is so powerful that the agent is psychologically unable to resist it. Hare writes that this kind of

> psychological inability . . . makes it impossible to act on . . . [the moral] prescription . . . and so explains how [the] prescriptivity [that is, the motivational force of the accepted moral judgment] . . . is still compatible with disobedience. . . . [The agent] cannot do the [moral] act. This is clearest in cases of compulsive neuroses in which "psychological" impossibility comes close to "physical"; but it also holds in more normal cases of weakness of will, as the very word "weakness" indicates. (82/5.9)

That last sentence is crucial, because it implies that in most incontinent actions of this kind, the inability of the "can't" is not complete, even in the restricted psychological sense. It is not that the agent has *no* ability to resist the temptation (80/5.8). She simply reaches a certain point at which her self-struggle with the temptation exhausts her, and she surrenders to it. Further, there is a certain laxity or weakness implied in her quitting her resistance at just such-and-such a point—could she not have held out a bit longer? And, if so, why did she not? That is why this kind of weakness (normally) is not simply neurotic compulsion, and why it is still correct to say that the agent *intentionally* acted against her moral judgment (Hare, "WW" 1306).

Let me clarify how this weakness occurs by returning to the example concerning Fred Nietzebaum's lost wallet. Suppose that I do not plead excuse for myself, but do, in fact, specify and prescribe to myself the particular intuitive moral judgment, "I ought to return Fred's wallet." However, suppose also that I am deep in the clutches of a lust for a new stereo system—my old system is failing, the warranties are (of course) expired, and I cannot go on much longer without hearing my Frank Zappa albums. I *need* a new stereo! I *must* have it! And being destitute (which sadly seems the lot of most parking-lot-attendant philosophers), I am obsessing about acquiring the money for my purchase. In an instant, I see that Fred's lost money will meet my need. That puts my lust for the new stereo into direct conflict with my moral judgment to return the money. Now, I *want* to tell Fred that I have his wallet; I *try* to tell him. But the temptation to keep the money is too strong, and I cave in under its pressure. I cannot resist my lust for the stereo system, and I tell Fred that I have not found his wallet (or perhaps that I did, but that it was empty).

However, it might be objected that there is nothing particularly psychologically overwhelming about my lust for a new stereo; I must not have been sincere in my moral judgment, since this case does not really seem to be one of "ought but can't." But while it is true that my interest in the stereo is not inherently overwhelming—that is, necessarily overriding—in itself, it is also true that this kind of weakness does not require such strength in the temptation-interest. If the interest opposed to the moral judgment *were* overwhelming in itself, then I would not be blameworthy or weak-willed in succumbing to it. As it is, though, I *can* be blamed as weak-willed "for not being strong-minded enough" to be able to resist what is, in fact, an eminently resistible temptation (Hare, "WW" 1306). Thus, Hare can say that my moral judgment was sincere, but simply was not held, or affirmed, strongly enough to prevent the stereo-interest from overriding it. My action, then, seems to be a true case of ought-but-cannot incontinence.

Further, we should note how this kind of incontinence exploits the intuitive moral judgment's vulnerability to being overridden. There is no excuse being made here, as was the case with special pleading; the moral judgment *does* apply, and it is an accepted prescription that I return the wallet. However, since, as we saw earlier, intuitive moral judgments must be overridable—so that conflicts between intuitive moral prescriptions can be resolved—that trait leaves the judgments open to being overridden by *non-moral* prescriptions, as well (Hare, *MT* 59–60/3.7). For, as Hare writes,

> What happens when I decide that I ought to break a promise in order
> to [meet a conflicting intuitive moral obligation] . . . has quite close

affinities with what happens when I decide to break one in order not to disappoint my own appetites. (59–60/3.7)

The latter sort of instance is what occurs in ought-but-cannot incontinence. Moreover, Hare easily can account for the intuitive moral judgment's being overridden, since its motivational force is provided by a mere feeling or disposition. As long as the temptation-prescription expresses a preference stronger than the moral prescription's feeling of obligation, then it is entirely possible, in Hare's view, for the temptation to override the moral judgment and to keep that judgment from being able to motivate action.

1.3.5 Impossibility of Weak-Willed Action at the Critical Level

With his explanations, then, of the special pleading and ought-but-cannot scenarios, Hare has proposed two ways in which "it is indeed possible" for a person to akratically act against an intuitive moral judgment ("WW" 1306). However, we need to understand that neither of these kinds of *akrasia* would be possible in the face of a *critical* moral judgment. As we saw in examining the connection between the rationality and overriding-ness of critical moral prescriptions, there is *no possibility* of exception in regard to those judgments. So special pleading could not work against a critical moral judgment, since there is no allowance for the exceptions special pleading utilizes. Moreover, because the rational process of critical thinking yields a necessarily overriding rational superpreference to motivate its moral judgment, there could not be a preference that could override that moral judgment. For that reason, no temptation-interest could create an ought-but-cannot situation at the critical level. In short, critical moral judgments still are "not allow[ed] to be overridden" (Hare, *MT* 60/3.8). So in Hare's account, it remains impossible to exhibit weakness of will in the face of a critical moral judgment. Any instance of moral *akrasia* signals an intuitive moral judgment.

That completes our picture of Hare's proposed solution to his theoretical difficulty in explaining moral incontinence. But before we move on, let us review: Hare distinguishes two levels of thought at which a moral judgment can be made. At the critical level, moral judgments are rationally informed and express overriding rational superpreferences. At the intuitive level, though, moral judgments merely are rationally justified, in a secondary sense. Hare concedes that these moral judgments *can* be overridden; that is, he is forced to loosen his characterization of what constitutes a moral judgment, and to allow that intuitive-level instances need not be overriding

(60/3.8). Hare's distinction then eases his theoretical difficulties by permitting him, first, to postulate two ways—special pleading and ought-but-cannot—in which incontinence could occur against an intuitive moral judgment, and second, to maintain that rational critical moral judgments never are violated by incontinent actions (60/3.8). Thus, he claims, weak-willed actions do not present a counterexample to his view of moral intentional action, as his theory does admit that weakness of will can occur ("WW" 1306). Also, by the same maneuver, Hare hopes to preserve his view of moral intentional action as action that the agent judges to be rational, since the rational critical moral judgments are not subject to weakness of will. With that, we conclude our exposition both of Hare's account of rational action and of his justificatory explanation of incontinent actions. Now, we may begin assessing the strengths and weaknesses of Hare's view.

2

HARE'S THEORY
IN THE CRUCIBLE

At this point, we may begin assessing the strengths and weaknesses of Hare's view. In doing so, we shall pursue two main lines of questioning. First, we shall compare Hare's explanation of weak-willed action against the measure afforded by human experience. That is, we shall investigate how well Hare's portrayal of weakness of will can account for what we experience among the phenomena of incontinent actions. Second, we shall examine what impact any newfound implications of Hare's view of incontinence might have on the suitability of his overall theory for serving as a model for rational action.

2.1 SPECIAL PLEADING'S
DEPENDENCE ON OUGHT-BUT-CANNOT

However, before we examine those issues, we need to clarify an important point—that of the connection between special pleading and ought-but-cannot incontinence. Hare presents these two as distinct and independent ways in which an agent can act against her moral judgment. But, in taking a closer look at special pleading, we shall see that it is not as independent as it first appears.

Now, we recall that in utilizing special pleading, an agent makes an exception for herself, so that her intuitive moral principle's judgment does not prescribe for *her* on *that* occasion (Hare, *FR* 76–7/5.6; *MT* 59/3.7; "WW" 1306). So by means of some excuse, the agent rationalizes that her case is special, that it does not fall under the moral judgment's rule. Say, for example that someone judges that she ought to protect her children from harm.

But, even though she believes that secondhand smoke can be harmful to children, she frequently smokes around her children anyway, because "anything less than two packs a day really will not cause any harm to *my* healthy-as-horses children." Further, since this instance is a case of akratic action, then, presumably, her excuse is illegitimate, and the rule of her moral judgment actually does apply to her specific action. Here, we must pose two questions: Does the agent honestly accept her rationalizing excuse—does she truly believe that it "works"? Or does she realize that the excuse is faulty, even though she makes use of it? Those questions trouble Hare, because if the agent *does* believe in her own rationalization, then she is not incontinent in acting upon that excuse; but if she does *not* believe in it, then special pleading cannot stand on its own as an explanation for her weak-willed action.

2.1.1 Sincerely Believed Rationalizations

For suppose, first, that our agent believes that her rationalization is correct. Then, she falls under Hare's description of the person "who thinks that in general *one ought*, but has not gotten as far as realizing that [*her*] present case falls under this principle" [Emphasis in original] (*FR* 83/5.9). In other words, if she honestly believes that—as long as she smokes less than two packs a day—she is not harming her children by smoking in their presence, then her doing so is a case of "it seemed like a good idea at the time." She does not realize that she is acting contrary to her moral judgment. We have already seen that Hare agrees that such an action does not qualify as "weak-willed," or "incontinent" (83/5.9). Therefore, if an agent sincerely accepts her own excuse in specially pleading, then the action—which she does, and which is explained by means of that special pleading—is *not* an incontinent one. Hare would thus lose special pleading as an explanation of how morally akratic actions can occur, since special pleading would no longer apply to such actions.

2.1.2 Hypocritical Rationalizations

But suppose, on the other hand, that the specially pleading agent *does* recognize that her rationalizing-excuse is faulty; would her smoking then qualify as an incontinent action? Perhaps, but before we can answer with certainty, we need to ask another question: if the agent realizes that her excuse is faulty, how could it keep her from applying and acting upon her moral judgment? Hare has two possible answers. His first possibility, for an agent who does not sincerely believe in her rationalization, is to say that she may be acting *hypocritically*, rather than incontinently. That is, she does not sincerely prescribe the moral judgment to herself; she just mouths the platitude that she ought to guard her children from harm, as if noting what *society* prescribes. In acting hypocritically, the agent uses the word "ought" insincerely or nonprescriptively, and thus illegitimately—exceeding even the backsliding that the intuitive "ought" can allow. She can make use of an insincere rationalization, because her moral judgment is already insincere. So in the case of a *hypocritical* agent, Hare claims, "there is something wrong with what [she] says [that is, with her judgment], as well as with what [she] does" (82–3/5.9). Again, Hare has already stipulated that such actions do not count as incontinent (82–3/5.9). For that reason, if the action involves hypocrisy, Hare would be unable to use special pleading as an explanation for weakness of will.

2.1.3 Self-Deceptive Rationalizations

The second possibility to which Hare could appeal in the case of an agent who realizes that her excuse is faulty is that the agent accepts the excuse out of *self-deception*. This explanatory tack looks more promising, since it can construe our agent's smoking as weak-willed. For—as we shall see shortly—if the agent is self-deceived, then she must have some kind of recognition that her rationalization is faulty, that her action *does* fall under the moral judgment's rule. So it would not be out of ignorance that she acts contrary to the judgment. Also, through her self-deception, she can suppress that recognition and believe in her excuse, so that acting upon it would not require her to be insincere in her moral judgment. Those points would allow Hare to maintain that she intentionally acts against her sincere moral judgment—that she acts *incontinently*. However, this scenario does not seem able to account for that akratic action solely through special pleading.

The problem in maintaining special pleading's explanatory independence arises because its action would be done under the influence of self-deception. "Incontinence," as I have characterized it in my introduction, excludes actions performed through self-deception. Moreover, the reason behind my introductory stipulation was that self-deception itself seems to involve *akrasia*. Given that point, it seems explanatorily unhelpful to try to account for how an incontinent action can occur by attributing its possibility to another incontinent action's prior occurrence. Now, in order to press Hare on this point about self-deception, I must offer some support for this claim; and Amelie O. Rorty's explanatory work on self-deception can give us a solid base for that support.

In describing self-deception, Rorty states that it involves a person's be-lieving a certain thing, *p*, and then either (1) believing *not-p*—or what she ought to recognize as *amounting to*, or implying, *not-p*; or (2) denying that she believes *p* (*Mind in Action* 365). So, for example, in the case of our smok-ing agent, she believes *p*, that the secondhand cigarette smoke of less than two packs a day will not harm *her* children. She also believes, given what she knows about the effects of secondhand smoke and the comparatively nor-mal health of her children, what amounts to a rejection of *p* (so she takes the first option described by Rorty). Further, Rorty writes, self-deception seems to involve more than the agent's simply being in error—she has not just mistakenly failed to make the connection between her inconsistent be-liefs; at some second-order level, the agent *does* recognize that the beliefs conflict (*MA* 213, 365). Moreover, it is not that the agent—confused by her belief-conflict and unable to tell which side to affirm—simply "falls back" on *p*, the prosmoking belief; rather, she adopts some trumped-up or ad hoc strategy to ensure that she can affirm *p* (213, 365). That trumped-up sup-port for the prosmoking belief is what moves our agent beyond mere error or self-conflict, and into self-*deceit*. Rorty says of such *p*-supporting strate-gies that they "should not themselves be mistaken or conflicted: as tailor made, trumped-up, ad hoc rationalizing maneuvers, they are themselves de-ceitful [that is, recognized by the agent as incorrect or untruthful]" (213). That is where *akrasia* enters the explanation for self-deception.

For the agent brings herself—by recognizedly dubious methods—to affirm *p*, the prosmoking excuse. Assuming that she morally judges that she ought not to be deceitful (which, I think, Hare would grant as a standard intuitive moral judgment), her coming to believe *p* is an akratic act. In com-ing to hold the prosmoking belief, she is acting intentionally and making use of a means that she recognizes as deceitful. Thus, she intentionally af-firms as true a belief that she realizes she has arrived at by a method yield-ing falsehood; she intentionally does what she identifies as morally wrong—namely, deceiving herself so as to believe *p* is true. Rorty calls that kind of thing "akrasia [she avoids the italics] of belief," and offers this scenario for its occurrence:

> A person can akratically come to believe something against her better judgment. . . . someone can akratically cut off inquiry or investigation, knowing that if [she] pressed on [she] would revise [her] beliefs. (236–7)

In our example, then, the agent might incontinently refrain from connect-ing her beliefs about secondhand smoke and about her children's general health in order to avoid acknowledging an *explicit* refutation of *p*, her prosmoking belief. Or she might akratically refrain from assessing the rational weight of that refutation in order to be able to disregard it, and so on. The point is that the self-deception, which enables the agent to "believe in" her rationalizing excuse, involves—or is made possible by—this prior *akrasia*. That is what I have claimed. In Rorty's words, "Often akrasia works as a strategy toward self-deception. . . . Akrasia of belief and self-deception often go hand in hand" (237).

2.1.4 The Dependence Relationship

Thus, we come to a vexing question for Hare: if special pleading relies upon self-deception, which itself involves a prior occurrence of weakness of will, what is the explanation for—what kind of incontinence is present in—that prior action? What troubles Hare is that he has only two possible answers: "special pleading" or "ought-but-cannot." If he responds with the latter, special pleading loses its independence as an explanation for incontinent actions. But he cannot answer with the former without falling into a regress that would remove any meaningful explanation for the action. For suppose that Hare did assert that special-pleading incontinence is what enables the agent's self-deception; then he would have to propose *another* self-deception behind *that* special plea, and then a third special plea to explain the second self-deception, and so on. Hare would fall into a trap, what Rorty calls a "suspicious regression," in continually having to postulate prior instances of special pleading and self-deception in order to account for the first ones (366). Really, that would amount to no explanation at all of how the incontinent action could happen in the first place.

Indeed, in order to be able to stop—or to avoid—the regress, Hare would have to answer that the self-deception behind the special pleading must be made possible by an instance of ought-but-cannot incontinence. As we saw earlier, ought-but-cannot weakness of will occurs when an agent makes an intuitive moral judgment about a specific action—in our example, that she ought not deceive herself about the secondhand effects of her smoking—but then has her moral prescription overridden by a stronger preference, here, to smoke no matter the consequences. The agent judges that she ought not perform the action of deceiving herself, but she cannot resist the temptation—her stronger opposed preference—to do so (Hare, "WW" 1306). So with that scenario's set starting point, Hare could characterize our agent's whole smoking-action sequence, stemming from the ought-but-cannot *akrasia* involved in the self-deceptive affirmation of the faulty excuse, as an explainable instance of weakness of will. However, it is now clear why special pleading can no longer be used as an independent explanation for weak-willed actions; it is a *secondary* move, which can work only on the basis of a prior occurrence of ought-but-cannot incontinence.

2.1.5 Special Pleading's Remaining Uses

That is not to say, though, that special pleading is left with *no* explanatory use for Hare. Rorty, for example, notes,

> Akratic actions are often unsettling because their occurrence gives the agent a sense of vertigo about [her] qualifications as an agent [that is, as controlling her own actions]; that is one reason why self-deception often rides on the back of akrasia, to steady the vertigo of an agent who seems unable to command [herself]. (*MA* 260)

So Hare could appeal to the whole special-pleading scenario to show how an agent might "push back" her ought-but-cannot incontinence in order to cover that unsettling experience with self-deceit about why she acts as she does. Or again, Hare could propose special pleading as an "end-around" incontinent maneuver; in this case, an agent—whose akratic desire is not strong enough to override her opposed moral judgment—might pit that desire, instead, against a weaker moral judgment that, when overridden, prevents the stronger judgment from being applied. Thus, our smoking agent might use special pleading because her prescription to protect her children is "stronger" than her preference to smoke; but the latter is "stronger" than her prescription to be truthful, which is a "weaker" moral judgment, since she thinks that being deceitful is not as bad as harming children. In those ways, then, Hare could use special pleading to explain phenomena related to the experience of *akrasia*. He could show how incontinent actions can lead to further incontinence, or how incontinence connects to self-deception.

But still, all special pleading would have to be rooted in ought-but-cannot incontinence. Ultimately, Hare has to attribute any incontinent action to some instance of ought-but-cannot weakness of will. And so, as we investigate how well Hare's explanation can account for what we experience with *akrasia* itself, we shall focus on Hare's portrayal of ought-but-cannot incontinence.

2.2 EXPLANATORY SUCCESSES

Now, when we try to fit the phenomena of our experience with *akrasia* into the framework of Hare's conception of ought-but-cannot weakness of will, what we first see is that there are some important aspects of that experience that Hare's account can indeed accommodate.

2.2.1 Phenomena of Mental Conflict and Anguish

One of those aspects is the mental conflict and anguish that the agent experiences in performing the incontinent action. Hare can give a good account not only of how it feels to act akratically but also of why that is so. We can refresh our memory of this aspect of incontinence by returning to our introductory illustration of Leontius and his perverse desire to ogle the corpses. Leontius struggles with himself—he oscillates between trying to ogle and trying to refrain. When he finally succumbs to temptation and rushes forward to view the corpses, he is distraught and angry at his action. Even in the midst of his performance, he is still resistant to, and anguished over, what he is doing (Plato, 439e–440a). Further, Leontius's inner conflict clearly seems connected to the fact that he judges he ought not ogle the corpses, *even as he does so*, anyway. We can note the push-pull of opposing or contrary judgments, which are both active motivators, present in Leontius's mind. Each of his judgments has a specific action as its end: his perverse appetite's judgment of desire directs him to leer at the corpses, and his moral feeling's judgment commands him to refrain. Moreover, each of those judgments apparently moves Leontius to take the action that it advocates. The mental disorder Leontius experiences is the evidence of that contrary judging. This mental conflict and its resultant anguish, then, seem typical of weak-willed actions, since they signal the conflicted nature of the actions themselves.

Further, Hare's concept of ought-but-cannot incontinence can well account for that mental disorder. For in instances of ought-but-cannot weakness of will, the agent has in mind specific opposed prescriptions. Given that, it is easy to make sense of the mental tug-of-war that an agent experiences in acting akratically. The agent's mental disruption is simply a result of her affirming prescriptions for her both to do, and not to do, a certain action. Each affirmation motivates her to act, but the acts so motivated are mutually exclusive, and that leaves the agent conflicted—wanting and trying to do contrary actions. Moreover, when her stronger akratic preference overrides her moral disposition's prescription, that leaves her unable to act upon that moral prescription, but it does not remove her *affirmation* of that prescription—her *desire* to so act. Her continuing desire to act morally then leads her to feel anguished—or angry or confused or frustrated or so on—at how she does act. Thus, Hare's portrayal of incontinent action can indeed account for this key aspect of the phenomenon of weakness of will. His conception of ought-but-cannot incontinence explains the mental conflict and anguish associated with akratic action. Moreover, since that mental disorder is based in the nature of ought-but-cannot actions, the explanation for it flows smoothly from Hare's characterization of those actions.

2.2.2 Phenomenon of Personality Division

Moving on, we can see a second important, related aspect of the phenomenon of weak-willed actions that Hare's theory can accommodate, at least provisionally. This point is that an agent, in acting incontinently, often sees herself as experiencing not just mental conflict, but suffering a more serious division of her very mind or personality. The apostle Paul, in his epistle to the Romans, offers a striking illustration of this facet of *akrasia*; he writes:

> [14]For we know that the law is spiritual; but I am of the flesh, sold into slavery under sin. [15]I do not understand my own actions. For I do not do what I want, but I do the very thing I hate. [16]Now if I do what I do not want, I agree that the law is good. [17]But in fact it is no longer I that do it, but sin that dwells within me. [18]For I know that nothing good dwells within me, that is, in my flesh. I can will what is right, but I cannot do it. [19]For I do not do the good I want, but the evil I do not want is what I do. [20]Now if I do what I do not want, it is no longer I that do it, but sin that dwells within me. [21]So I find it to be a law that when I want to do what is good, evil lies close at hand. [22]For I delight in the law of God in my inmost self, [23]but I see in my members another law at war with the law of my mind, making me captive to the law of sin that dwells in my members. [24]Wretched man that I am! Who will rescue me from this body of death? (Rom. 7:14–24, NRSV)

Paul's example typifies this phenomenon in several ways. He distances himself both from the desire to do the unlawful actions (vv. 15, 16) and from the agency for performing those actions (vv. 17, 20). But he also makes the seemingly contrary acknowledgment that it is still he who is responsible when he does wrong, that the motivation to do so comes from within himself (vv. 18, 23). Thus, he does realize that it truly is he who is doing the wrong actions

(vv. 15, 19). Paul sees a deep division within himself, and he makes an ago-
nized plea to be free of that part that draws him to evil (vv. 22–4).

Moreover, this experience of division appears quite common in agents
acting akratically. Indeed, as the mental conflict found its basis in the nature
of incontinent action, so also does this seeming division of the agent's personality signal important parts of the explanation of *how* such action occurs.
For that reason, it is crucial for an account of weakness of will to be able
not only to admit this phenomenon's occurrence, but also to explain how
it happens.

Now, Hare can indeed take note of this facet of weakness of will; he cites
Paul's plight as an example of it (*FR* 78/5.7; "WW" 1,306). Hare treats this
divided-mind scenario as one way in which incontinence can occur. He also
apparently sees it as a kind of ought-but-cannot situation, since he thinks the
agent *does* sincerely prescribe the moral action to herself, but is prevented from
performing it by a "part of [her which] resists" ("WW" 1,306). The ought-
but-cannot basis of this phenomenon is clarified when Hare remarks on

> the curious metaphor of divided personality which, ever since this sub-
> ject [of incontinence] was first discussed, has seemed so natural. One part
> of the personality is made to issue commands to the other, and to be an-
> gry or grieved when they are disobeyed; but the other part is said either
> to be unable to obey, or to be so depraved as not to want to, and to be
> stronger than the part which commands. (*FR* 81/5.8)

Hare's last clause obviously describes an ought-but-cannot conflict in the
agent's action. Paul's example does seem full of the frustration and sincere
desire to follow the moral judgment, which Hare would point to as the signs
of ought-but-cannot incontinence. So it looks like Hare can rightly place
this phenomenon within the parameters of his conception of ought-but-
cannot *akrasia*.

However, Hare does have some problem in explaining just how this
kind of ought-but-cannot situation might work. He notes, "The difficulty is
to interpret [this divided-personality metaphor]. For we do not really believe
that it is no longer I who am the agent [of my wrongdoing]. . . . Otherwise
I would not be to blame" [Emphasis in original] ("WW" 1,306). Now, we
noted above that Hare can explain why an agent, in acting akratically, might
experience mental conflict; that is easily attributable to the agent's affirming
contrary prescriptions. But the question here is what could be occurring that
would bring the agent to a state in which she sees her very personality as divided? That is what Hare has trouble answering. He proposes a few possible

responses: perhaps the agent has a "recalcitrant lower nature" that resists her moral judgment; or perhaps she is not prescribing to herself with her "whole personality or real self" (Hare, *FR* 81/5.8). Each of those options, though, is nearly as opaque as the divided-personality image itself; Hare does not offer any substantive explanation of what either of them would entail.

His problem is, I think, that there does not seem to be any element of ought-but-cannot incontinence that could easily be extended to explain why the agent might experience this more serious personality division. For as Hare said, ought-but-cannot situations are merely moral instances of prescription conflict, and so fit into the characterization of that broader conception (*MT* 60/3.7). However, on Hare's account, if an agent should affirm contrary nonmoral preferences—such as, to go to a movie, and to stay home and finish reading a novel—we might expect her to feel torn in acting upon one of those preferences. But we would be surprised if she began to see herself as having a divided personality simply on account of her conflicting desires. Since what counts in cases of conflict is neither the nature of a prescription's source-disposition, nor the moral value of its directed action, but rather that prescription's strength, why should conflict instances involving moral prescriptions differ on this point from the nonmoral ones? Why should the moral conflict cases give rise to that more extreme phenomenon?

That is not to say that Hare is unable to explain the divided-personality phenomenon by appealing to ought-but-cannot scenarios. But he has not done so yet, and such an explanation does not seem to emerge naturally from his characterization of what happens when an agent's prescriptions conflict. Perhaps, for example, Hare could argue that accepted moral prescriptions are fundamental enough to a person's identity—to her sense of who she is—that to violate them creates division in that sense of self; but this is mere speculation, since no hint of that currently appears in Hare's theory. So, as I stated earlier, Hare can provisionally account for this divided-personality aspect of incontinence. Before we can grant that he has done so, however, he needs to offer more explanation, to show how the agent's affirming conflicting moral and nonmoral prescriptions could bring her to think that her very self is divided.

2.2.3 Davidson's Mistaken Attack

Unfortunately for Hare, though, what he has done so far in describing the helplessness that the agent experiences in these ought-but-cannot situations appears to make his position vulnerable to attack. Donald Davidson, for example, argues that Hare's model of incontinent action cannot be correct.

Davidson thinks that it is misguided to take as a "paradigm of all cases of weakness of will" situations in which the agent is "overcome by passion or unstrung by emotion . . . [that is,] cases [in which] the agent is psychologically unable to do what [she] thinks [she] ought" (*Essays on Actions and Events* 27).

Davidson objects that this view of incontinence engenders two problems. He thinks those difficulties become evident when we try to portray the situation that Hare describes:

> The image we get of incontinence from . . . Hare is of a battle or struggle between two contestants [that is, between two interests of the agent]. Each contestant is armed with [her] argument or principle [that is, with a prescription]. One side may be labeled "passion" and the other "reason"; they fight; one side wins, the wrong side, the side called "passion" (or "lust" or "pleasure"). . . . On [this] story, not only can we not account for incontinence; it is not clear how we can ever blame the agent for what [she] does: [her] action merely reflects the outcome of a struggle within [her]. What could [she] do about it? And more important, the . . . image does not allow us to make sense of a conflict in one person's soul, for it leaves no room for the all important process of weighing considerations. (35)

Davidson, then, is arguing, first, that the ought-but-cannot model of incontinence removes the agent's action from being her responsibility. The action occurs mechanically, the outcome simply being a function of whichever of the agent's interests is the strongest. Second, Davidson thinks that Hare's mechanistic ought-but-cannot model is unable to allow the agent to weigh her options and rationally *decide* which action to do. Again, what the agent does seems determined simply by which of her interests has the most strength or force. However, Davidson sees that as a problem. For one aspect of the phenomenon of weak-willed actions that needs to be explained is the agent's ability to assess her options and rationally decide which action should be done or which to actually do—so that when she acts incontinently, she is deciding for the action that is worse to do.

Now, I think Davidson is correct in asserting both that what the agent does intentionally—even in the case of akratic actions—is a matter of her decision, and also that an agent *is* responsible for her incontinent action. However, Davidson has misunderstood Hare in claiming that Hare's conception of weakness of will cannot account for these aspects of an incontinent action. For while Hare maintains that an agent will act upon whichever of her preferences is the strongest, he also holds that which preference is the strongest is *subject to the agent's rational assessment and decision*. What makes

Davidson's attack plausible is Hare's repeated claim that when an agent prescribes and acts, she does so based on her "greater present desires" (*EET*
211). That is, Hare says, she will "in any case do what the balance of [her]
present preferences requires" (*MT* 104/5.6). So there is a straightforward relation between what an agent most prefers to do and what she then intentionally does. However, that does not make the agent's action merely mechanical or removed from her responsibility. For the agent can consider her
preferences and rationally strengthen or weaken—or even abandon—them
through doing so (Hare, *EET* 249). In other words, the agent can rationally
weigh her preferences, her various and perhaps contrary interests; and in
submitting those interests "to logic and the facts," she can alter their
strengths to determine which will be the strongest (Hare, *MT* 104/5.6). On
that account, Hare claims,

> It is true that both the agent and others can *change* their preferences or
> inclinations . . . [because it is] the freedom and the responsibility of the
> moral thinker to change [her] preferences if the moral thinking leads
> [her] to. [Emphasis in original] ("Comments" 212)

Moreover, we have already seen, in our discussion of the critical-thinking
process, how this rational preference-alteration works.

But how can that be squared with all of Hare's talk about "overridingness" and "psychological inability," which makes it seem the agent is at the
mercy of her preferences? In Davidson's defense, I must say that Hare is not
always completely clear about this point; but we can glean a hint of what
Hare would say, in his very definition of "overriding." He writes, "To *treat*
a principle as overriding . . . is to *let* it always override other principles when
they conflict with it and . . . [to] *let* it override all other prescriptions" (*MT*
56/3.6) [my emphasis]. Hare apparently means that even in the case of a
critical moral judgment—which is overriding since it is formed in such a
way that its underlying interest is made into the agent's strongest—it is still
a matter of the agent's rational choice whether that judgment will function
at that strength. She could reconsider the judgment, question her critical
reasoning, and so on; in short, she could rationally "talk herself down" from
holding the judgment so strongly. Moreover, she could do the same kind of
thing to her akratic preferences. So an agent's incontinent preference, left as
it is, might be too strong for her intuitive moral judgment to override—
hence Hare's claim that she is psychologically unable to resist her
temptation-interest. However, the agent could reduce that temptation's
strength by rationally considering it—what it would cost her and others if

she pursued it, and so on—hence Hare also can claim that she is blame-worthy and that her action is weak-willed, but not compelled.

Davidson, then, is mistaken in his accusation against Hare: Hare's ought-but-cannot model does make the agent's incontinent action her re-sponsibility, and it can account for an agent's rationally considering and weighing her preferences. Thus, Hare's theory admits and explains these facets of the phenomenon of akratic actions, as well. However, we should remember Davidson's concern with this issue, because when we examine Davidson's own view, we shall see that he wants it to correct Hare's *perceived* problem.

Also, before we move on, I want to make a few parting remarks about the helplessness that the agent experiences in the divided-personality cases of weakness of will. I think, first, that while Hare is heading in the right di-rection in admitting this phenomenon, we should examine it more carefully, because a fuller explanation of how incontinence occurs still lies "hidden" within it. Second, we need to explore the implications of that more com-plete account. For Davidson's concern is not unfounded, as Hare himself sees: if an agent's action proceeds from a divided mind or from a less-than-wholehearted will, it does seem at least questionable whether the agent can be fully responsible for that action ("WW" 1306). Or more precisely, we might wonder: is what the agent does in such an instance truly intentional, or is her action's intentionality compromised? If the latter should be the case, what are the general implications for explaining *akrasia* in terms of in-tentional action? We shall return to these issues later, but for the moment, we can only note them and must continue examining Hare's account.

2.2.4 Phenomenon of Continent Actions

We are almost ready to begin dealing with the problems in Hare's the-ory, but first we must address one last important point that he can explain: how *continent* actions can occur. That may seem like a nonissue; if *incontinent* actions are the problem for rational-action theories to explain, surely continent actions are already obvious as a kind of rational action? However—as we shall see later, with Davidson's view—that is not always the case. For that reason we should note how Hare handles this issue. Now, as Aristotle has pointed out, the key aspect of continent actions is that the agent does do what she judges to be rational, but she is still *conflicted* in do-ing so (*NE* 1145b10–15, 1146a10–15). A continent agent does not fail to "follow through" with her rational judgment, as an incontinent agent does; but the continent agent still has an interior struggle such that she might have acted *in*continently. So the question here is: in performing a continent action, where does the agent's success lie? That is, what does she do right that the incontinent agent gets wrong?

For Hare, the answer is simply that the continent agent utilizes her ability to subject her preferences to reasoned consideration. As we recently noted, the agent can use logic and the facts of her situation to examine her akratic preference; in doing so, she can reduce its strength. For instance, consider the smoking mother who faces an ought-but-cannot problem with regard to deceiving herself. If she should carefully consider what her self-deception would entail—for her self-respect, her children's health, her finances in buying all those cigarettes—she might find that she then wants less to deceive herself in order to smoke. As a result, her moral judgment that she ought not be deceitful would be comparatively stronger than her desire to deceive herself in order to smoke. Her moral judgment could then override the desire, rather than vice versa. By that means, the agent could refrain from deceiving herself—but not without conflict, since the overridden desire would still be in force, just as the moral judgment was in the weak-willed action. In this way, an agent could act continently, according to Hare's theory.

Further, Hare's view also can make sense of continent behavior in situations involving special pleading and even critical moral judgments. First, at the secondary level of special pleading, Hare could say that an agent, in submitting her preferences to rational examination, might thereby deconstruct whatever plausibility her special-pleading excuse had. In the case of the smoking mother, she could consider how much smoke her children would be exposed to if she kept to just under two packs a day; how at school they would reek of that smoke; how they would see smoking in a positive light, and so on. Her self-deceptive excuse, that her smoking would not harm the children, would then lose believability. That would allow her to see that her moral judgment, to protect her children from harm, *did* apply, so that judgment could override her desire to smoke. But, again, that desire might still remain and leave her with some interior conflict in refraining from smoking.

Moreover, Hare could maintain that moral judgments at the critical level might be overriding yet still face some resistance. As we saw earlier, critical thought "prunes back" interests opposed to the moral judgment, to ensure that judgment's supremacy compared to the agent's other preferences (Hare, *MT* 42/2.6, 215/12.4; "Comments" 249). But that does not require those opposed preferences to be completely eliminated; they even might retain enough strength to make the agent feel conflicted in overriding them and acting upon her moral judgment. So Hare's view can explain how an agent could act continently—by utilizing her ability to rationally analyze her preferences—with respect to both critical and intuitive moral judgments, and including both ought-but-cannot and special-pleading cases.

2.3 EXPLANATORY FAILURES

Now, having seen that continent actions can be performed in accordance with critical moral judgments, we can assess the first crucial failure of Hare's theory. For as we recall, Hare denies that critical judgments can be violated by weak-willed actions (*MT* 60/3.8). But this denial requires him to say that it never happens that an agent truly morally judges an action to be irrational but then intentionally performs the action anyway. We shall see that Hare is thereby left in a dilemma: either he is unable to account for a significant aspect of the phenomenon of incontinent actions, or he relegates his conception of rational action to being an unattainable ideal rather than a model of human moral action.

2.3.1 *Incontinent Violations of Fully Rational Judgments*

The root of Hare's problem is a point we have already seen: that intuitive moral judgments are based in feelings, dispositions, and the like (38–9/2.4). Such judgments are not deliverances of reason, except in the derivative sense that rational critical thought has commanded those underlying dispositions to be cultivated. In our example, when the smoking mother makes the intuitive moral judgment that she ought to protect her children from harm, she is not reasoning that harming her children would be irrational, but only *feeling* that doing so would be wrong. Hare puts it this way:

> [Only] the [critical] moral judgement is the conclusion of rational moral thinking. . . . That is why we have to pay much more (indeed a different sort of) regard to the moral deliverances of our own and others' critical thinking than to our and their intuitions. ("Comments" 212–13)

So the intuitive moral judgment itself is not generated by reason, nor does it assess the judged action's rationality.

Of course, the critical moral judgments *are* products of reason, and they *do* identify specific actions as rational or irrational to perform. But again, Hare maintains that such judgments are never overridden, that an agent never intentionally acts against her critical moral judgments (*MT* 60/3, 8). Further, that apparently leaves Hare in the position of saying that an agent can perform a weak-willed action only if her moral judgment against that action is not a reasoned verdict that the action is irrational. That is, an agent never intentionally does what she morally judges to be irrational.

However, that thesis seems plainly false; it does not fit our experience of weakness of will. Augustine of Hippo, in his autobiographical *Confessions*, describes his own struggles with weakness of will; and his account offers a striking illustration of why Hare seems mistaken here. Augustine tells not only how he had a transcendent vision that fully convinced him of the irrationality of his immoral actions, but also how he continued to act immorally anyway. He writes,

> [Upon achieving the transcendent understanding] I heard [the truth] in the way one hears within the heart, and all doubt left me (*Confessions* VII.x.16). . . . But I was not stable. . . . I was in no kind of doubt [about how to act] . . . but was not yet in a state to be able to do that. . . . I did not possess the strength to keep my vision fixed. My weakness reasserted itself, and I returned to my customary condition [that is, to acting immorally] (VII.xvi.22). . . . My desire was not to be more certain . . . but to be more stable [in action]" (VIII.i.1). . . . But while [acting morally] was pleasant to think about and had my notional assent, [acting immorally] was more pleasant and overcame me. (VIII.v.12)

More than that, Augustine goes as far as comparing his condition to that described by Paul in the divided-personality scenario of Romans 7 (VIII.v.12).

Now, I think that given Augustine's comparison and lament about not possessing the strength to follow the moral course of action, Hare would claim that Augustine suffers from ought-but-cannot weakness of will. But there is a problem with that characterization: for ought-but-cannot incontinence can occur only if the moral judgment to be violated is an *intuitive* one, and Augustine's moral judgment seems to be more than that. Augustine does not judge his actions to be wrong because of a feeling or disposition. Rather, the moral course of action has his "notional assent"; he has "no kind of doubt" about it and is as "certain" as he could desire to be (VII.xvi.22; VIII.i.1, v.12). In other words, he makes a sincere, rationally informed judgment that he ought not continue his immoral behavior. Augustine acts incontinently in the face of what seems to be a *critical* moral judgment; but that would make his action impossible, according to Hare.

Furthermore, I do not think that Augustine's weak-willed action is atypical in its violation of a fully rational judgment. Instead, I submit that his difficulty exemplifies another important aspect of the phenomenon of incontinence. Sometimes we perform actions that we judge we ought not to, even though our judgments against them are rationally informed and identify those actions as irrational. We do not lack rational *comprehension* of what we are doing, but we lose rational *control* and act incontinently—that is, irrationally—anyway. Given that, what can Hare say? If his fully rational judgments are critical ones, how can he explain this phenomenon?

As I see it, Hare can respond in either of two ways; but neither can satisfactorily solve his problem. First, Hare could answer that we may sometimes undercut the prescriptive force of our critical moral judgments through rationally criticizing them. Perhaps such a "weakened" critical judgment could then be overridden. Now, the kind of rational criticism involved here would be reflexive consideration of how certain or trustworthy one's own critical thinking was. For instance, critical thinking requires the agent to assume hypothetically the positions of others who would be affected by her proposed action. She then uses her understanding of the direction and intensity of her preferences, were she in those others' shoes, to help her form her own critical moral preference and judgment. But really, is it rational for her to suppose that she has assumed those hypothetical roles accurately enough to arrive at the correct critical judgment?

Hare's answer would seem at first to be "no." As Zeno Vendler has argued,

> [N]o perfect representation of another mind is possible. Short of being an organism at a given moment of its life, no one can fully know what it is like to be that organism at that time. [Emphasis in original] (173)

Hare concurs, at least with regard to *human* hypothetical representations. He writes, "I agree that no human can *fully* know what it is like to be another organism" [Emphasis in original] ("Comments" 282). He further states,

> [W]e lack the necessary information [for critical thinking] nearly always; in particular, we are very bad at putting ourselves in other people's shoes and imagining what it is like to be them. Secondly, we lack the time for acquiring and thinking about this information; and then we lack the ability to think clearly. These three handicaps make it all too easy for us to pretend to ourselves that some act is likely to be for the best (to satisfy preferences maximally and impartially) when in fact what commends it to us is our own self-interest. (*EET* 188)

Therefore, Hare laments, "we are always incompletely informed and always subject to other human failings" (111).

For that reason, human critical moral judgments seem to be generated under cognitive limitations that would render them less than ideally certain. Bernard Williams interprets the situation this way:

> Hare . . . cannot see critical, non-intuitive thought exclusively in archangelic terms [that is, as requiring full hypothetical knowledge and complete preferential impartiality], since he thinks that it is something that most of us can conduct some of the time. (191)

Moreover, recognizing those limitations could allow an agent rationally to undercut her affirmation of her own critical judgment. It is not that she then thinks the judgment is wrong and no longer holds it. Rather, she then considers the *possibility* of the judgment's being wrong, and so holds the judgment defeasibly. Her affirmation of the judgment becomes a bit more tenuous, and the judgment thereby becomes overridable. In such a case, Hare might say, the agent could experience ought-but-cannot weakness of will in the face of that *critical* moral judgment.

However, there are strong indications that Hare would not accept this construal of critical judgments. The first is that Hare explicitly denies Williams's claim. In responding to Williams's assertion that human critical thinking must be less than ideal, Hare writes, "I find this confusing . . . the critical thinking that we do is, so far as it goes, archangelic in form, only subject to our human limitations" ("Comments" 290). In other words, the "human limitations"—of lacking time and cognitive ability, and so on— must affect how often and how easily we can perform critical thinking, but not the results when we do engage in it. If we cannot perfectly envision what it is like to be in another's place, we can still do it well enough that, if we are careful and honest, our critical judgments will be trustworthy. So the reflexive doubts about sincere critical judgments would be unwarranted.

A second indication shows why this view is unacceptable, since it does not fit with Hare's account of the critical-thinking process. Critical thinking is supposed to yield a *prescriptive judgment* of reason that a certain action ought, or ought not, to be done. But if the critical judgment's accuracy is rationally doubted, then it seems one of two problems must be present. On the one hand, given the rational questions about the critical result, can that result still count as the judgment—the verdict, the unreserved or full decision—of reason? Hare argues, "since the [critical] moral judgement is the conclusion of rational moral thinking, it cannot be abandoned without impugning the reasoning and having to do it all over again" (212–13). I believe he would similarly object that the reflexive doubts would be sufficient to impugn the critical reasoning underlying the questioned conclusion. So the critical thinking would have to be redone to reach a judgment of critical reason, which also would remove the doubts and restore full prescriptive force.

But on the other hand, even if the doubted critical reasoning were to yield a judgment, can that judgment still count as *wholehearted* or *sincere*? The point, after all, is that this doubted judgment is overridable, that it has less prescriptive force than it might have. Yet, to Hare, that would just mean that the agent is holding it less than sincerely or fully. For, as we have seen repeatedly, it is the nature of critical thinking to guarantee overriding prescriptive strength to its resultant judgments. So if a "critical" judgment were to be less than overriding, it would have to be the case that the agent was backsliding in her commitment to the judgment. In such an instance, the agent must be less than wholehearted or sincere about what she morally judges. Either of those possibilities would defeat the purpose, because, for Hare, acting against such less-than-wholehearted judgments would not exemplify weakness of will, but rather hypocrisy or acting-in-uncertainty (*FR* 82, 83/5.9; "WW" 1305, 1306).

So then the idea that critical judgments might be less than certain conflicts unavoidably with Hare's account of the nature of critical thinking and judgments. Besides, that construal still would not explain incontinent actions like those of Augustine, who—as we noted—explicitly states that his moral judgments in no way lacked certainty.

Moving to his second possible avenue of response, Hare might argue that intuitive moral thinking *can* include rationally informed judgments. That is, perhaps there could be reasoned moral judgments that would identify specific actions as irrational, and those judgments would yet be intuitive, and not critical. That would allow Hare to admit that there could be akratically violated, rational, moral judgments, even while maintaining that such rationality and judgments do *not* qualify as critical. Arguing this interpretation, J. O. Urmson writes:

> Since the only other form of moral thinking that Hare recognizes is what he calls the intuitive level, it presumably follows that when anyone is engaged in what would be generally regarded as moral thinking but recognizably fails to conform to the canons of the critical level, [she] must be engaged in intuitive moral thinking and Hare's account of intuitive thinking must be intended to cover all such deliberation. (161)

On this view then, acting incontinently would imply operating from less-than-critical rationality, and "critical" rationality would apply *only* to thinking that *exactly* corresponds to Hare's stipulations about the critical process. So re-garding phenomena like Augustine's action, Hare might say that such a rational—but yet not critical—moral judgment could be overcome in in-stances of ought-but-cannot weakness of will.

I think this option is what Hare would indeed take. It fits with his re-jection of Williams's view and with his insistence that human critical think-ing must be "archangelic in form" ("Comments" 290). Moreover, this po-sition would make "critical thinking and judging" *success* terms, applicable only when the *specified* process is done *exactly* right. Hare seems to agree with that, as he contends, "The person who adopts a moral principle know-ing what the principle is, and what its acceptance concretely involves [that is, through critical thinking], is being as rational as [she] could be" (*EET* 46). But does this interpretation solve Hare's problem?

I think not. There are two serious difficulties for Hare's taking this route. The first is that intuitive thinking seems stretched beyond what it was designed to cover. Intuitive moral judgments are supposed to be based in feelings, dispositions, and so on. But I do not see, for example, how Augus-tine's rich understanding—his deep rational conviction—of how he ought and ought not to act could be relegated to the epistemic status of a feeling or intuition. Also, Augustine's rational judgment certainly is not generated in the way Hare describes for intuitive judgments. Rather than having it in-culcated over time and through social influences, Augustine reaches his judgment through extensive rational inquiry (*Conf* VII.x.16). The intricate difficulty and time-consuming process of that seeking further distinguish Augustine's case from the simple, nonreasoning fashion in which intuitive judgments supposedly are invoked. In short, I do not see any similarities be-tween Augustine's rational moral judgment and Hare's "intuitive judgment," except that neither meets the exact procedural stipulations for a "critical judgment." So Hare can defend his position by rejecting any incontinently violated judgment from being a "critical" judgment; but how he can make that defense hold by successfully categorizing all overridden moral judg-ments as "intuitive" is not apparent to me.

Furthermore, there is a second difficulty linked to this interpretation, and it is a consequence of the narrow construal of critical judgments. If Hare's strategy is to eliminate any sort of rational judgment that can "falter" during weakness of will from being a "critical" one, then—given the kinds of robust rational understandings, like Augustine's, that *can* be acted against—Hare fashions critical rationality into an ideal so rigid and de-manding as to be humanly unattainable. We have seen that critical judg-ments must, for Hare, be absolutely certain and overriding; and they can achieve that only by emerging from a practically flawless process of extensive hypothetical reasoning of a very particular kind. Now it must be asked: who ever successfully makes such a critical moral judgment? Even further, for any complex moral encounter involving more than a few people, who could ever succeed in making such a judgment?

Thus, Hare is left with two unworkable solutions to his problem; he cannot account for weak-willed actions performed against rationally informed moral judgments. The first idea, of allowing critical judgments to be less than certain and so less than overriding, does not fit Hare's characterization of the critical-thinking process and fails to account for all the phenomena. The second idea, that any rational judgments not explicitly critical should be categorized as intuitive moral judgments, can admit the phenomena in question; but it now does not fit Hare's description of intuitive thinking, and it relegates critical thinking to being an activity humans (at least) almost never undertake.

We leave this issue with a final question, which I shall only ask now but shall return to at the conclusion of this section. Moral intentional action is supposed to be rational action, according to Hare. That is because the prescriptive judgments that drive moral actions—properly speaking—are formed through the critical reasoning process that identifies actions as rational or irrational to perform. But if—as we have now seen—making critical judgments is practically out of reach for human beings, what good is critical reasoning-and-judging as a model of how rationality is linked to *human* moral intentional action?

2.3.2 Similar Rational Failure in All Incontinent Actions

Moving on, we now can turn to a second crucial failing of Hare's theory. He cannot make sense of incontinence as a problem of a single or unified nature that also applies to the whole range of intentional actions, and not just to certain moral actions. Let me explain by example. Suppose I have just learned a bit of particularly unpleasant and embarrassing news about an acquaintance I do not much like. I hold that maliciously gossiping is morally wrong, and I tell myself that I ought not to spread this tidbit around, but I do so anyway, in spite of my moral judgment to the contrary. Yet also suppose a seemingly nonmoral question of action: I am deciding what to make for dinner by considering what is available for the next four meals, which—since I am low on groceries—is three portions of ready-to-bake lasagna and one hot dog. I know that if I now eat the hot dog, which is easier and quicker to make, I will have to eat three lasagna meals in a row (which would be exceedingly distasteful by the third meal). So I judge that what I should do is eat lasagna—in spite of its more involved cooking requirements—*this* meal, to break up the later monotony; but, in the interests of time, I eat the hot dog anyway. What I think is obvious here is that the same problem is present in both my actions; in each action, I intentionally do what I have identified as irrational—both actions are *incontinent.* So it looks as if, in the words of Donald Davidson, "incontinence is not essentially a problem in moral philosophy, but a problem in the philosophy of action" (*EAE* 30, n.14). However, it is exactly that sort of unified-nature problem for intentional action that Hare is completely unable to explain.

Indeed, Davidson sees this problem in Hare's theory. Unfortunately, Davidson attributes the trouble to the wrong cause. He thinks Hare supposes weakness of will to be solely a difficulty for an adequate account of specifically moral judgments; the problem supposedly relates to the *content* or *meaning* of moral judgments (26). That is, Davidson maintains that Hare's distinction—between judgments about what *ought* to be done and those about what merely is *desired* to be done (where the former, the moral judgments, have to be universal)—frames incontinence as a conflict between what we selfishly *want* and what is our moral *duty* (27). That leaves Hare mistaken about where the real problem lies, as Davidson explains:

> [When discussing incontinence] two quite different themes . . . interweave and tend to get confused. One is that desire distracts us from the good, or forces us to the bad; the other is that incontinent action always favours the beastly, selfish passion over the call of duty and morality. (29)

For Hare is caught up exclusively with the latter theme, according to Davidson; but the former, more general theme is what shows incontinence to be the broadly applicable problem that it is.

However, Davidson's diagnosis of Hare's trouble is mistaken. Hare does not think weakness of will is limited to the narrow scope of the moral actions that he has described. He recognizes that we behave incontinently in other aspects of our lives, too. He notes, "Indeed . . . weakness is most typically exhibited in falling short of our *ideals*, which need not . . . have anything to do with other people's interests [that is, with the kinds of moral questions on which Hare has focused]" (*FR* 72/54) [emphasis in original]. And Hare gives an example of someone who wants to be—who has an ideal of being—physically fit, and so judges that he should go running, but who then sleeps in, instead (154/8.6). To be fair to Davidson, I should point out that for Hare, judgments about ideals do fall under the "moral" heading as it is commonly used (147–8/8.4). However, actions dictated by ideals are based on different kinds of judgments from moral actions, properly speaking; as we shall see, judgments about ideals do not generate duties the way moral judgments do. So Davidson's point, that Hare thinks weakness is tied to duties, is still wrong. No, Hare's difficulty is that he cannot make sense of the fitness buff's weakness as the same kind of problem present in cases of moral weakness, such as lying to evade punishment.

The true heart of Hare's failure lies in his inability to extend his rational-action standards and requirements beyond the narrow confines of those moral actions that involve others and their interests. Hare himself realizes part of that limitation and writes,

> [M]oral judgements [considered in a broad sense which includes the distinct ideals-judgments], though they are not confined to situations where the interests of others are affected, have their predominant use in such situations. For cases where the interests of others are not affected, I make no claim to provide canons of moral reasoning. But for cases where they are, the two properties of universality and prescriptivity [worked out through critical thinking] suffice to govern the reasoning. . . . [Yet in regard to actions not affecting others' interests] arguments based on these two properties cannot get a grip on such questions. (*MT* 54/3.5)

To understand that quotation, we need to recall how it is that, for Hare, moral action is rational action. Because of the process of critical thinking required in making a moral judgment, a moral action is, by nature, performed from and according to a judgment of reason. As a result of this standard, or canon, of rationality that underlies moral actions, incontinent moral actions represent a rational breakdown, a failure to meet that standard—which is exactly the sort of problem that concerns our investigation.

But the canons of critical reasoning play their role in moral action because such actions are motivated through prescriptive judgments that must be universalizable *by taking into account the interests of others* affected in the actions. The fact that putting ourselves in others' places—which is the job of critical reasoning—is a necessary part of forming a moral judgment, is what makes critical rationality a standard for moral action. So in regard to actions whose underlying prescriptive judgments need *not* be formed through consideration of others' interests, critical reasoning is not inherent in making those judgments. Therefore, the standard of critical rationality does not apply to performing those actions. Nonmoral actions are still performed from prescriptive judgments, which may even be universalizable; but since their judgments—unlike moral ones—are not necessarily rationally informed, acting against those nonmoral judgments does not imply doing what is judged to be irrational.

In short, because there is not the same standard of rationality required in any other kind of action, weakness of will cannot be the same sort of rational failure in those actions as it is in moral ones. For as Amelie Rorty has astutely pointed out, "Where there is no presumption of, or capacity for, rationality, there are no failures of rationality" (*MA* 219). That is, if a standard of rationality does not apply to the performance of some action, that performance cannot violate, or be a breakdown of, the standard.

We can see how Rorty's point is borne out by taking a closer look at what we previously examined briefly in explaining Hare's view—the way rationality is or is not connected to nonmoral actions. Since actions dictated by ideals are related to moral ones in Hare's scheme, let us first examine what happens when someone fails to act on her ideals. According to Hare, questions about ideals may commonly be called "moral" ones, but they cannot be answered by appeal to critical reasoning. Again, that is because ideal-driven questions of action do not involve consideration of other people's interests (Hare, *FR* 147–8/8.4). Hare maintains that because ideal-directed goals "are logically independent of the needs [of others]," their "grounds must be kept distinct" from those of moral directives (149/8.4, 8.5). So if I am trying to decide what kind of person it is good for me to be, whether I should be an early riser or a late sleeper, no one else's interests enter into my decision. Hence, Hare's disclaimer that he does not provide canons of reasoning for actions driven by ideals:

> [With regard to ideals a] factor is lacking, in the absence of which the logical requirement of universalizability [used in critical thinking] cannot . . . get a hold on the questions. . . . This other factor is the bearing of a question on another person's interests. (138–9/8.1)

So it looks as if no significant rational standard is required in making an ideal-based judgment, and thus that there is no rational breakdown in the agent's acting against such a judgment.

But perhaps Hare has too quickly excluded the possibility that actions dictated by ideals may conform to a rational standard; after all, these judgments can generate a kind of *hypothetical* "ought" (154/8.6). That is, if I want to be an early riser, then I judge that I *ought* to set my alarm for, say, 6:30 AM and get up the first time it rings. Hare does say that ideal-based judgments are universalizable, similar to moral ones (138–9/8.1). When I judge that, since I wish to be an early riser, I ought to get up at 6:30 AM, I am committing myself to more than wanting to rise early on just one morning; rather, my judgment refers to mornings *universally* considered. So, given that I hold the ideal of rising early, maybe my specific ideal-driven actions—like whether or not I get up early tomorrow—should be judged rational or irrational according to whether they do or do not meet the standard—the kinds of consequences demanded—of my ideal.

This line of interpreting action based in ideals seems promising, and I think Hare leans toward it. He recounts different ways in which actions dictated by ideals could be subjected to rational measure:

> There certainly are arguments that would be cogent in . . . [cases where the agent has] already accepted some ideal of human excellence; facts could then be adduced to show that such and such a line of conduct would or would not be in accord with the ideal. . . . There are also arguments which . . . may make use of the requirement of universalizability; . . . we can seek to show inconsistencies . . . between [a] judgment [of ideals] and other prescriptions to which [the agent] assents. If, for example, as a result of accepting certain singular prescriptions (the expressions of [her] desires), [she] habitually acts in a way that conflicts with [her] professed ideals, there comes a point at which [her] advocacy of [her] ideals altogether loses force. (150–1/8.5)

However, the problem that arises for this interpretation of actions dictated by ideals is that the hypothetical "oughts" generated are only of the *intuitive* level. The signal is that these ideal-generated "oughts" clearly are not exceptionless. If I happen to have slept in today, I can still consider myself an early riser (I was harried all day yesterday, and so was more tired than normal). We can see the allowance for exceptions even in Hare's own words: we may make a charge of rational inconsistency in someone's ideal-based actions when she "habitually acts" in conflict with her ideals; then there "comes a point" where we can charge inconsistency or insincerity. That is, it is only after *repeated* and *habitual* failure to act on ideals that the agent's rationality in acting becomes questionable. Obviously, then, my ideal-based judgment that as an early riser I ought to get up at 6:30 AM tomorrow, does not imply that I am judging that sleeping past 6:30 AM tomorrow would in itself be irrational. Indeed, as we saw in the earlier criticism of Hare, that is simply the way intuitive judgments work—they do not involve judging specific actions to be rational or irrational. So acting against an "intuitive" judgment of ideals does not constitute a rational violation or breakdown.

Is there some way, though, to "tighten" the force of the "ought" regarding ideals, so that it can be exceptionless and possess a critical-level rationality? One possibility might be for Hare to appeal to the influence of
prudence. He says that "it is rational to choose prudently, i.e. to treat one's
own future preferences as of equal weight to one's present" (*MT* 100/5.5).
He then spells out the "*requirement of prudence*": "This [requirement] is that
we should always have a dominant or overriding preference now that the
satisfaction of our now-for-now and then-for-then preferences should be
maximized" (105/5.6). What these two quotes mean is that in being prudent, an agent imposes on her action the stipulation that it must be the best
thing to do—the deed that best satisfies her preferences—given not only
what she now wants, but also what she will later want, both of which are
treated on equal footing, as if all were present preferences. Further, the way
to achieve prudence is by creating an *overriding* preference to pick that max-
imally satisfying action. In other words, an agent would have to engage in a
kind of critical thinking where, rather than hypothetically considering the
preferences of other people, she instead considers her own hypothetical
preferences in the future. This process would then "prune" her preferences
to give her an overriding one for doing the prudent action. So a judgment
of prudence would be like a critical moral judgment; it would have a hypothetically endowed specificity, overridingness, and a rationally informed
nature.

On that account, it seems that if an agent's ideals are pursued *prudently*,
then her actions dictated by those ideals are a product of rationally informed
judgments and are subject to a rational standard, similar to moral actions.
Acting against such ideal-based judgments would therefore be the same
kind of rational problem as acting against moral ones. Thus, if I were a prudent early riser, in getting up this morning I would have considered what I
now (and tomorrow and so on) would want to do. Since what I did this
morning affects what I can do now and later (am I running on schedule, or
laboring under a backlog?), my now- and tomorrow-preferences not to be
running behind would have outweighed my preference-this-morning to
sleep longer. I would have thus constructed an overriding, rational prescriptive judgment to rise early. My oversleeping in spite of that judgment would
seem to be a rational breakdown like moral incontinence.

Unfortunately, however, prudence cannot do this job asked of it. The
problem lies in the fact that Hare's conception of prudence cannot direct
actions with the certainty required to make its judgments bindingly prescriptive like critical moral judgments. That is, whatever course of action
prudence commends concerning an ideal is rationally uncertain enough

that not acting on the prescription does *not* necessarily represent a violation of what the ideal directs, or even of prudence. For that reason, such a failure to act would not represent a rational breakdown, either. The root of this trouble is that the "others," considered hypothetically in prudential thinking, are only *possibly* going to be affected by a proposed action, because those "others" are only possibly going to exist, at least as specified in the projection.

For example, suppose someone is stranded on a deserted island. She has enough food for seven meals, and she knows that a rescue ship will find her in seven days or less, since she sent a distress signal including her rough location. She also has an ideal of being a survivalist, of getting along smoothly and living the best she can in any primitive setting. Now thinking prudently, counting her present and future preferences equally, she arrives at the ideal-based judgment that she ought to eat one meal a day, so that the "others" of each future day can each have a meal. But she also realizes that she may not be on the island all seven days—the rescue ship could find her tomorrow or the next day, which would leave her needing less than seven days' food. Or again, one of her future "others" might find a tree full of ripe coconuts as she explores the coastline, so that there would be food for more than seven meals. Or yet again, she might be eaten by a shark as she bathes in the bay this afternoon, in which case those future "others" would not exist at all. That leaves her wondering, is it countersurvivalist and irrational for her to go ahead and eat three meals today? She cannot be truly sure. She is left with unavoidable doubts as to whether the future will match up with her projection, and thus as to whether her prudential prescription applies to her present question of action. Hare calls such doubting "discounting [the future preferences] because of unpredictability," and he admits that it is rational to do (100–1/5.5).

Moreover, the problem with doubts like that is that they undermine the binding nature of affirming the prescriptions of prudently generated judgments of ideals. It is not that prudent ideal-based judgments are not specific enough prescriptions; such judgments could identify specific actions as rational (or irrational) to do, given certain future conditions and adherence to a certain ideal. Instead, the uncertainty of the prudential projection prevents any resultant ideal-based judgment from identifying that the rational pursuit of the ideal *requires* the specified action to be performed (or not) on *this* occasion. The agent could sincerely affirm her prudent ideal-based judgment and yet not act upon it because of her doubts as to whether the prescription truly applies *now*. Her uncertainty "loosens" the prescription so that it does not bind her to take the action it directs. In contrast, moral critical reasoning yields an "escape-proof" bond, in which the agent affirms what is definitively rationally required of her in her given situation. But prudential reasoning cannot yield such binding prescriptivity, because in its calculations the "given" conditions include the situation's future effects, which are never closed to rational reconsideration. Prudence's recommendation might also be revised with any change in the projected "given." In short, the question can always rationally be asked: which possible prudential projection of the future is the one that applies to *my* situation *now*? Therefore, in making a prudent ideal-based judgment, an agent never prescribes to herself that this specific action x is definitively rationally required now, in the way that she does through moral critical thinking.

At first glance, it may seem that such a prudential prescription is not truly prescriptive at all, given that an agent can affirm it and not act upon it, without its needing to be overridden. But I think it better to call this kind of prescription "conditional," since these prescriptions effectively say, "*If* the facts—including future ones—are such and such, *then* I ought to do *x*." On that account, even though an agent accepts the description of the facts as they pertain to her present surroundings, she may so seriously doubt those facts as they pertain to her future that she questions whether the prescription *does* apply to her present situation. Thus, her affirmation remains truly prescriptive; she simply is unsure whether her prescription applies.

But if that is the case, her failure to act upon the prescription exemplifies the already discussed scenario of an agent who is uncertain whether her prescription applies to her considered action. Then either her uncertain affirmation of the prescription allows it to be overridden, or her doubts prevent her from applying it at all. Yet, as Hare stipulated, neither occurrence would count as a truly incontinent action (FR 83/5.9; "WW" 1305, 1306). More than that, since her doubts are rational, her inaction in spite of her prescription would *not* count as a rational failure on her part.

Furthermore, given the inherent uncertainty of predicting the future, there seems to be no way to change the conditional prescriptions of prudential ideal-based judgments into binding prescriptions like critical moral judgments. Prudentially formed ideal-based judgments, therefore, cannot identify a specific present action as definitively required for the rational pursuit of the ideal. Hence the aid of prudence cannot sufficiently "tighten" the "ought" of ideals to exclude exceptions to ideal-based judgments. Given that, we can now see why prudence cannot augment an ideal-based prescription so that a failure to act upon it would constitute a rational breakdown by the agent affirming the prescription.

So the stranded survivalist can reason to herself that rationally pursuing her ideal still allows her to eat three meals today. "If the future were set and prudence could discover it," she muses, "then my survivalist ideal would indeed require me to eat only one meal today. But the future is unclear, and it might be the better part of careful survival to eat well today, in case I have to swim out to the rescue ship tomorrow." She then can eat today's three meals, in spite of her prudential judgment that she ought not do so, without having to rationally condemn it as failing her ideal or even as irrational.

Thus, although augmented in specificity by prudence, the "ought" of ideals cannot be tightened enough to meet the requirements of *exceptionless*, critical-level rationality. That "ought" cannot generate a rational standard for action, in the sense that to fail to act upon an ideal-based judgment would be to do what is judged to be irrational, constituting a rational breakdown. Indeed, I do not see how Hare can circumvent this failure of prudence to provide a critical-level rational standard for actions dictated by ideals. Judgments regarding ideals, then, cannot possess more than intuitive rigor, and acting against them is *not* the same kind of rational failure as occurs in cases of moral incontinence.

Moreover, other kinds of nonmoral actions cannot be provided with a significant rational standard for their performance, either. For as we saw long ago in the exposition of Hare's view, merely desire-based actions—whose prescriptive judgments do not include "ought" in any sense—have no universalizability requirement. Acting on a simple hunger for, say, a piece of key lime pie utilizes only a *singular* prescriptive judgment, which does not commit the agent to holding that the action is universally desirable (Hare, *FR* 71/5.4, 157/9.1). So the whole approach, of exploiting the rationality inherent in "ought" judgments, is unworkable here.

For that reason, Hare again makes some effort in the direction of prudence. We recall Hare's claims that with regard to any prescription for action, there is at least this rational assessment: whether the prescription is informed with the understanding, first, of what is being prescribed, and second, of what that concretely entails (*EET* 37). In other words, the agent must understand what it is that she wants to do and what will happen if she does it. Further, Hare seems to want to include prudential calculations in the understanding of "what will happen in doing *x*." He gives an example of a man who is depressed over being seriously ill and who decides to commit suicide. Hare contends,

> Such a man *is*, perhaps, choosing irrationally; but if he is, it is because . . . he is not fully cognizant of the relevant facts [about what he is doing]. For the relevant facts include facts about what will be his state of mind if he does not die, recovers from the depression (as we may suppose is

probable), and thereafter lives a long and happy life. If he is not fully aware of this possibility, to the extent of giving weight to his possible future happiness and to his present temporary unhappiness in proportion to their intensity and duration [that is, by thinking *prudently* about the action], then he is not choosing rationally. This is because he is choosing in disregard of relevant facts. (39)

Hare's point seems to be that by acting against, or by not engaging in, prudential calculation, the man is ignoring "relevant facts"—namely that he will frustrate his future preferences for happiness, and so on—about what will happen to him in committing suicide. The man would thereby fail to meet even the minimal rational assessment of acting intentionally.

But Hare is not entitled to that accusation of irrationality. For as we saw above, the uncertain nature of the future appealed to in prudential reckoning implies that the effects on future preferences, used in a given projection, are only *possibly relevant*. That is, the prudential calculation's facts— about what will happen if a certain action *with a certain future projection* is performed—may or may not be relevant to the actual action being considered. That means there simply are not the grounds to say that acting in spite of a prudential prescriptive judgment, or not bothering with prudential thinking at all, must disregard relevant facts and constitute a rational breakdown, or failure of even Hare's minimal requirement.

With that, we finish the demonstration of my point here. Hare cannot account for weakness of will as *one* problem whose nature involves a rational breakdown in acting that applies to all kinds of intentional action. The source of his failure is his inability to extend his rational-action requirements to any intentional actions but moral ones involving the interests of others. Since no other kind of action can be cast as rational action, none of those other actions can be subject to the rational breakdown of incontinence. That leaves us with a question: can Hare's conception of rational action—such a narrowly applicable link between practical rationality and intentional action—be a good model of how human intentional action is supposed to be rational?

2.4 CONCLUSIONS

Now, as we conclude this analysis of Hare's view, we can answer both that question and the one posed at the finish of the prior point: Hare's theory does not provide a useful model of human rational action.

2.4.1 Rational-Action Standard Too Strict and Demanding

The problem is that Hare's requirements for rational action are too demanding, too rigid, too narrow in their application. That rigidity forces Hare into the two major explanatory failures we just examined. In the first failure, the strict requirements of critical thinking, which supplies the standard of rationality in action, compel Hare to claim that no one could ever both make a judgment that meets that standard and also act against it. Indeed, that puts Hare's conception of rational action in an even worse position than we previously noted. For Hare must keep rational-action judgments and judgments for actions-that-can-exemplify-incontinence in distinct categories that *do not overlap*. In other words, no judgment that meets the rational standard can be overcome by incontinence, and no vulnerable judgment can count as meeting that rational standard. That results in Hare's second failure; he cannot explain *nonmoral* weak-willed actions as *rational breakdowns*. But more than that, it also means that he cannot explain *morally* weak actions in such a way either. That is, moral judgments that are subject to weakness cannot be the kind of rational judgments needed for rational action. So no incontinent moral action represents a rational failure any more than any incontinent ideal-based or desire-based action does. Weak-willed *critically* moral actions would require such a failure, but they can never occur.

In Hare's view, then, the human problem with incontinent action has no connection to rational action; and incontinently violating a rational-action-judgment is impossible. So Hare's conception of rational action cannot accommodate weak-willed action at all. It has to say that the kind of acting that can be subject to incontinence is never the kind that could be rational action. For this investigation's purposes, that is a drastic failing of Hare's theory, because it gives up on the whole point of our investigation—finding a way that incontinent actions can be understood within a scheme of rational action.

Further, the extremely demanding requirements of critical thinking keep Hare's conception of rational action from being applicable to (virtually) any intentional action humans ever do. Now, some arguments—like Zeno Vendler's claim that truly accurately representing others' feelings and preferences cannot be done—have tried to show that Hare demands something *conceptually* impossible (173–4). R. B. Brandt, for another example, has also pursued such a strategy; he contends that it could not be true that by imagining other people's preferences, an agent could form preferences of equal strength for the same outcome. After all, the original and imagined preferences have completely different causes; and how, Brandt asks, could imagining dying of thirst in a desert really give someone the same strength preference for water that someone has who actually experiences that suffering (34–5)? Those are indeed promising arguments, but we do not need to claim so much. For our purpose is to find a model of rational action that can apply to what humans do, including their weak-willed actions. I submit as obvious from our arguments that the rigors of critical thinking make it something that humans, at least, could never do in any significant way. Hare's conception of rational action fails, therefore, to provide the kind of explanatory model for which we search.

2.4.2 Moral Theoretic Failings

At this point, I should note that Hare would, I believe, brush off much of my criticism as resulting from my pushing his theory to a use for which it was not intended. "You knew from the start," he might rebuke me, "that I was presenting a theory of *moral* action, not one of action in general. Having stretched my view onto your Procrustean bed of 'rational action,' is it any wonder that you see it as ungainly or inadequate?" Now it is true that I have approached Hare's view from an oblique angle, but that will not really exonerate his theory. For my criticisms about the experiential inadequacy of Hare's portrayal of the problem of moral weakness of will are still pertinent. That is, Hare's moral theory fails to explain how agents can act against rationally informed moral judgments. More than that, Hare proposes critical thought as the rational process justifying and grounding human moral judgments; and if humans cannot—or at least *do* not—engage in critical thinking, then that central moral-theoretic assertion is false.

Further, in his presentation of what he takes to be the canons of critical moral thought, Hare is trying to present a method of yielding reasons for *why* we behave morally. Critical thought is supposed rationally to justify moral actions, and to provide the motivation that explains their performance. Hare is, in Thomas Nagel's words, presenting "a conception of morality as a set of claims about how everyone has a reason to behave" (112). As I noted in the introduction, this provision of reasons to explain and justify moral action is one of the applications of a successful conception of rational action. That is, attaining this kind of rational justification for morality is one of the rewards that a theory of rational action might be able to offer. Again as I said before, that is one reason why rational-action theories are worth investigating and defending. However, it would be a valuable aspect of such a rational moral justification if it could fit with an overall scheme of reasons why we act, in general. Or as Nagel puts it, "The search for the foundations of morality ought to be part of a general theory of reasons for action" (112). That way, reasons for moral action could be compared to, and measured against, reasons for nonmoral action, since they would all be considered under one "schematic," and the moral justification would thereby gain a broader basis. Yet, as we have seen, Hare's rational basis for moral action *cannot* be extended into a more comprehensive scheme to cover reasons for action in general, which means that the criticisms leveled here show a further drawback to Hare's moral-theoretic justification.

2.4.3 Points for Further Consideration

In any case, I think it is now clear that Hare's conception of rational action is deeply problematic—enough so that we should turn to Donald Davidson's attempt to connect practical rationality to intentional action, in order to see if it is more successful. However, before we move on, we should recap some good aspects of Hare's account. One is that Hare explains quite well the agent's internal struggle in acting incontinently; Hare can give a good sense of how it *feels* to experience weakness of will. Another good point is that Hare's concept of critical thought offers a crisp and sharp standard of rationality in action. That is, he proposes a well-defined method by which an agent could confidently tell whether a given action would "measure up" and count as rational action. When we examine Davidson's view, we should keep these points in mind and see if his theory retains these strengths.

Finally, I need to point out one more correct, but troubling, aspect of Hare's account. That is his observation—which we noted when explaining Hare's position—that intentional actions fall into a *continuum* of rationality, with those at the bottom end being not very rational at all. This point is simply too obviously right to deny, but it seems to have grave implications for any project of rational action. For how could any meaningful standard of rationality include those bottom-end intentional actions? We can only ask this question at the moment, but later we shall see what can be said in response. Right now, we have arrived at Davidson's view and his address of Hare's problems.

3

DONALD DAVIDSON'S THEORY

For two reasons, we shall next examine Donald Davidson's view of rational action and his auxiliary explanation of weakness of will. The first reason is that since Davidson sees himself—at least in part—as responding to problems perceived in Hare's account, our examination of Davidson's own theoretical position flows naturally out of our consideration of Hare. We can proceed smoothly to Davidson's view while his criticisms of Hare are still fresh in memory. That will enable us to sharpen the focus of our questioning, when we examine those aspects of Davidson's account in which he addresses the problems he attributed to Hare. The second reason is that in spite of his efforts at improvement, Davidson's view is problematic in several new ways. As we did with Hare, we shall identify these theoretical pitfalls, so that we can further delineate the "path" that a more successful rational-action theory would need to follow.

3.1 DAVIDSON'S CONCEPTION
OF RATIONAL ACTION

To begin our examination of Davidson's view, we need first to lay out his conception of rational action. Unlike Hare, Davidson is a theorist not just of moral action, but rather of action generally; so we can reconstruct Davidson's picture of rationality's role in intentional action more directly than we could Hare's. However, Davidson's view of the nature of action—or more specifically, of *intentional* action—is complex. Hence, we had better start by clearly understanding exactly what Davidson means in using the term "intentional action."

3.1.1 Action and Intentionality

First, we need to note what Davidson means by "action" itself. Davidson thinks that humans do, or cause or bring about, a multitude of different events, but that not all the events we bring about can count as actions. For instance, a person attracts the Earth to herself, in a minute way, with the gravitational force that she exerts on it by virtue of her mass. Her attracting the Earth is thereby something that she brings about, or "does" in a broad sense. But Davidson would not call that an *action* of hers. Nor would the person's growing older or taller, or other similar things that she "does," count as actions. Davidson maintains that in order for an event that a person brings about to qualify as her "action"—as something she does, in the narrower sense of her being the *agent* of the event—it "require[s] that what [she] does is intentional under some description" (*EAE* 50). So she "acts," or is the "agent" of what she brings about "if what [she] does can be described under an aspect that makes it intentional" (46). A person is the agent, then, of those things that she does that are her actions; agency and acting imply each other. An "action" is "anything [she] does intentionally . . . including intentional omissions [that is, when she intentionally *refrains* from doing something—such refraining is an action, too]" (5, n.2).

But what does it mean for something that a person does to be intentionally performed, if that means that it is "intentional under some description" (50)? This idea of being intentional under some description is a crucial point in Davidson's view, so let me attempt to make it clear. Davidson holds that actions can be intentional or *un*intentional, depending upon how they are described. In other words, depending upon which aspect of the event is used to describe what occurs—that is, from which perspective the action is viewed—that action may appear intentional, or it may not. For an example of this idea, suppose that someone is putting up wallpaper and is becoming quite frustrated with the task. Because of her irritation, she furiously slaps the glue onto the paper with her brush, thereby covering not only the paper but also the surrounding floor in glue. Now, if we describe what she brings about as "her spreading glue on the wallpaper," then her action appears intentional—she meant to do that. But if we describe what occurs as "her scattering glue all over her clean floor," then it seems *unintentional*—she did not mean to do that. Yet both phrases can correctly describe the same event—the same action—that she brings about; and whether we call what happens "intentional" depends upon which description is applied. That is, her action is intentional only under, or according to, some, but not all, description[s] of it.

The idea here becomes clearer when we consider mistaken actions. Suppose I answer a geometry test question with "pi times diameter." The question required the formula for the area of a circle, which is "radius squared, times pi." I did not intentionally bring about "my giving the formula for the circumference of a circle." But the action was intentional under some description, since I did intentionally bring about "my giving what I [mistakenly] believed to be the formula for area." And for that reason, Davidson writes,

> The mistakes [such as mine] are not intentional, then; nevertheless they are actions. To see this we need only notice that making a mistake must in each case be doing something else intentionally. (45)

Davidson's point seems to be that in order for an event that a person brings about to be her action, it must be intentionally performed; but the intentionality of performance will only be apparent in—or even, in a strict sense, apply to—the action when it is presented either in light of a certain description or from a certain perspective. That is why Davidson, even though he speaks of both intentional and unintentional actions, can say,

> It is a mistake to suppose there is a class of intentional actions [that is, a distinct subset of actions, with different properties from the rest]: if we took this tack, we should be compelled to say that one and the same action [such as my geometry mistake] was both intentional and not intentional [that is, that it both had and did not have certain distinct properties]. (46)

Or again, he writes, "the concept of being intentional cannot mark out a *class* of actions. If an event is an action, then under some description(s) . . . it is intentional" (emphasis in original) (61). So every action, in order to be an action, must have intentionality present in its performance; and there must be some perspective of what occurs from which it could appropriately be called intentional.

However, in calling an action "intentional," or in saying that a person is "acting intentionally," Davidson must mean something more specific: he must be describing the action *from the perspective from which the intention applies to the action*. Thus, if Davidson were to say that our wallpapering agent's action was intentional, he would have to be taking her action to be "her spreading glue on the paper" (or some other phrasing of that same view of the action), since only according to that description is what she does intentional.

Furthermore, we need to be clear that while an action's intention may apply to the action only under certain descriptions of it, that does not mean the intention is just a name slapped onto what happens. The label "intentional" cannot simply be attached, after the fact, to whatever a person chances to bring about. Our agent from the gravity example could not say, "I *want* to attract the Earth to myself; I mean to do it. So 'my attracting the Earth' is an intentional performance." Rather, unless the event is brought about, or caused, in a particular manner, there will not be intentionality present in the performance, and the intentional-label will not be applicable to any description of it.

3.1.2 Intentional Performance

At this point, then, we must examine the issue of what *does* make it appropriate to label as "intentional" what an agent brings about. We can do so by investigating what sorts of causes and conditions must be present in the action's performance. The first necessary condition is that the agent must realize what she is doing. Davidson writes that the action's being "intentional under some description . . . requires, I think, that what the agent does is known to [her] under some description" (50). So, given that the person is bringing about an event, there must be some perspective or characterization of what occurs that she has in mind as an understanding of what she is doing. Moreover, although we must wait until later to see the reason why he makes this connection, Davidson means both "some description" phrases to refer to the *same* description. That is, given that the agent realizes what she is bringing about according to a certain description of what occurs, if her performance is intentional, then the intentional-label must be applicable to that same description of the event. Thus, with the person hanging wallpaper, in order for her spreading of the glue to be intentional, she must be aware of what she is doing. But the understanding and the intentionality both need to fit the same description of the action—that is, the action as "her spreading glue on the paper." With regard to the presence of intentionality in what she does, it seems irrelevant whether she grasps more than that about the action—whether she understands her action when viewed in the unintentional aspects, such as "her scattering glue on the floor." For Davidson, then, while it is necessary to the action's intentionality that the agent realize what she does, it is only necessary that she grasp her action as it is described in its intentional aspect.

Davidson indicates a second necessary condition for intentionality in an action's performance when he writes that acting intentionally implies acting for a reason (32–3). He puts it this way:

> [Suppose that the agent's] action is intentional. We must therefore be able to abstract from [her] behaviour and state of mind a piece of practical reasoning the conclusion of which is, or would be if the conclusion were drawn from the premises, that the action . . . performed is desirable. (32–3)

In other words, in order for an intentional-label to be applicable to what she does, the agent must have in mind a reason, or reasons, that both justify her action as rational and explain why she performs it. Given his words above, Davidson apparently does not mean that the agent must *consciously* work through her reason(s) to reach a conclusion by the practical reasoning process (although, sometimes, she might); but, rather, what is necessary is that the reason(s) be present in her mind, and that it (they) should play a role in how and why she acts. So we can now see that in order to understand Davidson's view of intentionality in action, we must turn to the questions of just what these reasons are, and of how they bring about action— or in short, of what Davidson means in saying that someone is "acting for a reason."

3.1.3 Action for a Reason

Davidson, in addressing the question we have just posed, indicates that "acting for a reason" implies the presence of two reason-components in the agent's mind. One component is some kind of desire to perform a certain type of action—say, for example, a longing to be cooler by "running the air conditioner at maximum during hot days." The other component is some kind of belief that the specific action about to be, or being, performed satisfies the desire—say, a perceptual belief that "this action x is a maximum running of the air conditioner during a hot day." So, in effect, the desire stipulates a goal for action, and the belief points out a particular action that meets that goal. In Davidson's words,

> Whenever someone does something for a reason . . . [she] can be characterized as (a) having some sort of pro attitude toward actions of a certain kind, and (b) believing (or knowing, perceiving, noticing, remembering) that [her] action is of that kind. (3–4)

"Pro attitude" is the phrase Davidson uses to convey the idea of the desire component, and soon we shall examine pro attitudes more carefully.

But for the moment, let us note that Davidson means for this pro attitude and belief to constitute the "reason" according to which a person acts. He writes,

Giving the reason why an agent did something is often a matter of naming the pro attitude (a) or the related belief (b) or both; let me call this pair the *primary reason* why the agent performed the action. [Emphasis in original] (4)

He formally characterizes a "primary reason" thus:

R is a primary reason why an agent performed an action A under the description d [that is, in understanding the action from a certain perspective, d] only if R consists of a pro attitude of the agent towards actions with a certain property, and a belief of the agent that A, under the description d, has that property. (5)

Further, he cements this connection between the primary reason and acting for a reason when he notes that the former can fulfill his general requirement for the latter; he writes,

Corresponding to the belief and attitude of a primary reason for an action, we can always construct . . . the premises of a syllogism from which it follows that the action has some . . . "desirability characteristic" [that is, that there is something desirable about the action]. (9)

In other words, from the primary reason we can abstract a piece of practical reasoning that concludes with the desirability of the action—which is what Davidson earlier said was needed in order for someone to be acting for a reason (32–3).

From the primary reason about running the air conditioner, for example, we could draw this syllogism: (1) it is desirable to become cooler by running the air conditioner at maximum during hot days; (2) this action x is a maximum running of the air conditioner during a hot day; therefore, (3) this action x is, based on (1) and (2), desirable. In Davidson's view, then, an agent is acting for a reason if she has in mind a primary reason. We have yet to see, though, what role the reason plays in bringing about the action; but we must put that issue aside for now.

3.1.4 Pro Attitudes

For at this point, we need to set out the nature of Davidson's "pro attitudes." Davidson's notion here seems quite similar to Hare's idea of "interests." For the pro attitude—like "want," in Hare's definition of the interests underlying prescriptive judgments—accommodates a broad array of kinds of desire.

Davidson stipulates that anything from briefly passing fancies or bodily urges like hunger, to moral compunctions or lifelong character dispositions like generosity, can "in so far as these can be interpreted as attitudes of an agent directed toward actions of a certain kind [that is, as they can be translated into directives about actions]," be the basis of the pro attitude (4). So there is a wide variety of wants and desires that can serve as a pro attitude.

Moreover, in any practical reasoning that the agent engages in while acting—whenever the agent consciously works out a primary reason's syllogism, as with (1)–(3) above—the pro attitude is represented in the agent's mind by a judgment. Since the conscious-practical-reasoning cases will be important to Davidson's account of incontinence, we had better take a moment to examine the nature of the pro attitude's representative judgment, as well (the primary reason's belief component is already a judgment, so it needs no outside representation in order to play its role in practical reasoning). The pro attitude's judgment is similar to Hare's conception of prescriptive judgments, for it does not serve simply to *describe* the desire that it represents; rather, this judgment must *express* the desire (86). In order to do that, these judgments must have the form—like (1) in the above syllogism—of evaluations; as Davidson writes,

> The natural expression of [the agent's] desire is, it seems to me, evaluative in form . . . explicit value judgements represent pro attitudes, [and] all pro attitudes may be expressed by value judgements that are at least implicit. (86)

Thus, for example, a character disposition like love of family might be a pro attitude and be expressed by the value judgment "Caring for my family is good to do." Or again, a pro attitude such as a distaste for broccoli could be expressed in an evaluative judgment like "Eating broccoli is a horrifying crime against the taste buds."

Further, because these evaluative judgments express the pro attitudes they represent, the agent can make use of the judgments "to arrive at an action" (86). That is, in expressing a want, disposition, or so on, the judgment expresses an attitude that has *motivational force*, which can bring about action. A pro attitude—represented in this judgment—can, thus, be a *cause* of action. For example, we might, with Davidson, say of someone's action, "Desire was the cause of [her] doing it," and thereby could indicate a pro attitude of hers that brought about the action (65). Davidson's pro attitudes, then, are the agent's desires, longings, and so forth, which are represented by, and expressed through, evaluative judgments that carry the motivational force to bring about action—again, making them very much like Hare's "interests" and "prescriptive judgments."

3.1.5 The Primary Reason's Function in Action

At this point, having examined the nature of the pro attitudes and their representative judgments, we can proceed to the issue of what role a primary reason has in explaining how and why a person acts. One way in which a primary reason explains an action is by *justifying* it, by showing *why* the action was performed and that it was *reasonable*. Davidson writes that the primary reason's components

> *rationalize* an action, in the sense that their propositional expressions [that is, the belief-judgment and the judgment that represents and expresses the desire] put the action in a favourable light, provide an account of the reasons the agent had in acting, and allow us to reconstruct the intention with which [she] acted. [Emphasis in original] (72)

We shall more carefully examine that last phrase in a moment; but right now, let me further clarify how the primary reason justifies the action. Take, for example, the primary reason concerning running the air conditioner. Also suppose that I have just turned on the air conditioner, up to maximum, and have done so with the specified primary reason in mind. If I am then asked *why* I performed that action, I might reply that "I wanted to be cooler on this hot day," or that "I believed that doing so would cool me off on this hot day." With either answer, I am indicating part of the primary reason—pointing to the pro attitude with the former, and to the belief with the latter—in the hope that doing so will answer the question put to me. The primary reason makes sense of my action, by telling *why* I acted as I did.

Moreover, the primary reason does not simply give a motive—a mere explanation of why—for the action; it also shows the action to be reasonable, or rational. Davidson maintains that the primary reason's belief and pro attitude must be "appropriately related to the action as viewed by the actor. [In order for them] [t]o serve as reasons for an action . . . the action must be reasonable in light of the [pro attitude and belief]" (84). The primary reason must treat as a given the perspective of what occurs from which the agent understands what she does. Then the primary reason—in order to be able to justify the action as rational—must "fit," or appropriately explain, the action, as viewed from *that* perspective. So with my action, given that I understand what I do as "running the air conditioner at maximum on a hot day," the belief and pro attitude about air-conditioner-running will be able to serve as the primary reason for my action. But if I saw myself as, say, "playing with the fascinating wall switches," then that particular belief and pro attitude could not reasonably explain why I acted as I did. Further, having appropriately applied to the action as understood by the agent, the primary reason then must show the action to be rational, *when viewed in light of that reason.*

That last phrase is crucial, because it indicates an important caveat that Davidson attaches to this point about rationalizing: the primary reason does not have to show the action to be rational, simpliciter, but only to be rational when viewed as the agent understands it, and when viewed as being justified by [only] that reason. Davidson puts his warning this way:

> The falsity of a belief, or the patent wrongness of a value or desire, does not disqualify the belief or desire from providing an explanatory reason. . . . [The action needs merely to be rational when considered *only* in light of that reason] (naturally, it may not be reasonable in the light of further considerations). (84)

So a primary reason that—when considered in light of the larger picture or in light of further reasons—is, itself, irrational, can still show an action to be reasonable, in the sense that the action is rational in light of the narrow consideration of that reason.

Suppose, for instance, that city electrical usage is nearing overload, and that by running the air conditioner I will, and do, cause a citywide blackout. My primary reason and action, then, are not reasonable when considered in the light of further reasons about city electrical use. But I am still acting for a reason; and my action is still rational when considered in the restricted scope of only my primary reason. Therefore, Davidson's contention that the primary reason justifies an action as reasonable seems to boil down to this: first, the action must be considered in the aspect from which the agent understands what she is doing; thereupon, the primary reason—and *only* the primary reason—is adduced or cited to justify the action; and only then must the action, based on the particular grounds of that reason, be rational to perform. We need to keep this point in focus, because it will be critical to Davidson's explanation of incontinent action, and to our own subsequent examination of that.

Right now, however, we must complete Davidson's account of how a primary reason explains its action. Davidson writes that explaining an action cannot be just a matter of

> the agent hav[ing] certain beliefs and attitudes in the light of which the action is reasonable. But then something essential has certainly been left out, for a person can have a reason for an action, and perform the action, and yet this reason not be the reason why [she] did it. Central to the relation between a reason and an action it explains is the idea that the agent performed the action *because* [she] had the reason. [Emphasis in original] (9)

In short, the primary reason not only explains *why* the action occurred, it also explains *how*, since the primary reason *causes* the action (4). Davidson, here, is simply spelling out the logical consequences of his assertion that the motivational forces of the pro attitudes are capable of bringing about action. If the pro attitudes can drive action, then it easily follows that a primary reason—of which a pro attitude is a part—can cause an action. But the belief, too, plays an important role in the causation, since it provides the pro attitude's motive force with a specific target. For instance, when I—having in mind the primary reason about air conditioner running—turn on the air conditioner, the primary reason's belief and pro attitude jointly bring about my action. Davidson, then, can explicitly assert that "A primary reason for an action is its cause" (12).

Further, Davidson thinks that a primary reason must do more than merely cause its action; somehow the action must be brought about in accord with the reason, as well. Davidson holds,

> The point is that not just any causal connection between rationalizing attitudes and a wanted effect suffices to guarantee that producing the wanted effect was intentional [that is, that intentionality was present at all in the performance]. The causal chain must follow the right sort of route. . . . [The problem is that] [b]eliefs and desires that would rationalize an action if they caused it in the *right* way—through a course of practical reasoning . . . [that is, causing the action by, and in accord with, their content]—may cause it in other ways. [Emphasis in original] (78–9)

Moreover, events caused in those "other ways" will *not* have intentionality present in their performance (79). So, then, the reason must cause the action in such a way that the agent acts from, and somehow in approval of or through agreement with, the content of the reason; it is not enough if the event is caused simply by the presence of the reason.

To illustrate what Davidson means by failing to act in accord with a reason, suppose that someone surprises a robber in her house, grabs the stunned criminal's pistol, and holds him at bay at gunpoint. In considering her options, she feels an angry urge to kill him and notices that she could do so by shooting him. Shocked at her violent thoughts, she twitches and pulls the trigger, thereby shooting the robber dead. Now, the shooting was brought about by her pro attitude and belief, which could make sense of the event. But the pro attitude and belief are *not* the shooting's primary reason, because they did not bring about the action in the right way, in *accord* with what they direct. Rather, they simply prompted an *involuntary* movement of the agent; the trigger-pulling was *not* intentional. The shooting could not count as an action, since the person was *not* acting for a reason—that is, acting according to a primary reason.

In any case, now we are in a position to see *why*—as was simply stated much earlier—the description of the action under which it is intentional must match the agent's understanding of the action. For the agent's perspective of what she does determines the description that the primary reason must "fit," and the primary reason then "determine[s] the description under which [the] action is intended" (98). We can see how that last connection occurs by recalling Davidson's statements that from the primary reason, we could both "reconstruct the intention" of the action (72) and show that the action has some "desirability characteristic" (9). The pro attitude–desire, in conjunction with the belief that this certain action would satisfy the desire, labels the action as having a desirable characteristic (98). From that desirable characteristic of the action, we can draw the agent's intention in performing it (98).

3.1.6 Intentions

Reconstructing the intention from the primary reason works like this: suppose someone has both a pro attitude, an aesthetic yearning to possess a teal-colored car, and also a belief that by spraying teal paint onto her white car, she will gain a teal-colored car. Then suppose that she sprays her car with teal paint. Now, from the primary reason above, we can conclude that for her, "spraying my car with teal paint" would be a desirable action, in that she would thereby have a teal-colored car. From that desirability in the action, we can "read off" her intention, *because the intention corresponds to the conclusion that could be reached by the primary reason's syllogism.* What was the agent's intention in spraying her car with teal paint? She intended, by so acting, to gain a teal-colored car. Based on that connection, then, between the primary-reason-given desirability of the action and the action's intention, Davidson can conclude, "To know a primary reason why someone acted as [she] did is to know an intention with which the action was done" (7).

Moreover, the agent's intention is expressed as a judgment, which—as we shall see later—must be present in her mind (regardless of whether she consciously uses practical reasoning to reach it) in order for her to act. Thus, our agent's intention here might be represented in the judgment that "it is desirable to gain a teal-colored car by spraying teal paint onto my white car." Further, this "intention-judgment" not only expresses the primary reason's conclusion, it also expresses—again, as we shall see later—the reason's motivational force (much as the pro attitude's representative judgment can). In this way, the primary reason causes the action through, or by means of, its representative intention-judgment.

At this point, we finally have seen all of Davidson's view concerning what is required in order for an event that a person brings about to have intentionality present in its performance—to qualify as intentional, under some description. But the account was rather complicated, so before we move on, let us recap: First, the agent must realize what she is doing; there must be some description of what she is bringing about that is present in her mind as an understanding of that action. Second, the agent must be acting for a reason. That means that she must have in mind a belief and a related pro attitude—a primary reason—that, given her view of the action, can both explain why she acted and show that her action was reasonable. That also means that the primary reason causes her action and that she is acting—in an appropriate way—in accord with it. Lastly, both the rational justification and the motive force of the primary reason must be expressed through the agent's intention-judgment. If the agent's performance meets these requirements, then what she does is an action and is intentional under some description.

3.1.7 The Rationality-Intentionality Connection

That summary brings us to Davidson's conception of rational action, which we are at last in a position to spell out. For Davidson, every action, in order to be an action, must be intentionally performed. This intentional performance requires both that the agent must have in mind a primary reason, and that her action must be brought about by, and in accord with, that primary reason. It also requires that, given the description of the action that the agent has in mind as her understanding of what she is doing, the primary reason must be presentable as a justification that the action is reasonable or rational. The motive force and rational justification of the primary reason then are expressed through a judgment in the agent's mind—as her *intention*, which represents the primary reason's syllogism's conclusion. In Davidson's view, then, whenever an agent acts, she must be acting from, and according to, a judgment that rationalizes her action. That is, every action must be brought about by, and in accord with, the agent's judgment that assesses the action as rational to perform.

3.2 THE APPARENT IMPOSSIBILITY OF INCONTINENCE

Now we have laid out Davidson's conception of rational action, but we have yet to see how akratic actions pose a problem for his view. In order to discover the nature of that problem, we need to look at two additional points by Davidson that further link acting to rationality.

3.2.1 Theses P1 and P2

First, Davidson asserts that, whichever of her action-options an agent wants more to perform, that action is the one that she does perform if she intentionally acts on any of those options. Calling this crucial point "P1," Davidson describes it in this choice between two actions, *x* and *y*:

> P1. If an agent wants to do *x* more than [she] wants to do *y* and [she] believes [her]self free to do either *x* or *y*, then [she] will intentionally do *x* if [she] does either *x* or *y* intentionally. (23)

To illustrate this idea, suppose that someone is considering how to spend her summer afternoon; she finds that she both desires to go to the beach for a swim and desires to see a movie matinee. She has the money and transportation to do either action, so she thinks she *can* do either, as she chooses. But which to do? Davidson would say the key is which action she *wants more* to do—that is, which action she wants more intensely, or to a greater degree, to perform. As it turns out, she wants more to go to the beach. So, if she acts on either of those two options—if she does not think of additional things she might want even more to do, or if her employer does not call her to work, or so on—she will go to the beach to swim. In Davidson's view, then, the degree to which an agent wants to perform a certain action in comparison to other considered options is linked to whether the agent will intentionally perform that action, rather than the other possible actions.

In his second point, Davidson maintains that the degree to which a person wants to perform a certain action is proportional to how much reason she judges that she has to perform that action. Davidson, calling this idea "P2," writes,

> P2. If an agent judges that it would be better to do x than to do y, then [she] wants to do x more than [she] wants to do y. (23)

Elsewhere, Davidson makes plain that by "judging that x is better to do," he means that the agent judges that she has better, or more, reason to do x (40). Thus, for example, when our agent goes to the beach, she must decide whether first to lie in the sun or to swim. She then judges that, since lying in the sun will make her hot and thereby make a cool swim even more refreshing, she has more reason, for a start, to take in some sun—she judges that lying in the sun is better to do first. According to Davidson, therefore, as her first action she wants more to lie in the sun. So in Davidson's view, the more reason an agent judges she has to perform a given action, the more she wants to perform it.

3.2.2 Incontinent Actions

Now, we have the pieces of Davidson's theory that make it difficult for him to account for incontinent actions; but before assembling them to show the problem, we need to see just how Davidson characterizes incontinence itself. He writes quite straightforwardly,

> An agent's will is weak if [she] acts, and acts intentionally, counter to [her] own best judgement; in such cases we sometimes say [she] lacks the willpower to do what [she] knows, or at any rate believes, would, everything considered, be better. [We also] . . . call actions of this kind incontinent actions . . . [and] say that in doing them the agent acts incontinently. (21)

Davidson further specifies his view by offering this formal definition—which he refers to as "D"—of incontinent action:

> D. In doing x an agent acts incontinently if and only if: (a) the agent does x intentionally; (b) the agent believes there is an alternative action y open to [her]; and (c) the agent judges that, all things considered, it would be better to do y than to do x. (22)

So with our agent at the beach, if she has thought it over and judged that, all things considered, it would be better to lie in the sun before swimming but instead has intentionally gone swimming first, Davidson would say that she has acted incontinently. Again, then, Davidson thinks that a person acts akratically if she intentionally performs an action in spite of her judgment that, all things considered, she has better, or more, reason *not* to perform that action—either by simply refraining or by doing some other action instead.

Further, Davidson makes clear that his view of weakness of will is much the same as the one I have proposed. For he writes that it need not be a matter of the agent's *knowing* that she has better reason to act other than she does: she needs only to "judge" or "hold" that the weak-willed action is counter to her better reason (21). But that judging or holding must be the sincere expression of the agent herself—it would not be an akratic action if she merely acted contrary to a judgment of what society or common morality said was better reasoned (27). Moreover, the agent must have an unclouded judgment, *at the time of action*, that she has better reason to do otherwise (28). Nor can the action be performed from self-deception or other such "shadow zones" of incomplete sincerity or understanding of the action (28–9). Her action cannot be coerced or out of control, either; she must *intentionally* act as she does (27). Indeed, Davidson hammers home his construal of incontinence by asking,

> Does it never happen that I have an unclouded, unwavering judgement that my action is not for the best, all things considered, and yet where the action I do perform has no hint of compulsion or of the compulsive? (29)

He answers his own question by stating that "it seems to me absolutely certain that [such actions] do [occur]" (29).

However, we also need to note a distinction between Davidson's and my construals of incontinence: by saying that someone judges that she has reason to perform an action, Davidson is not saying that she judges that she *ought* to perform the action—or that the action is right or good (4). For we recall from his attack on Hare that Davidson does not want the construal of incontinence to limit it to being a problem solely for moral actions. Davidson thinks that such limitation confuses incontinence with another difficulty—the human tendency to favor "beastly, selfish passion over the call of duty and morality," which is a problem of much more limited scope than incontinence (29). Instead, Davidson holds that, "incontinence is not essentially a problem in moral philosophy [that is, only for moral actions], but a problem in the philosophy of action [that is, affecting the whole range of human actions]" (30, n.14). That is why Davidson maintains,

> [I]n dealing with the problem of incontinence ... [we must] divorce the problem entirely from the moralist's . . . [construal, and instead we should] dwell on the cases where morality simply doesn't enter the picture. (30)

For that reason, Davidson distinguishes between judgments that an action has *good reason* and judgments that an action *ought*—or is right or good or so on—to be done.

Thus, by employing the broader construction of judgments of how well reasoned an action is, Davidson can treat incontinence as a problem for action generally and not as one limited to moral actions. He then hopes that—whatever difficulty his theory has in explaining akratic actions—he will at least have the advantage of dealing with a more accurate account of what *akrasia* is. This move is also one way in which Davidson tries to correct a problem that he attributes to Hare: Hare's account portrays weakness of will as a rational problem only for moral actions, while Davidson's account can describe weak-willed actions—in any area of human activity from aesthetics to housekeeping—as contrary to the agent's reasoned judgment about what to do. As I said, Davidson's construal also differs on this point from my introductory characterization of incontinence, which involved the agent's acting against what she judged she *ought* to do. However, since I use "ought" in a much broader sense than Hare's restrictive moral use, I think that Davidson's difference from me is partly terminological; we both think incontinence is a rational problem for the whole range of human action. We do disagree on the connection between weakness of will and morality, but we shall examine that disagreement later, when I present my own conclusions. For now, it is enough that we see that Davidson and I consider the same extensional set of problematic actions.

3.2.3 Theoretical Paradox over Incontinence

But what exactly, in Davidson's view, is the problem posed by weakness of will? That problem arises because of his commitment to P1 and P2, which—when added into his conception of rational action—apparently imply that weak-willed actions are impossible. We have already seen that for Davidson, any action must be performed from, and according to, the agent's primary reason, which implies both that she wants to perform the action, and that she assesses it as reasonable. But from P2 we have the additional thesis that the more reason the agent judges herself to have for performing an action, the more she wants to perform that action. And P1 says that whichever of her options an agent wants more to perform, that action is the one (if any) of those options that she will intentionally perform. Between them then, P1 and P2 imply this: if a person judges that a certain action is better—that she has more reason to do it—than another, then, if she intentionally does either of those actions, she will perform the one that she judges is better to do. Yet in acting incontinently, an agent would intentionally perform the action that is *not* the option that she judges that, all things considered, it is better to do. We can see, then, that according to P1 and P2 such an intentional performance appears impossible.

That is why Davidson—who thinks that we do, in fact, act incontinently—posits this "P3" in opposition to the first two:

> P3. There are incontinent actions. [He continues and explains that] . . .
> for someone (like myself) to whom the principles expressed by P1–P3
> seem self-evident, the problem posed by [their] apparent contradiction is
> acute enough to be called a paradox. (23)

So Davidson, like Hare before him, recognizes the problem that his theory of rational action has in explaining akratic actions. He also realizes that it is incumbent upon him, in order to relieve the tension of P1–P3's "paradox," to correct that seeming theoretical error.

3.2.4 Added Explanatory Requirements

However, before we investigate Davidson's proposed explanation of weakness of will, we need to note an extra requirement that Davidson himself imposes upon it. We recall that Davidson had criticized Hare because he saw Hare's account of incontinence as being too mechanical, as making incontinent acting simply a function of which of the agent's interests or preferences were stronger, thereby eliminating any real choice on her part. So now Davidson, for his own explanation of *akrasia*, requires that it be able to account for an agent's

> evaluating the relative force of various desires and beliefs in the matrix
> of decision [that is, it must account for how the agent uses reason to de-
> cide which of her options she should—or will—act upon]. . . . [And,
> therefore,] a reconstruction of practical reasoning . . . involves [explain-
> ing] the weighing of competing reasons. (16)

In other words, Davidson not only wants his explanation to be able to show how akratic actions are possible, he also stipulates that it must show how the agent uses practical reasoning to arrive at which of her possible actions would be better to do. We should keep that additional requirement in mind as Davidson presents his account, so that in our subsequent examination we can assess his success or failure.

3.3 EXPLAINING INCONTINENCE

Now, we can set out Davidson's explanation of weak-willed actions. As we shall see, Davidson's primary move is to distinguish between two levels of practical reasoning judgments. He writes,

> The major step in clearing up these matters is to make a firm distinction between the kind of judgement that corresponds to a [generalized] desire like wanting to eat something sweet and the kind of judgement . . . that can correspond to an intentional action. (97)

Moreover, Davidson labels the former kind of judgment "prima facie," and the latter kind "unconditional" (98). So our first task in examining Davidson's explanation of *akrasia* is to lay out the natures of these two types of judgment. Since Davidson's descriptions of the judgments are so intertwined, we shall look at them side by side, point by point.

3.3.1 Prima Facie versus Unconditional Judgments

We shall begin with the judgments' form and basis. First, both kinds of judgment are evaluations that, in some way, assess actions as desirable. At the prima facie level, that desirability is based in a particular single attribute of an action—usually the action's defining aspect, or main characteristic by which the agent views it. That is, prima facie judgments

> are judgements to the effect that *in so far as* an action has a certain characteristic it is good (or desirable, etc.) . . . [or are judgments] that actions are desirable in so far as they have a certain attribute. [Emphasis in original] (97–8)

So, for instance, if—in the example we used earlier for "acting for a reason"— I defined my turning on the air conditioner as a way of becoming cooler and saw the action as desirable insofar as it could cool me, then my judgment to that effect would be prima facie. Further, in conjunction with the prima facie judgments' basis in only certain attributes of actions, these judgments typically have the form of *general* evaluations. That is, since prima facie judgments focus on a desirable characteristic, they issue a general recommendation for whatever range of actions might possess that characteristic. Because of that generality, these judgments "have the form of a law: [for instance] [*pf*] any action that is an eating of something sweet is desirable" (97–8) (the *pf* signifies that what follows is prima facie, that the desirability is based only on the named characteristic). Or for another example, my prima facie judgment about being cooler would run like this: "(*pf*) any action that cools me by running the air conditioner at maximum is desirable." We can see from the examples that many different actions would fall under the offered recommendations. Eating chocolate cake and eating sweetened arsenic would both be desirable under Davidson's judgment; and under mine, running the air conditioner is desirable even at the expense of a citywide blackout. The judgments simply do not discriminate beyond stipulating that the desired property be supplied.

That is not the case with the unconditional judgments, though. Davidson thinks that this kind of judgment does more than evaluate an action as having a desirable characteristic; rather, it assesses the action as desirable overall, or as a whole—that is, as desirable *unconditionally* (98). So these judgments take an entire action into account in gauging its desirability. Moreover, given the completeness of their consideration, unconditional judgments are more specific in their evaluations. They apply only to a narrow range of actions—basically, to only *one* action and to its variations in performance (such as whether someone opens the package with her right or left hand in acting on her unconditional judgment to "grab a new stick of butter"; technically, such variations would be different actions). Thus, unconditional judgments would unreservedly approve actions, as, for instance, by declaring that "'This action [say, 'washing my dog, today'] is desirable [period].'" (98).

Now, moving to the next point while continuing with unconditional judgments, it is that "whole-hearted" quality of these judgments that apparently gives rise to the second facet of their nature: unconditional judgments are the ones that bring about actions. Davidson asserts, "Intentional action . . . is geared directly to unconditional judgements" (39). In fact, he goes as far as tentatively identifying the agent's actions with her unconditional judgments; that is, the judgment and the action connect so closely as to be virtually one and the same (99). For that reason, then, we can safely assume that when an agent acts, she must have in mind an unconditional judgment, which is bringing about that action.

But on the other hand, with regard to prima facie judgments, because of their generality and direction toward a characteristic rather than an action *as a whole*, there is a gap between making such judgments and acting. At the prima facie level, there has been a "loss of relevance" to action (39). So if an agent makes a prima facie judgment that an action is desirable, that, in itself, will not be able to bring her to act. Davidson puts it this way:

> Prima facie judgments cannot be directly associated with actions, for it is not reasonable to perform an action merely because it has a desirable characteristic. It is *a reason* [my emphasis] for acting that the action is believed to have some desirable characteristic, but the fact that the action is performed represents a further [unconditional] judgement that the desirable characteristic was enough to act on—that other considerations did not outweigh it [that is, that the action, *as a whole*, was desirable, given the characteristic of interest]. (98)

In other words, in order to act, the agent must move beyond prima facie judgments about an action and make an *unconditional* judgment for it. Therefore, Davidson concludes, "Reasoning that stops at [prima facie] judgements . . . is practical only in its subject, not in its issue [that is, it will not bring about action]" (39).

At this point we have seen the natures of prima facie and unconditional judgments, and by noting some examples that Davidson gives of each type, we can start to understand what roles these judgments play in his explanation of incontinence. First, the prima facie examples: several aspects—such as the emphasis on desirability characteristics—of these judgments may have seemed familiar, given what was said earlier about primary reasons. That familiarity has a solid basis, for Davidson fleshes out his account of the prima facie level by stating that pro attitudes, such as wants and prejudices and felt duties and so on, "are expressed by prima facie judgements" (102). That is because pro attitudes are best represented by *general* value judgments. If someone feels an obligation to contribute to charity, her pro attitude can suitably be expressed in the prima facie judgment, "(*pf*) any action that is a giving to charity is good." Or if I wanted new clothes, my pro attitude could be represented by this general evaluation: "(*pf*) any action that is an acquiring of new clothing is desirable." So when an agent reasons about her wants and desires—when she expresses those pro attitudes to herself as judgments and weighs them against each other—those representative judgments, and any consideration about them, will occur at the prima facie level.

Second, as examples for the unconditional level, Davidson points to those judgments that express the agent's intention in acting—to what I, in the earlier discussion of Davidson's view of rational action, called "intention-judgments." He notes two types of these intention-judgments:

> [1] intentions [he means "intentions" to refer to particular judgments here, a special use that will be explained in a moment] and [2] the judgements that go with intentional actions are distinguished by their all-out or unconditional form. (102)

The reason Davidson distinguishes between the two kinds of intention-judgments is that he seems to reserve "intention" for referring to only those judgments that an agent—in "forming an intention" based on her beliefs about the future—makes *before* the action (99). The differences between the judgments are simply that the "intention" is generated, given the agent's future beliefs, noticeably before the action is performed; while the "judgment that goes with intentional action" is made at the time of action and is based on the agent's beliefs about that present moment.

For example, suppose I were to claim, "I intend to wash my dog tomorrow." Davidson would call my just-announced unconditional judgment, that "washing my dog is, on the whole, desirable," an "intention," because the judgment was reached before, and apart from, the action of dog washing. But suppose that I simply washed my dog—I had not planned earlier to do so; I just noticed he smelled and straightaway dragged him to the tub. Then Davidson would label my action-causing, unconditional judgment— again, that "washing my dog is, on the whole, desirable"—with the cumbersome "judgment that goes with intentional action." However, the two judgments can, for our purposes, be considered as the same, because Davidson states that "[a judgment of] intention of exactly the same kind [as present when forming an 'intention'] is also present when the intended action [occurs]" (89). Each judgment, then, expresses an agent's intention in acting—hence my use of "intention-judgment" for both. Furthermore, since "intentions" and "judgments that go with intentional actions" are the only sorts of judgments that Davidson describes as unconditional, it is just such a judgment that must be present when the agent acts. At this point, we can see why I also said earlier that an intention-judgment must be present in the agent's mind when she acts.

Now, let us recap and note how what we have so far gives us a general framework that Davidson will use in explaining weakness of will. At the unconditional level, a judgment must express the agent's intention in acting.

Such a judgment also must assess an action as desirable as a whole, and it can bring about that action. Moreover, given those characteristics, Davidson will be able to use unconditional judgments to make sense of P1 and P2. If an agent judges *unconditionally* that she has more reason to do *x* than to do *y*, then we can see why Davidson would say she then wants to do *x* more than she wants to do *y*, since she is judging *x*, overall, to be more desirable than *y*. And if the agent *unconditionally* wants to do *x* more than she wants to do *y*, then it certainly follows that—if she intentionally does either—she will do *x*, for that is where her overall desire leads.

However, that confirmation of P1 and P2 means that unconditional judgments alone cannot be used to account for incontinent actions, because P1 and P2 are what create the tension in Davidson's paradox regarding incontinence. Further, the immediate link between unconditional judgments and acting keeps those judgments from being used to explain how a person weighs competing reasons. At first, it looks as if a person's unconditional judgment *can* show her reasoning in acting. Since it expresses her intention, the agent's unconditional judgment can be derived from her primary reason's syllogism; and that can give us a syllogism-model expressing *the* reason she had in acting. But that first appearance is deceptive, for, as Davidson writes,

> What emerges, in the *ex post facto* atmosphere of explanation and justification, as *the* reason frequently was, to the agent at the time of action, one consideration among many, *a* reason. [So neither the unconditional judgment, nor the primary reason's syllogism, which leads to it, can be used as a model] . . . for a normative account of evaluative reasoning. [Emphasis in original] (16)

In other words, the unconditional judgment and the primary reason from which it stems only explain what happens once the agent has decided which of her options to act upon; they do not tell anything about how she came to choose that action from among her options.

Davidson proposes the prima facie level of practical-reasoning-judgments to make up for these limitations in the explanatory power of unconditional judgments. For the prima facie judgments, which express the agent's general pro attitudes, merely assess actions as having a desirable characteristic, and, alone, they are not capable of bringing about action. Thus, a prima facie judgment that one action is better to do than another does not, in itself, lead to the agent's acting on the former option rather than the latter. Davidson, then, will be able to use prima facie judgments to make sense of P3 and to explain akratic actions. Further, since the prima facie judgments represent pro attitudes toward single traits of actions, the desirability or undesirability of various characteristics of a given action can yield competing reasons—competing prima facie judgments—for and against the action. So, by appealing to the prima facie level, Davidson will also be able to offer a model for how the agent weighs her reasons for action.

3.3.2 Incontinent Action and Practical Reasoning

We can now see the machinery of Davidson's solution to his theoretical problem with weakness of will. But how does this "machine" function? I think the best way to show that is by working out how *akrasia* occurs in the context of a particular akratic action. We need to start with an example of weak-willed action: suppose that the long years of procrastination are over, and that I, having removed my apartment's hideous wallpaper, am, at last, going to paint said apartment. I am perusing the paint-store aisles and find a sky blue that I like greatly. But I also notice that this paint costs more than I want to pay. Then I see a display for a much cheaper brand. Unfortunately, all that is left in this brand is puce green, which I think is unbecoming for a wall. I search the store, but stocks are low, and the sky blue and puce paints are the only ones I find that, in any way, appeal to me. The blue is beautiful and soothing—but the expense! The puce is rather grating—but, oh, the price is so right! Also, I know that I must choose one of them, and act *now*, or I will lose both my momentum and my window of painting opportunity for who knows how many more years. So I consider my options; I weigh the urging of my aesthetic sense against the prompting of the thrift ideal from my Dutch (read: cheap) heritage. I then judge that, all things considered, it is better to buy and paint with the sky blue, and to suffer the short-term "spendthrift" guilt feelings (that is, to disappoint the thrift ideal), rather than to endure the long-term aesthetic shame and oppression that painting with the puce (and disappointing the aesthetic desire) would yield. However, in spite of my judgment, I act to avoid that guilt, buy the inexpensive brand, and paint myself into a puce corner. Thus, I have behaved incontinently by intentionally acting contrary to my judgment that— all things considered—it would be better to paint my apartment with the expensive sky blue.

So how could that happen? According to Davidson, it would work like this: I have a pro attitude (an aesthetic desire) toward painting my apartment with a pleasing color; and I have a pro attitude (an ingrained cultural ideal) toward inexpensively accomplishing that painting. Further, I believe that by painting with the sky blue rather than the puce green, I will be painting my apartment in a pleasing color; but I also believe that by painting with the puce rather than the blue, I will be inexpensively painting my apartment. Now, when I consider what to do, the two pro attitudes are expressed in my mind as judgments. The generality of the two pro attitudes—any pleasant color satisfies the former, any cheap paint the latter—means that their representative judgments will be prima facie. The two prima facie judgments can then be joined to the beliefs to yield syllogisms that are possible reasons for acting. Davidson might formally portray my thoughts thusly (38):

[Pro attitude] (P1) *pf* (*x* [painting in a pleasant color] is better to do than *y* [painting in a grating color]).

[Belief] (B1) *a* [painting with the sky blue] is an act of painting in a pleasant color; *b* [painting with the puce green] is an act of painting in a grating color.

[Conclusion] (C1) *pf* (*a* is better to do than *b*, [based on] (P1), (B1)).

And also:

(P2) *pf* (*v* [inexpensively accomplishing the painting] is better to do than *w* [accomplishing the painting at great expense]).

(B2) *b* [painting with the puce] is an act of inexpensively accomplishing the painting; *a* [painting with the blue] is an act of accomplishing the painting at great expense.

(C2) *pf* (*b* is better to do than *a*, (P2), (B2)).

My initial consideration, then, yields two seemingly contrary judgments: (C1) that *a* is better to do than *b*, and (C2) that *b* is better to do than *a*.

But Davidson is careful to insist that both (C1) and (C2) must still be prima facie; he writes,

[W]e must give up the idea that we can *detach* conclusions about what is desirable (or better) . . . from the principles [in this case, the prima facie natures of (P1) and (P2)] that lend those conclusions colour. [Emphasis in original] (37)

And, elsewhere, he states,

[J]udgements [like (C1) and (C2)] to the effect that *in so far as* an action has a certain characteristic it is good (or desirable, etc.) . . . must not be construed in such a way that detachment [of the prima facie nature] works, or we will find ourselves concluding that the action is simply desirable when all that is warranted is the conclusion that it is desirable in a certain respect. (98)

Or in plainer words, when reasoning from prima facie judgments, only prima facie conclusions can be reached. The *pf* signifier/operator applies to the conclusion-judgment as well as to the grounds-judgment (38). Further, Davidson points out, that means that (C1) and (C2) do not contradict, but only address *different aspects* of *a* and *b* (97–8).

So neither (C1) nor (C2) assesses *a* or *b* as better or worse *as a whole*; and it is this property of prima facie judgments that allows Davidson to propose such reasoning as a model to account for how an agent evaluates and weighs her possible reasons. For, given (C1) and (C2), I can compare them to decide which desirable characteristic counts for more, to see which action has more desirability (or less *un*desirability, in the sense that each action disappoints one of the two desires) in its favor. I can then judge the rational "weight" of these two reasons for and against *a* and *b* to decide which action is better "all things considered." Of course, I may possess additional reasons, and those are weighed into the "all things considered judgment," as well: perhaps the blue paint provides smoother coverage, which would make the work easier; or perhaps the puce has a Dutch boy on the label, and my grandmother has admonished me to buy Dutch products. In any case, eventually, I can arrive at a judgment that takes into account "all the relevant considerations known to [me]" (38). Thus:

(C3) *pf* (*a* is better to do than *b*, (P1), (B1), (P2), (B2)" (P*n*), (B*n*)).

Now, (C3) is my "all things considered" judgment. Davidson states that it represents my "better reason"—the better judgment to which my akratic action is contrary (36).

So how can I act counter to this judgment, which accounts for all my relevant considerations? I need not act from, and according to, (C3), because for all its breadth of consideration, (C3) *is still prima facie*. The same connection of the prima facie nature from grounds to conclusion holds for (C3), as well as for (C1) and (C2). Since (C3) is prima facie, it will not lead to action without my making a further *unconditional* judgment for *a*, painting with the blue.

What seems to be required at this stage is that I, the agent, must decide that given a certain prima facie judgment—such as (C1) or (C2) or (C3)—in favor of an action, that action is desirable, as a whole. In doing so, I drop that judgment's prima facie qualification and begin holding it *unconditionally* (98). The resultant intention-judgment *can* bring me to perform its specified favored action, and when I do perform that action, it will be for the reason expressed in that judgment. Davidson describes the process thus:

> Practical reasoning does . . . arrive at unconditional judgements that one action is better than another. . . . The minimal elements of such reason-ing are these: the agent [in this case, Keith] accepts some reason (or set of reasons) *r* [such as (P1), (B1)], and holds that [(C1)] *pf* (*a* is better than *b*, *r* [that is, based on (P1), (B1)]), and these constitute the reason why he judges [unconditionally] that *a* is better than *b* . . . [and if he does *a*, then his] reason for doing *a* rather than *b* will be identical with the reason why he judges *a* better than *b*. (39)

So the agent acts on an unconditional judgment that expresses her inten-tion, but the reason within that intention comes from a prima facie judg-ment. That is why Davidson—earlier, in describing an "intentional performance"—could say that the agent's intention in acting, which is an *unconditional* judgment, can be derived from the desirability, or prima facie, characteristic of the action (98).

That extra decision required to reach an unconditional judgment from a prima facie—that gap between any prima facie judgment and action—brings us to the heart of Davidson's solution to his theoretical problem. First, it allows Davidson to propose that his model of practical reasoning is superior to Hare's. We have already seen that Davidson thinks the prima fa-cie level can provide a model to explain how an agent evaluates her motives for action, how she can *reason* to which of her options she should act upon. Now he can add that the gap between making prima facie judgments and acting keeps his account of action from being mechanistic, like Hare's. For no matter how much weight any pro attitude's desirability characteristic might carry—say, enough that an agent always would judge that character-istic, rather than any other, to give her more reason to act—the agent, in making the unconditional judgment, still *chooses* whether to act from that pro attitude. So in Davidson's view, it is *not* the case that if someone sincerely desires to perform an action—even if she (prima facie) judges that desire to count for the most among her various wants—that she then must perform that action (15). Thus, Davidson can claim that his account of practical rea-soning and action makes what an agent does a matter of her *choice*, and not simply of which of her desires is the strongest.

Second, because no prima facie judgment can, itself, bring about the unconditional judgment that would lead to action, Davidson can use that "inability" to explain how weak-willed actions occur. For while acting requires an agent to begin unconditionally holding one of her prima facie judgments, none of the prima facie judgments can *compel* her as to which judgment she decides to hold unconditionally. This point allows Davidson to escape the *akrasia*-paradox rising from propositions P1 and P2. If an agent judges, prima facie, that one action is better to do than another—even if that judgment considers all her relevant reasons—that does *not* mean that she wants more to do the former, at least in the sense that drives P1 and that would lead to her doing the former rather than the latter. Thus, in my case, I have three prima facie judgments—(C1), (C2), and (C3)—about whether doing *a* or *b* would be better. None of those—not even (C3), which represents my better reason—can compel or control my choice as to which I shall unconditionally hold. Because of that, it is possible for me to decide that inexpensively accomplishing the painting makes *b*, painting with the puce, desirable overall, and to begin holding (C2) unconditionally as

(C4) *overall* (*b* is better to do than *a*, (P2), (B2)).

My unconditional judgment (C4), then, is my intention-judgment. It expresses the motive force and rationalization of the primary reason represented by (P2) and (B2); also, it brings about my "painting my apartment in puce green," which is counter to my better judgment, as expressed in the prima facie (C3).

However, we should note that Davidson does not believe that he is abandoning propositions P1 and P2. Prima facie judgments my not jibe with P1 and P2, but unconditional judgments do. Thus, in (C4), I unconditionally judge that *b* is better to do than *a*; I then want to do *b* more than I want to do *a* (thereby fulfilling P2), and I do *b* rather than *a* (thereby fulfilling P1).

Further, even though my painting with puce is counter to my better judgment (C3), that deed is still an action, is still intentionally performed. For, given what Davidson said earlier about how reasons rationalize actions, we can see that my action only needs to seem reasonable viewed in the light of (C4) alone. Considered from that narrow perspective, my action is rational; I want to inexpensively accomplish the apartment painting, and painting in puce green achieves that end. On this point, Davidson writes, "The incontinent [person] believes it would be desirable on the whole to do something else, but [she] has a reason for what [she] does, . . . [and so her] action is intentional" (32–3). Thus, even though I am not acting according to my *better* reason (C3), I am still acting for, and according to, *a* reason (C4). My action is, therefore, intentional. It thereby fulfills Davidson's requirement for *akrasia*, since it is not only counter to my better judgment, but also intentionally performed.

Davidson can conclude, then, that his view successfully resolves the paradox. He defends propositions P1 and P2, while admitting the truth of P3; it *is* possible to act incontinently. Because the "all things considered" judgment is prima facie, it is possible both to judge that one action, *a*, is "all things considered, better to do" than another, *b*; and to make an unconditional judgment in favor of *b* and, thereby, to do *b* rather than *a*. Davidson could finish by claiming that he offers a model of rational action that not only can accommodate the occurrence of weakness of will, but also can correct the problems attributed to Hare's account. Davidson's construal of incontinence casts it as a rational problem for the whole range of intentional actions, not just for moral ones. Further, Davidson can explain how an agent rationally evaluates her reasons and chooses which reason to act upon; in this way, he avoids Hare's apparent problem of removing the agent's meaningful choice in what she does.

But has Davidson truly argued his case that successfully? At this point, we have seen Davidson's whole view of rational action and incontinence, and now we can begin to assess the strengths and weaknesses of his account.

4

DAVIDSON'S THEORY
IN THE CRUCIBLE

As we begin critically assessing Davidson's account of rational action and weakness of will, we shall first explore its successes, which consist mainly in avoiding some of the problems noted by Davidson in Hare's view. Then, having seen the strengths of Davidson's account, we shall compare this portrayal of incontinence to common human experience of that phenomenon, thereby enabling us to see crucial shortcomings in Davidson's position. Next, we shall continue our assessment by examining the impact of Davidson's failures in explaining incontinence upon his strategy for connecting intentional action and practical rationality. Finally, we shall conclude this chapter by reaching a verdict on the adequacy of Davidson's conception of rational action.

4.1 EXPLANATORY SUCCESSES

But first, Davidson's explanatory successes: one point that Davidson well accounts for is that incontinent actions represent a rational failure, or breakdown, by the agent. We recall that Hare was unable to show rational failure in any kind of incontinence but that involving critical moral judgments.

4.1.1 Rational Failure in Incontinence

For Davidson, though, any incontinent action involves the agent in rational inconsistency. We have seen that in Davidson's view, practical rationality is inherent to acting intentionally, because the actions performed must be rationalized—or rationally explained and justified—for the agent by her primary reasons in doing them. But that rationalization requirement does not seem to guarantee that *akrasia* must represent a rational failure; as long as an agent has a reason for her action, she might be performing one of her less rational options, but she might not be irrational in doing so. However, Davidson also includes as a fundamental norm of practical rationality the directive to "perform the action judged best on the basis of all available relevant considerations" (*EAE* 41). He calls this norm "the *principle of continence*" (41).

The principle of continence, then, directs the agent to act in accord with her properly formed "all things considered" (hereafter "ATC") judgments (Davidson, "Deception and Division" 81). Further, Davidson holds that in order for an agent's actions to be interpretable and explainable *at all*, her actions must (for the most part, at least) fit into and help to compose a pattern of thoughts and actions that is rationally coherent and consistent as a whole ("DD" 84). That "backdrop" of coherence allows individual actions to be rationally placed into the "scene" of the agent's beliefs and judgments. We shall delve deeper into that idea later; but at the moment, let us see what it implies about the role of continence in practical rationality. Davidson maintains that in directing action in accord with an agent's ATC judgments, the principle of continence "enjoins a fundamental kind of consistency in thought, intention, evaluation and action" (81). That is, following the principle of continence ensures that an agent's intentions will correspond to her best evaluations, thus helping to create the needed overall-coherent pattern of thoughts and actions. This basic function in forming the rational pattern, which is a prerequisite of actions' being rationalizable, makes the principle of continence one of the "constitutive elements" of practical rationality; it is a norm that every agent, in order to act intentionally at all, *must* affirm for herself (84).

On that account, an incontinent action must represent a rational failure in the agent, because the action is *inconsistent* with the principle of continence, which she rationally must accept. In Davidson's words,

> [W]hat is irrational in an akratic act is, then, that the agent goes against [her] own second-order principle that [she] ought to act on what [she] holds to be best, everything considered. ("Paradoxes of Irrationality" 297)

Or again, Davidson says, an akratic action shows irrationality in the form of a "failure, within a single person, of coherence or consistency in the pattern of beliefs, attitudes, emotions, intentions and actions" ("PI" 290).

However, we need to be clear that this rational failure does not involve the agent's believing or judging anything directly logically contradictory (Davidson, *EAE* 41). After all, the general, desirable-aspect-oriented prima facie judgments are not logically comparable to the specific, whole-action-oriented unconditional ones. So there is no *logical* conflict in making a prima facie ATC judgment in favor of an action *a*, but then forming an unconditional judgment to do a different action *b*. Instead, the rational breakdown is simply in not forming the intention directed by the principle of continence, based on the ATC judgment. That constitutes a failure "to form attitudes [that is, intentions] in a rational, coherent way" (Davidson, "Replies to Essays I–IX" 206). An incontinent action, then, flouts the rational norm of the principle of continence (which the agent *must* affirm) and decreases the necessary rational consistency of the overall pattern of the agent's thoughts and actions. It is that sense of "going against the agent's best judgment" that makes an akratic action inherently irrational (Davidson, *EAE* 41).

4.1.2 Incontinent Irrationality Applies to Any Kind of Intentional Action

Moreover, it is important to note that the rational failure in incontinence is not tied to moral actions alone (41). *Any* weak-willed action—regardless of whether it involves moral concerns, or where in a room to place a sofa—includes the same kind of rational fault. If I like the color contrast of my sofa with the living room door frame, and so position the sofa in front of the door in spite of my better judgment that this placement blocks the door and should be avoided, then I have failed to follow continence's directive. My action is irrational in the same sense, and on the same basis, as if I had acted against my better *moral* judgment. Thus, Davidson can substantiate his claim to avoid Hare's problem of not being able to show an inherent irrationality in incontinence, other than with respect to moral actions. That prevented Hare from explaining other kinds of akratic actions as exhibiting the same rational failing as morally incontinent ones. Davidson, though, can cast incontinence as a rational breakdown that applies to the *entire range* of intentional actions.

4.2 EXPLANATORY PROBLEMS WITH THE ATC JUDGMENT

However, Davidson's most important claim to superiority—that his theory *does* allow for the possibility of genuine weak-willed actions—is not borne out. Davidson declares that he explains those actions as intentional, all the while preserving his connection between practical rationality and intentional action (which is embodied in his principles P1 and P2). But that he fails here becomes obvious when we compare Davidson's portrayal of akratic actions to the phenomena of human experience with weakness of will. We can show that inadequacy by exploring the answers to two questions: first, does Davidson's picture of incontinence accurately reflect our experience of that problem? Second, given an accurate description of the phenomenon of akratic actions, can they be fit into Davidson's scheme of intentional, rational action? To answering those questions, we shall now turn.

4.2.1 Construing the ATC Judgment as Prima Facie

The first point of contention in Davidson's portrayal of incontinent actions arises over his characterization of the "all things considered," or ATC, judgment. According to Davidson, the ATC judgment is prima facie. But that means the ATC judgment must be *noncontradictory* with other prima facie judgments or with unconditional judgments. It is in the nature of all prima facie judgments to have a defeasible character. That is, making a prima facie judgment in favor of an action does not preclude making further judgments—even unconditional ones—*against* that action; for a prima facie judgment focuses only on a desirable characteristic, or aspect, of an action. This prima facie nature of the ATC judgment is crucial to Davidson's explanation of akratic actions; that allows him to contend that the agent *can* act against an ATC judgment, since such a judgment neither constitutes nor entails an unconditional judgment.

However, the ATC judgment must be based upon a reason, *r*, that includes *every consideration* that the agent should consider *rationally relevant* to the action (Davidson, *EAE* 38, 40). So Davidson's problem here is to explain how the ATC judgment can have the kind of comprehensive consideration of an action required for *r*, and yet still remain defeasible and prima facie. Indeed, at first glance, it appears that Davidson is already off-track in even attempting to cast the ATC judgment as prima facie. For as Michael Bratman has pointed out, if *any* judgment seems by its very nature to be unconditional—to assess an action *as a whole* as desirable—it would be the judgment that regards the action *all things considered*. Therefore, it seems "arbitrary and ad hoc" to stipulate that the ATC judgment must be prima facie (Bratman, 160, 161).

But Bratman has overstated the case. Admittedly, the burden of proof falls on Davidson to show that there is an acceptable sense of "all things considered" that could be applied to a prima facie judgment. However, if Davidson can do that, then his classification of the ATC judgment as prima facie would be neither arbitrary nor ad hoc, but would emerge naturally from his basic prima facie–unconditional distinction. Moreover, as we noted above, it is imperative for Davidson that the ATC judgment qualify as prima facie, because if it does not, his explanation of incontinent action collapses. Yet the question remains of *how* the ATC judgment can be merely prima facie. More specifically, Davidson needs to explain both what is meant in saying a judgment is made "all things considered" and how much consideration or evidence has to be included in *r*.

4.2.2 ATC Judgment's Reason, r

Let us first examine how much needs to be included in *r*, the reason that is the basis of the ATC judgment. The first possibility is that *r* may require the totality of facts relevant to performing the action(s) in question. In that case the ATC judgment would be based upon consideration of every possible aspect of what would occur in performing the chosen action. Such a judgment surely would meet the criterion for being "all things considered."

However, two major problems immediately preclude this option. The first is that the totality of supporting facts would almost certainly include points unknown, unavailable, and even unknowable to the agent (Grice and Baker, 35–7). For instance, if I am contemplating whether to fan myself vigorously in order to shoo away a pesky fly, then one fact relevant to the desirability of that action is that it subtly will alter air currents, which ultimately will have the effect, say, of producing flood rains in Texas. But I could not possibly discover such a fact, or the myriad others like it that relate to any given action. So making an ATC judgment that fulfills this requirement for *r* looks impossible for me or any other human.

The second problem is that an ATC judgment based on every relevant fact seems to entail a corresponding *unconditional* judgment (Grice and Baker, 35–7). If an action is judged to be desirable in light of every possible consideration for and against performing it—which is what this kind of ATC judgment would require—then it appears that the action must, on the whole, be desirable. But that is the content of an unconditional judgment about the action. In that case, either the ATC judgment is unconditional, or the incontinent agent makes a logical error by not reaching the entailed unconditional judgment from her ATC judgment. However, in Davidson's view, the ATC judgment *cannot* be unconditional, and, as we recently saw, that sort of logical inconsistency is *not* part of the rational failure of incontinence. Indeed,

Davidson acknowledges both of the above problems for this construal of the ATC judgment, and he rejects it accordingly (*EAE* 40, 41).

Another possible interpretation of the ATC judgment has been offered by Paul Grice and Judith Baker, who think Davidson may mean for the ATC judgment to have something like the form *pf* (Given *all before me*, it is desirable/better to do *a*) (43). In that case, *r* simply would need to include whatever facts or reasons the agent happens to have considered. Given that kind of *r*, which might well leave out much to be said both for and against the assessed action(s), this ATC judgment seems to avoid the problem of entailing the favored action's unconditional desirability. This version also gives a sense of the agent's assessing a kind of sum total of her considerations (35).

On the other hand, if *r* is construed as including all the facts/reasons that the agent *happens* to bring into her decision, then a crucial failing makes this option unsuitable. Such an *r* would not account for the distinction between all the evidence an agent does have and all the evidence she thinks she *should* have (35). That is, calling a judgment "all things considered" and designating it as satisfying the principle of continence's requirement make clear that the ATC judgment's *r* must meet some *normative* standard. The "all things before me" characterization of *r* does not require that. If I am lazy, I might cut short my reasoning about what to do; I know I ought to consider more aspects of my proposed action, but I do have an "all things before me" judgment that summarizes my admittedly meager deliberations. To say that I have reached an ATC judgment flies directly in the face of the normative requirement essential to the sense of "all things considered." For that reason, I believe Davidson cannot accept the ATC judgment's *r* as applying to any set of reasons that the agent happens to have considered.

That imposes a minimal condition upon how much consideration an ATC judgment's *r* must include: *r* must contain enough facts that the principle of continence would direct an intention to be formed from the judgment. Yet we also saw that *r*'s contents must be less than maximal: "enough" evidence must be something short of requiring *all* the facts relevant to the action(s) in question. Thus, the agent must reach a point in her deliberations such that, despite there (probably) being other relevant factors she has *not* assessed, she has deliberated enough that her judgment in light of those considerations is rational to act upon. Indeed, after sifting the options, Davidson seems to agree; he writes,

> The phrase "all things considered" must . . . refer only to things known, believed, or held by the agent, the sum of [her] relevant principles, opinions, attitudes, and desires. (*EAE* 40)

So Davidson restricts the evidence required for *r* to facts the agent is *capable* of considering, but he also demands that *r* constitute the sum of what the agent relevantly *could* consider.

However, while it may avoid the difficulties of the other options for *r*'s requirement, this construal has a serious problem of its own. The agent needs to know just how much evidence is "enough." For if she cannot reliably identify when she has deliberated "enough"—when she has factored in "enough" of her possible reasons for action—then neither can she reliably identify her ATC judgment. In that case, intractable problems would arise for the agent, both in attempting to act continently and in recognizing her own incontinence. Further, as we shall see, Davidson's theory places the agent in just that forlorn position of not knowing when to say "when" in her deliberations. But we must leave the thorough exploration of this difficulty for later; for now, let us continue as if how much consideration is "enough" were clear, so we can complete our examination of the ATC judgment's nature and role.

4.2.3 Agent's Recognition of the ATC Judgment's Sufficiency

What we need to look at now is the question of what is included, not in *r*, but in the ATC judgment itself. Grice and Baker cut to the heart of this issue when they write,

> The question [is] whether, to discharge its role in Davidson's scheme, an "all things considered" judgement can be regarded as specifying a set of propositions which *in fact* constitute the body of evidence [for the agent's summary judgment], or whether it has to be regarded as referring to such a set of propositions *as* constituting the body of evidence. [Emphasis in original] (33)

That is, the natural reading of "all things considered judgment" implies that the agent recognizes that in *r*, she has all the evidence she needs to consider. The agent's ATC judgment then would read something like this: *pf* (Given *r*—which includes sufficiently comprehensive assessment of what to do—action *a* is better to do than action *b*). But it is not clear that such recognition can be included in the ATC judgment without destroying Davidson's explanation of weakness of will.

Again, it seems obvious that this recognition ought to be present; otherwise the ATC judgment loses its essential sense of considering the *sum* of the available, relevant evidence, of being a *summary* judgment (35). However, it looks as if that recognition cannot be fit into the ATC judgment while retaining the judgment as prima facie. The primary difficulty has been pointed out in various ways by Paul Grice and Judith Baker, Christopher Peacocke, and Thomas Spitzley.

Essentially, the problem is that even if r needs only to include *enough* (not all) relevant facts, the ATC judgment still seems to entail an unconditional judgment as long as it includes the agent's regarding r as rationally sufficient, as "enough" evidence. Grice and Baker call the assessment of r's sufficiency the *optimality* clause of the ATC judgment (38). They note that in making a judgment counter to her ATC judgment, an agent contradicts the optimality claim. For the agent, in judging for an action other than that favored in the ATC judgment, effectively rejects as incorrect the claim that r—the ATC judgment's reason-basis—is optimal for her (39, 40). However, that contradiction shows that the ATC judgment, including the optimality clause, must no longer be prima facie or defeasible (41). Spitzley concurs; he argues that when the belief in r and the affirmation that r meets the evidence requirement are included in the ATC judgment, that judgment is *not* conditional in the sense needed for being prima facie (325, 326).

I think that Peacocke, though, best explains the heart of the problem. He notes that in specifying that r must include enough, rather than all, relevant evidence, Davidson is trying to avoid having the ATC judgment entail an unconditional one. But, Peacocke argues, this strategy just plays off the possibility that another set of reasons larger than r might reverse the ATC judgment's verdict (61). However, when the agent affirms r as sufficient or—more explicitly—judges that r is not in danger of being overturned (which is what regarding her judgment as "all things considered" seems to imply), then for the agent such an ATC judgment would preclude the reversal possibility and would entail an unconditional judgment. That is, judging not only that a certain set of reasons r favors a given action a, but also that r would not be overturned by further consideration, is effectively equal to judging that a is favored by the *totality* of relevant facts. That leaves this construal of the ATC judgment facing the same difficulties as the earlier rejected option of including all relevant facts in r (Peacocke, 62).

Furthermore, even the already unsatisfactory "all things before me" construal of the ATC judgment seems to become unconditional when the agent recognizes that it represents all her considerations. For unless the agent thinks further reflection would reverse her ATC judgment—and if she does, then she would not be truly incontinent in acting against it—it seems to require "extreme logical incoherence" to favor another action than that directed by the ATC judgment (Grice and Baker, 44). That indicates that when recognition of r's evidential sufficiency is included, this ATC judgment is not defeasible or prima facie, either. So Davidson cannot retreat to the lower evidential requirement of this version to avoid the problem.

Grice and Baker propose that Davidson solve this difficulty by stipulating that the now admittedly unconditional ATC judgment is somehow *not fully present* to the agent's mind (44, 45). That is, the agent is somehow not fully conscious of, or attending to or certain about, the ATC judgment. In this way, the ATC judgment would be able to be ignored or overruled by the agent, so that she would be able to act against it in spite of its unconditionality.

However, this option clearly is one Davidson cannot take. First, it breaks the close connection Davidson has made between unconditional judgments and the intention-judgments that drive actions (*EAE* 89). This problem is shown when Grice and Baker work out the implications of their "solution." In order for the unconditional ATC judgment to be overruled, it must not be, or even entail, an intention-judgment, so as to allow for the opposing intention's presence (Grice and Baker, 48). However, given Davidson's connection between them, an unconditional ATC judgment and an intention-judgment would possess an identical form. Both would assess an action *a*, as a whole, as desirable. But in that case, the unconditional ATC judgment for *a* would entail an intention-judgment to do *a*. Suppose, then, that the agent does *not* draw an intention-judgment from her "not fully present" ATC judgment, thereby allowing her to form the opposed akratic intention-judgment. In her inattention to her ATC judgment, she has committed a logical error. Yet we have seen that Davidson rejects the option of explaining incontinence by means of a logical error on the agent's part. So to avoid relying on such an error, Davidson would have to break the formal connection between unconditional and intention-judgments. However, what sort of distinction he might create and exploit between them, I do not know.

Second, this strategy would force Davidson either to admit the presence of opposing unconditional judgments in the akratic agent's mind, or—by supposing that there is no unconditional judgment, but only an intention, for the incontinent action—to deny that reaching an unconditional judgment is necessary to act (48, 49). Yet neither of those suggestions is consistent with Davidson's general theory of intentional action. Further, even if theoretical consistency could be maintained, the presence of opposed unconditional judgments and/or intentions raises the problem of casting incontinent actions simply as the result of a mechanistic interior struggle between judgments, because the agent's decision making concludes in her reaching unconditional judgments. But in that case, akratic actions would not be the culmination of practical reasoning and so would seem not to be intentional

(47, 48). Indeed, that was a perceived trouble of Hare's that Davidson wished to avoid.

Third, the very notion of making the ATC judgment "not fully present" to the agent's mind conflicts with Davidson's conception of true incontinence. For he stipulates that incontinence need not involve "shadow zones" of incomplete comprehension or clouded judgments (*EAE* 28, 29). Accordingly, Davidson rejects Grice and Baker's offered "solution" and possible interpretations of the ATC judgment ("RE I–IX" 205).

Yet rejecting the option of a not-fully-present ATC judgment apparently forces Davidson to deny that the recognition of the ATC judgment's sufficient and summary nature can be part of that supposedly prima facie judgment's content. Spitzley proposes that Davidson accept this consequence. In this construal, the ATC judgment is *based* on *r*—which does contain all the available, relevant prima facie reasons concerning which action to do—but neither *r* nor the identification of *r*'s sufficiency is part of the ATC judgment (Spitzley, 328).

Indeed, Davidson also favors this view of the ATC judgment. He stresses that "The [evaluative judgment] concept of prima facie . . . relates propositions . . . [that is] pairs of sentences related as (expressing) . . . [evaluative] judgement and ground" (*EAE* 38). Or in other words,

> [W]e cannot interpret a "pf" judgement as saying something like "Prima facie, relative to such and such evidence," since the relevant relation is *between* the propositions expressed, and so cannot be expressed by one of them. [Emphasis in original] (Davidson, "RE I–IX" 203)

That is, in a prima facie judgment such as *pf* (*a* is better to do than *b*, *r*), the "*pf*" signifies that in what follows in the parentheses: (1) the information before the comma is an evaluative judgment of prima facie nature, and (2) following the comma is the reason that is the judgment's basis. So the judgment's *content* is restricted to what precedes the comma. While the prima facie judgment might be written "*pf* (*a* is better to do than *b*, *r*)," all that the agent *thinks* in making this judgment is, "Prima facie, *a* is better to do than *b*." On that account, Davidson claims,

> But, and this is the important point, nothing whatever can be put inside [the content of a prima facie judgment] . . . to give the force of an "all things considered" judgement. For . . . no "pf" judgement in itself gives a reason for an evaluation: "pf" judgements simply say what would count as a reason. To have a reason, one must add something to the "pf" judgement. (204)

Or more simply, no prima facie judgment—even the ATC variety—includes in its content the reason that serves as its basis; nor does that content include any affirmation of that reason's truth or rational sufficiency. So neither the recognition of its reason's sufficiency nor even the reason itself appears as part of the content of an ATC judgment. Thus, the ATC judgment's prima facie nature is apparently preserved, since the judgment now does not contain the information that seemed to render it unconditional.

However, this strategy does not really get Davidson off the hook. Suppose we grant that neither the belief in the ATC judgment's reason *r* nor the affirmation of *r*'s rational sufficiency is in the content of the ATC judgment proper. It still would be ad hoc and counterintuitive to deny that this belief and affirmation are normally present, at least as natural concomitants of the ATC judgment. For that denial would remove the essential *realizedly summary* aspect of making an ATC judgment. That is, as we saw earlier, in labeling a judgment "all things considered," we indicate both that the judgment utilizes the requisite breadth of consideration of what is believed relevant, *and* that it is understood by the agent to be a summary evaluation of those considerations. Thus, when the concomitant beliefs in *r* and in *r*'s rational sufficiency are included (to justify the use of "all things considered"), the agent reaching an ATC judgment now makes the ATC judgment *and* believes *r*, the judgment's reason(s), *and* believes that *r* is rationally sufficient (or not in need of further consideration). In fact, Davidson admits that the agent does believe all three of these (205). Yet if the concomitant elements are present, then Davidson's difficulty is not significantly ameliorated. For the conjunction of judgment and concomitants seems to entail an unconditional judgment much the same as the inclusive ATC judgment would have. Indeed, Peacocke sees this point and includes it in his criticism; he writes that by "all things considered,"

> we don't mean anything about what influences [the agent's] judgement [that is, about what reason(s) it *happens* to have,] but rather something about its content, and that in some cases the judgement may be as strong in content as the conjunction [above]. (62)

So the ATC judgment proper might be prima facie; but since it seems naturally tied to the concomitant beliefs, an unconditional judgment still seems entailed in making the ATC judgment. Again, that leaves the incontinent agent either making a logical error or holding contradictory unconditional judgments—neither of which fits into Davidson's explanation of weak-willed actions.

4.2.4 Saving the ATC Judgment as Prima Facie

However, I believe there remains one response open to Davidson. In order to take it, he would need to abandon the assertion that if the ATC judgment's reason r should contain the totality of relevant facts, then an unconditional judgment would be entailed. But I think Davidson was mistaken in admitting that in the first place; he failed to apply his basic contention that a prima facie judgment focuses only on a desirable aspect or characteristic of an action. With that in mind, I propose that since an ATC judgment is intended to account for the considerations of all the agent's available and relevant prima facie judgments, then in order to remain prima facie, the ATC judgment must assess the favored action as being desirable *only in the aspect of having the most reason, or being the most rational.* That is, the ATC judgment does account for the agent's various reasons (in the bare sense of pro attitude "motivations") for and against acting in a certain way. And it does "add up" those reasons, but not in the sense of accumulating desirability-aspects and agglomerating motivations. If the ATC judgment did that, then including any level of sufficiently comprehensive consideration in r would indeed entail that the favored action was desirable overall or on the whole or unconditionally.

Instead, I see the ATC judgment as assessing the various pro attitude reasons solely in terms of their *rational weight,* or of how rationally compelling they are. It is only the rational weights—not the desirability aspects or motivational forces of the contending prima facie judgments—that are added up in the ATC judgment. Thus, an ATC judgment recommends a certain action only in that this action has better reason in the sense of being the *most rational* option. In the sofa-placement example used earlier, my ATC judgment between the two actions a (my placing my sofa against the wall) and b (my placing the sofa in front of the door) might then look like, ATC: *pf* (a is better to do than b, r) and r (*pf* [x is better to do than y if its pro attitude motivation has more rational weight] and [a's pro attitude motivation has more rational weight than b's]). In that case, even though a is favored by the ATC judgment, a can still be desirable or undesirable in other aspects than being the most rational option. Say, a might be undesirable in that it is less aesthetically pleasing to place the sofa against the ugly wallpaper-covered wall. For only the rational weight, not the consideration-aspect, of that undesirability has been amalgamated into the ATC judgment's verdict of desirability.

Given that, we can see that my construal of the ATC judgment is prima facie. It addresses the desirability of only an aspect of performing a

versus performing *b*. That would be true regardless of how many considerations for and against *a* and *b* were assessed in the ATC judgment's *r*. Even
if *r* (superhumanly) included the totality of facts relevant to doing *a* versus
doing *b*, the resultant ATC judgment would still merely recommend one of
the two as desirable in being more rational.

Further, suppose that this ATC judgment proper is normally accompanied both by a belief in *r*—which meets the "enough" evidence
requirement—and by a belief that *r* does meet that requirement, so that the
agent holds all of these in making an ATC judgment. In that case, the inclusive ATC judgment would grant the agent recognition of her judgment's
summary and evidentially sufficient nature. Moreover, even that inclusive
conjunction would neither constitute nor entail an unconditional judgment
for the ATC judgment's favored action. For the entire conjunction still only
addresses a desirability aspect, not the on-the-whole desirability, of doing *a*
versus doing *b*.

Therefore, this version of the ATC judgment *does* accurately represent
the phrase "all things considered," and does remain prima facie. That means
Davidson could rebut Bratman's charge that it is simply ad hoc and counterintuitive to designate the ATC judgment as prima facie. Also, this construal is the only way that I can see to make sense of the ATC judgment
within the constraints of Davidson's action theory and explanation of incontinence. However, although it solves his immediate problem regarding
the ATC judgment's prima facie nature, this version also raises some fundamental questions about Davidson's necessary connection between rationality and intentional action. But we must postpone examining those questions
until later.

4.2.5 ATC Judgment Itself Seems to Cause Action

For at this point, we need to explore one more challenge regarding the
prima facie nature of the ATC judgment. Bratman argues that if the ATC
judgment is prima facie, then it is not true that only unconditional judgments can bring about actions. There are cases, he says, where an agent can
reach only an ATC judgment but must act on that without reaching an unconditional judgment (160, 161). For example, suppose someone is choosing mystery prizes on a TV game show. She knows that a car and a box of
Rice-a-Roni are hidden behind two doors but does not know which door
conceals which prize. She has some prima facie considerations for and
against choosing each door—the audience cheers most for door #1, bigger

prizes are usually hidden behind door #2, and so forth. She runs through her considerations and reaches an ATC judgment that it is better to pick door #2. But she does not *unconditionally* favor choosing door #2, because what she unconditionally wants is to choose the car, and she is not certain the car is behind door #2. So she has apparently chosen door #2 only from her ATC judgment, since she would attest that she did *not* have an unconditional preference as to which door to pick (160, 161). Now, if Bratman is right about this kind of case and ATC judgments can, themselves, bring about action, then Davidson's explanation of incontinence collapses. For Davidson depends on the ATC judgment's not being able to bring about action without a further unconditional judgment in order to make sense of how an agent might *not* act on the ATC judgment.

However, Davidson could respond to this objection by asserting that Bratman has misunderstood what it means to unconditionally judge in favor of an action. It does not require that the agent judge the action, based on her reasons, to be unconditionally desirable in the sense of having no reservations. Instead, to make an unconditional judgment for an action is to move beyond prima facie judgments about aspects of the action and to identify the action as desirable in the sense of worth doing. The unconditional judgment need be no stronger than "that the desirable [prima facie] characteristic was enough to act on—that other considerations did not outweigh it" (Davidson, *EAE* 98). Thus, it can be admitted that the game show contestant did not desire without reservation to choose door #2; her judgment to act was not unconditional according to the first meaning, above. Hence, Bratman's claim that the agent acted from a less-than-unconditional judgment. But that interpretation is mistaken. The very fact that the agent does choose door #2 shows that she has decided that the desirable aspects of choosing door #2 were enough to act on. So she does make an unconditional judgment according to the second meaning above. That is all Davidson needs; he can claim that prima facie ATC judgments alone cannot bring about action, and that Bratman's objection fails.

It looks, then, as if Davidson successfully can defend his designation of the ATC judgment as prima facie and also as unable to bring about action on its own. So his characterization of the ATC judgment itself is not manifestly empirically inaccurate. That judgment can still play its needed role in his explanation of akratic action. But, as I mentioned earlier, that success here is not without cost elsewhere to Davidson's theory. Part of that price is Davidson's failure to be able to account for significant aspects of the phenomenon of weakness of will. To the first aspect of that failure we now turn.

4.3 EMPIRICALLY BASED EXPLANATORY FAILURES

One consequence of Davidson's adamancy that the ATC judgment be prima facie is that, in his view, weakness of will is only possible against prima facie judgments. Yet crucial aspects of the phenomenon of incontinence seem explicable only if an unconditional judgment is violated in the akratic action. Davidson's view, however, cannot account for such experience. There are three distinct points of explanatory failure here.

4.3.1 Phenomenon of Akrasia *Violating Unconditional Judgments*

The first problem arises because some instances of incontinence apparently involve acting against intentions, not just prima facie judgments (Mele, 34). We saw a clear instance of that in our earlier example of Leontius's akratic ogling of the corpses. Leontius does not merely judge that ogling is against his better reason; he acts to restrain himself from looking, even though his resistance ultimately fails (Plato, 439e–440a). But if Leontius acts to restrain his shameful urge, then—in Davidson's view—he must have an intention-judgment to do so, and that must be unconditional. However, as Alfred Mele points out,

> Davidson's account of akratic action does not help us here [to explain incontinence in the face of intentions]. Indeed, this case is inconsistent with [Davidson's central rational-action principles] P1–P2. . . . For Davidson, weakness may explain why an agent fails to intend to do what [she] judges to be best, all things considered; but it cannot explain an agent's failing to act in accordance with a here-and-now intention, that is, with an "unconditional judgment" about what it is best to do here and now. (35)

In other words, the very factors about Davidson's theory that made it imperative to cast the ATC judgment as prima facie make it impossible for him to explain this kind of incontinence. For that explanation would require positing that the agent holds conflicting unconditional judgments, and as we saw earlier, Davidson's theory cannot accommodate that.

Instead, as Mele notes, Davidson can only explain weakness in the face of prima facie judgments, since they are not bound by principles P1 and P2. For if an agent judges unconditionally that she has better reason to do *a* than to do *b*, then P1 and P2 imply that she wants more to do *a* and *will* do *a* rather than *b*. So if Leontius makes an unconditional judgment that it is better to refrain from ogling—and he clearly does, since he acts to restrain himself—then, on Davidson's view, Leontius's incontinent action is impossible.

However, Mele thinks Davidson could offer a partial explanation for *akrasia* against intentions by adding temporal references into P1 and P2. That is, P1 and P2 would then stipulate that whichever action the agent unconditionally judges best *at the moment of action* is the one that she will do. This way an agent could act against an unconditional intention–judgment by changing it over time (42, 43).

Unfortunately, that does not give Davidson any real help. For changing unconditional judgments over time would involve the agent's changing her mind about which action was better to do. Thus, it would not be clear that she acts incontinently at all, in that her pursuit of the "incontinent" option requires her to abandon her judgment for the continent option; she no longer acts against a judgment she holds. Further, even if it were supposed that an ATC prima facie judgment remained from the rejected continent intention–judgment, it still would never be the case that the agent acts against an unconditional judgment.

That brings us to Davidson's second related explanatory failure. In Davidson's view, incontinent actions are counter only to prima facie judgments. But as we have noted several times, such judgments—even the ATC judgment that represents the agent's violated "better reason"—focus solely on aspects of the action(s) in question. These judgments are defeasible regarding the desirability of the action as a whole. Yet that means making an ATC judgment against an action is *not* the same as judging that the specific action in question should *not be done*. Instead, the ATC judgment merely says that the rational weight of the desirable aspects of the incontinent option is less than that of the continent option, and that the incontinent option is undesirable in this aspect.

On the other hand, I submit that the common human experience of weakness of will involves acting against judgments that identify certain actions as flatly wrong or irrational or such as ought not to be done. That is, if I judge that I ought to work on my manuscript this morning instead of playing basketball, then I take myself to be judging that the action of playing basketball—whatever its attractions—is not worth doing this morning. But that is an unconditional judgment, in Davidson's theory. When I grab my shoes and ball and go out to the court, it is that kind of unconditional judgment that I violate. As we have seen, though, Davidson must deny that incontinence can occur in the face of unconditional judgments. So if I am right that *akrasia* does happen, at least sometimes, in spite of unconditional judgments about actions, not just traits, then Davidson's theory cannot account for such phenomena.

Mele tries to correct that explanatory failure by proposing that

> unconditional judgments are *not* (Davidson's contention notwithstanding) identical with intentions; for, one may retain an unconditional judgment without retaining an intention. [Emphasis in original] (43)

In this way, an agent might make an unconditional judgment for the continent option but still unconditionally judge for, or at least intend (since they are not the same thing) the incontinent option.

However, as we found earlier in discussing Grice and Baker's interpretations of the ATC judgment, Davidson's theory cannot accommodate the proposed split between unconditional judgments and intentions. That distinction would leave the agent committing a logical error in acting akratically. It would also require admitting either that the incontinent agent holds conflicting unconditional judgments, or that an intention can be reached without making an unconditional judgment. Again, *none* of these points is compatible with Davidson's general theory of action or with his explanation of weakness of will. So it seems Davidson is at a loss to account for the obvious occurrence of *akrasia* in the face of an unconditional judgment (Audi, 194).

4.3.2 Phenomenon of the Incontinent Agent's Inner Conflict

Furthermore, that restriction of incontinence to countering only prima facie judgments also results in Davidson's third explanatory failure: he cannot account for the phenomena of inner conflict that seems so characteristic of incontinent actions. As we observed in examining Hare's view—and as was so clear in the example of Leontius—the akratic agent experiences a conflicting push-pull toward both the continent and incontinent actions. But in Davidson's picture of weakness of will, the continent action is favored only by a prima facie judgment. Because prima facie judgments cannot bring about action and are not even logically comparable to unconditional judgments, the ATC judgment for the continent option is not truly "in play" against the unconditional judgment for the incontinent option. That is, the ATC judgment does not conflict with the unconditional one, nor can it yield the kind of urge to act that would produce a "push" against the unconditional judgment's "pull."

Davidson might respond, though, by pointing out that the prima facie ATC judgment does represent a pro attitude—a motivation to act. Leaving that pro attitude unsatisfied by not acting upon it might well produce regret, a sense of dissatisfaction, and so on. Thus, it would be explicable for an agent to experience unhappiness or regret or frustration over her performing her incontinent action. So, Davidson might claim, his theory can explain why an agent feels conflicted over her incontinent action, and that accounts for the inner conflict characteristic of experiencing weakness of will.

Yet that assertion would be only partially true. Yes, Davidson could explain the incontinent agent's conflict *over* what she does, in that she is dissatisfied and frustrated with how she acts—which is an important aspect of the phenomenon of weakness of will. But, no, he still could not account for the agent's conflict *in* what she does—for the opposing urges to act with which she struggles, for her feeling of being torn, caught in trying to do contrary actions. Again, that kind of inner struggle only seems explicable in Davidson's terminology if the agent holds opposing unconditional judgments—a scenario not possible within Davidson's theory. So from these three failures, we have seen that by restricting the possibility of incontinence to acting counter to prima facie judgments, Davidson "seems to go against our experience . . . [of] the most full-blooded" cases of weakness of will (Audi, 194).

4.3.3 Phenomenon of Self-Division

Furthermore, the inadequacy in explaining the phenomena of inner conflict implies yet another empirical failing of Davidson's theory: it cannot account for the phenomena of self-division. The incontinent agent's seeing her very self or personality as divided—as we earlier saw described by the apostle Paul in Rom. 7—seems predicated upon the inner struggle that occurs in acting akratically. That is, the phenomenon of self-division seems to grow out of the agent's experience of inner conflict; as that struggle worsens or becomes intractable, the agent sees not just conflict but division within herself. If Davidson cannot even account for the phenomenon of the mental conflict, how could he possibly explain phenomena rooted in the worsening of that conflict?

Indeed, as the earlier exposition of Davidson's view detailed, Davidson does not discriminate between kinds of pro attitudes in how they help to bring an agent to action (*EAE* 4). Habits, inklings, lusts, lifelong dispositions, and so on are all represented in the agent's mind as prima facie judgments about how to act. They can all be appraised comparably in making the ATC judgment, and all are converted into unconditional judgments in bringing the agent to act. In other words, the different kinds of action-motivations all operate and interact in the same fashion. So there does not even seem to be a foothold in Davidson's theory to give him the explanatory leverage needed to show how some conflicts between pro attitudes might be intractable while others would not be. Given that, Davidson is apparently unable to explain how an agent's inner conflict in acting incontinently might become so entrenched that she experiences the more serious conflict of a divided self.

Yet Davidson may have a response to my charges on this count. He supplements his portrayal of weakness of will with an account of *mental partitioning*, in order to help explain how the former occurs. Perhaps, then, Davidson can explain the phenomenon of self-division by appealing to partitions in the agent's mind. However, Davidson intends for mental partitioning to solve other difficulties of his theory as well; so before we look at his proposed solution, let us examine one more empirical failure the theoretical addition is meant to correct.

4.3.4 Phenomenon of the Agent's Recognition That Incontinent Action Is against Her Better Reason

This new difficulty is that Davidson cannot seem to account for an incontinent agent's understanding that she is acting against her better reason. We recall that, for Davidson, intentionally acting requires that (1) the agent understand what she does, and (2) that she act from, and according to, a primary reason that rationalizes what she does (*EAE* 50, 84). Further, we saw that in rationalizing an action, the primary reason—the belief and pro attitude pair—needs to show that the action was reasonable to perform, at least when viewed in light of that reason *only*. In other words, even a reason that, given added considerations, would be seen to be faulty still can rationalize an action (84). Supposedly that allows the inadequate reason that drives an incontinent action to rationalize the action and make it intentional. But, and this point is crucial, the primary reason needs to rationalize the action *given the agent's understanding of what she is doing*. For as Davidson writes, "rationalizing [by the primary reason] . . . enable[s] us to see the [action] . . . as reasonable from a point of view of the agent" ("PI" 289).

Yet a central aspect of acting incontinently is that the agent *understands* that she is doing what is against her better reason (Grice and Baker, 45). Davidson puts it this way:

> The standard case of *akrasia* is one in which the agent knows what [she] is doing, and why, and knows that it is not for the best, and knows why. [She] acknowledges [her] own irrationality. ("PI" 304)

And he intends his analysis of incontinence to apply to these kinds of situations ("RE I–IX" 205). Now the problem for Davidson is that, given this understanding of the inappropriateness of what she is doing, the agent's primary reason *cannot rationalize* her incontinent action. But that is exactly what the primary reason is required to do if the incontinent action is to be intentionally performed—which of course it must be, in order to satisfy Davidson's construal of weak-willed actions (*EAE* 22, 32, 33). That leaves Davidson either unable to account for the agent's understanding that she acts against her better reason, or unable to explain incontinence as intentional action.

An example should help demonstrate Davidson's dilemma. Suppose I am going to walk (or, more likely, run, since I am probably behind schedule) to work. Since it has rained nearly every day this month, I judge that even though it is cumbersome, it is best, all things considered, to carry an umbrella with me. However, because of the umbrella's unwieldiness, I leave it at home. I act, then, from a primary reason something like this: *pf* (*x* is better to do than *y*, if *x* involves less carrying of cumbersome objects) and (*a* [leaving behind the umbrella] involves less carrying of cumbersome objects than *b* [bringing the umbrella with me]). Since I am acting incontinently, my grasp of what I am doing is something like "against my better reason, leaving behind the cumbersome umbrella." But my proposed primary reason cannot rationalize my action, given that understanding. The pro attitude–belief pair about avoiding carrying cumbersome objects does not make it reasonable that I should do so *against my better reason.* Yet that last clause is an essential part of my understanding of what I am doing if my action is to count as "incontinent."

So on the one hand, if Davidson grants me that understanding, then my leaving behind the umbrella is *not* rationalized by the pro attitude–belief pair that brings about the deed. In that case, my leaving behind the umbrella is *not* something I *intentionally* do; it cannot count as intentional, or even as an *action* under Davidson's scheme. On the other hand, suppose Davidson excludes the realization of the action's inappropriateness from my grasp of what I am doing. My understanding now focuses only on the desirable aspect of what I do; I am merely "leaving behind the cumbersome umbrella," which in fact is against my better reason. In this case, my pro attitude–belief pair does rationalize what I understand myself as doing; the pair can serve as a primary reason for my intentionally performed action. But my action no longer seems to be incontinent, for I do not understand what I do as being against my better reason. Without that understanding, my action may be foolish, but it does not qualify as incontinent.

Davidson's dilemma, then, is that he can either exclude the wrongness-grasp from the agent's understanding of what she does or admit that incontinent deeds are not intentionally performed. The first option fails to account for the phenomenon, since true incontinence certainly seems to include the agent's grasping the inappropriateness of her action. The second option fails to explain incontinence as an intentional performance or as fitting into Davidson's scheme of rational action.

4.4 MENTAL PARTITIONING AS A POSSIBLE DEFENSE FOR DAVIDSON

However, Davidson stresses that he does want the agent's understanding of her incontinent action to include an awareness of its rationally inappropriate nature ("RE I–IX" 205). Yet if he is to avoid the dilemma's first horn of admitting that incontinent performances are not intentional, then he needs to explain how a primary reason can rationalize such performances. To do that, he must again appeal to mental partitioning. In order, then, to see what aid that idea can offer, we shall now turn to Davidson's explanation of how and why the incontinent agent's mind is partitioned into functionally distinct segments.

4.4.1 Rational versus Causal Strengths of Reasons

To begin, Davidson claims that the *causal* strength of a reason is not necessarily proportional to the agent's evaluation of the reason's *rational* strength. That is, a pro attitude might have a brute causal force—a strength of motivation to act—that is disproportionate to the rational weight it has when expressed *as a reason* in a prima facie judgment. Davidson writes, "a reason that is causally strongest need not be a reason deemed by the actor to provide the strongest (best) grounds for acting" (*EAE* xii). Or again, Davidson more strongly asserts,

> [A] person sometimes holds that all [she] believes and values supports a certain course of action, when at the same time those same beliefs and values cause [her] to reject that course of action. If *r* is someone's reason for holding that *p*, then [her] holding that *r* must be, I think, a cause of [her] holding that *p*. But, and this is crucial here, [her] holding that *r* may cause [her] holding that *p* without *r* being [her] reason; indeed the agent may even think that *r* is a reason to reject *p*. (41)

In other words the rational content of a reason may point to a certain course of action, while the reason's motive force points to—and brings about—a different action.

Suppose for example that someone is considering whether to send her children to Catholic schools. However, this mother harbors a powerful resentment against nuns, because of her own overly strict Catholic education. Yet she believes Catholic school also would provide a value-rich, theologically based environment of learning. So she thinks that r (*pf* [education under the religiously based teaching of nuns is desirable] and *pf* [education under the strictness of nuns is to be avoided] and [sending my kids to Catholic school will educate them under the nuns' strict, religiously based teaching]). After consideration of r, she arrives at ATC: *pf* (sending my kids to Catholic school is desirable). So r's rational force directs sending the children to Catholic school. Yet in spite of her desirable assessment, the thought of nuns educating her children actually brings the mother to reject the option of Catholic schooling. Thus, the causal or motive force of r is not in line with the agent's evaluation of its rational weight. Therefore, although r is a reason for action, it is not in the role of a reason that r brings the agent to act.

Davidson claims that occurs in incontinent actions. The judgment that determines an akratic action does so partly from causal force, and not entirely through its rational justification, as it should. Davidson says, "there is a mental cause that is not a reason for what it causes" ("PI" 298). The motive force of desire expressed in the judgment overpowers the agent's adherence to the principle of continence, to acting according to her better reason. The judgment expressing the incontinent desire is considered in the ATC judgment; there, the desire's rational weight is duly evaluated. But then, apart from its rational justification, the desire's causal strength brings the agent to override the principle of continence and to act on the incontinent desire instead of the ATC judgment (297).

Indeed, the *only* way to overrule the principle of continence is through appeal to brute causal strength. As we saw earlier, because it is fundamental to practical rationality, no motivation could "be a *reason* for neglecting the requirement [of continence]. Nothing can be viewed as a good reason for failing to reason according to one's best standards of rationality" (Davidson, "DD" 92). So the incontinent desire works as a cause only, not as a reason, in bringing the agent to judge unconditionally according to it instead of according to her ATC judgment (Grice and Baker, 30, 31). On that account, Davidson says that when the question is asked,

[W]hat is the agent's reason for doing *a* when [she] believes it would be better, all things considered, to do another thing, then the answer must be: for this, the agent has no reason. [And Davidson explains in a foot-note:] Of course [she] has a reason [that is, a rationalizing justification in the form of the incontinent desire's representative primary reason] for doing *a*; what [she] lacks is a reason for not letting [her] better reason for not doing *a* prevail. (*EAE* 42, n.25)

Thus, an akratic desire (represented in a primary reason judgment-pair) functions as a justifying reason in explaining why the akratic action is per-formed, but it functions only as a brute cause in explaining why the action was performed *against the agent's better reason*.

4.4.2 Mental Partitioning

Further, Davidson maintains that some kind of mental partitioning is a necessary environmental condition of this not-as-a-reason mental causation. He writes, "Only by partitioning the mind does it seem possible to explain how a thought or impulse can cause another to which it bears no rational relation" ("PI" 303). He thinks the usual instance of this kind of causation occurs between different minds (300). For example, suppose I want to lift my wife's spirits. I therefore tell her some jokes and some good news that make her smile. My desire to cheer her is then a cause of her smiling; but it is not a reason for her action of smiling. Davidson explains how *akrasia* works similarly in the context of one mind:

Mental phenomena [like pro attitudes] may cause other mental phe-nomena [like intentions] without being reasons for them, then, provided cause and effect are adequately segregated. . . . I suggest that the idea can be applied to a single mind and person. Indeed, if we are going to ex-plain irrationality at all, it seems we must assume that the mind can be partitioned into quasi-independent structures that interact. . . . The idea is that if parts of the mind are to some degree independent, we can un-derstand how they are able to harbour inconsistencies and to interact on a causal level. (300)

So Davidson offers this picture of the incontinent agent's mind:

[S]uppose two semi-autonomous departments of the mind, one that finds a certain course of action to be, all things considered, best, and another that prompts another course of action. On each side, the side of sober judgment and the side of incontinent intent and action, there is a supporting structure of reasons, of interlocking beliefs, expectations, assumptions, attitudes and desires. (300)

Thus, the incontinent pro attitude can act as a cause only, not as a reason, in overruling the principle of continence, because the causation occurs between quasi-independent "departments" of the agent's mind.

Davidson fleshes out his picture of these mental structures and notes first that each structure is *internally rationally consistent.* He writes, "To constitute a structure of the required sort, a part of the mind must show a larger degree of consistency or rationality than is attributed to the whole" (300). So there is inconsistency in the agent's mind as a whole, between her action and her affirmation of the principle of continence; but each subdivision is consistent and rational in itself. Indeed, in explaining a view almost identical to Davidson's on this point, David Pears asserts,

> [T]hough the subsystem [that drives the incontinent action] is more limited than the main system [with the ATC judgment], . . . it is from its own internal standpoint equally rational. ("The Goals and Strategies of Self-Deception" 64)

The main system, then, univocally directs and rationalizes the continent action; and the rebel subsystem does the same for the incontinent action.

That is not to say, however, that the two systems' contents are completely distinct and separate. In fact, since the incontinent pro attitude's rational weight is considered in reaching the ATC judgment, that pro attitude must be represented in the main system as well as in the subsystem (Davidson, "PI" 301). So the different mental structures map out the contents of the mind in such a way that they are "overlapping territories" (300, n.6). But the key is that there must be enough "functional insulation"—enough functional independence of each structure—that the incontinent subsystem can have "elements that do not interact [as reasons] with all of [the main system's] elements" (Pears, "GSSD" 70, 71). Hence the incontinent pro attitude can act as a nonreason cause against the principle of continence, while still functioning as a reason in forming the ATC judgment. On that account, "The breakdown of reason-relations defines the boundary of a sub-division" (Davidson, "PI" 304). Thus, even though there are some elements shared between divisions, there is enough functional independence in each structure that the subsystem alone can bring the agent to act, and that its contents "can operate on [the main system's] . . . in the modality of non-rational causality" (301).

4.4.3 Davidson's Proposed Defense

Given that picture of how an akratic action occurs, Davidson can offer responses to some of the criticisms I raised earlier. First, he can claim that the agent's understanding of her incontinent action as "against her better reason" appears in the main system with the ATC judgment, but not in the subsystem. Therefore, this understanding might be prevented from interacting as a reason with what the subsystem directs. The acknowledged irrationality then would not make the incontinent action irrational *in light of the subsystem's contents*, nor would it prevent the subsystem from bringing about the action. Since the understanding of the incontinent action contained in the subsystem only portrays what is done in its favorable aspect, that action—brought about by the subsystem's elements—can be intentionally performed. Thus, Davidson might say, his theory allows that the incontinent agent *can* realize that what she is doing is counter to her better reason; yet that need not keep her action from qualifying as an intentional performance.

Further, Davidson could claim that his theory postulates a real division within the incontinent agent's mind. That would give him a basis from which to explain the phenomenon of self-division which the akratic agent may experience. Moreover, perhaps Davidson could add that since weakness of will involves mental causes operating *not-as-reasons*, then that causation by motivational strength alone might disrupt the mind (in some way yet to be explained) and lead to the phenomenon of mental conflict experienced in incontinence. So by supplementing his explanation of weakness of will with an account of mental partitioning, Davidson might claim that he does have the theoretical resources to account for the crucial phenomena of inner conflict and self-division.

4.5 FAILURES OF THE DEFENSE

4.5.1 Prior Objections Still Stand

Unfortunately for Davidson, though, his theory's explanatory failures are not effectively corrected by adding mental partitioning to his account. In the first place, Davidson still cannot give an acceptable explanation of how an agent can intentionally perform the incontinent act when that includes understanding the performance as against her better reason. The problem remains because mental partitioning places the realization—that the incontinent action is rationally inappropriate—into a mental subdivision functionally separated from the one that brings about the action. As Mark Johnston points out, this move rather implausibly seems to make a normal incontinent agent like a sufferer of multiple personality disorder (82). That is, in the psychological disorder, dormant personalities do not control the dominant personality's actions, yet may have knowledge it does not. That looks similar to Davidson's view, in which parts of the agent's mind know things other parts do not, and a given part can cause action on its own, apart from the knowledge or interference of other parts. Moreover, this picture of what occurs does not seem to represent true incontinence. The part of the agent's mind that brings about the action does *not* contain the realization of the action's inappropriateness; that understanding is segregated into a "dormant" mental partition. In other words, it seems the agent does not have an "active," or functionally accessible, realization of her action's wrongness. Yet it is just such an "active" understanding that Davidson has agreed is central to whether an action counts as "incontinent."

However, Davidson responds to this first problem by stipulating that these mental subsections are *not* experienced *as divisions* by the agent. Davidson writes, "Such boundaries [of mental partitions] are not discovered by introspection; they are conceptual aids to the coherent description of genuine irrationalities" ("DD" 91, 92). On that account, while the agent's identification of her action's inappropriateness is in fact isolated and functionally inert with regard to her performance, she does not experience—or sense or feel—that dividedness. To the agent, it seems that her wrongness-grasp is "active" in her decision of what to do. Regardless of the actual partitioned state of her mind, then, the incontinent agent does not experience anything like what the multiple personality victim does, in the sense of experiencing her knowledge and actions as held and controlled only by parts of herself. Again, to the agent it feels as if she is of undivided mind, and acting in spite of a functionally interactive understanding that this action is rationally faulty. Thus, Davidson might claim that he *can* account for the phenomena in question.

But even if Davidson can account for the *phenomenon* of the incontinent agent's understanding her action as wrong, he still faces a dilemma in explaining such an action as intentional. For the incontinent action is rationalized in regard to the rebel subsystem *only*, not in regard to the main system or to the agent's mind as a whole, which includes both subdivisions. So on the one horn, if Davidson attributes the incontinent deed to the agent—as seems sensible—then the performance is not rationalized in her understanding, and thus cannot count as intentional. But that would fail to explain weakness of will under Davidson's conception of intentional action or within his scheme of rational action. On the other horn, if Davidson characterizes the akratic action as intentional because it is performed from the subsystem's primary reason and rationalized according to the understanding contained in the subsystem, then the action seems to be the *subsystem's*, not the agent's. That is, it seems that the subsystem acts, but the agent does not. But that would make Davidson guilty of proposing *homuncularism*—the implausible doctrine that inside a person are "little men" who think and act through her. Moreover, on this view it would not even be clear that the deed performed would count as incontinent, since the "actor" producing it does not "regard" it as irrational (Johnston, 85). We shall further explore the homuncularist objection later; but for now, having noted this dilemma, we need to move to Davidson's second problem.

For as we just saw, since Davidson denies that the incontinent agent notices the partitions in her mind, she does not experience the mental division as such. But if mental partitions do not produce any phenomenon of dividedness in the agent's consciousness, the difficulty arises in that mental partitioning does not offer an explanation for the agent's *experience* of her self's being divided. Indeed, since for Davidson *every* case of *akrasia* involves mental subdividing, partitioning offers no basis for why only *some* instances should be accompanied by this experience, or for why it should be perceived as a heightened level of inner conflict.

Now I do not think Davidson is helpless against this objection. He might, for instance, propose that in cases of prolonged suffering of weakness of will, an agent may begin to perceive her mental subdivisions or to experience those divisions and their effects. However, Davidson would need to offer a detailed account of how such perceptions and experiences might arise, and of why they would do so only in certain cases. Therefore, he needs to supply a more comprehensive defense to rebut this objection.

Furthermore, given the denial that the incontinent agent experiences her mental divisioning, Davidson still possesses no explanation for the more common phenomenon of inner conflict. Granted that the ATC judgment for the continent option and the unconditional judgment for the incontinent one are now in different—but unnoticed—mental structures. Yet how can that account for the agent's experience of real conflict? There remains only a prima facie judgment favoring the continent action; no new source of true opposition has been added to explain conflict between the judgments and attempts to act.

But suppose Davidson were to respond by postulating that since each mental subdivision is functionally insulated, both the subsystem and the main system might contain unconditional judgments for and against the incontinent action, respectively. For Davidson has already proposed that the akratic pro attitude determines which action shall be done, not by rational weight but by pure causal force instead. On that account, it seems only a small step to claim that the rebel subsystem might bring about the incontinent action by causally overpowering an unconditional judgment in the main system. In that case, the incontinent agent's opposing unconditional judgments would provide a basis to explain the inner conflict she faces.

Also, perhaps this tactic might not violate Davidson's principles P1 and P2. For even though the agent would be acting on her own more poorly reasoned unconditional judgment, the mental partitioning would make that similar to being browbeaten by a rationally insubstantial—but forcefully presented—argument *from another person*. This case, then, seems significantly different from the P1–P2 contradicting instance in which the agent simply would act for what she, without conflict, unconditionally judges is more poorly reasoned.

However, we have already explored this strategy of conflicting unconditional judgments and have rejected it as not feasible for Davidson's theory; the addition of mental partitions does not substantially change that verdict. Davidson would still be proposing that the incontinent action, rather than the continent option, is done simply because the unconditional judgment for the former causally overpowers that of the latter. Unfortunately, that would remove from the agent's control any effective *decision* about what to do. For the agent's decisions occur in reaching the unconditional judgments. Yet from there, it would remain to be determined which action is to be performed, and that determination would be made by the judgments' brute causal force alone.

That leaves Davidson facing several unacceptable consequences. First, it again subjects him to the charge he already made against Hare. The agent's incontinent action now seems to be *mechanistic*, and not a result of practical reasoning. But, as Davidson declared, that apparently removes the voluntariness and responsibility from what the agent does. Yet those traits are central to the conception of what it is to act incontinently.

Second, if Davidson maintains that the akratic action can be voluntary and responsible because it is performed from the reasoning and unconditional judgment reached in the subsystem, then the action again seems to be the *subsystem's*, not the agent's. The homuncularist objection returns. For the main system and the agent-as-a-whole now seem like "innocent victims," compelled by the subsystem, a "straightforward," unabashed, and unrepentant wrongdoer. Indeed, from the subsystem's perspective, the action does not appear weak-willed, either (Johnston, 85). Even from the perspective of the agent-as-a-whole, the action does not seem weak-willed, unless the main system were somehow colluding with, or negligently succumbing to, the subsystem's coercion. However, that would only advance the charge of homuncularism by requiring a further subdivision. The main system would then have to be partitioned into one segment purely directing the continent option and one directing collusion or succumbing. That would start a regress of subdivisioning so that the weakness would never be explained (84).

Therefore, proposing that each subdivision might contain an unconditional judgment either makes the incontinent action mechanistic and nonvoluntary, or it deepens the homuncularist difficulties by requiring a regress of subdivisions in order to explain the action as weak-willed. On those accounts, the proposal seems unacceptable within Davidson's view—thus leaving Davidson with no feasible explanation of the phenomenon of inner conflict, even when mental partitioning is added to his theory.

4.5.2 The Intentionality of Incontinent Actions

Furthermore, Davidson's postulation that the incontinent action is brought about by a reason that is not operating *as a reason* but only as a cause gives rise to a new problem. This proposal jeopardizes Davidson's assertion that akratic actions are intentionally performed, because such actions are now seen to be brought about by *wayward causal chains*. That is, if an incontinent action is brought about because of a reason's causal force rather than its rational content, then the action is not performed *for*, or *in accord with*, the reason. Yet we recall from the exposition of Davidson's view that an intentional performance requires not only that a reason brings about the action, but also that the action is performed because of, and in accord with, the reason's content. For Davidson wishes to exclude deeds brought about by "nonstandard or lunatic *internal* causal chains" from counting as intentionally performed (*EAE* 79). Davidson explains,

> Beliefs and desires that would rationalize an action if they caused it in the *right* way—through a course of practical reasoning [that is, from and according to their rational content] . . . may cause it in other ways. If so, the action was not performed with the intention that we could have read off from the attitudes that caused it. . . . [Therefore] since there may be wayward causal chains, we cannot say [merely] that if attitudes that would rationalize *x* cause an agent to do *x*, then [she] does *x* intentionally. [Emphasis in original] (79)

However, it is now plain that in a case of incontinence, the agent only has judgments that would rationalize her action *if* they brought it about through their rational content, which they do not.

That waywardness becomes clearer when we recall Davidson's earlier statement that since the principle of continence is *constitutive* of practical rationality, this principle could never be violated *for* or *according to* any reason ("DD" 92). Given that, it is obvious that in bringing about an action counter to the dictates of continence, the agent's supposed primary reason cannot be doing so from and according to its rational content. But in that case, an incontinent deed is *not* intentionally performed, since it is brought about by a nonstandard, internal causal chain. However, that means Davidson fails to explain incontinent action as a kind of intentional action and cannot account for it within his scheme of rational action.

In addition, I do not see any effective responses that Davidson could make to this criticism. He might try retracting his claim that intentional performance requires acting for, and in accord with, a reason. Then performing an incontinent action could count as intentional. Yet that would force Davidson to accept as intentional just the sort of clearly *nonintentional* performances (such as the example used in the Davidson exposition of the person nonintentionally shooting a burglar) that his stipulation was specifically designed to exclude. This response, then, seems unworkable with Davidson's general action theory.

Or again, Davidson might press his claim that the incontinent action *is* intentional, because it is brought about by and according to the reasoning of beliefs and pro attitudes contained in the subsystem. But that just brings the homuncularist objection to the fore. That is, it seems even more clear that the incontinent action is the subsystem's, instead of the agent's. It is the reasoning and perspective and unconditional judgment of the subsystem that bring about the action and that make it intentional. It is only when seen from the *agent's* perspective—represented in her ATC judgment and affirmation of the principle of continence—that the action appears nonintentional and unrationalized. For that reason, this response also seems unhelpful, since it does not preserve the action's intentionality with respect to the agent.

Moreover, an additional aspect of this intentionality problem arises from Davidson's reliance on mental partitions to explain incontinent action. We recall that in beginning our analysis of Davidson's view, we observed that the principle of continence is fundamental to practical rationality because it helps to create the background of overall rationality in the agent's thoughts and actions. This overall rational coherence is a necessary condition of being able either to assess any individual action's rationality, or to understand why the action is done (84). Davidson calls the assumption that an agent has such overall coherence of thought and action the *principle of unavoidable charity*; we must make that assumption if we are going to be able to understand or interpret another person's thoughts or actions *at all* ("Expressing Evaluations" 18). Now Davison admits a problem in using mental partitioning:

> There is no question but that the precept of unavoidable charity in interpretation is opposed to the partitioning of the mind. For the point of partitioning was to allow inconsistent or conflicting beliefs and desires and feelings to exist in the same mind, while the basic methodology of all interpretation tells us that inconsistency breeds unintelligibility. . . . [So] we [must not] merely compromise our ability to diagnose irrationality by withdrawing the background of rationality needed to justify any diagnosis at all. ("PI" 303)

In other words, mental partitioning is used to account for nonreason mental causes that then operate between mental subdivisions; but that creates a significant rational incoherence in the agent's *overall* thought-action framework. Because of that, the principle of charity cannot be applied well to that framework; instead it only truly applies to the internally rational *subdivisions* (Evnine, 172). On that account it again becomes problematic to interpret an incontinent action as intentional from the overall perspective of the agent. Rather, an akratic action only seems intentional if attributed to the internally coherent subsystem that produced it. Unfortunately, that just reinforces the homuncularist objection we have been developing.

Furthermore, this problem is rooted in Davidson's basic idea of mental causes that operate as other-than-reasons. For as Simon Evnine points out, Davidson's principle of charity demands that mental content must be connected to rationality, that it must fit into a normatively governed holistic pattern. Yet Davidson also requires the causes of incontinent actions to be mental, since he sees nonmental causes as nonrational, as excluded from questions of rationality or irrationality. However, by proposing *nonreason* mental causes, Davidson has guaranteed that they will *not* fit into the normative pattern (Evnine, 171, 172). That results in incontinent actions' not being explicable as intentional for the agent. Evnine describes the problem thus:

> If beliefs and desires are constituted by normative standards of correctness and rationality, as Davidson holds, then failure to be rationally explainable at the level of beliefs and desires must mean failure to be explainable at

that [intentional] level at all. We must . . . descend to a non-rational level (i.e. a level that does not involve intentional mental states) to explain, or even describe, what happens [in a case of incontinence]. (172–3)

Or again, as Johnston notes, "For where we can find neither a coherent intention in acting nor a coherent intention to be acted upon we cannot discern intentional action" (76).

Yet, as mentioned above, Davidson's only recourse seems to be to attribute the incontinent action to the subsystem that produced it, rather than to the agent as a whole. Then the action consistently fits into the coherent framework of beliefs and pro attitudes contained in the subsystem, and the action is explicable as intentional behavior—but only for the subsystem. Davidson, therefore, must either admit that incontinent actions are not intentionally performed, or attribute the performance to a seemingly homuncularist subsystem. So let us now examine in more depth the difficulties of this homuncularism itself.

4.5.3 Homuncularism

Davidson's basic problem is that in order to avoid the objections I have been raising, he must propose subdivisions of the agent's mind that are themselves implausibly anthropomorphic. The subdivisions seem to be *mini-agents*, which create "a host of psychological puzzles" about how they can function and bring about action on their own (Johnston, 64). For instance, Johnston points out that the subsystem seems required to be sufficiently agent-like that it can manipulate the main system. As an example, suppose that I were to form an incontinent intention to neglect my work and watch TV later this evening. It seems like the subsystem containing my incontinent desire and intention must be able to ensure that no serious reconsideration occurs between now and the time of TV watching, so that the intention will not be changed. But that appears to demand something like *consciousness* and *introspection* on the part of the subsystem, to check whether any resistant reconsideration is occurring in the main system and, if so, to squelch it (82).

This aspect of the subsystem's capacities also becomes more prominent in akratic actions involving *self-deception*. In such cases, the subsystem needs both "representations" of what occurs in the main system and the ability to act or react based on that information to make sure the main system does not make the undesired rational connections and penetrate the deception (Pears, "GSSD" 76). Indeed, according to Pears, since the akratic pro attitude is represented in the main system but is seen there as rationally unacceptable, the subsystem based around that pro attitude then "is motivated" by a kind of "altruism" to satisfy the main system's desire (63). All of that leads Mele to complain that the subsystem "is unnecessarily anthropomorphic . . . rather than simply being constituted of wants, beliefs, and the like, [it] *has* wants, *is aware* of certain things, and so on" [emphasis in original] (82).

Yet both Davidson and Pears deny that their views are tainted by homuncularism. Davidson claims,

> The [mental] parts are defined in terms of function; ultimately, in terms of the concepts of reason and of cause. The idea of a quasi–autonomous division is not one that demands a little agent in the division; again the operative concepts are those of cause and reason. ("PI" 304)

Or in other words, the subdivisions are not homuncularist but are only groupings of reasons causing actions. Pears claims that subdivisions do not have consciousness, but merely something he calls "preconsciousness" that functions similarly enough to consciousness to let the subsystem do its reflective work ("GSSD" 75).

But what support do Pears and Davidson have, other than the words of their denials? My objections have shown that in order to avoid other problems, Davidson must attribute so much autonomy and action to the subsystem that it, rather than the agent as a whole, seems to be the author of the incontinent action. Given that, how can Davidson's disavowal of homuncularism be maintained?

Marcia Cavell attempts to offer Davidson some needed support. She disputes the charge that his view requires positing subagents in the incontinent agent's mind. Cavell appeals to the "transitive" parts of the stream of experience in acting, that is, to "things like feelings of activity or the process of reflecting or drawing a conclusion" (305). Cavell holds that while these experiences are not part of the *content* of what is thought or reasoned, they *do* affect what an agent concludes or does. These transitive experiences, then, obviously are not miniagents. However, Cavell maintains they can result in the reflective or manipulative effects attributed to the homuncularist mental subsystems (304, 305).

Cavell seems to picture something like this: *how* an agent perceives her possible actions, the manner in which she reflects on her competing reasons to act, such things affect what the agent decides to do. An agent's habits of perception, say, may result in her focusing on the pleasure associated with eating her friend's piece of cake, rather than on the action's weightier negative social consequences. That might "hook her up" to the mental subsystem containing both the pro attitude toward eating the pleasurable cake and the understanding of the incontinent action as satisfying that desire. Then the subsystem's primary reason components can bring about her swiping and eating the cake. In this way, it is not the subsystem alone that determines the agent's action; rather, the *agent* does the determining, by means of the way she has perceived her action, and so on. On that account, the subsystem need not constitute anything more than a grouping of beliefs and attitudes ready to have their motive force "activated" by the agent's transitive experiences.

Unfortunately, a serious problem underlies Cavell's proposed solution; this difficulty surfaces in Johnston's similar view. Johnston thinks that self-deceived and weak-willed actions are brought about under the influence of mental processes "that are purposive but not initiated for and from a reason" (65). Johnston calls such processes "mental tropisms" and describes them as "nonaccidental, purpose-serving mental regularities" or as "characteristic pattern[s] of causation between types of mental states" (66, 86). He gives as an example this perceptual tropism: "an automatic filtering process that is ordinarily inaccessible to introspection and which determines that what is salient in perception will be what answers to one's interests" (87). In other words, this tropism would ensure that what the agent notices about her prospective actions would correspond to the aspects singled out in her pro attitudes.

Moreover, Johnston's described perceptual tropism seems very much like the perceptual habit that, on Cavell's account, influenced the agent to focus on her action in ways that fit her akratic primary reason. The problem is that Johnston points out that mentally tropistic behavior has an important similarity to the tropistic behavior of plants in leaning toward the sun: neither kind of behavior is intentional. Mentally tropistic processes have purposiveness; but if they are normally below the threshold of introspection and not the sort of activity that the agent *consciously intends* to do, at best we might call them *subintentional*. That would mean that incontinent actions are brought about subintentionally, a consequence Johnston affirms (65).

Admittedly, Cavell wants to distance herself from Johnston's reliance on the subintentional, so that her view may maintain that incontinent actions are intentionally caused (304). However, she lacks any discernible firm ground for the distinction she claims. It seems that the transitive experiences Cavell appeals to are *exactly* the kind of mental processes that are going to be shaped—or at least greatly influenced—by mental tropisms. How a person perceives or reflects or considers is very much affected by that person's perceptual habits, by the degree of reflexivity in her mind-set, and so on.

Those are the sorts of mental traits that are normally unobserved by the person, and that are not normally intentionally invoked. Given Davidson's picture of intentional action, our akratic cake eater does not intentionally focus on the deliciousness of the devil's food and frosting. Instead, because she is a cake lover, that is simply where her perceptions *automatically* gravitate. Perhaps she has a pro attitude guiding her perceptual process, but no complete primary reason, since the tropism picks out action-aspects that only then lead to the formation of beliefs about what actions fit her situation. That is, the tropism does its work before the agent has enough information to form a true primary reason about what she is doing. So Cavell has not shown that her view significantly differs from Johnston's. Cavell's proposal, then, would only shift Davidson back to the problem of not being able to portray weak-willed actions as intentional. For that reason, Cavell seems not to offer a viable response to the charge of homuncularism, since her view does not sufficiently guarantee that an incontinent action must be brought about at the intentional, rather than the subintentional, level.

Perhaps, however, Davidson might offer a last defense along a completely different line. He might retreat to his claim regarding the necessity of mental partitioning in order to explain mental causes operating not-as-reasons. Then even if they are homuncularist, these mental subsystems are explanatorily necessary to a theory of incontinent action. Homuncularist mental partitioning might be implausible, but it may be the *only* possibility to explain akratic actions as intentionally performed.

Yet Mele argues that this defense will not work either. He attacks it by pointing out that it is *not* necessary to postulate a mental partition every time a mental cause operates other than as a reason (77). Mele gives an example of a man wanting to resist the temptation to smoke a cigarette; the man employs a self-control technique of visualizing a calm, pleasant scene and associating it with not smoking—and the smoking urge then recedes. The man's mental visualization plays a *causal* role in his resisting temptation, but it does not supply a *reason* for that resistance. Yet, Mele notes, no mental partitions need be posited to understand how that could happen. Till we are shown otherwise, we may assume the same to be true for nonreason mental causes in incontinent actions, as well (77–9). But then it seems that mental partitioning is *not* theoretically necessary in explaining incontinence. So, barring further justification, Davidson could not argue for his homuncularist subdivisions by this route either. As Davidson himself wants to avoid homuncularism, anyway, he is left facing the objections I have been raising about his ability to characterize incontinent actions as intentional behavior.

4.5.4 Summary of Mental Partitioning

That concludes our argument concerning mental partitioning and Davidson's attempt to use it to better explain incontinence. In summary, then: mental partitioning does help Davidson account for the phenomenon of the agent's understanding her akratic action as against her better reason. But partitioning does not significantly lessen Davidson's problems in explaining the phenomena of inner conflict and self-division. Moreover, the use of mental partitioning and nonreason mental causes also places Davidson on the horns of a dilemma. On the one horn he must attribute the intentionality in an agent's akratic action to a mental subsystem that brings about the action. Yet that implausibly posits homuncularist, nonincontinent miniagents and implies that the agent does not intentionally bring about the weak-willed action—a position Davidson explicitly disavows. However, on the other horn, if Davidson denies that the subsystem itself acts intentionally, he cannot characterize incontinence as intentional action *at all*. Such action seems mechanistic rather than voluntary; it is unrationalized and is brought about by a wayward causal chain that not only makes the action conflict with the principle of charity, but also renders it inexplicable at the intentional level.

Since the proposal of mental partitioning completes Davidson's explanation of incontinent actions, I therefore conclude that Davidson fails to account for genuine *akrasia*—for an accurate construal of incontinent action—either as a kind of intentional action by the agent, or as covered under the Davidsonian scheme of rational action.

4.6 EXPLANATORY FAILURES
REGARDING PRACTICAL REASONING

That said, we must also examine explanatory failings in other areas of Davidson's theory. The first problem regards the evaluative reasoning used to rationally weigh one prima facie judgment against another. We recall that Davidson rejected Hare's view partly because it could not explain how an agent sifts through her reasons to arrive at a rational decision about what to do. Davidson requires that "Any serious theory for predicting action on the basis of reasons must find a way of evaluating the relative force of various desires and beliefs in the matrix of decision" (*EAE* 16).

4.6.1 Lack of a Measure to Compare Reasons

More specifically, Davidson needs a measure for evaluatively comparing the rational weights of prima facie judgments representing the various diverse pro attitudes. The agent must be able to make use of such a measure, given that she needs to evaluatively compare and rank her competing prima facie reasons in order to reach an ATC judgment. Beyond that, she requires that evaluative measure if she is to follow the principle of continence and to perform the action she judges *rationally best*, all things considered. Davidson explains,

> Shoulds, oughts, goods, and evils compete for our final approval or choice of a course of action; therefore we need to be able to construct "pf" sentences [like the ATC judgment] that combine considerations. . . . Now we will need a principle of inference corresponding to each evaluative word which says that if something is a reason for holding something to be obligatory, or good, or desirable, etc., then it is a [comparable] reason for holding the thing . . . to be intention-worthy. ("RE I–IX" 210–11)

Or, in short, "It is not enough to know the reasons on each side [of the question of what to do]: [the agent] must know how they add up" (Davidson, *EAE* 36).

Unfortunately, Davidson provides no explicit, practical, evaluative measure to compare prima facie judgments' rational weights. Indeed, he laments that in practical reasoning we lack

> a general formula for computing how far or whether a conjunction of [prima facie judgments] . . . supports a conclusion [about what to do] from how far or whether each conjunct supports it. . . . We have no clue how to arrive at [the ATC judgment] from the reasons. (39)

Thus, we cannot be clear on how to rationally form an ATC judgment (Davidson, "Reply to Spitzley" 332). That seriously harms Davidson's view; for he has no explanation of how an agent might compare the rational weights of, say, a hunger pro attitude toward eating right now against a desire for the companionship of friends in eating later with them. Yet if she cannot rationally sift those competing reasons, how can the agent form an ATC judgment? Further, how can she act continently or even *in*continently— how can the agent identify her *better* judgment, in order to act either for or against it?

Davidson does attempt to provide *some* answer to the question of how an agent can rationally evaluate her competing prima facie reasons. This answer involves the principle of charity in interpretation. As was mentioned before, this principle directs us to assume that others are largely rationally coherent in the frameworks of their thoughts and actions, because that is a requirement for interpreting their behavior in terms of intentional and rational content. This "policy of rational accommodation"

> necessarily requires us to see others as much like ourselves in point of overall coherence and correctness—that we see them as more or less rational creatures mentally inhabiting a world much like our own. . . . In so far as people think, reason, and act at all, there must be enough rationality in the complete pattern [of their thoughts and actions] for us to judge particular beliefs as foolish or false, or particular acts as confused or misguided. (Davidson, "EE" 18)

So in interpreting your behavior, I must assume that you are largely correct in your evaluations, the rational rankings you give your pro attitudes. To do that,

> I must also match up your values with mine; not, of course, in all matters, but in enough to give point to our differences. This is not, I must stress, to pretend or assume we agree. Rather, since the objects of your beliefs and values are what cause them, the only way for me to determine what those objects are is to identify objects common to us both, and take what you are caused to think and want as basically similar to what I am caused to think and want by the same objects. . . . There is no room left for relativizing values, or for asking whether interpersonal comparisons of value are possible. The only way we have of knowing what someone else's values are is one that . . . builds on a common framework. (19)

Thus, Davidson here asserts that charity requires us to assume large-scale agreement between our evaluations, and that we must take that agreement as the standard that determines—or at least offers a basis for determining—the correctness of evaluations.

In other words, the measure of how evaluations are to be made, of how prima facie reasons are to be rationally ranked, is constituted *intersubjectively*—that is, in the *agreement between us*. We must be guided by "the ineluctably objective and intersubjective elements . . . in evaluation" (3). Or again,

> [E]verything depends on our ability to find common ground. Given
> enough common ground, we can understand and explain differences, we
> can criticize, compare and persuade. The central point is that finding the
> common ground is not subsequent to understanding [how to rank and
> compare pro attitudes], but a condition of it. (20)

So by starting from points of intersubjective agreement, we have a basis for
assessing how evaluative judgments like prima facie reasons should be
ranked and compared. At points of disagreement, our common ground provides a starting point for determining which of our evaluations are
deviant—that is, which ones are anomalous and depart from the shared rational pattern of evaluative ranking and comparison. We will then be in a
position to label deviant evaluations or comparative rankings as *irrational*, because they depart from the intersubjective standard.

With that in mind, Davidson might say that he at least offers a foundation for a measure to rank and compare the rational weights of prima facie
judgments. By appealing to points of intersubjective agreement, an agent
could determine whether her judgment-rankings and subsequent intentions
were in line with the shared standard. If they were, then she could affirm that
she acted continently; if not, she would have to investigate the possibility that
she is being irrational in acting against the shared standard of better reason.

However, this intersubjective agreement does *not* effectively meet
Davidson's theoretical need. Two serious problems plague this standard.
First, the evaluative measure's intersubjective nature indicates that incontinence would often be apparent to the agent only *after the fact*. That the agent
has violated her own rational standard might well be visible only when her
action is considered in the *communal* judgment, when she can see whether
it fits into the rational pattern of the intersubjective agreement. It would be
as if the agent were a member of a club. She agrees to the club's rules; but
exactly what those rules require is a matter interpreted by the club as a
whole. She might find for an individual action that she alone cannot tell
whether or not it breaks the rules. That is only clear when the action is considered in the club's communal judgment. Even if the club ruled that her
action broke a rule she had agreed to, that would not be like incontinence.
In an akratic action, the agent needs to be able to tell *on her own at, or before,
the time of action* whether her intention is in line with her better reason,
whether her evaluation is in accord with her rational standard. But that
might often not be the case with Davidson's proposed intersubjective evaluative standard. So use of this standard would not stay true to the common
experience of weakness of will.

The second problem stems from the same root as the first. The need to appeal to intersubjective agreement—in order to assess whether prima facie judgments are being correctly compared, ranked, and combined— ensures that this evaluative measure is going to be *unusable in daily practice.* That is, this intersubjective standard will not be helpful to the agent in trying on her own to decide what to do now, in reaching her own ATC judgment now. It would be a practical impossibility for an agent to discover and reason from intersubjective agreement in making everyday decisions about what she rationally ought to do. On that account, I do not believe Davidson has provided anything like the concrete, practically workable measure of evaluative rank and comparison that he, himself, requires of an adequate theory of practical rationality and rational action. Davidson offers no practically useful method for an agent to sift her prima facie reasons in reaching an ATC judgment, or in establishing a "better reason" to act for or even against.

4.6.2 Impossibility of Identifiedly Continent Action

At this point, we may proceed to the next area of difficulty for Davidson's theory, since this new problem connects to his troubles in explaining evaluative practical reasoning. This related failure concerns Davidson's inability to offer an adequate account of *continent* action. Now, for Davidson, an agent acts continently if she acts upon, or forms an intention based upon, her properly generated ATC judgment. Or more precisely, Davidson writes,

> [A]n action x is continent if x is done for a reason r, and there is no r' (that includes r), on the basis of which the agent judges some action better than x. (*EAE* 40)

In this description, r is the ATC judgment's reason-basis, while the exclusion of any larger reason r', which would overturn r, reflects that the agent's ATC judgment has satisfied the rational requirement for "enough" consideration. Hence the principle of continence's requirement to "perform the action judged best on the basis of all available relevant considerations" (41).

We should also note that Davidson slightly modifies his construal of incontinence in order to allow that the mere presence or possession of a reason r' is sufficient to ensure that the agent "has a better reason for doing something else [other than x]" and is incontinent in doing x (40). This modification, Davidson claims, represents "an improvement . . . since it allows (correctly, I think) that there are incontinent actions even when no judgement is made in light of all the reasons [that is, in light of *r'*]" (40). So the agent need not make an explicit judgment based on *r'*; if *r'* is simply *present or available*, then the agent cannot act continently on *r*, which directs another action than that favored by *r'*. The modification then tightens the requirement for "enough" consideration in establishing the ATC judgment's *r*; no overturning, larger reason *r'* can even be available to the agent for judgment.

Given those conditions, then, our main question becomes: how is an agent to reach an *identifiedly* continent intention from her various prima facie reasons? That is, suppose an agent wants to ingrain in herself the virtue of continence, wants to perform the continent action *because* it is the continent action. At what point does the principle of continence enter her reasoning? How can she be sure that she is acting in accord with continence?

I believe Davidson would explain the process this way: It may seem as if the principle of continence would enter the agent's reasoning in reaching an unconditional judgment from the prima facie ATC judgment. For, as Davidson says, prima facie reasons cannot prompt actions, since they focus only on a desirable characteristic, which is insufficient to make an action reasonable. The latter step requires "a further judgement that the desirable characteristic was enough to act on—that other considerations did not outweigh it" (98). But it *is* reasonable to act based upon the judgment that the considered action is continent, because that implies that the action is the agent's most rational option. So it seems that the principle of continence would enter into the agent's decision to judge unconditionally.

However, that impression is mistaken. As Evnine points out, Davidson's theory requires all the reasoning to be part of reaching the prima facie ATC judgment (Evnine, 57). Thus, the judgment that an action is continent and thereby desirable must somehow enter the reasoning in the prima facie stage. Davidson makes that clearer by asserting that the reason why an agent unconditionally judges a certain action better than another is "identical with" the reason why she prima facie judges the former to be better to do (*EAE* 39). But if the judgment that an action is continent were to enter *after* the prima facie reasoning had concluded, then the unconditional judgment's reason would have that added element and would not be identical with the prima facie judgment's.

Instead, if an agent wants to act continently—whether she has a one-time urge or a habitual disposition—she will possess the principle of continence as a *pro attitude* (4). As the principle of continence issues a general directive for action, it recommends any action that is favored by a properly sufficient reason *r*. So when the agent reasons about what to do, the principle of continence will be represented by a prima facie judgment (97, 98, 102). Further, the judgment would have a general form, something like this: pf (x is desirable if x is recommended based on r, such that there is no available r'—including r and more—that recommends an action other than x). Thus, even though the principle of continence would, in effect, favor an action as rational enough to perform, its recommendation would still focus only on the action's characteristic of having a sufficient r. Therefore the prima facie operator would not detach (37). The principle of continence's recommendation would be considered in making the ATC judgment—probably as the last reason considered, since it presupposes that the agent recognizes that her considerations have been sufficient.

Further, in making an unconditional judgment for the continent action, the agent is employing no new reasoning. Yet it cannot be the case that the unconditional judgment just *causally* arises once the prima facie reasoning is complete, because that would destroy the prima facie–unconditional distinction in respect to acting, upon which Davidson insists (Evnine, 57). For in that case, prima facie judgments, themselves, could bring about actions, by causing action-driving unconditional judgments.

So it must be pure *choice* on the agent's part; but not simply *random* choice—the agent's deciding that such and such a prima facie desirability provides "enough reason to act" is her making an unconditional judgment. Thus, any prima facie judgment of desirability can be made unconditional if the agent chooses to do so. But such a choice would only be appropriate if continence is satisfied, and there truly is sufficient desirability to constitute "enough reason to act." The person trying to be continent, then, only will make the unconditional judgment when it is appropriate—not for any new reasoning, but because the prima facie reasoning she has already done shows her that this action (as the continent option) is the one she wants.

I believe, then, that Davidson thinks a continent action *should* occur in the aforementioned way; unfortunately, that cannot happen, given Davidson's theory. For as we have already seen, Davidson offers no evaluative measure with which the agent might sift her prima facie judgments to arrive at a judgment having a sufficiently comprehensive reason r to satisfy the principle of continence. That also means that, in practice, an agent could not rank and compare and combine her prima facie reasons to reach an ATC judgment. Yet if the agent could not reach the required sort of summary judgment, she could not reliably identify any of her options as continent, or favored by her better reason. Therefore, she could not knowingly act for her better reason. So intentionally acting continently would be impossible, or at least impracticable, given Davidson's lack of a usable evaluative measure.

Indeed, the situation is actually worse than that. For even if we supposed that Davidson *had* provided a measure for comparing the rationality of prima facie judgments, he still has offered no clear or concrete or explicit standard by which an agent could tell when she had accumulated enough considerations to satisfy continence or to form an ATC judgment. We mentioned this difficulty much earlier; now we can see its consequences. In fact, Davidson admits,

> Under what conditions is it rational to accept [that enough has been considered to satisfy continence or to form an ATC judgment]? There are some things you can say that seem clearly right. Everything that you believe to be relevant evidence you certainly ought to take into consideration. But now should you also have hunted down further evidence if you know that there is, or may be, further evidence to be discovered? Available relevant evidence—well, what does "available" mean, how available does it have to be? . . . Well, the trouble is that there doesn't seem to be any clear answer to this question. What does rationality demand of us under these circumstances? . . . [W]e must say that it is not completely clear what rationality demands of us. ("RTS" 332)

Davidson's honesty is admirable. Unfortunately, his admission only demonstrates why his theory fails to explain how continent actions can occur. Again, if Davidson provided a means to rank and compare evaluations, an agent could tell when one reason would be better than another. But without some clear guide as to when to cry "enough" consideration, the agent still could not reliably identify any judgment as her "better reason," in the sense of being sufficient for continence or an ATC judgment. That means it would be impossible, in practice, for the agent to intentionally act continently, since she could not be certain whether she had considered enough in her prima facie reason's r to satisfy continence's requirement.

Furthermore, that uncertainty is exacerbated by Davidson's stipulation that the mere presence or availability of the larger, overturning reason r' is sufficient to render incontinent actions based on r. That is, if no explicit judgment from r' is required, and if the agent is already uncertain as to how much consideration is needed in r, then how could she ever be sure—or even moderately satisfied—that no overturning r' is available and that she is continent in acting upon any given, proposed r?

For we already saw from our discussion of the ATC judgment that it would be impossible for a human agent to acquire *all* the information relevant to her choice of action. So an agent could not assure herself by that method that there was no r' in danger of overruling her r. Yet suppose she were just to stop her consideration and say "enough"—and it *happened* that there was no overturning, larger r', although she had not assured herself of that. Then her r seems not to account for the sense of meeting a rational norm in acting continently. In other words, it appears arbitrary that she stopped when she did, rather than that she ceased considering because she recognized that she had met the rational requirement. But that aspect of fulfilling a rational norm is essential to what it means to act continently. Therefore this option provides no help, either.

Moreover, any appeal Davidson might make to the intersubjectivity of continence's rational requirement will suffer the same sorts of problems we saw with the standard of evaluative reasoning. For suppose that in setting her rational requirement for continence, an agent referred to the intersubjective agreement over how much consideration is needed to constitute an r sufficient for continent action. If she tried to use this agreement as a standard by which she could tell when she had reasoned "enough," it might well be that whether she had satisfied that requirement would only be apparent after the fact of her action, when she could compare her r to what is intersubjectively or communally acceptable. Yet our experience is that in acting continently, an agent needs to be able to tell on her own, at—or before—the time of action, whether her proposed r is rationally sufficient. Again, if an agent tried to make use of the intersubjective standard in formulating a sufficient r, that would be unworkable in practice. It simply is beyond human ability to make practical use, while in the midst of acting, of that kind of standard. So neither can Davidson find real aid in this strategy.

Therefore, Davidson's theory leaves the agent unable to reliably identify her better reason, and unable to act continently—or at least to do so intentionally. Moreover, that inability also casts serious doubt on the agent's power to diagnose her own *in*continence. If she cannot identify her better reason, then she cannot tell when she is acting *against* it any more than when she acts *for* it. I conclude, then, that Davidson cannot account for continent action, and that this problem also worsens his troubles in explaining akratic action.

4.7 PROBLEMS IN THE CONCEPTION OF RATIONAL ACTION IN P1–2

Now, having explored Davidson's difficulties in explaining continent and incontinent actions, we may turn to more general questions about the success or failure of Davidson's rational-action scheme itself. We recall that Davidson requires more than simply that intentional action be performed from, and according to, a primary reason. After all, that would merely link intentionality to acting for a *purpose* or *motivation*; a primary reason's rationalization does not guarantee that an action's performance is rational, even in the agent's own eyes. Incontinent actions demonstrate this fact. So in order to link intentionality to acting from, and according to, reason—in the sense of what the agent takes to be rational—Davidson also stipulates that intentionality demands affirmation of the principle of continence.

I believe that the consequence of that necessary affirmation is displayed in Davidson's principles P1 and P2, which, we recall, are

> P1. If an agent wants to do x more than [she] wants to do y and [she] believes [herself] free to do either x or y, then [she] will intentionally do x if [she] does either x or y intentionally. . . .
> P2. If an agent judges that it would be better to do x than to do y, then [she] wants to do x more than [she] wants to do y. (*EAE* 23)

P1 and P2 together imply that in acting intentionally, an agent will perform whichever of her options she judges is better to do—that is, whichever option she judges she has better *reason* to do. That links acting intentionally to acting continently, to doing what is judged to be most rational. It also indicates that in intentionally acting, an agent is operating from, and according to, reason, not just a motive. On that account, I think P1 and P2 represent the heart of Davidson's scheme of rational action.

4.7.1 Abortive Attacks on P1–2

However, P1 and P2 have been attacked on several grounds. First, C. C. W. Taylor disputes P2 on the assumption that it implies what Taylor calls P2′. P2′ stipulates that if an agent judges that, all things considered, x is better to do than y, then she wants to do x more than she wants to do y (Taylor, 500). After all, Taylor reasons, the ATC judgment seems like "a paradigm instance" of judging better; but if that is the case, P1 and P2 rule out the possibility of incontinence (500–2). For P1 and the implied P2′ forbid exactly what occurs in Davidson's construal of *akrasia*; that is, P1 and P2′ stipulate that an agent could not intentionally act against her ATC judgment, which she does in acting akratically. So P2′ must be false; but then, argues Taylor, P2—since it implies P2′—must also be false. Thus, Davidson's framework of rational action seems to collapse.

However, Taylor is mistaken, not having paid sufficient attention to Davidson's construal of the ATC judgment. As we saw earlier, Davidson successfully insists that the ATC judgment must be prima facie. And as has been demonstrated at great length—since it is the core of Davidson's explanation of *akrasia*—P1 and P2 apply to unconditional judgments only, not to prima facie judgments. Therefore P2 does *not* imply P2′ and is not falsified by the occurrence of incontinent actions against ATC judgments.

A second attack comes from Gary Watson, who charges that P1 and P2 *equivocate* over the phrase "want more." Watson points out distinguishable *evaluational* and *motivational* senses of "want more." The former meaning involves ranking something higher on a scale of values—for example, "I want world peace more than I want the end of world hunger." The latter meaning implies being more strongly motivated to act—for instance, "I drank because, being thirsty, I wanted the water more than I wanted the saltine cracker" (Watson, 320–1). But, Watson claims, P1 is only true if "want more" is understood motivationally; we intentionally do what we are more strongly motivated to do in preference to what we are less motivated to do. Yet as incontinent actions show, we can rank one action higher on the scale of rational value than another and still intentionally do the latter in preference to the former. However, P2 seems true only in the evaluational sense; when we think one action has better reason than another, we rank it higher on the scale of rational value. Yet as instances of *akrasia* again make clear, it is *not* true that judging one action to have better reason than another requires that we are more strongly motivated to do the former. Therefore Davidson's connection between P1 and P2 seems to depend on an equivocation (Watson, 320, 321). If the connection between P1 and P2 dissolves, so does Davidson's requirement for rational action.

I think that Davidson would respond that, like Taylor, Watson has erred in supposing that P1 and P2 apply to prima facie judgments. Yes, Davidson might admit, when a person prima facie ranks an action higher on the scale of rational value, it does not mean she is more motivated to perform that action than those lower ranked, nor that she will intentionally perform that one instead of the others. But if we consider the *unconditional* level, perhaps the evaluational P1 and the motivational P2 may be true after all. For if a person unconditionally ranks an action as having a higher rational value, or unconditionally judges that it is better to do, then—Davidson would assert—she is more motivated to perform it and *will* intentionally do it in preference to other options.

In that case, P1 and P2 both could be considered motivationally or evaluationally, to the same result. Thus, motivationally understood,

P1(m). If an agent is more motivated to do *x* than *y* and believes herself free to do either, then she will intentionally do *x* if she does either intentionally.

P2(m). If an agent unconditionally judges that *x* is better to do than *y*, then she is more motivated to do *x* than to do *y*.

Or, evaluationally:

P1(e). If an agent unconditionally ranks *x* as having a higher rational value than *y* and believes herself free to do either, then she will intentionally do *x* if she does either intentionally.

P2(e). If an agent unconditionally judges that *x* is better to do than *y*, then she unconditionally ranks *x* as having higher rational value than *y*.

Moreover, either version upholds Davidson's scheme of rational action, while clearly allowing incontinence, as Davidson portrays it.

4.7.2 Failure to Necessarily Connect Intentionality and Rationality

However, I do not think this response frees Davidson of problems with P1 and P2 (including both *m* and *e* variants). For one thing, since P1 and P2 do not apply to prima facie judgments, they do not seem, after all, to require intentional action to be rational action, beyond being rationalized by a primary reason. That is, all the substantive evaluative reasoning—the judging that x is "better to do" or "has better reason"—occurs at the prima facie level. As we saw in exploring continent action, no reasoning occurs in making an unconditional judgment; it is merely a choice. Further, we recall that any prima facie judgment can be made unconditional by the agent, regardless of whether it is or is not the best reasoned. So judging "better to do" at the unconditional level is not subject to a standard of rationality; such evaluation can represent the approval contained in any prima facie reason the agent just decides is worth acting upon.

In other words, at the prima facie level at which reasons are compared and ranked, the ATC judgment represents the agent's assessment that a certain action is in fact her most rational option. In making the ATC judgment that it is better to do *x* than *y*, the agent labels *x* as the action reason recommends. But in making an unconditional judgment that it is better to do *x* than *y*, or even that *x* has higher rational value than *y*, the agent labels *x* as worth doing over *y*, merely because *a* reason recommends it. Yet that means that neither P2(m) nor P1(e) links motivation to act with the agent's judgment of what it is rational to do, of what reason recommends. For the requirements of unconditionally judging that *x* is "better to do" or "has higher rational rank" are trivial and without rigor.

Therefore, P1–2(m) and P1–2(e) do not demand anything beyond what is already required from the primary reason. Davidson's scheme of rational action, represented in P1 and P2, collapses into nothing more than acting for a motive or purpose, rather than according to reason. Moreover, as we recognized from Davidson's initial proposal of P1 and P2, a link between acting intentionally and acting for a motive does not constitute a sufficient requirement for rational action. So it seems that in Davidson's theory there is no necessary connection such that an intentional action must be performed according to reason; Davidson seems not to be a rational-action theorist after all.

Worse, our earlier objections to Davidson's account of incontinence give us good grounds for suspecting that P2(m) and P1(e) are false anyway. First, in P2(m), the unconditional judgment that *x* is better to do than *y* amounts to the agent's judging *x*, on the whole, to be more desirable than *y*, on the whole. But "more desirable" is ambiguous and can be understood in two ways. In the first sense, of assessing *x*'s performance as more strongly desired than *y*'s, P2(m) seems trivially true; and P1–2(m) are left making no connection to rationality at all. So Davidson must mean the second sense of "more desirable," that is, assessing the performance of *x* as more worthy to be desired—as more rational—than the performance of *y*. However, one of our objections to Davidson's portrayal of incontinence was that at least some akratic actions seem to violate unconditional judgments about which action is more rational to do. Since P1(m) seems unproblematic, the existence of incontinent actions violating unconditional judgments would falsify P2(m).

Further, a corresponding problem plagues P1(e). P2(e) seems safe enough as a definitional stipulation about how unconditional judging works. But the above sorts of weak-willed actions apparently provide counterexamples against P1(e)'s claim that unconditionally ranking *x* with a higher rational value than *y* requires intentionally doing *x* in preference to doing *y*. At the very least, the occurrence of akratic actions in violation of apparently unconditional judgments renders P2(m) and P1(e) highly questionable and dubious—far from the "self-evident" status Davidson claims for P1 and P2 (*EAE* 23). It seems, then, that in addition to providing no necessary connection to acting according to reason, both P1–2(m) and P1–2(e) are false conjunctions.

However, several of Davidson's critics have proposed ways of changing or correcting P1 and P2. Unfortunately, as we shall now discover, none of the "corrections" salvage a scheme of rational action. Mele, for instance, writes, "That the motivational force of a want may be out of line with the agent's [rational] evaluation of the object of that want seems to me obvious" (37). Therefore, he claims,

> We may, and should, reject Davidson's P2 [and, presumably, P2(m) and P1(e)]. . . . The connection between better judgments and the balance of an agent's motivation is more complex than Davidson thinks; and this holds as well for the connection between intentions and motivation. (49)

Mele proposes, instead, that we should think of P2's requirement as an "ideal condition"; that is, an agent should *strive toward* being most motivated to do what she unconditionally judges to be best or most rational (44).

However, that means that for Mele, the agent's motivation to perform an action and her rational evaluation of that action are *not* necessarily connected. He supplies no essential link between acting intentionally and acting from, and according to, reason. So while Mele's proposed change may allow a Davidsonian theory to be more empirically accurate by accounting for incontinent actions that violate unconditional judgments, it also entails completely abandoning the construal of intentional action as, by nature, rational action.

Bratman's approach makes similar concessions. He supposes that P2 must be mistaken, on the grounds that the unconditional or intention-judgment does not have an evaluational form, such as "It would be best to do *a*." Bratman links that form to the evaluative reasoning that culminates in the ATC (or in Bratman's terms, "best") judgment. He assigns the intention (or "action") judgment the form of a simple *self-command*, such as "Do *a*" (161–7). In this way, Bratman leaves no rational implication or logical connection between an agent's evaluational-form best judgment and her self-command-form action judgment. On that account, then, an agent may form her action judgment without rationally needing to base it upon her best judgment.

Again, though, that approach severs the necessary connection between acting intentionally and acting according to reason. Like Mele, Bratman may offer some aid to Davidson—in this case, Bratman's alteration allows the agent's best judgment to consider an action *as a whole* rather than only in an action *characteristic*, thus giving a more plausible construal of that summary judgment. But that change has the cost of admitting complete defeat for the idea of intentional action being, by nature, rational action. For the agent now has no rational connection between the evaluation she makes in her best judgment and the self-command she makes in her action judgment. Her best judgment carries no rational implications as to which self-command she should affirm, thus leaving no rational requirement or standard applying to those action-causing self-commands.

Further, Taylor's proposed corrections fare no better. Taylor rejects P2 on the objection that judging that *x* is better to do than *y* does not imply wanting more to do *x*, or intentionally doing *x* in preference to *y*. Instead, Taylor submits P2′, which is much like P2(e); that is, P2′ stipulates that judging *x* better to do than *y* implies ranking the performance of *x*, on this occasion, higher than the performance of *y*. In that case, the agent regards *x* as more valuable in some way, but is not required to be more motivated to perform *x* (Taylor, 518). Again the conjunction of P1 and P2′ would allow the occurrence of some kinds of akratic actions that have been shown to conflict with P1 and P2. For instance, incontinence that violates unconditional judgments about which action would be better to do is now consistent with P1 and P2′. However, like the others', Taylor's solution destroys any necessary connection between acting intentionally and acting according to a rational judgment about what should be done. Once more the notion of intentional action as rational action simply is dropped.

Lastly, Audi's "corrections" also follow this well-worn path. He argues that P2 is false, for the same reasons given above: some incontinent actions demonstrate that judging an action to be better than another does not entail wanting more to perform the "better" one ("WWPJ" 190–2). Rather, Audi proposes, judgments of practical rationality seem to create a *tendency* to do an action; so there is a tendency for an agent's motivation to be in accord with her practical judgments about what actions are better to do (194). Audi's version, then, can allow the incontinent actions countermanded by P2. His view leaves at least some connection between acting intentionally and acting according to judgments of practical reason. However, that connection is not necessary or essential to intentional action. That is, the connection is not such that an action's intentionality is conditional upon its being performed in accord with those practical judgments of what it is rationally best to do. So yet again, the idea that intentional action is, by nature, rational action has been abandoned.

To sum up this point, all of the changes proposed by the various critics fall along the same lines. They alter P1 and P2 in ways that allow explanation of previously problematic aspects of incontinence. But far from tightening P1–2 into a sufficient requirement for a scheme of rational action, all the alterations serve only to make more explicit that such a scheme neither is present nor even could fit into a Davidsonian theoretical explanation of weak-willed actions. Neither Davidson's P1 and P2 nor any of the offered changes or variations provide Davidson's theory with an acceptable construal of intentional action as rational action.

Furthermore, we recall Davidson's failure to offer a concrete, practically useful measure of rationality in action. Davidson cannot explain how an agent might compare or rank her reasons to reach an ATC judgment. Nor can his theory offer the agent a practically recognizable endpoint to her deliberations; she is left unable to reliably identify her better reason in order to act either continently or incontinently. Now we can see a further implication of that failure: even if P1–2 (or some variation) could be made into a requirement sufficient to characterize rational action, Davidson still could not explain how an agent might get from having *a* reason recommend an action to having *reason* recommend an action. That is, even if a rational action standard were provided, it would be a practical impossibility to meet that standard within Davidson's theoretical framework.

So Davidsonian explanation requires merely that an intentional action be performed from, and rationalized according to, a primary reason. But we have seen that this requirement boils down to acting for a motive or purpose, which is insufficient to generate a conception of rational action. For this requirement does not discriminate between acting for well or poorly reasoned motives. Yet a standard of rational action needs to ensure that intentionality is linked to acting *according to* reason (in the sense of measuring up to a norm), and not simply to acting *for a* reason (in the sense of having some motive). Therefore, Davidson's scheme of intentional action possesses insufficient rigor to qualify as a theory of rational action; or if the scheme is viewed as an attempt to provide such a theory, it fails.

4.8 SUMMARY OF FINDINGS ON DAVIDSON'S VIEW

Let us then conclude our examination of Davidson's position with a short summary of what we have uncovered. First, Davidson's account of incontinence is deeply troubled. He cannot explain much of the phenomena surrounding weakness of will, including the agent's inner conflict and sense of self-division. Davidson can give no account of those incontinent actions apparently performed in violation of unconditional judgments and intentions. Further, given the akratic agent's understanding of her action as rationally inappropriate, Davidson cannot explain incontinent actions as intentional, even under his loose requirement of being rationalized by a primary reason.

Davidson's only recourse in construing such actions as intentional seems to be a homuncularist scheme of mental partitioning that attributes those actions to mental subsystems rather than to the agent. But then, the actions no longer seem incontinent. So Davidson is forced either to offer a radically incomplete explanation of incontinent actions or to portray those actions in an inaccurate and implausible way. I am reminded of a comment R. M. Hare made when he kindly agreed to meet with me and discuss his views. Regarding Davidson and those espousing related positions, Hare shook his head and remarked, "I sometimes wonder if these people have ever *experienced* weakness of will."

Moreover, Davidson does not meet his own requirement to explain how an agent sifts and compares her reasons to reach an ATC judgment. Nor can Davidson give an account of how an agent could reliably, practically identify her own "better judgment" in order to act either for or against it. Finally, under the combined weight of these objections and of the vacuousness of P1–2's supposed connection between intentional action and rationality, Davidson's framework of rational action, itself, collapses. So not only does Davidson fail to account for incontinent actions as intentionally performed by the agent, he also cannot account for them under a workable construal of rational action.

What, then, have we learned from Davidson? What guidelines for a successful account of rational action can we draw from our examination? From Davidson's successes, we can see that incontinence needs to be understood as a rational *failure*, or breakdown, as involving practical *irrationality*. Also, that rational problem needs to be *widely applicable* to various kinds of intentional actions, so that incontinence in different areas of life can be explained equally.

From Davidson's failures, we can see that a good rational-action theory must work from an *accurate and robust portrayal* of incontinence and needs to be able to *explain the diverse phenomena* associated with the experience of weakness of will. Also, the theory must provide *a specific, practically usable, evaluative standard*, so that it can explain better than Davidson's view how an agent could sift her competing reasons to identify an action as the option reason recommends. Finally, a successful rational-action theory needs a more *rigorous connection* between intentionality and practical rationality than is offered by Davidson. The link between acting intentionally and acting from, and according to, reason must be *necessary*—essential to the intentionality of any performance.

That leaves us with a troubling question, related to the one yielded by our examination of Hare's view. If Davidson's theory—whose P1–2 did not even provide a sufficiently rigorous connection between intentionality and practical rationality to begin with—could not account for all incontinent actions as intentional, how could any theory proposing a stricter requirement hope to do so? To discover a possible answer to that question, we must now turn to Thomas Aquinas's view and the conclusions we can draw from it.

5

THOMAS AQUINAS'S THEORY

To reach the solutions provided by a Thomistic theory of rational action, we must first identify the problems that incontinent actions pose for such a theory. Initially, then, we shall set out Aquinas's view of the connection between practical rationality and intentional action. Next, we shall examine Aquinas's characterization of incontinent actions, and the difficulties such actions present for his position. Finally, we shall examine Aquinas's proposed solution to those problems, and note some crucial implications of that proposal.

5.1 AQUINAS'S CONCEPTION
OF RATIONAL ACTION

First, we must lay out Aquinas's construal of rational action. To do that, though, we need to understand his account of action, including both the psychological components involved in action-production and the step-by-step process that constitutes intentional action—which Aquinas characterizes as "human action." That will allow us to see how practical reason operates in human actions, and what Aquinas's standard for rational action is like.

5.1.1 Psychological Principles of Action

The most basic aspect of his rational-action conception concerns the psychological capacities that are brought to bear in producing a human action. Aquinas calls these capacities, these faculties from which the guidance and motivation of action originate, the *principles* of human action; and he says there are four. The first is *reason*, the second is *will*, and the third and fourth are the *concupiscible* and *irascible appetites* that generate *passions* (Aquinas, *Summa Theologica* I–II q.78, a.1, resp.). These, Aquinas maintains, "are the only powers that can be the principles of a human or a voluntary act" (*Disputed Questions on Virtue* q.2 [on the cardinal virtues], a.1, resp.).

Of the four, reason—or *intellect*—is the capacity primarily responsible for the *guidance* of action. Included within reason are the cognitive abilities to apprehend possible objects of action, and to consider and compare those objects in order to judge and direct the best course of action (*ST* I q.82, a.4, rep.3; *Treatise on Happiness* q.14, a.6, resp.; q.17, a.1, resp.; Kretzmann, 174).

On the other hand, the will—or *rational appetite*—is the power primarily responsible for the *motive force* that produces action (174). Will includes the capacities to form preferences and make choices, and to move the body into action (Aquinas, *TH* q.14, a.1, rep.1; q.15, a.3. resp.; q.16, a.2, resp.). However, the will possesses no cognitive powers, no thinking or understanding. Through its choices it simply provides motive force to ends and means presented to it as good by reason; that is, the will is an appetite activated specifically by rational conceptions of goods—hence its name (q.8, a.1, resp.). As John Driscoll puts it in commenting on Aquinas, "The will is a blind power. It tends towards objects as they are known by the intellect" (3204).

The third and fourth principles of action are both sources of passions. The concupiscible and irascible appetites are subdivisions within the *sensitive appetite*, from which passions come. The sensitive appetite is activated by, and provides motive force toward (or away from), goods (or evils) apprehended by the senses (Kretzmann, 174). That appetitive movement is experienced as a passion, which Juvenal Lalor defines thusly:

> [P]assion is an operation of the sensitive appetite consequent on sense knowledge and necessarily accompanied by some bodily transformation, in virtue of which a [person] either tends to some recognized sensible good which, having first stimulated (or acted upon) [her] organism, now draws [her] to itself, or tends away from some recognized sensible evil which, having first stimulated (or acted upon) [her] organism, now repels [her] from itself. (3,225)

Depending on whether what is perceived is directly attainable (or avoidable), or is hindered by obstacles, the appetite will fall into the category of concupiscible or irascible, respectively (3,224–5).

So, for example, when a sensed good, like food or sex, is directly attainable, a person will experience a concupiscible passion—in this case, *desire*—to get it. Once the good is had, the person will experience another concupiscible passion, *pleasure*. On the other hand, if the food or sex were only attainable after some extended, difficult effort, the appetitive passion felt would be irascible—in this case, *hope*, or perhaps *despair* if the good seemed practically unreachable (3,224–5). Or again, the person might experience *anger*—from which the irascible appetite takes its name—if some evil were foisted upon her and made difficult to remove (3,234). Aquinas calls the concupiscible passion of desire *concupiscence*, and from it the source appetite is named (3,230). Soon we shall see how passions can help produce action, but in passing let me emphasize the "bodily transformations" the passions engender; those physical changes, and their effects on reason's functioning, will be crucial to us later.

Now we can examine the roles these principles play in producing human actions. We will leave the details for later, but the basic interactive relationships between reason, will, and the passions are as follows: Reason plays an essential part in three ways. First, it always remains primary to any action, in that all actions must begin from some apprehension of a good. In Aquinas's words, "We must stop at the intellect as preceding all the rest. For every movement of the will must be preceded by apprehension, whereas every apprehension is not preceded by an act of the will" (*ST* I q.82, a.4, rep.3).

Second, reason possesses freedom in its consideration of the contingent particulars that make up the possibilities for action. That is, as reason sifts through possible ends to act on, and possible means to reach those ends, it can explore any of the opposing lines of consideration (Aquinas, *TH* q.10, a.2, resp.). Nothing necessitates or determines its thought path regarding such contingencies. Aquinas puts it this way:

> [I]n the case of some particular act ... reason ... [has] free judgment and [so the agent] retains the power of being inclined to various things. For reason in contingent matters may follow opposite courses. . . . Now particular operations are contingent, and therefore in such matters the judgment of reason may follow opposite courses, and is not determinate to one. (*ST* I q.83, a.1, resp.)

Moreover, Aquinas emphasizes the importance of this aspect of reason by pointing out a crucial implication, "And forasmuch as [humans are] rational is it necessary that [humans] have a free will" (q.83, a.1, resp.).

Third, because the will is an appetite specially fitted to reason, reason interacts *directly* with the will. For the will's movements derive from reason's presenting it with a good, an end for action (Stump and Kretzmann, 361–2). Aquinas writes, "In this way [as an end moves an agent] the intellect moves the will, because the good understood is the object of the will, and moves it as an end" (*ST* I q.82, a.4, resp.). However, we need to note that this "moving" is what Aristotle—and Aquinas after him—would call *final causation*; that is, it implies no motive force on reason's part. Reason does not and cannot coerce the will, as Thomistic scholars Eleonore Stump and Norman Kretzmann point out (361–2). Rather, reason, in a sense, dangles an attractive object in front of the will and waits for the will to move itself. Nevertheless, as we shall see, every act of will is tied to a prior act of reason.

As for the will itself, it plays an essential part in human action because, quite simply, the will is the "prime-mover" in a person. As Driscoll puts it,

> Now, all movement in [a human] has its human source in the will; the will is the human prime-mover; the will moves all other [voluntary] powers of the soul, including reason, to their objects. (3,210)

In other words, as the generator and applicator of the motive force to act, the will *can* make the other psychological (as well as the physical) capacities operate in accordance with the preferences it forms; the will acts on the other capacities as an agent—or in Aristotelian terminology, as an *efficient cause* (Stump and Kretzmann, 362). Aquinas says it clearly:

> In this way [as an agent] the will moves the intellect, and all the powers of the soul. . . . Therefore the will as an agent moves all the powers of the soul to their respective acts, except the natural powers [for example, autonomic bodily functions] . . . which are not subject to our will. (*ST* I q.82, a.4, resp.)

Obviously, then, all human action emerges from the will.

Moreover, the will's independence is exhibited not only in its ability to move other faculties into action, but also in its ability to *resist* direction from those other faculties. Stump and Kretzmann point out that "the will can refrain from acting, rejecting . . . [an] end presented to it by the intellect" (361–2). Driscoll concurs, writing, "No matter what particular good is presented by the intellect, the will can reject it" (3,206). Aquinas himself offers abundant support for these commentators. He declares, "[the will's] capacity is not subjected to any individual good. And therefore it is not of necessity moved by it" (*ST* I q.82, a.2, rep.2). Or again, he claims that the will can turn away from any good-conception reason offers (*TH* q.1, a.7, rep.1; Stump and Kretzmann, 362). Furthermore, there is no particular kind of good that necessarily draws the will's choice (Aquinas, *ST* I q.82, a.2, rep.1). Indeed, even a perfect and complete good—because our reason could not perfectly conceive of its complete desirability—cannot necessitate the will (q.82, a.2, resp.; *TH* q.5, a.8, resp.). Similarly, Aquinas maintains that the will also can resist whatever influence the sense appetite's passions may exert, which again affects the will as a kind of final causation (Kretzmann, 175). In his words,

> [A person] is not moved at once, according to the irascible and con-cupiscible appetites: but [she] awaits the command of the will, which is the superior appetite . . . wherefore the lower appetite is not suffi-cient to cause movement, unless the higher appetite consents. (*ST* I q.81, a.3, resp.)

On that account, Aquinas concludes, "It is therefore clear that the will does not desire of necessity whatever it desires" (q.82, a.2, resp.).

Hence Aquinas also takes the will to be the central locus of freedom in human actions. For "choice is principally an act of the appetitive power [namely, the will]. And thus free-will is an appetitive power" (Aquinas, *ST* I q.83, a.3, resp.). With that in mind, when we later investigate questions concerning whether or not freedom and agency are diminished in incontinent actions, we shall have to pay close attention to Aquinas's account of the will's status and activity in such actions.

However, before we can advance to the passions to complete the exposition of the principles of human action, we must address a puzzling point in what has been said so far. Aquinas seems to attribute freedom to both reason and will, yet he also says that the will can cause reason to act. How can those statements be consistent? The question concerns freedom not so much of the will as of reason. On the one hand, as we just saw, Aquinas clearly supposes will to have the power to cause reason's acts (q.82, a.4, resp.). Stump and Kretzmann characterize this causal control as extensive; they speak of "the will's occasional *coercion* of the intellect" [emphasis added] and its capacity "to direct the intellect's attention" (362). That seems to imply that reason's considerations are determined by the will in both their direction and outcome. Reason becomes a mere tool under the will's control, and the will becomes effectively "self-directed" (360, 362).

Yet that interpretation seems not to fit Aquinas's description of reason's operation. For one thing, we saw that Aquinas asserts that every movement of the will occurs under some kind of guiding apprehension from reason (*ST* I q.84, a.4, rep.3). For another, he repeatedly proposes that the freedom of will and choice are dependent on reason. That is, he portrays the will's freedom as, to some extent, emerging from reason's ability to consider opposing possibilities with regard to courses of action (q.83, a.1, resp.). For example, he claims,

> [A person] does not choose with necessity. . . . The reason for this lies in the very power of reason. For . . . in all particular goods, reason can consider the good that is in something and the lack of good in it, that is, which is accounted as evil, and thus it can apprehend any one of these goods as something to be chosen or avoided. (*TH* q.13, a.6, resp.)

He also writes, "no object moves the will necessarily, for no matter what the object may be, it is in [a person's] power not to think of it, and hence not actually to will it" (*TH* q.10, a.2, resp.). Or again, Aquinas says that because "reason is a power that compares several things together," the will "may be moved; but not of necessity from one thing" (*ST* I q.82, a.2, rep.3). Moreover, he claims we are free in our actions because we "can deliberate about them, for when deliberating [which is an act of reason] reason is related to opposite alternatives, and the will can tend to either" (*TH* q.6, a.2, rep.2). Further, as we shall later see, Aquinas characterizes incontinence as involving a failure by reason to hold to its judgments about what ought to be done (*Commentary on the Nicomachean Ethics* VII.L.6: C1393–4; VII.L.7: C1420). He even calls reason "the regulative power of all the internal affections [that is, appetites]" (*On Evil* q.3, a.9, resp.).

How then shall we understand Aquinas on this matter? I think we need to revise Stump and Kretzmann's position. Given what Aquinas says, it is undeniable that the will *can* prompt reason to act. However, it is also clear that not all acts of reason—particularly reason's initial apprehensions—occur because of the will's bidding. Indeed, I think that reason possesses some spontaneity, or indeterminacy, and self-guidance in what it thinks of, or apprehends, in its consideration of both ends and means. For the power of attending to an idea is cognitive, belonging not to will but to reason.

I do not mean to imply, though, that will has no influence over reason's considerations. For instance, having thought of some object of action appealing (or repellent) to the will, reason may be prompted to consider it more (or less). But if additional consideration is called for, I do not think the will controls the thought path that consideration follows; rather, reason does. Again, though, it certainly is the will that controls when reason stops considering and deliberating, and full action begins. As Driscoll observes, "The last practical judgment of reason which decides that this particular good should be chosen, *is* the last only because the will wishes it to be so" (3,206). This interpretation, I hope, preserves aspects of freedom and independence in both reason and the will, while leaving their functions connected.

In addition, we recall that one of Davidson's problems was that his view kept tending toward homuncularism, the attempt to explain agency by postulating "little men" inside the agent. And Davidson's position had to provide safeguards against this tendency. So must Aquinas's. Thus, I want to make sure that will and reason both retain sufficient power and distinctiveness that neither functions in itself as a "little agent." Rather, each constitutes a *component* of a functioning agent. I think that Stump and Kretzmann's position, with a "self-directed" will that controls all other faculties, comes perilously close to homuncularism. On the other hand, I hope that my own interpretation, according to which reason possesses a type of guidance-ability that is independent of the will, yet in which the will possesses sole powers of choice and motivation, stakes out ground that safely avoids homuncularist territory.

Finally, on this point, we need to note that, for Aquinas, reason and will are intricately and inextricably bound together. He says they "include one another in their acts, because the intellect understands that the will wills, and the will wills the intellect to understand" (*ST* I q.81, a.3, resp.). Indeed, Aquinas sometimes includes both rational cognition and rational appetite under the name of "reason" or "intellect." For example, he speaks of "reason" as "*consenting*," although consent, strictly speaking, is an act of will (*In Epistolam ad Romanos* chp.7, lec.3). In another passage, he makes this inclusion more explicit, writing, "Therefore consent to the act belongs to . . . reason, yet in the sense in which reason includes the will" (*TH* q.15, a.4, resp.). This usage unfortunately results in some unclarity in places, and we shall have to sort out such statements carefully when they appear. But I believe we can do so without doing violence to Aquinas's view.

That said, we can at last complete our exposition of the principles of human action, by laying out how passions, whose source is in the irascible and concupiscible appetites, interact with will and reason. First, passion is *not* necessarily involved in every human action, as reason and will are; passions are not essential to agency of action. Second, though, passions *can* help to produce human actions, because—similar to reason—they can incline the will by *final causation* (Kretzmann, 175). That is, because a sense appetite for some object makes it appealing, that object can then seem good to reason and thereby may incline the will as an end or goal for action. Again, though, as it was with reason, this influence is *resistible* by the will (Aquinas, *ST* I q.81, a.3, resp.).

Moreover, unlike reason, passions affect the will only *indirectly*, through reason (Kretzmann, 175). Later we shall examine this point in more detail, but for now let us content ourselves with the basic relationship: As Lalor pointed out, sensible goods (or evils) have to be recognized, or apprehended, as such in order to excite passions (3,223). But that apprehension allows the passions "indirectly [to incline the will], through the medium of the intellect which [thus] knows goods of the sense order and presents them to the will" (Driscoll, 3,205). Finally, we should note that, aside from cases of insanity, this influence is not coercive on reason, either; reason's freedom-in-consideration means it is not forced to present a passion's "proposal" to the will for choice (Aquinas, *ST* II–II q.156, a.1, resp.).

5.1.2 Human Actions

With that picture in mind of the principles of human action, we can now move to an exposition of exactly how those principles—particularly reason and will—operate in producing a human action. Our first point concerns Aquinas's definition of "human actions." Aquinas points out that not everything done, or caused or brought about, by a person counts as a *human* action, that is, as something she does in a way characteristic of her *as* a human being. She digests food; she sweats. But Aquinas characterizes such activities by the lesser label of "*actions of a man.*" In order for an agent's activities to qualify as "human actions strictly speaking," the agent must be "master" over them; she has mastery over actions that proceed from the "free judgment of choice" that she possesses through her reason and will. Aquinas calls that required interaction between will and reason "deliberate will." "Therefore," he asserts, "actions that are deliberately willed are properly called human" (*TH* q.1, a.1, resp.).

We shall explore the elements of human action in a moment, but let me first quickly explain how Aquinas's concept of "human" action fits with the notion of "intentional" action we have been using. Indeed, Aquinas describes the process of deliberate willing as involving an intention, without which an agent could not act (*TH* q.1, a.2, resp.) So every human action includes an intention of the agent, from which intention the action proceeds; in that strict sense, then, every human action must be intentional.

However, we must recognize a distinction between Aquinas's use of the word "intention" and the use so far in the present argument. By "intention," I (and Davidson) have meant a judgment directing the performance of a specific action. Aquinas, however, uses "intention" to refer to a step in the human action process that is prior to judging specific actions. For Aquinas, "intention" refers to a will-act in which the will affirms a *general* rational judgment that directs a *type* of action.

But that difference over "intention" does not mean that Aquinas's characterization of human action fails to correspond to the present argument's notion of intentional action. For each human action also essentially incorporates and follows from a reason-act called "discretive judgment," which does correspond to our usage of "intention." In a discretive judgment, reason directs the performance of a specific action. Thus, for Aquinas "discretive judgment" fills the role of "intention" (in the sense that Davidson and I have meant). I therefore believe we can justifiably consider Aquinas's account of human action as a theory of intentional action—in the sense used by the current argument—and as pertinent to our inquiry.

As to the basic nature of human action, Aquinas first reiterates his assertion that human actions must be *voluntary* (q.6, a.1, resp.). Voluntariness requires both that the agent's action proceed from causes internal to her, and that she have understanding of an end for which she acts (q.6, a.2, resp.). In other words, she must act from a motive force within her and within her control—which is the will, as we shall detail in a moment (q.6, a.3, rep.3). Also, she must rationally grasp what she does, at least as it satisfies or fulfills her intention in acting (q.6, a.2, resp., a.3, rep.3; *CNE* VII.L.9: C1438).

Moreover, Aquinas contends, the freedom of voluntariness results from the distinctive manner in which will and reason interact. For as we saw in the last section, the will is a "rational appetite"; that is, it provides "inclination," or motivational force, toward what reason proposes to it as good to do (Aquinas, *ST* I q.82, a.4, resp.; *TH* q.8, a.1, resp.). And again as we noted, in considering various courses of action to determine what would be good to do in a given situation, reason moves between "opposite alternatives," thus leaving the will free to incline toward any alternative that reason offers (q.6, a.2, rep. 2; q.13, a.6, resp.; *ST* I q.82, a.2, rep.3). Hence the requirement that human actions must proceed from deliberate will.

5.1.3 The Process of Deliberate Willing

But how, specifically, does deliberate willing produce action? Like this: First, reason, or intellect, notices or recognizes some good (Aquinas, *TH* q.9, a.2, resp.). Driscoll describes it this way:

> [S]ince nothing can be desired unless it is known, human action must begin with an act of the intellect. This movement is called *simple apprehension*—a simple knowing of [an apparent good]. (3,208)

For example, someone's reason might apprehend that "charity is a good thing."

Once reason has such a simple apprehension of a good, that apprehension favorably disposes the will to this good—the will's first act, called *simple volition* (Aquinas, *TH* q.12, a.1, rep.4). We should note, though, that this act yields "a mere complacency in the good. . . . By volition the will merely assumes a 'you look so good' attitude towards [reason's] object" (Driscoll, 3,208). In other words, no motivation toward concrete action has yet emerged; our agent merely likes the notion of charity.

That motivation comes from the next pair of reason- and will-acts. With the will arousing some interest in reason's apprehended good, reason acts on that interest by making its first *judgment*. The intellect considers this good in order to judge whether it is possible to obtain, and whether it is worth doing so, and when (3,208). If it judges the worth and possibility of achieving this good favorably, reason, in effect, proposes the object to the will in a general way as good for action. This proposal works like a "formal principle" moving the will (Aquinas, *TH* q.9, a.1, resp.). That is, it possesses a universalized evaluational form such as, "Any act of charity is good to do."

In being presented with this principle, the will inclines toward—or supplies motivation for—performing charitable acts. This is the will-act of *intention*, as Aquinas uses the term (q.12, a.1, rep.4). Aquinas asserts that reason orders the will's intentions by giving it an *end*, or *object*, for which to act (q.9, a.1, resp.; q.12, a.1, rep.3). So while will supplies motive force to perform actions, intending is itself initiated and directed by reason in presenting the will with an object (q.12, a.1, rep.3; *ER* chp.7, lec.3). Moreover, with intention the will now

> efficaciously desires the good, it intends it as an end which is to be attained by the very practical method of employing suitable means. . . . Intention . . . desires a good in a very businesslike way. (Driscoll, 3,208)

That is, now action is being motivated. But such intentions still only incline the will in a general way to action, not toward any specific action to be done here and now.

Next, then, *deliberation* must occur to reach a choice of a particular action. Deliberation begins when will, inclining toward a certain end—in this case, performing charitable acts—thereby moves reason to consider how to attain that end. Reason had moved the will by presenting it with an end, and the subsequent inclination now moves reason to investigate possible

means (Aquinas, *TH* q.14, a.1, rep.1). This inquiry into means is deliberation, or counsel (q.14, a.1, resp.). Reason starts from the general end
desired—here, the principle to perform charitable acts—and applies that
end as best it can to the facts about the agent's current situation (q.14, a.6,
resp.). Wanting to do some act of charity, our agent examines her circumstances and discovers that she has no spare money, but does possess spare
time. Given that, she reasons that she could better and more immediately
help the elderly next-door neighbor with his yardwork than she could support the missionary fund at church—both of which actions she views as
constituting particular instances of charity. Thus, reasoning from her general
end, the agent "arrives at what must be done at once" as the means to fulfill her end (q.14, a.5, resp.).

   This result of deliberation constitutes the second crucial judgment by
reason. Aquinas says it designates "that which presents itself as first to be
done," and that it is the "ultimate conclusion" to deliberation (q.14, a.6, resp.).
This conclusion is an act that "belong[s] to reason" Aquinas calls it "a 'decision' or a 'judgment,'" and *choice* is the will's act that "follows upon it" (q.13,
a.1, rep.2). In order to distinguish this judgment from reason's prior judgment
that preceded the will's intention, I shall adopt a term used by Driscoll and
call the judgment that concludes deliberation *discretive judgment*. Driscoll aptly
describes it as "a singling out of one of the many means proposed by counsel ... and the presentation of this means to the will as the most acceptable of
all" (3,210). Discretive judgment, then, proposes a specific action as good to
do; in our example, the agent's reason now judges that "charitably going next
door to offer to help my neighbor rake his yard is good to do."

   Now, the will actually has two possible acts that may follow discretive
judgment. We have already mentioned the normal follow-up, choice, and
the other option is *consent*. These dual possibilities will have some vital implications later, so let us carefully distinguish them. Sometimes deliberation
can conclude that more than one action would suitably fit as the first step
in reaching the desired end. In such a case, discretive judgment presents several means to the will as acceptable (3,210). Suppose, for example, that our
agent's deliberations had concluded that she could offer help either with
raking leaves *or* with weeding, that both were immediately possible charitable actions for the neighbor. In these instances, Aquinas says, the will responds with consent to both options:

> [I]t may be that through deliberation several means are found that are
> conducive to the end; as long as each of these is acceptable, consent is
> given to each one. (*TH* q.15, a.3, rep.3)

By consenting, the will begins to apply motive force toward actually doing the actions that are the approved means. In Aquinas's words, "Hence, the application of appetitive movement to a determination of the deliberation is consent proper" (q.15, a.3, resp.). So our agent's will consents to offering help both with weeding and with raking, and begins to "gear up" for action. Here, it is important for us to emphasize that in consent, the will affirms and begins to carry out the proposal of discretive judgment.

However, obviously, all the means cannot be enacted at once. Our agent has to pick either raking or weeding to do first; she accomplishes that by making a choice between the means to which her will has consented. Choice, then, is the will-act that picks out one means for performance (q.14, a.1, rep.1). Indeed, choice is basically consent narrowed to one option. As Driscoll says, "The only essential difference between these two acts of the will is the element of preference with is found in the notion of choice" (3,210). Or in Aquinas's own words, "among those [means] which are acceptable [and consented to] we give preference to one by making a choice" (*TH* q.15, a.3, rep.3).

In our example, the agent reasons by discretive judgment that she ought now to offer to help her neighbor with his weeding or raking, consents to both options, and then chooses, say, to offer to help rake, inclining her will specifically to that action and applying motive force toward accomplishing it. This application of appetite thereby begins to bring about the specified action (q.14, a.2, rep.2).

The relationship between consent and choice is close enough that in many cases the two become one act of will. Aquinas writes, "if we find that only one means is acceptable, then consent and choice do not differ in reality" (q.15, a.3, rep.3). That is, we often find reason to prefer one immediately available means over the rest; discretive judgment then proposes only that one to the will—as in our example, in which the agent judged that offering to help rake, only, would be good to do—and will affirms this means in one act of choice that includes consent's application of appetitive movement. Indeed, Aquinas notes that if the best means to an intended end is sufficiently obvious, even deliberation can be skipped, and discretive judgment and choice immediately follow (Aquinas's notion of) intention (q.14, a.4, rep.1). However, in those instances in which deliberation *does* yield equally acceptable alternatives in discretive judgment, it seems that the movement from consent to choice comes purely from the will through a simple and free expression of preference (Stump and Kretzmann, 361). We need to keep that in mind, because such cases will be of importance to us later in analyzing incontinent actions.

Also, at this point the justification for my earlier claim that human action is intentional action is apparent. Discretive judgment partially fulfills the
role that the present argument has, in respect to Hare's and Davidson's
views, characterized as an "intention"—for it is a *rational judgment directing
the performance of a specific action*. The will acts of consent and, especially,
choice supply the other aspect of (our sense of) an intention—a *desire to perform a specific action*. The inclusion of discretive judgment and choice confirms that human action equals intentional action (in this work's usage); all,
and only those, actions done through deliberate will are performed from a
discretive judgment and choice—that is, from an intention (in the sense I
have meant). That said, let us conclude the exposition of the elements of
human action.

The final stage in the production of action consists of executive, or
"follow-through," activities by reason and will. Moved by the choice of an
action, reason commands the physical and mental motions required to carry
out the act (q.17, a.1, resp.; a.5, resp.). That is, now the will's motive force to
act is carried over into, and precisely channeled by, reason in the form of a
command (Driscoll, 3,210). Thus, "Command is . . . a pointing out, a declaring of what is to be done; it is a blunt 'do this'—with emphasis on the
'this' as well as on the 'do'" (3,210). For our example, the agent's reason
commands, "Walk over and ask the neighbor if he would like help with his
leaf raking."

Lastly, "the will begins the [commanded] act [that is, the outward per-
formance] . . . by executing the command of reason" with its appetitive force;
the will makes *use* of whatever mental and physical faculties will accomplish
reason's command (*TH* q.17, a.2, rep.1; q.16, a.2, resp.). In the example, once
the agent's reason has commanded the walking and talking needed to go to
the neighbor's and offer aid in raking, her will uses her legs, mouth, motor
and speech skills, and so on, to actualize her offer of assistance.

Interestingly, Aquinas makes two comments about command that, I
believe, we can apply more broadly to summarize the relationship of all the
reason- and will-acts just described. Aquinas writes, "it is clear that command and the commanded act are one human act in the way that a whole
is one, yet is many in its parts" (q.17, a.4, resp.). In other words, command—
and all the other "subacts" like intention and deliberation—make up one
whole, and are constitutive of one human action. However, Aquinas next
says, "The fact that a command and a commanded act can be separated from
each other shows that they are many as to parts" (q.17, a.4, rep.2). As an example of the situation Aquinas describes, think of Samson waking to find
himself bound and—not realizing his hair has been cut—proceeding to act

as far as commanding his muscles to break the bonds, but use and the whole action fail since his supernatural strength is lost. More generally, we can say that the constituent parts of a human action are *separable*; and we may find instances where human acts abort at some point, because one part *cannot connect* to the next. We need to remember this separability, as it will figure prominently in our analysis of Aquinas's account of incontinent actions.

In any case, with the above process in mind, we can clearly see that human actions are brought about by, and in accordance with, what reason directs. Action starts from an apprehension in the rational intellect that sparks the rational appetite's volition. Reason presents the will with a formal principle that shapes the will's intention for action. Reason also deliberates to determine how to proceed in attaining the desired end. Further, reason's discretive judgment directs the will to a choice of a certain specific action, and reason's command guides the will's execution of the performance in using the faculties required. While will and reason obviously move each other reciprocally in this process, reason initiates the exchange and makes the judgments that direct its outcome. Given this picture of what it means to act *as a human*, it is not surprising when Aquinas claims, "Properly speaking, [a human being] is that which is according to reason" (*ST* II–II q.155, a.1, rep.2).

5.1.4 The Practical Syllogism

To display reason's role in the production of action, Aquinas makes use of Aristotle's practical syllogism; and although Aristotle's conception of the practical syllogism differs in some respects from Aquinas's, Aquinas sees himself as following Aristotle. Indeed, in the framework of our present considerations, the two philosophers' thoughts do largely coincide. However, there may be some differences regarding the syllogism's conclusion; in this section we shall note the nature of that possible disagreement, but we shall have to leave a fuller exploration of this issue to the next chapter.

For both philosophers, though, the premises of the practical syllogism summarize the route of reason's judgments in reaching a specific conclusion about what to do. The syllogism has both a universal and a particular premise (Aristotle, *Nicomachean Ethics* 1147a1–3). As Aristotle describes the syllogism,

> One belief [that is, the first premise, called] (a) is universal; the other [that is, the second premise] (b) is about particulars, and because they are particulars, perception controls them. [1147a26–7; note: the (a) and (b) are supplied by the translator, Terence Irwin, not by Aristotle]

In other words, the syllogism contains a major, universal premise that represents the end proposed by reason. A minor premise, concerned with the particulars of the agent's situation, brings an action under the scope of the major premise's end. This particular premise represents a conjunction of all the relevant facts, gained through sense perception. That is, the minor premise states particular facts relevant to achieving the good identified in the major premise, and that is information that figures in the agent's deliberations. So far, Aquinas and Aristotle seem to track smoothly, for in commenting on the above passage Aquinas writes,

> [Regarding] the natural process of practical science, we must take into consideration the two judgments in this process. One is universal, for example, "Every dishonorable act must be avoided"; the other, singular, is concerned with objects which properly are known by sense, for instance, "This act is dishonorable." (*CNE* VII.L.3: C1345)

Although Aquinas's example differs in its explicitly moral cast from those Aristotle gives, Aquinas and Aristotle do apparently agree concerning the syllogism's representation of reason's judgment about the end to be sought, and of information included in reason's deliberations about the particular means to action.

Regarding the syllogism's conclusion, however, potential disagreement arises. Part of the problem is that Aristotle's own position remains somewhat unclear on this point. First he says that when properly conjoined, the two premises

> result in (c) one belief, [from which] it is necessary . . . in beliefs about [action-] production (d) to act at once on what has been concluded. [Aristotle, *NE* 1147a28–9; note: the (c) and (d) come from Irwin]

But then, immediately following, he gives an example describing premises (a) and (b) as concluding directly to (d):

> If, e.g., (a) everything sweet must be tasted, and (b) this, some one particular thing, is sweet, it is necessary (d) for someone who is able and unhindered to act on this at the time. [*NE* 1147a30–1; note: again, (a), (b) and (d) are added by Irwin]

Some commentators, like Norman Dahl, thereby interpret Aristotle as claiming that the conclusion to the practical syllogism is not a judgment, but (d) the *action* to be done (206). Others, such as David Charles, assert that

Aristotle meant that the conclusion was (c), the "*one belief*" that conjoined premises (a) and (b) (120). Further complicating this argument is Aristotle's statement in another passage:

> What we deliberate about is the same as what we [choose] to do, except that by the time we [choose] to do it, it is definite; for what we [choose] to do is what we have judged [to be right] as a result of deliberation. (*NE* 1113a4–5)

As Aquinas observes, this passage makes it seem as if choice "is a sort of conclusion about practical affairs," since it occurs when deliberation reaches a definite answer about what to do (*TH* q.13, a.1, obj.2).

Which interpretive option to take? In the next chapter, we shall explore what may be the best interpretation—textually and explanatorily considered; but right now, we need to see how Aquinas resolves the question. Aquinas anticipates Charles in his view that Aristotle thinks that the practical syllogism's conclusion is a judgment that a certain action should (or should not) be done. He writes,

> But since there is one formality [that is, property] underlying these judgments [premises (a) and (b)], a conclusion [regarding what to do] necessarily follows. (*CNE* VII.L.3: C1345)

Aquinas therefore understands the passage about deliberation and choice to imply that choice follows the discretive judgment, which concludes the syllogism (*TH* q.13, a.5, rep.1; q.14, a.4, rep.1). Aquinas puts it this way:

> The decision of counsel, [Aristotle] says, precedes choice because after the inquiry of counsel a judgment concerning the things discovered must follow. Then what was previously judged is first chosen. (*CNE* III.L.9: C484)

So choice concerns a matter of action that "is definite" because "the result of deliberation" already has been "judged" (Aristotle, *NE* 1113a4–5). Elsewhere, Aquinas makes explicit that discretive judgment is "the conclusion of an operative [that is, practical] syllogism" (*TH* q.13, a.3, resp.). And again he says, "The conclusion of a syllogism about actions does belong to reason. It is called a [discretive judgment] ... and choice follows upon it" (q.13, a.1, rep.2). From that position, given the close relationship between discretive judgment and choice, Aquinas resolves the possible confusion in Aristotle by noting, "For this reason the conclusion seems to belong to choice, which [actually] follows upon [the conclusion]" (q.13, a.1, rep.2). Moreover, Aquinas explains Aristotle's indication that the syllogism concludes with the action by pointing out that since choice engages the will to a specific action, choice *efficiently causes* the action, unless something hinders performance (*CNE* VI.L.2: C1133). But since discretive judgment and choice are so closely related, once discretive judgment is reached, it then seems the agent "goes into operation immediately" (VII.L.3: C1346).

Finally, to illustrate Aquinas's position in our example, the charitable agent's practical syllogism would look like this:

(a) Any act of charity is good to do (that is, ought to be done).
(b) My elderly neighbor needs help with his raking, and I have the time and ability to help him, and I first need to offer my help, and offering to help him would be an act of charity.
Therefore,
(c) Charitably offering to help my neighbor with his raking is good to do (that is, ought to be done).

Reaching (c) prompts her choice to walk next door and offer her assistance. Also, we should note here that Aquinas routinely abbreviates the description of the deliberations, so that (b) would simply read, "offering to help my elderly neighbor with his raking would be an act of charity"—or even just "*this* is an act of charity." In this way, then, for Aquinas the practical syllogism represents reason's activity in bringing about human actions; it shows both reason's judgment about the end to pursue (a), and the pertinent information included in reason's deliberations (b), as well as reason's discretive judgment directing performance of a specific action to reach that end (c). On that account, when Aquinas explains practical reasoning in human action—and how that breaks down in incontinent actions—he does so using the tool of the practical syllogism.

5.1.5 Human Action, Morality, and Action's Rational Measure

However, before we can explore Aquinas's explanation of weak-willed actions, we need to examine further his characterization of human actions. Aquinas argues that all human actions also are *moral* actions; that is, every such action bears moral weight and is either good or evil. This moral value derives from the end for which the action is done (Aquinas, *TH* q.1, a.3, resp.). We can see why that should be so when we examine the measure, or standard, according to which reason operates in generating human actions.

In explaining reason's measure, Aquinas points out that everyone desires to satisfy her own will wholly, so that she would lack nothing that she wants. Such satisfaction would constitute a "perfect or complete good," or "happiness" (Aquinas, *TH* q.5, a.8, resp.). Moreover, Aquinas asserts that regarding every individual thing that a person desires, the person wants it because she sees it either as part of, or as leading toward, her happiness. For, Aquinas says, "every beginning of fulfillment is ordered to complete fulfillment, which is achieved through the ultimate end [that is, attaining happiness]" (q.1, a.6, resp.).

Furthermore, according to Aquinas, the facts of human nature as divine creation are such that only *one* thing can satisfactorily serve as the ultimate end for any person; a person must order her will toward this one ultimate end if she is going to actually achieve happiness (q.1, a.5, resp.). This ultimate end consists in an intellectual communion with God—in Aquinas's words, "Ultimate and perfect happiness can only be in the vision of the divine essence" (q.3, a.8, resp.). But this communion requires a person to be in right relationship with God, who "is the very essence of [moral] goodness," so the person needs "rectitude of the will" (q.4, a.4, resp.). Such rectitude, then, comes through ordering the will toward love of God and, in service to that, toward charity (q.4, a.4, resp; *On the Epistle to the Galations* chp.5, lec.6). Now a person imposes such order on her will by performing morally good actions (Aquinas, *TH* q.5, a.7, resp.). Evil, or sinful, actions then are "alien" or detractive to the needed rectitude (Aquinas, *EG* chp.5, lec.6). Thus, through good actions the will's inclinations become rightly ordered.

Yet Aquinas says that good actions involve not just "right desire," but also practical reason (*CNE* VII.L.1: C1294). For, in ordering the will toward the ultimate end of communion with God, actions performed must somehow be *proportioned* to that end. That is, whether, and how much, a certain action may lead toward happiness in God must be discovered. To do that, an agent needs a *measure* by which to tell whether a given action contributes to reaching the ultimate end (Aquinas, *TH* q.7, a.2, resp.). In human beings, the measure of the ordering toward God belongs specifically to reason (Aquinas, *ST* I–II q.85, a.4; q.71, a.2). For the final or true measure—the "first rule"—comes from *God's* reason, as expressed in the eternal law, specifically in the "natural" and "divine" laws, God's directives for rational humanity; yet we learn and apply God's law through *our* reason, the "proximate" rule (I–II q.71, a.6; q.91, a.2, a.4).

Thus, human reason should direct the will toward good and away from evil; and reason demarcates evil and good by checking whether actions lack conformity with God's law (I–II q.71, a.6; *ER* chp.7, lec.3). Reason should ask of any general course of action or any particular action: is it lawful or not? Or again, does it turn the will toward God or away (Aquinas, *ST* I–II q.77, a.8, rep.3)? For instance, suppose I am considering grading my students' essays in a quick and slipshod manner, in order to minimize that tedious activity. I reason to myself, would slipshod grading accord with God's law or not? On a number of accounts—that such grading exhibits sloth in me, that it breaches my obligation to my students, and so on—I determine that the action would violate God's law; reason tells me, therefore, that it would be evil to act so, and that I should refrain from such action. Indeed, Aquinas asserts that this activity, of making willed actions agree with God's law, constitutes part of the natural, practical function of reason (*ER* chp.7, lec.3, 4). So the judgment of God's reason, his law, is the primary rule for what reason should direct concerning action; and human reason presents an approximated rule derived from the ability to discover the primary one (Aquinas, *TH* q.19, a.4, resp.). In short, we measure the *rationality* of actions by whether, and how well, they accord with God's law.

Reason, then, properly functions in practical matters by bringing about actions through presenting the will with its ends, and by making sure those ends agree with God's law. Moreover, since every human action is done for some end of deliberate will—as we saw in detail in section 5.1.3—the conformity (or not) of each end with God's directives renders each human action morally good (or evil) (q.18, a.9, rep.3). Thus, we now understand Aquinas's statement that all human actions are moral actions; that completes our description of the process of human action.

At this point, we also can see why Aquinas's theory of human action presents us with a model of intentional action as rational action. The description of deliberate willing showed how human action proceeds from reason's judgments, which include the discretive judgment that—along with choice—functions as an intention (as we have used the term); the account of human action's rational measure shows how reason makes those action-guiding judgments in accordance with a standard of perfect rationality. As Aquinas writes,

> [A human being] acts from judgment, because by [her] apprehensive power [she] judges that something should be avoided or sought . . . this judgment, in the case of some particular act, is . . . from some act of comparison in the reason [against the standard of eternal law]. (*ST* I q.83, a.1, resp.)

Therefore, human, or intentional, action clearly requires acting from, and according to, reason.

5.1.6 Implications of the Rational-Action Model

However, before we move on to Aquinas's characterization of incontinent actions and the problem they represent, we need to notice some important implications of Aquinas's model of rational action. First, we should note that Aquinas's conception of the moral domain encompasses a far wider range of actions than Hare's did. Hare's notion of a "moral" action included only those actions in which we must take into account the interests of others. But Aquinas's view would include actions even as seemingly nonmoral as my picking up a leaf while I'm walking alone. Now Aquinas recognizes that in itself an action like leaf picking "may not involve anything as relevant to the order of reason [in terms of God's law]," thus making the activity in itself morally "indifferent" (*TH* q.18, a.8, resp.). However, whenever I actually intentionally pick up a leaf, I do so with some end in mind, which thereby makes the leaf picking good or evil. Do I pick up the leaf to more closely admire a piece of God's incredibly beautiful creation? Then the act is good. Do I pick up the leaf to dawdle, because I do not want to finish my walk and arrive at my tedious job? My slothful end makes my action evil. The same holds for *any* action, no matter how trivial the activity, performed from deliberate will (q.18, a.9, resp.).

If, however, someone performs an action that does *not* proceed from deliberate will, then the action qualifies neither as moral nor as human (q.18, a.9, resp.). Suppose I fidget or twitch a foot as I sit and write this; or perhaps I absentmindedly scratch my ear. These trivial activities *could* proceed from a reasoned end—a baseball running coach might use them as signals—but in my case they do not. For the coach, those movements would be moral, human actions; for me, since they do not have a reason-determined end, "they do not result from . . . the proper principle of human acts" and so "are not properly human" (q.1, a.1, rep.3). Thus, Aquinas does not consign moral weight to acts of a man, but any action that qualifies as human also possesses moral value.

Further, while Aquinas's standard of rationality then applies only to moral actions, the far broader moral domain of Aquinas's view spreads that application to any action performed for a reasoned end—in short, to the whole range of intentional actions, as we just saw. Therefore, even if Aquinas should treat incontinence as a moral problem, that problem could still represent a failure of the same rational standard in actions ranging from adultery to overzealousness in brushing one's teeth. Thus, Aquinas's view can avoid Davidson's accusation against Hare that construing incontinence as a moral question must illegitimately limit the scope of the problem (section 3.2.2).

Moreover, Aquinas's view of the moral domain allows his standard of rational action to do what Hare's could not. Hare hoped that his model of critical reasoning would show not only how reason can yield moral judgments, but also how and why moral actions are rational to perform. Yet he failed to demonstrate the latter goal, at least in part because his rational standard was incapable of comparing the rational justification of moral actions with that of so-called nonmoral ones (see section 2.4.2). As Thomas Nagel described Hare's problem, "The search for the foundations of morality ought to be part of a general theory of reasons for action" (112). Hare could find no ground for such a foundation; but, happily, Aquinas can. For because Aquinas's moral domain encompasses the whole of intentional action— which is all performed in accordance with one rational standard—it is possible, in Aquinas's theoretical framework, to *compare the rationality* of any action with that of any other (given an adequately complete picture of one set of circumstances for both of the proposed performances), and the actions' *moral values will be directly proportioned to their rational values*. Thus, Aquinas's model of rational action seems to have extremely beneficial connections to his moral theory, which was one of the advantages proposed in the introduction as possible for a working rational-action theory.

Building on the last point, we discover a second crucial implication: Aquinas's measurement-standard for actions' rationality presupposes a *limited* form of *commensurability*. That is, if we measure the rationality of an action by whether, and how much, it leads us toward God, then we must assume that for any action we might consider taking, that action can be subsumed under the question of how much it will lead us toward (or away from) God. In addition, we must assume that this action's "leading-toward-God-ness" will be commensurate with other actions' "values" when considered under the same question; that way, we can decide which of our options will best lead us toward God. David Wiggins points out the need for some such kind of commensurability in order for practical reason to be able to do its work and identify more and less rational actions (255–6).

However, Wiggins also explains that this kind of commensurability does *not* require us to assume either that leading-toward-God-ness represents the *only* consideration of value in an action, or even that all other desirable aspects of an action can be reduced to, or measured in terms of, leading-toward-God-ness (255–7). In other words, Aquinas can allow that actions might have other desirable qualities—say, that they are pleasant or would gain wealth—that remain distinct from, and unmeasurable in terms of, how much they lead toward God. For instance, when I consider how carefully and thoroughly to grade my students' essays, I reject the quick and slipshod route on the grounds that it violates God's law and is therefore irrational. But such careless grading might still be easier and less unpleasant than the thorough effort I choose instead. Those desirable points do not enter the consideration of the action's rationality; they represent *incommensurate* values with respect to what makes the action irrational. Moreover, in choosing the more rational option, I *lose* those other valuable aspects (256–7). As we shall see, this allowance for the possibility of choosing between incommensurable desirable aspects of actions helps Aquinas in accounting for the irrationality of weak-willed actions.

A third critical implication we can note is that Aquinas's conception of the rational measure in actions *avoids* Hare's *overstrictness* and Davidson's *lack of specificity*. For we have seen that critical thinking, Hare's method of assessing the rationality of moral actions, presented too strict a standard. Critical thinking's difficulty prevented it from being practically useful; and its use of other people's interests in its calculations rendered it inapplicable to any actions outside Hare's narrow conception of the moral domain (sections 2.4.1 and 2.4.2). However, determining whether, and how well, an action would accord with God's law does represent the sort of rationality-standard a human agent could plausibly employ "in the field." Utilizing this standard may require gaining both knowledge of God's law and experience in perceiving what sorts of actions do and do not violate that law; but normal, adult humans could certainly meet such requirements. Moreover, the lawfulness-calculations themselves do not seem too difficult for those same human agents to carry out in the course of choosing actions in everyday life, even given our finite and error-prone minds. In the words of Alasdair MacIntyre,

> The practical life, as Aquinas portrays it, is a life of enquiry by each of us into what our good is, and it is part of our present good so to enquire. The final discovery of what our good is will indeed reveal to us the inadequacy of all our earlier conceptions. . . . But at every stage in this practical enquiry we have a knowledge of our good sufficient to guide us further. (*WJWR* 193)

So while we may not be able to know exactly what values our actions have with respect to leading-toward-God-ness, we can know approximately and to a degree sufficient to guide our actions well enough to draw closer to God, allowing us then to judge our actions still more accurately, and so on. In short, Aquinas's rational standard is sufficiently clear and simple to enable its practical use.

Regarding Davidson's opposite theoretical difficulties, we saw that he could not provide a rationality standard specific and precise enough to be usable in practice. Davidson's theory could not offer the agent specific, practically useful directives on how to compare the rationality of her various options, or on how to determine which option she could justifiably identify as the most rational to perform (sections 4.6.1 and 4.6.2). But again, Aquinas's system does involve a specific, usable measure of rationality. We already saw, in light of what Wiggins says, that Aquinas needs only a limited and plausible form of commensurability to allow the standard of lawfulness to differentiate the rationality of options for action. Moreover, as MacIntyre pointed out above, even our limited understandings can grasp our final end well enough to utilize it as the corrective measure or guide for our actions; so the rational standard's precision is sufficient for practical life. Therefore, Aquinas's rational-action model seems to avoid the problems of the extremes in both Davidson's and Hare's systems.

5.2 THE PROBLEM OF AKRATIC ACTION

5.2.1 The Definition of Akratic Action

Now, we are in a position to examine the problems that incontinent actions present for Aquinas. First, we must observe how Aquinas characterizes incontinent actions themselves. He constructs his position from Aristotle's discussion of *akrasia* in the *Nicomachean Ethics*. According to Aristotle's portrayal, an akratic agent acts willingly, having understanding both of what she does, and of the end for which she acts (*NE* 1152a16). Aquinas agrees, calling akratic actions voluntary (*CNE* VII.L.10: C1461). Moreover, Aquinas also asserts that akratic action occurs against, or in spite of, the agent's understanding that the deed ought not be done (*ER* chp.7, lec.3; *CNE* VII.L.8: C1425; *ST* I–II q.77, a.2). Aristotle further points out that this judgment to which the agent acts counter could represent either knowledge or merely belief on the agent's part (*NE* 1146b25–31). But it is required that the overcome judgment be sincere and undoubted by the agent (1145b35–1146a4; Aquinas, *CNE* VII.L.2: C1316). Aristotle and Aquinas, then, agree this far with the conception of incontinence that we have been using.

So an incontinent action is voluntary, and thus seemingly a human action and generated from, and according to, reason; but it somehow occurs in spite of—even in opposition to—the agent's sincerely affirmed rational judgment about what should be done. Aquinas and Aristotle both assert that the akratic agent does not act from the results of her deliberation, on her deliberate choice; but rather she acts because of her passions—that is, because of irrational feelings from the sense appetites (VII.L.10: C1461; *EG* chp.5, lec.4; Aristotle, *NE* 1145b10–14). Such an action, they say, could occur in two ways: (1) from *impetuousness*, in which the agent does not even deliberate at all; passion sweeps over her and she acts without stopping to deliberate (1150b20–2, 1152a19; Aquinas, *CNE* VII.L.7: C1419); or (2) through *weakness*, for this agent does deliberate and reach a result, but because of her passion she abandons that result and acts contrary to it (VII.L.7: C1419; Aristotle, *NE* 1150b20–2, 1152a18–29). Since the weak akratic case clearly coincides with incontinence as we have been characterizing it in our investigation, we shall focus on the explanation given for such cases.

Now, Aristotle and Aquinas differ from our accepted notion of incontinence on one key point—the problem's matter, or scope. Both stipulate that properly considered, "incontinence" refers to actions performed through being overwhelmed by concupiscence, or the desire for pleasure—specifically, physical pleasure; and "continence" too, properly speaking, deals with the same subject matter of desires for physical pleasure (1149b25; Aquinas, *CNE* VII.L.3: C1335, L.4: C1366; *ST* II–II q.155, a.2, rep.1). Thus, both thinkers view continence and incontinence, in their most proper references, as constituting middle stages between temperance, the virtue of rightly desiring and acting with regard to physical pleasures, and intemperance, the opposed vice (Aquinas, *CNE* VII.L.4: C1361; Aristotle, *NE* 1148a13–17).

However, this difference matters less than it first seems. For other passions than appetites for physical pleasures can overcome deliberation through the agent's weakness. Fear of pain, anger, desires for honor or gain, and so on—all of these passions can cause action contrary to the agent's deliberation (Aquinas, *ST* I–II q.77, a.3; Aristotle, *NE* 1147b30–2). Moreover, all such actions occur through a similar weakness in the agent's soul (Aquinas, *OE* q.3, a.9, resp.). On that account, by "similitude" and analogy we call all the other weak-willed actions "incontinent" as well (*CNE* VII.L.1: C1304, L.4: C1367; Aristotle, *NE* 1147b33–5). The appetites for physical pleasures, then, provide the most conspicuous, paradigm examples of incontinence, so that subject matter defines "incontinence," most restrictively or simply considered. But broadly or commonly considered, "incontinence" applies to any action in which the agent acts from an irrational passion or appetite instead of from rational deliberation (Aquinas, *ST* II–II q.156, a.2, resp.). And "continence" can assume the same range, applied "in a general sense and relatively" (q.155, a.2, rep.1).

We should note, too, that for Aquinas all these weak-willed actions are sins, making incontinence a moral problem (*ST* I–II q.77, a.3). But as I pointed out earlier, that does not harmfully limit the scope of incontinence (or continence), since all human actions bear moral weight. Moreover, Aquinas writes,

> In this way incontinence is a sin, not from the fact that one gives way to wicked desires, but because one fails to observe the mode of reason even in the desire for things that are of themselves desirable. (*ST* II–II q.156, a.2, resp.)

Thus, in Aquinas's view, incontinence—broadly considered—presents a problem, with a unified nature, for all of intentional action. That is, allowing for slight explanatory alterations to fit whatever passion is supplanting deliberation, Aquinas can construe incontinence—in matters ranging from eating too many cookies to competing too hard (out of an inordinate desire for victory) in checkers against one's small children—as recognizably the same rational breakdown in the normal process of human action. On that account, Aquinas can meet Davidson's challenge to characterize incontinence as a problem for the whole range of intentional action.

5.2.2 The Apparent Impossibility of Akrasia

Indeed, now we can clearly see that problem as it applies specifically to Aquinas's theory: since agents perform incontinent actions voluntarily, those acts would seem to qualify as human; yet if the actions do not proceed from deliberate choice but, instead, from passion, how can they be human actions? Aquinas calls akratic actions sins, but how can they be, since less-than-human actions—as incontinence seems to involve—do not qualify for moral consideration, either? Even more, if in cases of weak *akrasia* the agent does deliberate to a determinate directive of reason, how can that fail to incline the will and produce action? In short, how can reason's control of action break down as it does in incontinence, and how can the resulting actions still count as human and moral?

5.3 AQUINAS'S PROPOSED SOLUTION

In answering these questions, Aquinas first explains several disordered or vulnerable aspects of the human faculties for action. These "glitches" in human functioning will then help to show how the process of human action breaks down in incontinent acts.

5.3.1 Instability in Rational Consideration

Aquinas identifies a first factor of instability in reason's direction of action, in that reason can construe one and the same action as good or not-good, *depending on the aspect from which the action is viewed* (*TH* q.13, a.6, resp.). Happiness, which completely satisfies the will, must obviously look good from every "angle," since, by definition, it satisfies in every aspect. However, we never comprehend happiness's nature enough to form a concrete conception of it that actually has no aspects in which it might appear unsatisfying. So while happiness, as an abstract end, compels reason's evaluation of it as good, its abstractness prevents identifying any particular actions that would reach it. On the other hand, no end that is intellectually grasped sufficiently to connect to particular actions can appear perfectly satisfying. So reason can view any such end, no matter how good, in an aspect from which it appears not good, thus possibly inclining the will away from it (q.10, a.2, resp.; q.13, a.6, resp.). For instance, I view finishing my manuscript as an enormously satisfying good. Yet as I write this at 9:45 on a Sunday evening, after spending several hours already working, the grinding effort required to complete this much-longer-than-I-expected argument appears to my reason as a distinctly nongood aspect of completion. If I view the task in that light, then no matter how good it might seem in light of my serving God by developing my talents and completing the task set me, I can want *not* to continue to work.

As we previously saw (section 5.1.1), this point about reason actually contributes to the voluntariness of rational willing, since the will gains freedom at least partly through reason's ability to consider opposing aspects of a considered notion (q.10, a.2, resp.; q.13, a.6, resp.; *ST* I q.83, a.1, resp.; q.82, a.2, rep.3). The presence of such competing good and nongood action-aspects also follows from our earlier point regarding commensurability of values. If continuing to write for another hour represents a good as my most *rational* choice of action, since it brings me closer to completing my manuscript (and thereby serves God as noted above), that does not make it the best of my choices in terms of other values, like *pleasantness*. Watching the *X-Files* on TV may give me more pleasure, and so may appear good from that vantage. Neither goodness-value necessarily measures into the calculation of the other, since they are not commensurate. Aquinas then notes the pertinent implication of this incommensurability: "But because good is of many kinds, for this reason [deliberation and] will [are] not of necessity determined to one [kind]" (q.82, a.2, rep.1).

However, the possibility of reason's fluctuation between good and nongood aspects of an action presents a problem for action in that it makes deliberate choice *unstable*. A person's choice of whether or not an action should be performed will remain effective only as long as she focuses her rational consideration on whatever feature of the action pertained to her choice. If I deliberate and choose to continue writing my manuscript— since doing so would bring me closer to completion and its benefits—but then begin to consider the action in terms of the missed pleasure it could cost me, I may find myself wavering from my choice and perhaps watching TV after all. Thus, in the possibility of distracting or diverting the rational consideration directed toward a certain action lies the further possibility of the agent's deliberate choice crumbling.

Nor does the fact that happiness truly resides in the particular end of communing with God help to stabilize rational choice. It might seem that in focusing on an action as it leads us toward God, the complete satisfaction inherent in that end would determine the will toward the chosen course of action. However, in the first place not everyone recognizes that happiness can only be found in God, so not everyone desires happiness in that particular end. Secondly, even if we do see where happiness truly lies, we cannot adequately intellectually grasp the complete satisfaction had by communing with God; to our minds this activity does not look as good as it really is. So even if we choose according to that end, that will not guarantee the stability of our willing it (q.82, a.2, resp.; *TH* q.5, a.8, resp.). Thus, humans act for happiness, but only under partial and/or mistaken conceptions from which the will can still turn away (q.1, a.7, rep.1). That leaves us pursuing actions under ends that are "apparent" goods, "not desirable in an unqualified [that is, completely satisfying] way" (q.19, a.1, rep.1). Therefore, those goods— even happiness in God—that we actually propose as ends do not provide unshakable stability for deliberate choice (Aquinas, *ST* I q.82, a.2, rep.2).

5.3.2 Damage from Original Sin

The effects of original sin provide a second contributor to the instability of reason's control in human action. According to Aquinas, part of the divinely just punishment resulting from original sin "consists in the de-struction of the commensuration of man's desires" (*CNE* VII.L.1: C1275). That is, God has punished humanity by allowing a permanent disorder into the faculties of human action (Aquinas, *ER* chp.7, lec.3). In one conse-quence of that disordering, the appetites—the "inferior powers"—no longer are subject to reason (chp.7, lec.4). In humanity's originally inno-cent state—which is our *true, normal condition* and is called by Aquinas, *orig-inal justice*—sense appetites for physical pleasures would not even have arisen unless reason had directed it, and even then appetite would only have been as intense as reason required (*ST* I–II q.85, a.3; *OE* q.4, a.2, rep. to On the contrary 2). The rational appetite of the will, too, would not have been attracted to any end except those that reason deemed good through being most rational (q.4, a.2, rep. to On the contrary 7). But the "wounds" of original sin have removed that restraining obedience (q.4, a.2, resp.; *ST* I–II q.85, a.3).

As a result, our appetites can now arise without rational control. We experience sense appetites for objects regardless of whether reason deems them rationally appropriate; and those desires may possess intensity inordi-nate to the rationally calculated desirability of their objects (Aquinas, *OE* q.4, a.2, resp.). To describe this condition, Aquinas once again utilizes the term "concupiscence." So, particularly in discussing *akrasia* and its out-of-control desires, Aquinas means "concupiscence" to refer to "the proneness to *inordinate* concupiscence [in the basic meaning of a sense-desire], which may be called by the general name of concupiscence [in the new sense]" [emphasis added] (q.4, a.2, resp.). Thus, while concupiscence (meaning 1), considered as a mere desire for a sensed good, is normal to human nature even in its originally just ideal (q.4, a.2, rep. to On the contrary 2); concu-piscence (meaning 2), considered as a desire toward

> what is sensually enjoyable contrary [to] the order of reason, is contrary to the nature of [a human] inasmuch as [she] is a [human]; and therefore it pertains to original sin. (q.4, a.2, rep. to On the contrary 1)

Meaning 2, then, describes one of the "wounds" of original sin (Aquinas, *ST* I–II q.85, a.3).

Further, Aquinas also links concupiscence (meaning 2) with the con-cept of the *ineradicability* of sinful desire, due to original sin. Aquinas calls this inescapable urge, the *fomes*, that is, the *spark, or tinder, of evil desire* (*ER* chp.7, lec.3). That gives us yet another meaning of concupiscence (mean-ing 3), such that

> Concupiscence [3], according as it is something belonging to original
> sin, does not designate the necessity of *assenting* to inordinate movements
> [2] of concupiscence [1] but designates the necessity of *experiencing* them.
> [Emphasis added.] (q.4, a.2, rep. to On the contrary 10)

These three possibilities give us a deeply complicated usage of concupiscence. I shall keep them distinct in two ways: first, by identifying which option Aquinas means, when the word appears in quoted passages; second, by
utilizing different terms for the different meanings, when I refer to them. To
refer to the normal activity of the concupiscible appetite, I shall use "sense-
desire" or "desire (or passion) from the sense (or concupiscible) appetite." I
shall refer to meaning 2, the sense-desires that arise for objects contrary to
reason, as "inordinate/evil desires/passions." And for meaning 3, I shall simply utilize "the spark of evil desire."

Before we move to original sin's effect on the will, let me recapitulate:
Because of original sin, the concupiscible, and irascible, appetites can now
generate passions contrary to reason, both in their objects and in their in-
tensities. Those inordinate passions have their source in the spark of evil desire, so they *cannot* be completely eliminated. However, even if the spark of
evil desire necessitates that inordinate passions will arise, it does not in itself
make them irresistible. Such evil desires may assail our will and reason, but
it remains our own fault or weakness if we succumb.

Next, then, due to original sin, the will itself can now incline to
goods—such as physical pleasure—apprehended by reason, yet denied by
reason on this or that particular occasion to provide a rational basis for action. This disorder is the "wound of malice" in the will, "in so far as the will
is deprived of its order to the good" (Aquinas, *ST* I–II q.85, a.3). Having
lost its original justice, the will assumes malice, in which "it becomes subject to every proclivity to choose evil" (Aquinas, *OE* q.4, a.2, rep. to On the
contrary 7). Thus, the disordered will now "loves more the lesser good" and
chooses to suffer loss in respect to some rational good, in order to gain a
good proposed in—but not approved by—reason (q.78, a.1).

Aquinas also calls this disorder in the will "inordinate love of self," and
he posits it as the root of sinful action (q.77, a.4; *EG* chp.5, lec.5). For because of that disorder, the will can incline to actions that reason apprehends
as good, yet as violating divine law and as being irrational. However, this
point leaves us questioning how reason could propose a good to the will and
yet recognize that the proposal is counter to reason. The answer lies in the
vulnerability of reason to the power of the sense appetites. But before we explore that answer, we need to see the effects of *active* sin, as well as original.

5.3.3 Damage from Active Sin

For Aquinas points out that our sinful actions produce a new level of disorder beyond that of our sinful state itself. When we sin, we inflame our inordinate desires, and thereby incline our wills even more toward the lesser goods. In Aquinas's words, "concupiscence [2], if indulged, gathers strength" (*ST* II–II q.142, a.2, resp.). Also, that inflammation of desire makes it more difficult for practical reason to do its proper work in proposing the rationally best object to the will (I–II q.85, a.3). In short, performing sinful actions magnifies our internal disorder by increasing our inclination to sin, and by decreasing our inclination to do right (q.85, a.1).

One important way in which this increased sinful inclination arises is that repeated sin creates a sinful habit. For as reason repeatedly proposes to the will a certain kind of action, the will gradually becomes imprinted—it gains an enduring inclination, a habit to actions of that sort (Aquinas, *Treatise on the Virtues* q.51, a.2, resp.; *DQV* q.1 [disputed question on the virtues in general], a.8, resp.). Aquinas describes the process:

> [Repeated action] can . . . cause a habit, because the first act causes some disposition and the second act, finding the matter disposed, disposes it even more, and [the] third yet more and thus the ultimate act acting in virtue of all the preceding completes the generation of [the habit]. (q.1, a.9, rep.11)

Thus, forming a habit resembles the process of combing one's hair until it begins to fall "naturally" into the combed style. When sinful actions produce the habit, the evil habit acquired continually inclines the will toward sin. Moreover, the habit becomes "a sort of nature" for the agent, thereby making the habitual actions "lovable" and "delightful" and "natural" to perform (q.1, a.1, resp.; *ST* I–II q.78, a.2).

Furthermore, it is crucial for us to see, here, that if the repeated action also satisfies an inclination in a sense appetite, that appetite *also becomes habituated*. Aquinas writes,

> When reason repeatedly inclines the appetitive power [that is, *any* appetitive faculty] to some one thing, a disposition is implanted in it by which it is inclined to the thing to which it has become accustomed. (*DQV* q.1, a.9, resp.)

Not only the will's inclination, then, but also the sense appetites' can be strengthened and fixated by habits. And this habituation can cement our devotion to the good by adding the sense appetites' inclinations to the will's (Lalor, 3,227). However, it is damaging if the passions habituated are inordinate. For as Aquinas approvingly quotes from Augustine (from *Confessions* viii.5), "*Lust served [becomes] custom, and custom not resisted [becomes] necessity*" (*ST* II–II q.142, a.2, resp.). Such heightened evil desires can thereby have a devastating effect on reason's deliberations, as we shall soon see.

In addition, the claim of necessity is not mere overstatement; habits can *efficiently cause* actions (Aquinas, *ST* I–II q.71, a.3). For the habitual action becomes so natural to perform that it is as if reason no longer needs to consider and propose such an action as an object to the will; instead, reason can merely notice the habitually desired apparent good of an action, and the will inclines by "auto-pilot." Deliberation is unnecessary, since the will can choose without waiting for "inquiry" (Aquinas, *DQV* q.1, a.1, resp.). Further, this automatic inclination can grow so hardened through strength of habit that in certain instances, "especially in sudden or indeliberate actions," satisfying the habit "becomes necessity" (Aquinas, *OE* q.6, rep. 24). Aquinas limits this necessity by stating that careful deliberation can still prevent the habitual action in a given instance (q.6, rep. 24; *ST* I–II q.109, a.8, resp.). Still, though, when the habits are evil, this habitual necessity further disorders the process of human action. For evil habits can make a person "a slave of the carnal [or sinful] inclination" (Aquinas, *ER* chp.7, lec.3). Or more specifically,

> [W]hen surprised, a [person] acts according to [her] preconceived end and [her evil] pre-existing habits . . . although with premeditation of [her] reason a [person] may do something outside the order of [her] preconceived end and the inclination of [her] habit. But because a [person] cannot always have this premeditation, it cannot help occurring that [she] acts in accordance with [her] will turned aside from God [that is, from her sinful habits]. (Aquinas, *ST* I–II, q.109, a.8, resp.)

On that account, Aquinas observes, such an agent may be able to "avoid each . . . sin, and for a time. . . . But it cannot be that [she] remains for a long time without . . . sin" (q.109, a.8, resp.).

We need to realize, here, that the possibility of habituation is not, itself, the glitch in human acting. Far from it, for Aquinas makes clear both that the virtues "are habits," and that they need to be, so as to "stabilize" the bearer's moral goodness (*DQV* q.1, a.1, resp.). Rather, the possibility of evil habits creates the problem, since such habits may virtually eliminate reason's role in the performance of some sinful actions. Moreover, although the habitual condition may seem contrary to voluntary control of action, Aquinas maintains "there is nothing in this [habitual state] that is repugnant to free-will" (*ST* I q.83, a.1, rep.5). Therefore, actions done from evil habit will still count as human and sinful. Exactly how such habituated actions can still qualify as voluntary, we shall examine in the next chapter. For the moment, let us simply note that the necessity arising from sinful habits will figure importantly in our analysis of incontinence.

Now, however, we need to return to the question of how reason's proper functioning can be impeded by the passions of the sense appetites. Aquinas initially points out that, given humanity's composite nature of physical and mental faculties, pleasures that suit one faculty may have a distractive or unnatural effect on another (*CNE* VII.L.14: C1534). In particular,

> The use of reason requires the due use of the imagination and of the other sensitive powers [that is, physical perceptions], which are exercised through a bodily organ. Consequently alteration in the body hinders the use of reason, because it hinders the acts of the imagination and of the other sensitive powers. (Aquinas, *ST* I–II q.33, a.3, rep.3)

In other words, perceptions and visualizations of the imagination figure importantly in reason's considerations about action; they provide the raw material for deliberation about what is possible to do in a given circumstance. But perception and imagination connect intimately with a person's physical condition. Therefore, changes in a person's body can influence how her reason operates; and conversely, a person's rational focus can affect her experience of bodily passions.

Suppose, for example, that someone is reading a book while at the same time having her back rubbed. If she begins to catch herself up in the intellectual pleasure of her book's imagined events, she may find that her perception of the back rub's pleasure wanes. If she luxuriates in the rubbing sensations, she may be unable either to continue to stay involved in her story, or perhaps even to continue to read at all. Through this kind of interaction, the "alien" pleasures (or other strong passions) of the concupiscible and irascible appetites can hinder reason's focus on, and ability to proceed with, its own work of proposing goods to the will (Aquinas, *CNE* VII.L.12: C1495).

Further, the sin-induced disorder of the human action-mechanism exacerbates the deleterious effect the sense appetites can have upon reason's proper activity—so much so "that the enfeebled intellect can be easily mis-

led and hindered from operating perfectly" (Aquinas, *ER* chp.5, lec.5).
"Misled" provides the key here, because the concupiscible (or irascible)
appetite—in its capacity as a principle, or cause, of human action—
influences and corrupts reason's judgment when an inordinate passion actually arises (Aquinas, *ST* I–II q.78, a.1). For example, the passionate desire
for the pleasure of satisfying the concupiscible appetite for sex causes
satisfying-actions *to appear good to reason in that respect*. Indeed, the stronger
the passion, the more it draws reason's focus. Thus, the concupiscible appetite's pleasure-prospect can incline reason toward its object, and reason
can then incline the will to that object (q.85, a.1, rep.4). So as we saw earlier (section 5.1.1), the sense appetites' passions can move the will when
such a passion becomes active through the perception of its object (Aquinas,
TH q.10, a.3, rep. 3). In the case of an inordinate sense-desire, reason's assessment of an action's goodness is corrupted if reason proposes that action
to the will under the passion's goodness-aspect.

However, we must remain clear that no passion moves the will directly.
Aquinas explicitly stipulates that "the object of the will is not a passion of
the sensitive appetite, but rather the good defined by reason" (*ST* I–II q.77,
a.1). An inordinate passion, then, foists an *apparent* good onto reason, in that
it makes a nongood action (in terms of lawfulness and rationality) appear
good to reason (in terms of pleasantness—or relief from fear, etc.). Thus, reason fails by not attending to its own particular construal of what makes an
action good. Instead, under the influence of an inordinate passion, reason erroneously construes an action as good, because it appears so in respect to
satisfying that passion (q.77, a.2). In this way, reason's selection of what to
propose to the will lies open to the corruptive effect of inordinate passions.

5.3.4 Implications of Reason's Vulnerabilities

We should also notice that reason's vulnerability provides grounds for
making an important distinction regarding action-causation. Aquinas points
out that because "reason . . . is the principal thing in a [person] . . . it seems
that every single [person] is [her] own reason, or perhaps [her] own intellect" (*ER* chp.7, lec.3). We must be careful here, because this instance is one
in which Aquinas seems to be grouping reason *and* will under "reason,"
hence his "or perhaps" as if there might be a difference between intellect
and reason. With that in mind, Aquinas apparently asserts that we identify
ourselves and our agency with our rational powers—both cognitive and appetitive. To me, "I" refers most particularly to my reason, broadly considered
(chap.7, lec.3). And *I do* those things that are brought about by means of my

rational activity, namely, through my reason and will. Therefore, when my reason falters and passion subverts it to its own ends, I may distinguish the resultant passion-caused action from what *I* do. Or again, if habit causes my action without my deliberating or rationally approving of it, it may seem to me as if the action were done by someone (or something) other than myself. As we shall see, this distinction in the agent's appraisal of her own actions will aid Aquinas in explaining the divided-self phenomenon associated with akratic actions.

A crucial implication also attaches to the view the agent takes of herself. As Aquinas recognizes, it may seem to the agent that *she* (that is, her reason, in the broad sense) does not perform her actions done because of passion; but, truly, *she has*, since her reason falters by erroneously accepting passion's construal of the action as good. Her passion brings about the action through her "reason . . . since it consents to these things which the carnal inclination [that is, the inordinate passion] urges" (chp.7, lec.3). Again, the inclusion of consent with reason indicates that "reason" includes will here (Aquinas, *TH* q.15, a.4, resp.). We can see, then, that passion gives the action a desirable quality, but in accepting that desirable quality as an appropriate end for action, reason proposes the action to the will as good. That activity of reason provides the impetus necessary for the will to efficiently cause the action; reason still brings about the action, even in this kind of instance. Therefore, the distinction in the agent's view of herself is not entirely accurate.

However, while reason does serve as the "chief cause" of such actions, it no longer moves the will "according to its own characteristic feature"—that is, according to calculations of rationality or lawfulness; instead reason moves "according to the characteristic feature of another [namely, the sense appetite's object of pleasure], by which it is moved" (chp.7, lec.3). Thus, reason still causes the action, but not in its own special capacity—not as the assessor of rationality, not as reason qua reason. Rather, reason causes the action in its capacity to be misled by passion—as reason qua tool-of-the-passions. This difference allows us to distinguish between actions brought about by reason-*proper*, and those brought about by reason-*as-passion's-tool*. For the latter kind of act "is not attributed chiefly to reason," at least in its most proper sense (chp.7, lec.3). Therefore the agent's view is not completely mistaken, either; a real, if more subtle, distinction underlies the one she claims. Moreover, not only can this true distinction help us see why Aquinas attributes the performance of incontinent acts to passion instead of reason, but also it will figure critically in our examination of how akratic actions can count as human.

Now, one last point about reason's vulnerability to passion: we must recall (from section 5.1.1) that reason-proper *can* resist passion's controlling interference. If a passion were so strong as to overpower reason by sheer intensity, that would not be an instance of incontinence, but of insanity (Aquinas, *ST* II–II q.156, a.1, resp.). Otherwise, inordinate appetites cannot so totally dominate reason "that reason would never complain" (Aquinas, *EG* chp.5, lec.4). Passion may "cloud" reason, but reason's ability to consider options from various perspectives grants it the freedom to repel the passion's influence and consider the action according to its own rational concerns. Thus, it remains possible for reason to exercise restraint in its attention, to make sure to propose its own object—and not passion's—to the will (Aquinas, *TH* q.10, a.3, rep. 2; *ST* II–II q.156, a.1, resp.). Hence, we can see that acting under the influence of passion demonstrates *weakness* on the agent's part—that is, in her not judging according to reason-proper (Aquinas, *CNE* VII.L.7: C1419), and/or in her "not standing firm in resisting the passion by *holding* to the judgment formed by [her] reason" [emphasis added] (Aquinas, *ST* II–II q.156, a.2, rep.2).

5.3.5 Explaining Akratic Actions

Keeping in mind the preceding vulnerabilities of the human action-faculties, we can now lay out Aquinas's explanation of the occurrence of akratic actions. We have seen how passion can subvert reason's activity and thereby direct action. Yet as we focus on the "weak" akratic cases, we must still discover how passion can cause action even when reason has *already* concluded deliberation and directed a course of action. For in weak *akrasia*, the agent does reach a discretive judgment, but somehow she does not act on it (Aquinas, *CNE* VII.L.7: C1419).

In accounting for such actions, Aquinas offers this basic picture, which I shall illustrate through an extended example: The incontinent agent initially proposes a rational end to her will. This end directs her to avoid a kind of action that would fail to meet her standard of rationality and lawfulness—for instance, that she should refrain from the illicit activity of fornication. Using this end, she deliberates and concludes on a course of action—here, that she should not enter the bedroom of tonight's date, who is currently standing inside the door of that room and beckoning to her. However, she greatly enjoys her date's company, and he looks just like her favorite movie star. Having perceived his similarity to her "dreamboat," she experiences an inordinate passion of desire from the concupiscible appetite.

This passion then deleteriously affects her reason in three ways. First, it fixes her attention on the pleasures possible in her situation, thereby distracting her attention from her rational deliberation and its implication for her will (Aquinas, *ST* I–II q.77, a.1). For as Aquinas notes, "we attend much to that which pleases us," so that the prospect of pleasure "concentrat[es] the mind's attention on itself" (q.33, a.3, resp.). Second, by means of the avid attention given to its pleasure-prospects, the roused passion inclines the agent's reason to construe the option of a pleasurable sexual escapade as good. In effect, the passion foists a new end upon reason—here, to partake of any available sexual pleasures (Aquinas, *CNE* VII.L.6: C1393–4). Because this end arises from an inordinate desire, it is "contrary to the order of reason," and represents a breakdown from reason's proper estimation of action (Aquinas, *ST* I–II q.33, a.3, resp.). Third, the passion brings about physical changes in the agent—her heart races, her temperature rises, and so on. These physical alterations "fetter" reason; they make it difficult for the agent to think rationally at all (q.33, a.3, resp.; q.77, a.2).

Thus, the agent no longer attends to her rationally deliberated conclusion, but instead to the new end derived from passion. With her attention fixed on the aspects of her situation that bring it under the scope of passion's directive, the agent's proposed sexual action no longer "fits" under her deliberated conclusion (Aquinas, *TH* q.9, a.2, resp.). Therefore her deliberation loses its hold, and she akratically chooses and acts according to passion's end by entering the bedroom (Aquinas, *ST* II–II q.155, a.3, resp.).

From this explanation, we can see that the instability of deliberate choice, the disorder in the appetites, and the vulnerability of reason to passion all play a role in the generation of an incontinent action. Moreover, though, we need to see that reason's failure connects to a fault in the will. Attending to this or that end, or to this or that relevant action-aspect, falls under reason's operation. But since the will moves reason to its activities, if reason lacks focus in doing its job, that may trace back to an insufficient or mixed motivation from the will. Such is the case in *akrasia*; the will's malice—its weakness in being able to be attracted by recognizably lesser goods—undercuts its commitment of motivational force toward reason's proper considerations. As Aquinas observes, "The will stands between reason and the concupiscible [appetite], and may be moved by either. . . . [I]n the incontinent [agent] it is moved by the concupiscible" (q.155, a.3, rep.2). In fact, Aquinas claims that the "primary difference" between being incontinent versus continent lies neither in "right reason," nor in the "vehement evil desires"—which each are present in both conditions—but in the choice of the will; therefore those traits "reside in that power of the soul, whose act it is to choose; and that is the will" (q.155, a.3, resp.). The incontinent agent's will "forsakes" the "judgment of reason" (q.156, a.1, resp.). Hence the akratic agent "fails to resist a passion by the reason . . . [because she] does not stand to what has been counseled, through holding weakly to reason's judgment" (q.156, a.1, resp.). But holding onto reason's judgments is will's job, especially in its act of choice. Therefore, Aquinas charges, "the *direct* cause of incontinence is on [that] part of the soul," namely, the will [emphasis added] (q.156, a.1 resp.). As Aquinas's explanation of incontinent action further unfolds, then, we need to be alert to the full nature of the rational failure, both in the cognitive and in the executive rational faculties.

But again, Aquinas stresses that reason and will *can* resist any and all of these effects of passion. The agent could mentally shake herself to refocus her attention on the illicitness of her proposed action; she could concentrate hard enough to see through passion's "cloud," and so on. For, Aquinas maintains, "so long as the use of reason remains, [an agent] is always able to resist [her] passions" (q.156, a.1, resp.). And also, "It is in the will's power to give or refuse its consent to what passion inclines us to do" (Aquinas, *ST* I–II q.77, a.3, rep.3). If an agent fails to judge and choose properly, it is only "through a certain negligence" that is culpable and sinful on her part (*ST* II–II q.156, a.2. rep.2). The agent's evil desire *hinders* reason's proper focus and will's proper choice, but does *not necessarily prevent* them (*ST* I–II q.77, a.3, rep.3). On this account then, weak-willed actions exemplify just that— weakness on the part of the agent's reason and will.

The most critical instance of that weakness shows in the inordinate passion's effect on the agent's perceptions. The agent allows the passion to pull her attention to the pleasurable aspects of entering the bedroom; that ensures that the action will "match up" with the general end from reason-manipulated-by-passion, and not with that from reason-proper. At that point, Aquinas says,

> The result is that the [discretive] judgment of reason . . . follows the passion of the sensitive appetite, and consequently the will's movement [that is, choice] follows it also. (q.77, a.1)

Because of that, as we now consider Aquinas's use of the practical syllogism to give a more detailed account of the incontinent reasoning process, we shall concentrate on passion's effect upon the particular premise of the practical syllogism. For that premise deals with the agent's perceptions of her situation.

Aquinas bases his characterization of the incontinent agent's practical syllogism on Aristotle's. Both say that the akratic agent has a universal premise from reason-proper (q.77, a.2, rep.4; Aristotle, *NE* 1146a33). They also stipulate that the agent has a universal judgment that represents the appetite's inclination (1147a34; Aquinas, *ST* I–II q.77, a.2, rep.4). Given that, Aquinas explains that the agent's syllogism has four premises—two universal and two particular. Reason-proper and reason-as-passion's-tool each offer a universal premise; each universal has a particular premise to fit with it and bring the considered action under the universal's scope (q.77, a.2, rep.4). So the incontinent person reasons like this:

(a) Acts of fornication are unlawful and to be avoided.
(b) Going into the bedroom to have sex with my date is an act of fornication.

And:

(x) Sexual pleasure is to be pursued.
(y) Going into the bedroom to have sex with my date is sexually pleasurable.

However, the agent does not consider, or actively attend to, all these premises at once.

First, before her appetite rises and clouds her reasoning, the agent accepts (a), reason-proper's universal premise; she understands what, in general, she ought to do (Aquinas, *CNE* VII.L.3: C1347). Then, deliberating in light of that end, the agent surveys her current situation and formulates (b), the particular premise that regards the proposed action as it pertains to (a). In concluding her deliberation, the agent reaches a discretive judgment that "follows through" on the rational estimation of lawfulness (VII.L.3: C1345). The agent judges:

(c) Going into the bedroom to have sex with my date is an act of unlawful fornication and is to be avoided.

Thus, (c) tells her to refrain from the considered action (Aristotle, *NE* 1147a35–b1).

However, when the agent's inordinate passion arises, that inclines reason to the universal end (x) as well, because of the appeal of pleasurably satisfying the appetite for sex (Aquinas, *CNE* VII.L.3: C1347, 1348; L.6: C1389; *ST* I–II q.77, a.2, rep.4). Here, the evil desire "inclines to something contrary to what [the agent] knows in the universal" (q.77, a.2). Moreover, the passion also draws the agent's attention to the pleasurable aspects of her considered action, thus yielding (y), which regards the action as it pertains to (x). Further, the inordinate desire's capacity to fixate the attention and to make reasoning difficult enables it to "bind reason," so that reason views the action only in terms of (y) rather than (b) (VII.L.3: C1347).

This attention-fixation in regard to the particulars then devastates reason-proper's deliberations. For the agent no longer actively attends to (b); she sees her action as described in (y). But with (b) removed from active consideration, (a) does not "connect" with the proposed action anymore, so (c) drops from consideration too. Thus, (a), "now rendered impotent," does not apply to the agent's situation (VII.L.3: C1348). That allows her to form a new discretive judgment, opposed to reason-proper's universal (Aquinas, *ST* I–II q.77, a.2, resp., rep.2). She thereby concludes,

> (z) Going into the bedroom to have pleasurable sex with my date is to be done.

And she acts upon her new conclusion (Aquinas, *CNE* VII.L.3: C1348).

So the inordinate passion *obscures* (b), by fixing attention on (y). Since the agent ceases actively considering (b), that effectively *removes* (b) from her active knowledge. The loss of (b)'s particular knowledge, then, constitutes passion's most damaging effect, as it "paves the way" for (z) to be reached and acted upon (Aquinas, *OE* q.3, a.9, rep.7). Aquinas sums up the situation concisely:

> Hence passion fetters the reason, and hinders it from thinking [that is, considering premise (b)] and concluding [(c)] under the first proposition [(a)]; so that while the passion lasts, reason argues [that is, views the action in light of premise (y)] and concludes [(z)] under the second [universal, (x)]. (*ST* I–II q.77, a.2, rep.4)

Thus, we can now see how the weak-willed agent reasons; the inordinate passion's effect on the agent's consideration of the particular premises provides the key to her performance of the akratic act.

Furthermore, this effect underlies a crucial element of Aquinas's construal of incontinent actions. While the passion remains strong and in control of the agents' attention, the agent *changes her mind* about the action. She "acts contrary to what [she] formerly intended, but not contrary to what [she] now wishes to do" (Aquinas, *TH* q.6, a.7, rep.2). So even if she mumbles to herself, "I shouldn't be doing this," as she passes the door frame and begins to disrobe, she *no longer truly means it* (Aquinas, *ST* I–II q.77, a.2, rep.5). She may be "saying these words," but she is "pretending," because "in [her] heart [she] does not think this way" (Aquinas, *CNE* VII.L.3: C1344). With this claim, Aquinas denies the possibility of "clear-eyed" incontinence in which the agent recognizes and objects to her own wrongdoing even *as* she does it. In other words, while under the inordinate passion's influence, the agent acts in ignorance of the wrongfulness of the particular act she does. The ignorance lasts only as long as the evil desire holds sway, but the agent chooses while not actively recognizing that her action falls under reason-proper's prohibition (Aquinas, *ST* II–II q.156, a.3, rep.1). As soon as the passion subsides, the agent once again realizes the act's wrongfulness and repudiates it (q.156, a.3, resp.). However, while the passion affects her, the ignorance is real and relevant, although negligent and culpable (*ST* I–II q.77, a.7, rep.2). We shall have more to say about this point in analyzing Aquinas's view; but right now we should conclude the current exposition.

5.4 EXPOSITION CONCLUSIONS

5.4.1 Implications of the Explanation

We can complete the exposition of Aquinas's view of incontinence by noting two implications of Aquinas's account. First, Aquinas stipulates that incontinent acts are performed *without* deliberate choice (*CNE* VII.L.4: C1361). At this point, we can see how he justifies that claim. For we understand that given our distinction between reason–proper and reason-as-passion's-tool, an incontinent action does *not* proceed from the deliberation of reason–proper. Indeed reason–proper's deliberations conclude with the discretive judgment (c), which directs refraining from the action. If the agent had acted on (c), she would then have acted from deliberate choice, from reason–proper concluding under its own universal end. As she does behave, however, she abandons her deliberation and acts from the universal end foisted upon reason by passion, from reason–as-tool concluding under a universal unapproved by reason–proper. This production thus seems similar to, but precisely speaking cannot qualify as, deliberate choice.

Incontinent actions, then, appear *like* human actions, which must proceed from deliberate will, but seem *not* to *be* human actions—at least *not in the fullest, most proper sense*. I think that last phrase gives us the key to solving a problem that plagued Davidson. As we saw, Davidson—who had too weak a standard of rational action, anyway—could not account for incontinent actions under his model of rational action (sections 4.5.4 and 4.7.2).

Yet perhaps he erred in assuming that the intentionality of actions presented an all-or-nothing question. That is, I propose that we should view intentionality (or in Aquinas's terminology, "humanness") as a matter of *degree*. On this account "intentional," or "human," becomes a *success term*, indicating achievement of a *regulative, normative* ideal. The question over incontinent actions (or any of our actions) then becomes: to what *degrees* are they intentional or human—to what extent do they approximate the norm for what constitutes intentionality or humanness? We shall explore this notion in more detail later; but I believe it can help us not only to solve Davidson's problem, but also to account for Hare's troubling observation that the rationality of so-called intentional actions varies enormously (section 1.1.3). Aquinas's distinction—between deliberate choice, proper, and approximations of that choice—opens the door for his theory of rational action to construe intentionality as subject to degree.

The second implication of Aquinas's portrayal of incontinence is that he can show how incontinent actions involve a rational failure, without having to attribute them to simple logical error. Of the four premises that the incontinent agent reasons from, both minor premises are merely true observational statements. Nor does the incontinent agent accept contradictory major premises. Since her universal premises direct action based on goods that are incommensurate—lawfulness versus pleasantness, in our example—acceptance of one cannot imply anything about acceptance of the other; thus, neither entails rejection of the other. No logical contradictions, then, lurk in the premises of the incontinent agent's reasoning.

Rather, reason fails in its job of action-guidance by accepting and proposing to the will an *inappropriate* or *inordinate* end, one that does not focus on the action-aspects that are reason's proper considerations. Indeed, the true opposition to correct reason comes from the inordinate passion itself, which according to reason should not exist. But in accepting the passion's goal as a universal end, reason-as-tool makes a judgment out of line with its practical standard demanding that all accepted ends should lead toward God—that is, that leading-toward-God-ness should be the focus of reason's judgments about ends (VII.L.3: C1349). So reason fails in proposing passion's end as suitable for action, thereby making the resultant deed irrational, since its end is too. In this way, Aquinas can characterize any akratic action as involving a rational *breakdown* by the agent.

Moreover, the inclusion of that rational failure provides a defense against a charge made by Davidson against Aquinas's theory. For Davidson rejects the Thomistic view, in part because he thinks that in allowing the incontinent agent two unqualified major premises—which lead to contrary conclusions—Aquinas has erred. Davidson writes, "For how can premises, all of which are true (or [rationally] acceptable), entail . . . [such contrary conclusions] (*EAE* 34)?" But in fact, Davidson has erred in assuming that all the incontinent agent's premises are true or rationally acceptable. As we have now seen, the major premise foisted upon reason by passion does not qualify as rationally acceptable, and reason fails in accepting it—not in simple logical error, but in a failure to meet the standard of practical rationality for choosing ends. So the contrariety of the conclusions comes not from error in the system of practical reasoning used by Aquinas, but from the rational unacceptability of one of the major premises used by the incontinent agent.

Furthermore, through coupling the notion of that sort of rational failure with the prior point regarding intentionality-by-degree, we can generate a proportional scale for intentionality and rationality: the top-end, fully intentional actions are also completely, correctly rational; incontinent actions fall somewhere lower, that is, they have imperfect reason for their performance and possess only a certain degree of intentionality. But again, we shall return to this intentionality scale in the next chapter.

5.4.2 Summary

Before we analyze Aquinas's view, let us close this chapter with a quick summary of his theory of human action and his explanation of incontinence. First, for Aquinas, intentional actions are human actions, because discretive judgments—which correspond to our common notion of intentions—result from the deliberate willing required in human action. The process of deliberate will involves reason interacting with will, so that an action is brought about by, and in accord with, reason's judgment that it is good to do. Thus, Aquinas's conception of human action yields a model of rational action. The rationality of such actions is measured according to the value of whether those actions lead toward communion with God (and how much). This measurement presupposes a limited commensurability of options, in that any action must be comparable with respect to that value. The standard of that value is God's law (the expression of his reason), thus making all human actions good (rational) or evil (irrational), depending on their conformity to that law.

Second, because akratic actions are voluntary (and therefore seemingly human) and performed counter to the agent's rational deliberations, Aquinas must explain how such actions can occur. He appeals to three important facts about the faculties producing human action: instability in rational consideration, damage from original sin, and the further damage from active sin. With those in mind, he asserts that in an akratic action, the agent experiences an inordinate sensual appetite that distracts her reason from the situational-particulars of her properly rational deliberations, which then collapse. The appetite also foists a rationally inappropriate principle of action onto her reason; and with her new sensually focused perception of the particulars of her situation, reason-as-passion's-tool directs the akratic action. That action is no longer fully human, since it was not brought about by reason-proper; thus the act may be human, intentional, and rational, but only to a certain proportionate degree. Also, while the deed represents a rational failure—in the acceptance of passion's principle—it is not driven by a mere logical mistake on the agent's part, since passion's and reason's values may be incommensurate. However, Aquinas's explanation does exclude the possibility of clear-eyed *akrasia*, as the agent changes her judgment while acting. That said, we are now ready to analyze Aquinas's view for its strengths and weaknesses.

6

AQUINAS'S THEORY
IN THE CRUCIBLE

Now we can begin appraising Aquinas's conception of rational action and his auxiliary explanation of *akrasia*. As we shall see, Aquinas's account of incontinence possesses both distinct strengths lacked by Hare's or Davidson's theories and some explanatory weaknesses of its own. However, I shall propose some modifications that I believe Aquinas's theory can accommodate without destroying its model of rational action; those changes will allow a Thomistic position to deal with its flaws in accounting for weak-willed actions. Since Aquinas's view falters in fixable ways, I shall dispense with my previous format of separately grouping explanatory successes and unresolved explanatory failures. Instead, I shall serially examine the account's key aspects—including good points, problems, and possible solutions—with regard to both experiential and theoretical adequacy. Initially, though, we need to address a significant interpretive objection to the previous chapter's exposition of Aquinas's view. With that resolved, we shall then be free to consider how well Aquinas saves the phenomena associated with incontinence, looking first at his portrayal of continent action.

6.1 DEFENDING THE
EXPOSITIONAL INTERPRETATION

6.1.1 Kretzmann's Objection

The interpretive difficulty arises over what counts as incontinence and what does not, according to Aquinas. In my presentation, I have drawn significantly from Aquinas's commentary on Romans, particularly as it deals with chapter 7. In the latter half of that chapter the apostle Paul describes a condition that I—and tradition—have understood as a type of incontinence. Indeed, I have proposed those verses as a paradigmatic instance of the divided-self phenomenon associated with incontinent action (section 2.2.2). I have therefore understood Aquinas's commentary on that passage to be relevant to his view of incontinence and have presented that view in a manner that allows it to include under its explanatory umbrella the situation depicted in Rom. 7.

However, Norman Kretzmann has argued that Aquinas neither thinks Rom. 7 describes incontinence nor intends his own account of incontinence to cover the condition detailed there. Kretzmann maintains that Aquinas sees something different from *akrasia* occurring in the pertinent passage. If Kretzmann is correct, Aquinas's view on incontinence would differ significantly from the portrayal of it that I have given. Therefore, we need to look carefully at Kretzmann's objection; following that I shall lay out my reasons for preferring the interpretation I have used.

First, then, Kretzmann sets forth what he sees as Aquinas's view of incontinence. Incontinent action must emerge from an "initial disturbance . . . among the passions of the sensory appetite, which [then] affect[s] the will via the intellect" (174–5). When the disturbance occurs, "The passions affect the will indirectly, by distorting the intellect's proposal of an object of volition" (175). The resultant action exhibits weakness on the agent's part, because the will is able to resist such proposals from passion—and, indeed, any like proposal from the intellect (175). The upshot is that Aquinas's conception of incontinence *essentially* "involves the retention of ability [by the agent to resist passion], albeit at a level of diminished capacity" (176).

However, that means that for Aquinas, any situation in which the agent expresses psychological inability must *not* count as incontinence. That is, if the agent says, "I cannot resist my passions," then she is not experiencing *akrasia*. If what she says is actually true, then she suffers from a kind of *insanity*, "some sort of victimization of the will" that "ought not to count as a human action . . . at all, much less as immoral [incontinence]" (174). On the other hand, if her statement is sincere but actually false, then the agent's case is one of "*self-deception*—an instance of the will's coercion of (exercising efficient causation on) the intellect" (177). And of course, if the agent's statement were both false and insincere, then her action would be simple *hypocrisy*. Thus, none of the possible options regarding psychological inability seems to fit the condition Aquinas calls "incontinence."

Also, according to Kretzmann, Aquinas rejects the notion that incontinent acts are only *partially* voluntary, or voluntary "in-a-certain-respect." Rather, an akratic act must be *fully* voluntary, involving *complete* willings alternating in an "on-again off-again fashion" (179). By a "complete" or "absolute" willing is understood the full process of a human act, including discretive judgment, choice, and the rest—in other words, "we will absolutely that which we will in accordance with reason's [completed] deliberation" (Aquinas, *ST* III q.21, a.4, resp.). Now, Kretzmann comments, Aquinas cannot mean for incontinence to involve *concurrent*, opposed, complete willings, because that would be impossible in Aquinas's action theory, since it would require both doing and not doing an action at the same time. Kretzmann writes,

> If incontinence is taken to be . . . a person's performing a human action while willing—i.e. engaged in a complete volition—against performing that action, then incontinence cannot be instantiated. (189)

So opposed complete willings can only occur by *alternating*, which Kretzmann calls the "on-again, off-again" feature (179).

Further, though, the willings that occur in incontinence do need to be complete; they cannot simply be what Aquinas calls an "incomplete willing" or a "*velleity*." Aquinas explains the concept of a velleity as follows:

> [W]hat we will in accordance with the movement of sensuality, or even of the simple will [that is simple volition] . . . is willed not absolutely but conditionally . . . that is, provided no obstacle be discovered by reason's deliberation. Wherefore such a will should rather be called a *velleity* than an absolute will; because one would will (*vellet*) if there were no obstacle. (*ST* III q.21, a.4, resp.)

So, as indicated in the quote, if someone has only a simple volition for a certain good, or has only an intention (in Aquinas's sense) inclined by an end drawn from a passion, that agent wills incompletely. Also, if someone intends a good and discovers in her deliberations that it cannot be attained, her willing reverts to a velleity; because "the will that is [directed] at impossibilities . . . should be called *velleity* . . . for one does not will such things absolutely, but one would if they were possible" (Aquinas, *ST* App.1, a.1, a.2, rep.2). In short, an incomplete willing is just that, *incomplete*. The key is that the willing process stops at some point prior to completed deliberation and its resultant discretive judgment.

Given Aquinas's picture of incomplete willing, Kretzmann then maintains that Aquinas would not utilize velleities in explaining incontinence. For the incontinent agent recognizes that her particular action is against her rationally directed will; yet because one who wills incompletely never reaches a discretive judgment regarding that will, *no particular action* is identified as falling under it. So if someone acts contrary to an incomplete will for the rational good, hers is "a case in which the conflict between what the person thinks best and what [she] wills on a particular occasion goes unnoticed by [her]" (Kretzmann, 191 n.24). That is,

> [T]he incontinent person *does* know better while the [incompletely willing person] . . . *should* know better but does not . . . the contrariety between [her] uncompleted volition and [her] commanding [that is, completed] volition [to sin] goes unrecognized by [her] . . . and so there is no willing on [her] part to repudiate the uncompleted volition (as there would be if this situation were one of incontinence) . . . so there is not a full-fledged change in the will—in the conscious direction of the will . . . [she] does not have to say to [her]self "I'll [do the proscribed action] *anyway*," as the incontinent person would. [Emphasis in original] (193 n.51)

Therefore, Kretzmann thinks, actions involving velleities will not be seen by Aquinas as incontinent.

Now, in applying these points to Aquinas's commentary on Rom. 7, Kretzmann argues that Aquinas offers two interpretations, neither of which describes incontinence. The first interpretation is that Paul is speaking in an *assumed character*, that of the "man of sin" not yet saved. The second, which Aquinas sees as better, is that Paul speaks in his *own person*, the "man of grace" (*ER* chp.7, lec.3) In either interpretation the "I" in such phrases as "I am of the flesh sold into slavery under sin" (v. 14) refers to the speaker's *reason* [in the broad sense, this is the passage alluded to in section 5.3.4] (chp.7, lec.3; Kretzmann, 184). In the case of the man of sin, the "subjection to the flesh" portrayed throughout the passage refers to such a man's reason being subjected to his inordinate passions by his *reason's* "*consent*" to them (185; Aquinas *ER* chp.7, lec.3). Regarding the man of grace, his reason is subjected to the "flesh" of his inordinate desires in that *reason cannot prevent* them from arising and so is continually "under attack" from them (chp.7, lec.3; Kretzmann, 185). That is, the former interpretation depicts someone consenting to, and acting upon, inordinate desires; the latter portrays someone bombarded by inordinate desires (concupiscence 2) from the ineradicable spark of evil desire (concupiscence 3), but not consenting to, or acting upon them (Aquinas, *ER* chp.7, lec.3).

However, given those interpretive options, Kretzmann thinks Aquinas does not see either possibility as describing incontinence. The man-of-grace does not act impetuously on his inordinate desires, nor does he deliberate a course of action against them and then weakly crumble from his resolve. The man of grace completely wills and does the good; he does evil only in that he experiences inordinate desires from the sense appetites (chp.7, lec.3). Therefore, Kretzmann claims, the man of grace is "obviously not incontinent" (186). On the other hand, the man of sin completely wills and does the evil urged by his inordinate desires, but only wills the good with

> a certain incomplete willing . . . [in which people] will the good in the universal, just as in the universal they have correct judgment concerning the good. Nevertheless, through a habit or perhaps a perverse passion, this judgment is subverted, and such a willing is corrupted in the particular, so that [the man-of-sin] does not do what, in the universal he understands ought to be done and would have been willing to do. (Aquinas, *ER* chp.7, lec.3)

On that account, Kretzmann writes,

> [T]he man of sin means something like this: "I know what is good in general, and I am favorably disposed to do whatever will contribute toward it, but I fail to apply my understanding to certain particular cases, and so my uncompleted volition for the good in general is overridden by a completed, commanding volition for what only seems good on such occasions." (187)

Therefore, because the man of sin operates only from a velleity and doesn't know better, he does not exemplify incontinence, either (187, 193 n.51).

Kretzmann makes two additional points to support his take on Aquinas. First, he claims, Aquinas fills his Romans commentary with references to Aristotle's *Nicomachean Ethics*, but Aquinas makes none in commenting on the passage in chapter 7 and surely would have if he thought Paul was discussing *akrasia* (189). Second, the "on-again off-again" portrayal of incontinence does not seem sufficient to account for Rom. 7. If Paul says "I do not do the good that I will" (v. 19), Kretzmann points out that interpreted as incontinence, Paul would really have to mean "I do not do the good that I *used* to will," which would be "a pretty lame, disappointing analysis" of that anguished lament (179–80).

Finally, Kretzmann proposes that the man of sin in Rom. 7 actually represents a *new* condition *worse* than incontinence, but not yet as bad as the vice of intemperance. He describes this stage as "a kind of despair in which the agent consciously wills against [her] reason *without* having earlier willed in keeping with it" (191 n.24). That is, like a "self-loathing, unrepentant alcoholic," this person hates what she does—unlike an in-temperate person—but wills it continuously with an "I can't help it" quality, rather than in the "on-again off-again" fashion of incontinence (191 n.24). Thus, Kretzmann thinks that while Aquinas does not recognize this moral stage, it is clearly distinct from incontinence and temperance, as Aquinas understands them (191 n.24). For all these reasons, then, Aquinas would not see Rom. 7 and its divided-personality phenomenon as pertaining to incontinence.

6.1.2 The Objection's Rebuttal

Kretzmann presents a formidable objection; nevertheless, I think he is mistaken. Aquinas does mean for his view of incontinence to cover phenomena like the lament of a divided self in Rom. 7, because he definitely regards the situation described in that passage as pertaining to incontinent action. I shall demonstrate this contention in two steps: first, by showing how Aquinas's construal of *akrasia* does involve incomplete volitions; and second, by showing why he must conceive of Rom. 7 as portraying incontinence, under the man-of-sin interpretation.

On one important point, however, I agree with Kretzmann. Aquinas definitely does not intend the man-of-grace interpretation of Rom. 7 to portray a kind of incontinence. Aquinas regards Paul as fully virtuous, including being temperate. Because Aquinas sees human nature as possessing the spark of evil desire—that ineradicable propensity toward inordinate desires, due to original sin—he thinks that even someone who is "truly temperate," like Paul, will experience "depraved desires" (*DQV* q.2, a.1, rep.6). Aquinas also explicitly makes this point in regard to a similar passage from Paul's epistle to the Galatians. In the fifth chapter of that letter, Paul writes,

> [16]Live by the Spirit, I say, and do not gratify the desires of the flesh. [17]For what the flesh desires is opposed to the Spirit, and what the Spirit desires is opposed to the flesh; for these are opposed to each other, to prevent you from doing what you want [NRSV]. (Gal. 5:16–17)

These verses also describe the inner opposition and conflict, and the inability to do what is willed, that figure so prominently in Rom. 7. In commenting on Gal. 5, Aquinas makes the connection to Rom. 7 (*EG* chp.5, lec.4). He claims that both passages can apply to a temperate person, established under grace, if the evil "desires of the flesh" are understood as referring to appetitive movements from "the 'fomes' introduced by the first [that is, original] sin" (chp.5, lec.4). Therefore, Kretzmann is correct in his assertion that the man-of-grace interpretation of Rom. 7 portrays not incontinence but merely a wound of original sin, present even in those who, like Paul, are temperate.

Now, to begin the rebuttal: incontinence, as Aquinas views it, does utilize incomplete volitions. If we think of the incontinent reasoning process shown in the practical syllogism, we find two major, universal premises. In our example, these were

(a) Acts of fornication are unlawful and to be avoided.

And:

(x) Sexual pleasure is to be pursued.

Each represents a general end proposed to the will, one from reason-proper and one from reason-manipulated-by-passion. Moreover, if we consider the practical syllogism's representation-system, we recall that the major premise corresponds to reason's first judgment that follows simple volition and prompts intention (sections 5.1.3 and 5.1.4). Given that, we know that each major premise signifies the presence of a (so far) *incomplete volition* in the agent. That is, the major premise would not be judged if the agent did not already have simple volition for those goods; moreover, in judging those major premises, the agent normally proceeds to hold *intentions* to pursue—in a general way—those goods. Now, the will-acts of simple volition and generalized intention are exactly what Aquinas described as exemplifying a *velleity* (*ST* III q.21, a.4, resp.; *ER* chp.7, lec.3).

Moreover, as we recently saw (section 5.3.5), the akratic agent's inordinate passion shifts her attention regarding the relevant characteristics of the particular action she contemplates. In the example, the agent's sexual desire draws her attention to the pleasurable aspects of having sex with her date; that passion also thereby pulls her attention away from the action's nature as fornication. In doing so, the sexual desire effectively removes from active consideration the minor premise (b), Going into the bedroom to have sex with my date is an act of fornication, that fit with reason-proper's judgment (a). Now, when (a) and (b) were both present to the agent's mind, she concluded with the discretive judgment, (c) Going into the bedroom to have sex with my date is an act of unlawful fornication and is to be avoided. With (c) in mind, the agent was choosing not to enter the bedroom and have sex; she was willing *completely* to avoid the fornication. However, with

(b) removed from consideration, reason-proper's syllogism *breaks down*; (b)'s loss disconnects (c) from (a).

Therefore, once passion draws her attention away from (b), the agent judges only (a), with regard to avoiding fornication. She loses (c), so her will must stop short of choosing to avoid fornicating, for that choice would require (c)'s discretive judgment to prompt it. Further, she does not have (b), so she *has no rational deliberation* to point out how (a) applies to her present situation. She continues to will to avoid fornicating, but only in the general way associated with (a), which is "*impotent*" for producing action (Aquinas, *CNE* VII.L.3: C1348). In other words, when reason-proper's syllogism collapses, the agent's will to avoid fornicating reverts to an *incomplete* stage. So in acting incontinently she retains an incomplete will to avoid fornicating.

In addition, we also saw that with her attention removed from (b), the incontinent agent is *ignorant* of the "particular detail of choice" that her action is fornication (Aquinas, *ST* II–II q.156, a.3, rep.1). And since she therefore no longer judges (c), to avoid this unlawful fornication, she truly does *not know better* at the time of her action. Again, this quality of incontinent action conforms to the nature of incomplete willing, in which the agent does not notice that her action conflicts with her general will and judgment (Kretzmann, 187).

The upshot of these points is that the "on again, off again" willings in an incontinent action do not alternate between completely willed and not-willed-at-all, but rather between completely willed and incompletely willed. Kretzmann seems not to have made the connection between the akratic agent's passion-induced ignorance, and the implied incomplete state of that agent's will for the rational good. Therefore, contrary to Kretzmann's characterization of it, Aquinas's model of incontinent action does involve incomplete willings. When reason-proper's syllogism is intact, the akratic agent completely wills the good of reason-proper; but when inordinate passion arises and sways her particular judgments, she wills reason's good only incompletely. Moreover, if she were successfully to resist her inordinate passion's influence and to act continently, her complete willing from the syllogism of reason-manipulated-by-passion would break down and revert to an incomplete stage as her attention shifted back to the rationally pertinent aspects of the action. In fact, then, both incontinence and continence involve incomplete willings as the agent's attention moves back and forth between reason's and passion's pertinent aspects in the considered action.

With the above points in mind, we can now see that Aquinas's man-of-sin interpretation of Rom. 7 clearly *does* fit with his account of incontinence. The incomplete volitions characteristic of the man of sin's condition obviously fall under the umbrella of Aquinas's general description of akratic action. Indeed, Aquinas explicitly interprets the related passage from Galatians as applying to incontinence. In reference to Gal. 5:17, he writes,

> But incontinent persons, who resolve to abstain but are, nevertheless, conquered by their passions, do what they would not, inasmuch as they follow such passions contrary to what they resolved. (Aquinas, *EG* chp.5 lec.4)

With its language of "do[ing] what they would not, contrary to what they resolved," Aquinas's comment clearly parallels the condition described in Rom. 7:15, "For I do not do what I want, but I do the very thing I hate." Aquinas, then, explicitly interprets the parallel Galatians passage in light of incontinence; and he connects those verses to Rom. 7—as we saw earlier—with regard to the man-of-sin interpretation (*EG* chp.5, lec.4). The conclusion obviously follows that Aquinas's man-of-sin interpretation of Rom. 7 applies to incontinent action. Curiously, Kretzmann acknowledges the presence and pertinence of the Galatians passage but fails to make the connection between Aquinas's commentaries (189 n.1).

Finally, to respond to Kretzmann's other supporting arguments, Aquinas does refer to Aristotle's *Nicomachean Ethics* in commenting on Rom. 7, and Aquinas's portrayal of incontinence has a problem of adequately accounting for akratic experience, generally, and not merely in reference to Rom. 7. With regard to the former point, when Aquinas explains that the "I" in the Romans verses refers to the agent's reason that is assailed by the inordinate passions (section 5.3.4), he bases that on a quote from the *Ethics*; but he does not reference it (*ER* chp.7, lec.3). Elsewhere, when Aquinas makes the same point, in almost exactly the same words, he gives the reference (*ST* I q.75, a.4, rep.1; Aristotle, *NE* 1168b30–1169a3). Indeed, in that spot Aquinas also links the point to the "inward man" versus "outward man" terminology of Rom. 7 (*ST* I q.75, a.4, rep.1). Further, Aristotle first makes the identification of agency with reason, in conjunction with an assertion that

> someone is called continent or incontinent because [her] understanding [that is, her intellect] is or is not the master, on the assumption that this [the intellect] is what each person is. (*NE* 1168b35–1169a1)

Therefore, Aquinas not only utilizes Aristotle's *Ethics* to explain Rom. 7, he does so with regard to the passage's central explanatory distinction between reason-proper and reason-as-passion's-tool, and he quotes Aristotle where the Philosopher is dealing with a point about incontinence. Thus, contrary to Kretzmann's claim, Aquinas *does* think Aristotle's views on *akrasia* are relevant to interpreting Rom. 7, and Aquinas utilizes the Philosopher's insights accordingly.

With regard to Kretzmann's latter argument, Aquinas's denial of the possibility of clear-eyed incontinence creates explanatory problems that extend beyond giving a robust account of the situation from Rom. 7. We recall Kretzmann's complaint that the alternating volitions of incontinent action did not suitably describe what occurs in Rom. 7, in doing what one presently "wills"—not "used to will"—not to do (179–80). However, we can now see that Aquinas has characterized incontinence, generally, in such a way that any instance of clear-eyed incontinence will cause an explanatory problem for him. Therefore, if Rom. 7 portrays a kind of clear-eyed incontinence—as I think it does—it comes as no surprise that Aquinas's depiction of incontinence does not completely adequately cover this situation. So Kretzmann has not advanced a reason to think Aquinas's account of incontinence is not meant to apply to Rom. 7 but has only uncovered a significant difficulty in Aquinas's theory. Kretzmann even admits that Aquinas's

> on-again, off-again account seems to fail utterly to capture the inner conflict that moral people often experience even *while* acting incontinently. (179–80)

Kretzmann immediately attempts to deflect that criticism from Aquinas by claiming that Aquinas's account does allow for inner struggle, but not within the incontinent agent's will; rather the struggle occurs between the agent's will and her reason, so that she "acts out of concupiscence [sense 2] even though and even while [she] knows better" (180). Yet given what we just saw regarding the ignorance that occurs during the performance of an akratic action, Kretzmann's defense falls flat; the incontinent agent truly does not know better while she acts on her passion. So Aquinas cannot view the inner conflict as Kretzmann claims, because Aquinas does not admit the presence of such "clear-eyed" conflict. Therefore, Aquinas faces problems in explaining any phenomenon of clear-eyed incontinence, and his inability to completely capture the character of the situation in Rom. 7 is thus indicative of this larger difficulty, and not of Aquinas's regarding the man of sin as something other than incontinent.

To conclude the rebuttal, I think that Kretzmann's identification of the man of sin's condition with a new moral stage between incontinence and intemperance is unnecessary. In the coming sections, in analyzing Aquinas's position, I shall argue for some changes that will allow Aquinas's explanation of incontinent action to cover the phenomena associated with clear-eyed akratic acts. With those alterations in place, Aquinas's model of incontinent action should gain enough flexibility to account successfully for the man of sin's condition, as described in Rom. 7. The motivation for Kretzmann's proposal of the new moral stage then falls away.

6.2 CONTINENT ACTION

6.2.1 Rational Success of the Continent Agent

With the exposition of Aquinas's view now secure, we can proceed to analyzing the strengths and weaknesses of that account. To begin this task, we shall look at how well Aquinas characterizes continent action. When we examined continent action before in the contexts of Hare's and Davidson's views, we proceeded by asking the question: what does the continent agent do right that the incontinent agent gets wrong? In Aquinas's view, the difference lies not in the agents' experience of an inordinate passion, but in their reactions to it. For the continent person remains susceptible to the same kind of strong, inappropriate passions, or "vehement evil desires," as the incontinent person (Aquinas, *EG* chap.5, lec.4; *ST* II–II q.155, a.3, resp.). A fully virtuous, temperate person might have "pruned" such passions from her character, but a continent agent still finds herself with appetites such that she "is disposed to take unreasonable pleasure" (Aquinas, *CNE* VII.L.9: C1453). Moreover, the continent person's "reason has the same disposition" as the incontinent's (Aquinas, *ST* II–II q.155, a.3, resp.). In fact, the continent agent reasons within the same kind of four-premise-syllogism structure that the incontinent person uses. The continent person has a universal premise from reason-proper, a universal premise from reason-as-passion's-tool, and particular premises that bring her considered action under the scope of the two universals, respectively (Aquinas, *OE* q.3, a.9, rep.7).

The continent agent's success lies in her rational resistance against the effects of her passion. That is, "by the vigor of [her] reason [she] holds fast" to her discretive judgment that follows from reason-proper's universal (Aquinas, *EG* chp.5, lec.6). We must note that Aquinas's phrase the "vigor of reason" here refers to both rational intellect and appetite. For Aquinas describes the continent agent's success as lying in her "resisting the passion by *holding to* the [discretive] judgment formed by [her] reason" [emphasis added] (*ST* II–II q.156, a.2, rep.2). That is, by continuing to choose based on that judgment, the agent avoids falling into incontinence; the phrase "holding to" indicates the agent's will-act of maintaining her choice. "Hence," Aquinas writes, "continence must needs reside in that power of the soul, whose act it is to choose; and that is the will" (q.155, a.3, resp.). Yet he also speaks of how the continent agent must "resist [the] passion by [her] reason," or again, of how through "the use of reason . . . [she is] able to resist [her] passions" (q.156, a.1, resp.). So the intellect works with the will in maintaining the proper choice. Intellect, with its power to attend to various aspects of the action, must remain focused on the aspects that bring the action under the scope of reason-proper's universal, in order that the will may be "moved by the reason . . . [and not be] moved by the concupiscible [appetite]" (q.155, a.3. rep.2).

For an example, suppose that our fornicating agent (from the last chapter) had been continent instead of incontinent. Recognizing her situation as one ripe for fornication and feeling her sexual appetite begin to rise, she might have mentally shaken herself or "counted to ten" while considering the consequences of having sex with her date. By such rational techniques, she might have increased her confidence in her reason-proper's deliberation, might have resolutely fixed her attention on the aspects of the action that made it unlawful—the insult it would cause God, the inordinate self-love it would "feed"—and so on. Through such effort the agent could retain and focus on her discretive judgment not to do this unlawful fornicating, and thereby maintain her choice to refrain.

In fortifying her attentiveness, then, to the particular aspects of her action that connected that action to her rational injunction against fornication, the agent might have avoided having her attention swept along by the passion. This steadfastness would have allowed her to retain the conclusion of reason-proper's deliberation, and to have chosen and acted from that conclusion, instead of from passion's (Aquinas, *CNE* VII.L.7: C1420). Thus, the continent agent experiences the inordinate passion and the inner conflict over attentiveness to particulars of the action, just as the incontinent agent does. However, her rational faculties do not fail as thoroughly as the incontinent agent's do; the continent person's reason (inclusively considered) clings attentively to, and chooses to follow through on, its discretive judgment of what rationally must be done. This rational resistance demonstrates Aquinas's earlier point that reason can avoid succumbing to the effects of passion. Therefore, we can now see that Aquinas is able to give a good account of the rational success essential to the notion of continent action.

6.2.2 Mental Conflict Experienced by the Continent Agent

Also, Aquinas can explain the mental conflict experienced by the continent person. The force of the agent's passion would war against her attempts to keep her attention focused on the rationally relevant aspects of her proposed action. More than that, the contrarily directing ends of reason-as-tool and reason-proper would then incline her will to choose for or against the action, as her attention wavered between the pleasant and rationally relevant aspects, respectively. Thus, Aquinas describes a situation in which the continent agent would experience internal struggle: a "push-pull," away from and toward the action, involving a disconcerting erosion of her own control over what she does. Indeed, the phenomena surrounding continent actions would lead us to expect just that sort of internally torn feeling in the continent agent. So Aquinas seems successful on this point as well, and his portrayal of continent action looks experientially adequate.

6.3 INNER CONFLICT EXPERIENCED DURING INCONTINENCE

Moreover, the struggle Aquinas portrays in continent action would apply also to *in*continent actions. That is, in Aquinas's view, the incontinent agent will experience the same assault against her rational control over the direction of her attention, the same push-pull in her choice for and against the action, from the ends proposed to her will by reason-as-tool and reason-proper. Observationally speaking, we would expect the incontinent agent to suffer internal conflict similar to the continent agent's; and Aquinas gives an account of akratic action in which that related struggle occurs. Initially, then, Aquinas's theory gives us a model seemingly adequate to experience.

6.3.1 Failure to Explain Clear-Eyed Akrasia *against Intentions*

However, this model falls short of accounting for the full extent of internal conflict that we observe in weak-willed agents. For in our assessment of Davidson's view, we saw that the struggle included even the experience of acting against affirmed intentions, in our sense of judgments specifically directing performance of the rationally approved action (section 4.3.1). Yet Aquinas's model does not accommodate the possibility of such conflict. Indeed, the agent's *intending* (in our sense) to perform a *certain* action would have to coincide with Aquinas's conception of the discretive judgment resulting from deliberation; for discretive judgments direct the will to perform a specified action concluded upon by the agent as the appropriate means to her end. The problem arises because, in Aquinas's view, the akratic agent cannot *retain* a discretive judgment for her rationally approved action, while she acts on her inordinate passion.

To review what we saw in the last chapter, imagine an incontinent agent who has progressed to the point of completing her deliberation and identifying the rationally approved option. When her passion affects her, so as to impede reason's functioning and to fix her attention on the pleasant aspects of the akratic option, the practical syllogism of her rational deliberation crumbles. She no longer retains its result in mind, and therefore she no longer retains her discretive judgment to act. In order, then, for the agent to act akratically, her opposed deliberation and its result must already have been abandoned. Aquinas could then account for the experience of acting against what one *previously* discretively judged to do, but he does not explain how one could experience *akrasia* in the face of a *presently* held, opposed discretive judgment.

Perhaps Aquinas might counter that when the akratic experience begins, the agent's rational deliberation still holds until her attention is fixed on the pleasant aspects of the incontinent option; in that sense, the *akrasia* would occur against a current discretive judgment. However, even in this case, *while* the incontinent action is performed, only the agent's *universal* premise's rational end opposes her action. In other words, once her deliberation collapses with the removal of its attention-based particular premise, the agent no longer possesses any judgment that regards her *specific* action as not to be done. But, as we now see, that theoretical position of Aquinas's does *not* match up with experience, for it requires his denial of what we earlier called "clear-eyed" incontinence.

Indeed, Aquinas's denial of clear-eyed incontinence presents a serious problem, because the human experience of *akrasia* definitely includes examples in which the agent recognizes and sincerely condemns the wrongfulness of her action, even as she performs it. Yet Aquinas would have us reject the possibility of such recognition and condemnation; for according to him, the incontinent agent in the throes of her passion remains ignorant of her action's wrongfulness. Since the agent "under passion's influence" does not actively attend to the particulars of her action as it fits under the scope of reason-proper's universal directive to avoid such actions, she effectively loses or forgets the knowledge of her action's rational inappropriateness. So the self-condemnations uttered by the akratically acting agent are only "mouthed" without sincerity or understanding, because the agent no longer truly regards her specified action as wrong.

However, Aquinas's assertion here does not fit well with our experience. To return to Plato's example of Leontius, we recall that even as he ogles the corpses, Leontius angrily curses his action. That anger indicates not only sincerity in Leontius's repudiation of his action, but also an *applied recognition* of the act's baseness. Leontius does not merely "say the words"; he has enough awareness and acceptance of the wrongness of corpse ogling that such a performance makes him angry, and he directs that anger to his *own* performance *while* it occurs. If I am correct, then, regarding this implication of Leontius's anger, Aquinas's model fails to account for this kind of phenomenon. Further, if Aquinas's theory requires that he deny the possibility of such experiences as Leontius, that would constitute a critical empirical inadequacy in Aquinas's view.

6.3.2 Aquinas's Problematic Interpretation of Aristotle

But does Aquinas need that denial? Or can his theory accept some alteration that would allow him to account for clear-eyed incontinence? I believe Aquinas could answer no and yes, respectively; and I shall sketch out how he could change his model to allow the currently denied phenomena. Aquinas acquires his problem here through his interpretation of Aristotle's account of incontinence. Aristotle argues that the akratic agent, while in the grip of her inordinate passion, lacks knowledge in some crucial way. In explaining just how Aristotle thinks that is so, Aquinas constructs the problematic explanatory account of incontinence. I shall argue that Aquinas's view can solve this difficulty by using a different interpretation of Aristotle's point about akratic ignorance. To understand this proposed change, then, we must first set out what Aristotle says on this matter.

Aristotle remarks that we must be careful in attributing incontinent actions to ignorance, because *before* the action an incontinent agent does judge that she should not perform it (*NE* 1145b28–32). So Aristotle tries to explain this situation by positing three ways in which someone may have knowledge of something, and yet effectively not know it, as well. First, Aristotle distinguishes between merely having knowledge and *using*, or *attending* to, that knowledge; he says that it seems quite possible to act contrary to knowledge had, but not attended to or used (1146b32–5). For instance, a person might know that spicy food upsets her stomach, but not think of that when she is given a bowl of "five-alarm" chili.

Second, Aristotle points out that someone may have knowledge in the universal, and even use it, but yet lack knowledge in the particular, or perhaps not use it at this level. Since the practical syllogism uses particulars in reaching a conclusion about how to act, mere universal knowledge seems insufficient to produce action (1147a1–3). Moreover, the particular premise conjoins a number of different facts—that *I* am the kind of agent directed by this universal premise, that *this* action fits the type described in the universal, and so on—needed to bring a proposed action under the universal's scope; therefore, the agent might not know or not attend to the knowledge of *any* of the conjuncts, and that would derail production of the action (1147a4–9).

Third, Aristotle speaks of people who are "asleep or mad or drunk" or "who have just learnt something [but need] . . . for it . . . [to] grow into them, [which takes] . . . time" (1147a14–22). All of these can have knowledge, even to "saying the words that come from knowledge," and yet because of their state can truly *not have* the knowledge (1147a14–20). Again, such possession of knowledge cannot reliably guide action.

Then Aristotle puts these pieces together to explain how incontinent agents can lack knowledge they have shown they do possess. Aristotle says that, regarding the particular premise of reason's practical syllogism, the akratic agent "does not have [it] when [she] is being affected [by passion]. Or rather the way [she] has it is not knowledge of it, but . . . [merely] saying the words, as the drunk [does]" (1147b12–14). Moreover, this "last term" involving "only perceptual knowledge" is "not the sort that seems to be knowledge to the full extent," and during an akratic action that knowledge is "present" but "dragged about" by passion (1147b15–19). So the incontinent agent does not act on her knowledge, since she "is not in the condition of someone who knows and is attending [to her knowledge], but in the condition of one asleep or drunk" (1152a9–15).

Now, Aquinas—quite plausibly—interprets Aristotle's somewhat cryptic comments to mean this: the first distinction between having and using, or attending to, knowledge refers to the difference between simply possessing a piece of knowledge somewhere in one's mind and *actively, consciously* considering that piece of knowledge. Aquinas calls the former kind *habitual* knowledge and the latter, *active* or *actual* knowledge (*CNE* VII.L.3: C1338). For he thinks of a habit as involving a disposition toward, a readiness for, activity; habit implies a *potential* for activity (Aquinas, *TV* q.49, a.3, rep. 1). Hence the name "habitual" refers to knowledge ready for use, but not actively considered. Aquinas also notes that active, but not habitual, knowledge seems necessarily to guide action

(*CNE* VII.L.3: C1338). For example, I have habitual knowledge of the number that is 13 × 13; but unless I actively consider that by doing the math, I might well answer incorrectly that the square of 13 is greater than 169 (for some reason, I keep thinking it's 225).

Further, Aquinas elaborates on Aristotle's remarks about the importance of knowing in the universal *and the particular*. Aquinas points out that since actions deal with singulars (moving *this* sofa, drinking *that* glass of soda, etc.) the knowledge in the practical syllogism's particular premise holds "the foremost place" in determining action (*ST* I–II q.77, a.2, rep.1). He adds the habitual/active distinction to this idea and notes that it then seems quite possible to act contrary to both universal and particular knowledge, if only the universal is active, with the particular being known only habitually (*CNE* VII.L.3: C1339). In other words, if the particular knowledge is not actively considered but remains habitual, a person can act counter to even particular knowledge (Aquinas, *ST* I–II q.77, a.2).

Aquinas then uses these ideas to construct the kind of explanation that I discussed earlier and presented as problematic. The akratic passion distracts the agent's attention in the particulars; thus, while the passion holds sway, it prevents the agent from actively considering her particular knowledge that would link her action to reason-proper's directive (I–II q.77, a.2). So the agent in the throes of passion does not actively recognize that reason-proper's universal applies to her proposed action (Aquinas, *CNE* VII.L.3: C1340). That allows her to act contrary to her active universal and *habitual* particular knowledge; for to suppose that she could act counter to knowledge that is "actual, concerned with the particular" would "seem unreasonable" (VII.L.3: C1341). Indeed, Aquinas stresses repeatedly that given the habitual/active knowledge distinction and the emphasis on particular knowledge's importance for action, only reason-proper's universal premise can remain active during the akratic action; the passion must keep both the particular rational premise and the conclusion that would follow as nothing more than "restrained" habitual knowledge (VII.L.3: C1352; *ER* chp.7 lec.3). Thus, "the evaluation of the sensible [particulars] . . . is dragged along by passion" (VII.L.3: C1352). That leaves the agent no longer actively knowing the rational particulars or the rational conclusion, but—as we saw earlier—only "saying the words" to that conclusion, through being in a state like the drunk person mentioned in Aristotle's last point (VII.L.3: C1342). In this way, Aquinas arrives at his denial of the possibility of clear-eyed incontinence.

As much as his position will allow, however, Aquinas does try to admit the incontinent agent's recognition of her own wrongdoing. Aquinas stresses that the akratic agent's ignorance of her particular wrongdoing is *voluntary* and culpable on her part, since she could have resisted the passion (*ST* I–II q.77, a.7, rep. 2). Further, that ignorance lasts only as long as the passion holds sway; immediately before and after, the agent's state "quickly changes" so that her rationally deliberated conclusion becomes active (I–II q.77, a.2, rep. 2; *CNE* VII.L.8: C1430). Thus, the akratic agent does resist her action before-hand, and regrets and repudiates it after she performs it. Yet none of those kinds of recognition solves Aquinas's central problem; he still must claim that *while* she acts on her passion, the incontinent agent cannot even actively rec-ognize the pertinent aspects of her action's wrongfulness, let alone the con-clusion of that wrongfulness itself. Unfortunately, that clearly contradicts the phenomena of our experience with weakness of will.

6.4 CORRECTING THE ACCOUNT OF CLEAR-EYED INCONTINENCE

6.4.1 Alternative Interpretation of Aristotle

However, Aquinas's view can perhaps solve this difficulty by utilizing a different interpretation of Aristotle's argument about knowing and not knowing. For some modern commentators—R. M. Hare, Richard Robin-son, and Terence Irwin, for example—agree with Aquinas's interpretation (Hare, "WW" 1,305; Robinson, 80–3; Irwin, "Notes" 352). Yet others—like Norman Dahl, David Charles, and Sarah Broadie—do not. The latter group argues that Aristotle *did* allow for clear-eyed incontinence, in which the agent judges against her action even as she performs it (Broadie, 282; Dahl, 215). They point to statements of Aristotle's, such as "the incontinent per-son notices that [she] is incontinent," to confirm his general acceptance of clear-eyed incontinence (*NE* 1150b35).

More specifically, they claim that Aristotle's distinction between hav-ing and attending to, or using, knowledge means something different from Aquinas's interpretation. When understood correctly, this distinction not only confirms Aristotle's allowance of clear-eyed *akrasia*, but also helps to explain that phenomenon's possibility. Now since Aristotle's view is not our primary focus, we cannot take the time to explore the textual arguments here, so we shall have to make do with simply summarizing the conclusions.

First, regarding negative arguments against Aquinas's interpretation, David Charles reiterates that *akrasia* essentially involves voluntarily or in-tentionally acting against one's better judgment. Further, as we saw earlier (section 5.1.2), voluntariness requires that the agent intellectually grasp what she does. So she can voluntarily do only what she understands herself to be doing. Also, in Aristotle's account, the practical syllogism of reason (proper) would exemplify the agent's better judgment. However, Charles points out, if an akratic agent voluntarily acts against her better judgment, then she must understand that violation in her grasp of her action. Yet without some active understanding of reason's particular premise and conclusion, the agent has no better judgment in mind to understand that she is violating it. Hence she cannot *voluntarily* perform such a violation. Therefore, if Aristotle were relying on the agent's not actively recognizing her wrongdoing, his explanation would not fit akratic actions. So Aristotle's talk of the incontinent agent's "not knowing" must refer to some state other than purely propositional ignorance (Charles, 120).

Along the same lines, Dahl claims that "traditional" interpretations like Aquinas's would commit Aristotle to foolishly obvious errors. Right off, such an interpretation forces a denial of clear-eyed incontinence—as we have seen in depth. Further, though, the effective ignorance of reason's particular premise would require that the agent not notice basic aspects of her action. But that seems ludicrous, since it would demand that the agent somehow miss or forget obvious facts about what she does (Dahl, 152–3). For instance, the fornicating agent from our example would somehow have to remain *unaware* that she was fornicating, that her action was morally wrong, and so on. Yet the very idea of incontinence demands that the agent be aware of just such facts, which are, in any case, so basic to her action that it seems deeply implausible that she could not actively notice them. Again, then, we reach a charitable conclusion that Aristotle must have meant something different from the traditional interpretation.

Second, regarding positive arguments for an alternative interpretation, Dahl makes his case based on Aristotle's conception of practical knowledge. According to Dahl, Aristotle regards knowledge as practical in its capacity to motivate actions; that is, *practical* knowledge has the "function . . . to (help) produce action" (148). Such knowledge becomes perfected in *phronesis*, the virtue of practical wisdom, which is "*full* and *complete* practical knowledge" (148). The completely realized knowledge of *phronesis*, then, *cannot* fail to bring about action, because the rational directives have been fully incorporated into the agent's character, so that her desires and dispositions accord with them. But any level of practical knowledge less than that ideal *can* fail (202). Dahl explains how by appealing to Aristotle's practical-realm distinction between having and using knowledge. It refers to the difference between knowing something as a piece of information in one's head, and *integrating* that knowledge into one's character so that the information *must* guide action (209–10). For example, if I know from my dentist that I should brush my teeth because the activity prevents cavities, then I have that bit of practical knowledge. If I brush my teeth regularly until I like doing so, and observe my dental checkups improving, then I am *using* that knowledge. Indeed, I know that information more fully through my use—through my conforming my dispositions to it and through my confirming experiences. Both of those factors make the knowledge more efficacious in producing action; they make it more *practical*.

In the case of the akratic agent, Dahl says Aristotle does *not* mean that such a person "has" knowledge in the sense of possessing but not actively considering it. Rather, this agent merely "has" knowledge in the sense that she has not incorporated it into her character fully enough for it to necessarily guide action. Thus, she fails to "use" her knowledge, since it remains inactive in directing her behavior (209–10). On this account, Aristotle can allow the akratic agent to actively consider all the particular, perceptual knowledge relevant to her action; she may even actively consider the result of her rational deliberation. All that consideration now counts only as *having* knowledge, and can occur even while the agent akratically acts; for it is such particular knowledge (since the deliberated judgment concerns particulars, too) that Aristotle claimed was "dragged about by passion" (210–11). In this picture, the akratic agent resembles not the drunk so much as the new learners whose "practical principles have not yet become 'a part of themselves'" (210).

David Charles largely concurs with this portrayal. He sees Aristotle as claiming that akratic agents fail to accept their deliberated conclusions in a way that would motivate action; they hold the conclusions in an "off-color" way, practically speaking (120). They do not make the knowledge part of themselves, in the sense of curbing and modifying their desires to fit the knowledge's directive. Their *rational evaluations* of their desires are still out of sync with those desires' *motivational strengths* (149). Thus, these agents can know intellectually what they ought to do, even as they violate that knowledge because their passions prevent them from using the knowledge—from knowing practically, in the sense of accepting it in a way that brings their desires into line with it, so that the knowledge would motivate action (167).

Sarah Broadie, too, argues similarly. She claims Aristotle's view in no way depends upon the akratic agent's suffering some *cognitive* ignorance, since "having" knowledge includes the contemplation of it. Instead, the agent fails to use the knowledge by acting upon it; Aristotle calls that "acting in ignorance," because the agent acts *without benefit of the knowledge*—that is, *as if she did not know it* (Broadie, 288–9). So Broadie also maintains that

Aristotle meant "use" and "attend to" to indicate *using in action*, at least when referring to knowledge in practical matters (294–5). For she takes Aristotle to be defining practical knowledge as essentially involving *doing*; failure to do then indicates practical ignorance (291). The have/use distinction is similar, but not identical, to the potential/actual distinction (294). Use is the "final actuality of what is possessed" thus, using knowledge is truly "*knowledge* in the strict and primary sense of the term," and failure to use is *practical* ignorance "in the primary sense" (291). Moreover, Broadie attributes Aristotle's statement that *akrasia* occurs through ignorance of the particulars to the fact that the particular-level knowledge shows the opportunity for action; that point is where the akratic agent's use-failure occurs, in not taking the opportunity by acting (302). Thus, in Broadie's construal, too, Aristotle can allow clear-eyed incontinence (282).

From these commentators, then, we draw this view of Aristotle's position on practical reason: Fully actualized practical knowledge does not merely cover practical matters, questions of action, but is practical in its effect, by producing action. Anthony Kenny, whose overall interpretation of Aristotle on incontinence is actually closer to the traditional line, nevertheless characterizes practical reason best by saying that, "practical knowledge . . . thrusts towards action" (161). If an item of practical knowledge is used and not merely had—if it is "operative" and not merely "present"— then it brings on the next step in the action-process:

> A practical generalization, a universal premise, will be operative when consequences are drawn from it that are more particular [that is, when it leads to deliberation.] . . . A particular premise will be operative when it leads to a practical conclusion being drawn . . . when . . . [it] leads to the decision. . . . A practical conclusion, in its turn, is operative when it is actually acted upon. (161)

Moreover, the ends that reason uses as directives can only become fully known, and so become operative, over time. For such ends must be integrated into one's character by training and habituation that shape one's dispositions and desires into agreement with acting on the end (Dahl, 147; Charles, 180; Broadie, *EA* 269). Aligning the dispositions in this way then conjoins reason's guidance with motive power to act.

Thus, it is possible intellectually to affirm an end, and yet to need to integrate it more in order for it to effectively motivate action (Dahl, 147). No purely intellectual or merely cognitive grasp of an end can necessitate action (Broadie, 285). Such knowledge has not become fully actualized

(Kenny, 160–1). Agents at this stage still "lack knowledge in the sense that their practical principles have not yet become 'a part of themselves'" (Dahl, 209–10). Only when the knowledge infuses one's character can it count as practical knowledge in the fullest sense; only then will it suffer no danger of failing to produce action (Charles, 180; Dahl, 148).

Aristotle sums up this conception of practical reason when he says, "the function of what thinks about action [that is, practical reason] is truth agreeing with correct desire" (*NE* 1139a30). A person must repeatedly act on reason's ends, then, to align her dispositions with them, for

> [r]eason does not teach the origins [that is, the ends] . . . in actions; it is virtue, either natural or habituated [that is, through practice in doing right actions], that teaches correct belief about the origin. (1151a17–19)

Further, when reason's ends have not achieved full integration and complete realization, passions can intrude by foisting their own "ends" upon reason. In that way, a passion, unapproved by rational standards, can cause action (1149a35–b1).

Moreover, just as we saw with the traditional interpretation, the agent's acquiescence to passion represents a kind of *rational failure*, since passion's end falls short of the requirement for rationally acting (Broadie, 290). Yet passion's end does identify an apparent good—for example, pleasantness— about the action, so such action does not occur without some reason, and the action has some degree of rational explicability (Charles, 146, 149). Because that identified good is incommensurate with the good of rationality (which we saw earlier, section 5.1.6), acting on passion's end does not commit the agent to outright logical contradiction, even if the agent reaches and retains the results of her rational deliberation (137). That is, under the new interpretation proposed, the agent may have in mind at one time all four premises of her practical syllogism; she may even act out passion's conclusion while still keeping in mind reason's deliberated result. So the agent sees that her action falls under reason's end, even as she acts from her passion (Dahl, 206). Her irrationality is not a mere "failure to entertain or believe something proposition-like" (210). Further, while reason's and passion's final directives urge *contrary* courses of action, because the two focus on the incommensurate values of rationality and pleasure, respectively, they do not *logically* contradict. Thus, even this newly allowed case of clear-eyed incontinence involves a rational failure but does not depend on simple logical error. This alternative interpretation appears to cohere, then, with Aristotle's— and Aquinas's—views of how the akratic agent rationally fails.

Furthermore, the alternative interpretation not only allows for clear-eyed incontinence, but also may help to explain how people can act incontinently in the face of opposing intentions (in our sense). For in this view, the agent retains the results of her rational deliberation; she has in mind a deliberated judgment—a directive referring to a specific action. Thus, while the agent akratically acts, she may experience the more intense internal conflict deriving from reason's specifically directing one action and passion's specifically urging an opposed action. In Dahl's words, the agent enters "a genuine state of conflict" in which she is "prevented from doing . . . [what she rationally judges, by a] strong conflicting desire" (215). Indeed, Dahl's and the others' accounts of practical reason's relationship to an agent's desires and dispositions help to show how such conflict can occur. The commentators explicate how the rational evaluation of desires can diverge from their brute motivational strengths, until the latter are brought in line through experience and practice. In so doing, the interpretation forwarded by Dahl and the others both illuminates the manner in which reason can suffer from motivational insufficiency and exposes the possibility of effective opposition to reason's guidance in the presence of an agent's non–experientially integrated desires and dispositions. Thus, the alternative interpretation seems to augment the empirical adequacy and explanatory power of Aristotle's position.

6.4.2 Adapting Aquinas to Fit the Alternative Interpretation

Now, in the context of our current analysis of Aquinas's system, we need to investigate whether Aquinas can accommodate the new interpretation of Aristotle. So we shall not pursue the interpretive controversy between Aquinas and Dahl, Charles, and Broadie. Instead, in order to continue our primary examination, let us assume that Aristotle thought along the alternative lines plotted by Dahl and the others. Then we can see whether Aquinas's model of human action can successfully adapt to the changes required for incorporating this different interpretation of Aristotle.

I think the Thomistic explanatory framework *can* adapt. Given the enormous scope of Aquinas's writings, I cannot definitively prove my claim here; that would take a separate work of detailed, wide-ranging textual scholarship. However, I shall offer an argument showing why Aquinas's system should have the ability to accept the necessary changes.

First, then, Aquinas's view of practical reason suits the alternative interpretation. He writes, "practical reason . . . is directed to action" (*Treatise on Law* q.94, a.2, resp.). And for reason effectively to produce action, it has to work in conjunction with "right desire [which] is a good will" (Aquinas,

TH q.19, a.3, obj.2). In other words, to generate action and achieve "rectitude," or rightness or correctness, "reason depends upon its conformity to the desire of a due end," even though "this very desire of the due end presupposes a right understanding of the end, and this is the work of reason" (q.19, a.3, rep.2). So for Aquinas, reason first needs to correctly apprehend the ends for human action, the goods of human life; but then, in order to actually produce actions, the rational appetite must be right, in that it approves those ends and the particular actions which are the means to attain them (*CNE* VI.L.2: C1131). However, even in reason's initial apprehension of the ends, it needs the will to be "right enough" for those true goods to seem so, to be appealing, to the agent. In Aquinas's words, "rectitude of the appetitive faculty [that is, the will] in regard to the end is the measure of truth for the practical reason" (VI.L.2: C1131). That means that the perfection of practical reason, present in the virtue of prudence (which Aristotle called *phronesis*), is inextricable from a rightly oriented will (Aquinas, *TH* q.19, a.3, rep.2). Thus, as we saw in the alternative interpretation of Aristotle, "the good of the practical intellect is . . . the 'conformable' truth, i.e., corresponding to a right appetitive faculty" (Aquinas, *CNE* VI.L.2: C1130).

Moreover, Aquinas further explicates the reason–rational appetite relationship by affirming Aristotle's statement that reason's ends become fully known only through time and experience. Aquinas writes that understanding requires that information learned become "connatural" to the agent; the new beliefs need to "be confirmed" over time and by "much meditation"— only then are they "impressed perfectly on [the agent's] mind" (*CNE* VII.L.3: C1344). And again, Aquinas maintains that, although the ends that direct action are grasped *in* and *by* reason, we do not fully accept those ends *through* reasoning. That is, we do not merely think and reason our way to these ends; instead, an agent "acquires right evaluation regarding the principles of things to be done, i.e., the end, by the habit of virtue either natural or learned by custom" (VII.L.8: C1431). For that is how to orient the will rightly enough that correct rational apprehension can occur. So a person may learn a rational end—say, that fornication is unlawful and to be avoided—and believe it, but yet not *fully know* its truth until having practiced acting on it, over time.

Given that Aquinas accepts this point, he can accommodate the further notion that ends not known in the full experiential sense may not reliably guide action. In fact, we just saw that he regards prudence, practical reason's virtue, as requiring a rightly ordered will, which in turn requires practice in right action. In addition, Aquinas holds that knowledge of how to act becomes fully active, or actualized, through *use in action*. Aquinas writes,

"There is a twofold relationship of the will to what it wills" (*TH* q.16, a.4, resp.). Likewise, "reason can enjoin or declare something in two ways" (q.17, a.1, resp.). In the will, the distinction falls between the will's taking on "some proportion or order to [the] willed thing," and the will's "mov[ing] to possess an end really, which is to possess it perfectly" (q.16, a.4, resp.). In reason, the distinction lies between reason's directive to act being "expressed by a verb in the indicative mood," and reason's "impelling [a person] to [an action], and then [the directive] is expressed by a verb in the imperative mood" (q.17, a.1, resp.).

Commenting on this double relation, Ralph McInerny explains that Aquinas distinguishes the "order of intention" from the "order of execution" within a human action. The former process culminates in choice, and settles the will—or "orders" or "proportions" it—toward the action required to achieve the end proposed in the intellect. The latter process includes command and use, and concerns *actually acquiring* the desired good (McInerny, 182).

Aquinas draws the line between choice and command because up until choice, the action-process concerns specifying an intention (in our sense), narrowing the will's orientation from a general approval of a kind of action to an inclination to do *this specific* action. From that point on, reason does not make its directives any more specific, but changes the *manner* of its direction, as Aquinas says, from indicative to imperative. Discretive judgment, we recall from the elaboration of the action process (section 5.1.3), still only indicates, or points out, an action: "Action *x* ought to be done." The will's choice then completes the *intending* of the action; now the agent wants to do a certain, specified thing. Command, however, does just that: "Do action *x*!" This reason–act expresses motive force and kicks off the actual *doing* of the action. Reason becomes imperative by channeling the appetitive force of the will's choice. In Aquinas's words,

> And because the power of a prior act carries over into the act which follows, there can be an act of reason [namely, command] which retains something from the power of the will's act [of choice]. (*TH* q.17, a.1, resp.)

Then the will-act use simply applies that appetitive force to the various faculties involved in the action's performance. Thus, Aquinas puts discretive judgment and choice in the first order, of intending an action, and command and use in the second order, of doing or executing the action (q.16, a.4, resp.).

Now, since the order of execution "relates to the good as it exists and not simply as it is known," it is "more perfect" than the order of intention (McInerny, 181–2). After all, having is the goal of wanting, so having—or even getting—fulfills, or perfects, the wanting (Aquinas, *TH* q.16, a.4, resp.). Thus, the executive reason- and will-acts are more perfect than the intentional-order ones. In other words, reason's end becomes more actualized, more fully realized, in executing the action than in simply directing the act. Moreover, the difference between the indicative-mood discretive judgment and the imperative-mood command is not a matter of more perfect comprehension, but of more perfect actualization, by means of the acquisition of motive force to act. That corresponds to the alternative interpretation of Aristotle, in which practical knowledge becomes complete only when the agent's desires and dispositions are aligned with it. And for Aquinas, as we just saw, the way to produce that level of correct practical judgment is through habit and custom—in short, through *practice* (*CNE* VII.L.8: C1431). Again, that matches the alternative interpretation of Aristotle. Indeed, Aquinas thinks practice is so crucial that he writes, "That is why moral science is said to avail little for the acquisition of virtue, because even when it is had a [person] can sin against virtue" (*DQV* q.1, a.6, rep.1).

Therefore, Aquinas should be able to distinguish between "attending to," as implying use of knowledge in action, and "having," as implying complete awareness, but not involving acting. His conception of practical reason provides the groundwork ready to build on, in order to construct an explanation of *akrasia* by using the alternative interpretation of Aristotle's "have/attend to" knowledge-distinction.

Second, Aquinas's conception of a velleity, or incomplete willing, can be expanded to give a more comprehensive account of how an agent may have, but fail to use, practical knowledge. We recall (from section 6.1.1) that Aquinas regards a velleity as stopping short of reason's deliberations and discretive judgment; it is a willing limited, somehow, to intention (in Aquinas's sense) or even to the simple volition expressing general favorableness (*ST* III q.21, a.4, resp.). He also characterizes velleities as willings, particularly for something we recognize is impossible (App.1, q.1, a.2, rep.2; *TH* q.13, a.5, rep.1). For example, if I intend (in Aquinas's sense) to visit my extended family and begin deliberating about how to do so, but then realize that I have neither the time nor the money to make that 2,000-mile journey, the development of my intention is thwarted and it remains a velleity. Because deliberation revealed insurmountable obstacles, I am left with merely a general wistfulness toward visiting; that is, I am not "grieved" and frustrated at my failure to visit, as I would be if I had discretively judged for, and chosen, a road trip and had my car die just when I departed (Aquinas, *ST* App.1, q.1, a.2, rep.2). An incomplete willing, then, is a "feeble" thing that does not amount to a full intention (in our sense) to act (Aquinas, *ER* bk.7, lec.3).

We recall, too, that those limitations on velleities convinced Norman Kretzmann that incontinence must not depend on incomplete willings (section 6.1.1). For if an agent's rational directives were incomplete willings that did not extend to deliberation and discretive judgment, then her weak-willed action would never be clear-eyed, occurring "even though and even while [she] *knows* better" (Kretzmann, 180, 193 n.51). Yet we also saw that Kretzmann was mistaken, that Aquinas both did appeal to velleities in explaining incontinence and was, in fact, unable to account for clear-eyed *akrasia* (sections 6.1.2 and 6.3.1).

However, I maintain that Aquinas correctly appeals to incomplete willings, but that he should extend the umbrella of that concept to cover *any attempted human action that stops short of completion in the will-act use.* In fact, Aquinas has no compelling reason to limit velleities as he does, except his commitment to the traditional interpretation of Aristotle. His troublesome Aristotelian characterization, of the akratic agent's having knowledge but not actively considering it, forces Aquinas to restrict a velleity from reaching discretive judgment. Apart from that Aristotelian limitation, Aquinas says several things that actually support the more extensive conception of velleity. So with the old interpretation of Aristotle discarded, Aquinas faces no significant obstacle in expanding what counts as a velleity.

In support of the more extensive concept, Aquinas makes the very telling statement that was noted in the elaboration of human action (section 5.1.3):

> The fact that a command and a commanded act [carried out by use] *can be separated from each other* shows that they are many as to parts. [Emphasis added.] (*TH* q.17, a.4, rep.2)

For what does "can be separated" mean, except that a human act can abort even at the stage of command, so that use—and thereby the performance—do not occur? And, as I mentioned at the earlier citation, that separability applies more broadly than to command alone; human acts can stop short of performance by being aborted at any of the reason- and will-acts prior to use. Indeed, that may well constitute the rationale behind Aquinas's original division of the various will- and reason-acts involved in producing a human action. That is, some commentators have analyzed why Aquinas distinguishes so many different acts—like deliberation, choice, use, and so on—in the production of one human action. Among those investigators, both Alan

Donagan and Ralph McInerny have concluded that Aquinas does not base these act-distinctions on introspection; in most human actions, we could not discern so many separate acts. Instead, Donagan and McInerny maintain—rightly, I believe—that Aquinas distinguishes the parts based on points at which an agent *may fail to complete an action*, once begun (McInerny, 179; Donagan, "Thomas Aquinas on Human Action" 654).

Now, interestingly, after having applauded Aquinas's reason for subdividing a human action, Donagan accuses him of *mistakenly* proposing the subdivisions of command and use. Since, if Donagan is correct, that would eliminate the order of execution and would thereby seriously damage Aquinas's ability to adopt the alternative interpretation of Aristotle, we need to stop and examine Donagan's charges. Donagan claims that if use

> belongs to the second relation of the will to the thing willed . . . namely, the relation it has when the willed [thing] is something really possessed—then the executive power by which the willed [thing] has been brought about must already have been exercised. (652)

In other words, if use concerns having the thing willed, then that action that acquires what is desired must already be over. Hence, Donagan claims, use should reductively "be identified with choice. And [command] . . . should simply be identified with the [discretive] judgment with which deliberation terminates" (652). For that is where the *doing* of the action occurs.

Indeed, Aquinas seems to admit what Donagan charges. He writes that "choice is . . . a principle of action, and so of motion, i.e. in the manner of an *efficient* cause" [emphasis added] (*CNE* VI.L.2: C1133). So Aquinas himself seems to cite choice as the will-act that executes the action, since the nature of an efficient cause is to make the effect happen by application of motive force. In that case, though, the separate executive order collapses, and Aquinas seems left with no way to explain how an agent might fail to perform an action if she has an intention (in our sense) to perform it—once again, accounting for clear-eyed *akrasia* falls out of reach.

However, happily, such is not the case, because Donagan is mistaken. He misses the import of a subtlety in Aquinas's wording. For Aquinas describes the will's second relation to its object as "wherein the will *tends to the realization* of what is willed" [emphasis added] (*TH* q.16, a.4, resp.). That phrase, "tends to the realization," indicates that executing an action requires more than just a flick of the will's inclination-switch, like choice; it is a *process* that takes *continued effort* all the way through. McInerny, who defends Aquinas against Donagan, puts it this way:

> What Donagan has lost sight of here is the dynamic character of the or-
> der of execution. He takes it to be the order of having already been ex-
> ecuted. . . . [He] simply does not do justice to the difference Thomas sees
> between the intentional and executive orders. . . . Where Thomas sees
> the dramatic emergence of the existential, Donagan sees merely the ex-
> ternal appearance of the intentional chain. (182)

Use, then, does not occur after an action is over when its object is gotten,
but occurs during the action in the process of getting. And command then
marks the transition of crossing the existential "hump," moving from deciding to doing.

Moreover, distinguishing command and use does have observational
justification. As McInerny points out, it is clear that "sometimes the most
suitable means is found [that is, discretively judged] and chosen, and the act
is stopped" (181). For instance, Donagan's action-model would not be able
to account for our earlier illustration of Samson's choice to break his bonds,
which was foiled by his unnoticed haircut. Are we to believe Samson really
had not made up his mind to break free? Because "if choice were use, only
fulfilled acts could be said to involve choice" (181). Further, as mentioned
above, Donagan's model would wholly rule out the possibility of clear-eyed
incontinence; an agent could *never* maintain an intention (in our sense) to
act and yet not act despite a lack of external hindrance—which is exactly
what observation tells us occurs. So Donagan's reconstruction is empirically
implausible.

More than that, Aquinas says several things that not only validate the
distinctions of command and use, but also support the extended concept of
velleity, particularly as it pertains to weak-willed actions. In one instance,
Aquinas asserts that even command is not enough to ensure a complete
willing; he writes,

> An imperfect [that is, ineffective] command occurs when reason is
> moved by opposing motives to command or not to command, and so it
> fluctuates between the two and does not command perfectly. (*TH* q.17,
> a.5, rep.1)

So Aquinas clearly thinks choice—which precedes command—must not
involve executing the chosen action, since the action can fail even at a stage
past choice. When Aquinas refers to choice as action's efficient cause, then,
he must mean that choice generates the motive force that, *if* command and
use engage it, initiates action. In other words, if nothing goes wrong in command and use, choice's motivational impetus will cause action. Moreover,

the passage just quoted shows that Aquinas recognizes command as distinct from use, and not simply because of the possibility of external impediments to performance, as in the Samson example. Rather, Aquinas sees that command can fail due to *internal, voluntary* conditions.

He elaborates on that problem when he discusses the effects of lust on reason's guidance of action. Now for Aquinas, since incontinence most particularly refers to actions involving loss of rational control in the face of inordinate desires for physical pleasure, actions derailed by lust present paradigm cases of incontinence. For "concupiscence [in sense 2 of inordinate desire] . . . especially pertains to lust" (Aquinas, *OE* q.15, a.4, rep.1). Aquinas writes,

> Now sexual pleasure, which is the end or object of lust, is the most intense of physical pleasures. . . . [Accordingly, lust] has . . . daughters . . . [namely,] blindness of mind, thoughtlessness, inconstancy, [and] temerity. (q.15, a.4, resp.)

By "daughters" Aquinas means specific deleterious effects, and he distinguishes these four because they refer to lust's damage to the reason–acts involved in a human action. He explains,

> Now there are four acts of reason according to which it directs human acts: the first of which is an understanding by which a person judges rightly about the end which is . . . the starting point or principle in practical matters . . . and inasmuch as this is impeded "blindness of mind" is assigned as a daughter of lust. . . . The second act is counsel [or deliberation] about things to be done, which is precluded by [lust] . . . and in regard to this, "thoughtlessness" is assigned. The third act is [discretive] judgment about the things to be done, and this too is impeded by lust . . . and in regard to this, "temerity" is assigned, namely, when a person is inclined to consent [and choose] rashly without waiting for the [discretive] judgment of reason. The fourth act is command about the thing to be done, which likewise is impeded by lust, inasmuch as a person does not remain steadfast in [her] decision about what [she] should do . . . and in regard to this, "inconstancy" is assigned. (q.15, a.4, resp.)

Given this explanation, we can see that Aquinas recognizes that lust can derail reason's guidance *throughout* the action, including the executive order.

Lust's first daughter, blindness of mind, concerns not incontinence, but the vice of *intemperance*. For in this case the agent no longer grasps the correct ends for action. She does not know what to do; she acts on the irrational ends supplied by lust and is unconflicted in so doing. Lust's second daughter pertains to *impetuous* incontinence, since the thoughtless agent acts on her lust before thinking through what reason would counsel. The third daughter, *temerity*, also applies to the impetuous agent, since she consents and chooses without waiting for reason's verdict in discretive judgment. But the fourth daughter, *inconstancy*, clearly refers to the *weak* incontinent, our investigation's focus. And again, it is worth stressing that the reason-act foiled by inconstancy is *not* deliberation or discretive judgment—as would be expected in accord with Aquinas's interpretation of Aristotle—but *command*.

The upshot is not only that command yet again is distinguished from discretive judgment, but also that we have good reason to believe Aquinas would welcome an expanded concept of velleity, since he already seems to be employing it in spite of his stated, restricted definition. Further, utilizing the extended concept gives Aquinas the tools to explain how the rational *guidance* of action can fail without the rational *comprehension* being mistaken. Aquinas recognizes the possibility that an agent may finish her deliberation and choose an action, and still not perform the action, due to failure in the follow-through acts of command and use. But that connects immediately to the alternate interpretation of Aristotle, in that Aquinas strengthens the distinction between having in mind knowledge of how one ought to act, and using that knowledge to actually do the action. So again, it appears that Aquinas's system has the capacity to accommodate the alternate interpretation of Aristotle.

Third, Aquinas's psychology should be able to allow clear-eyed *akrasia*. Kretzmann, having maintained that incontinence must involve complete willings, pointed out that it would be impossible for those willings to be simultaneous, as clear-eyed incontinence requires (189). And truly, it would be impossible for an agent's will simultaneously to use her faculties to both perform and not perform an action. But if clear-eyed *akrasia* involves only an incomplete willing—even a nearly complete one—for reason-proper's end, then Aquinas's psychology can admit that. For only reason-acts and the will-acts *prior to use* would need to be present simultaneously, in contrary veins. And that should be possible.

Aquinas already accepts the possibility of an agent's simultaneously having in mind more than one intention (in his sense). Indeed, Aquinas thinks such simultaneous intentions need not focus on the same action—as for instance, if someone were to wash dishes not only to clean them, but also to play with soap bubbles. Instead, Aquinas writes, even "if two things are not ordered to one another [that is, they are not accomplished by the same action], [a person] can still intend several things at the same time" (*TH* q.13, a.3, resp.).

Now, to extend Aquinas's recognition, we can point to the ever-present facet of human labor that modern business has dubbed "multitasking." Given the obvious fact that people can and do perform more than one human action at once, Aquinas must admit the possibility of an agent simultaneously having in mind the discretive judgments, choices, and commands to perform different actions. For example, an agent might simultaneously make discretive judgments, choices, and commands to drive her car and also to talk on her cell phone. In this case, she can perform the actions simultaneously; both uses can occur together (although, perhaps, not well, as many drivers might attest). And nothing in Aquinas's view forces him to deny this kind of occurrence.

Of course, if the agent's discretive judgments directed *contrary* actions, she could not carry out both judgments simultaneously. But could she not at least possess such contrary judgments together in her mind? Perhaps even make the choices and issue the commands? Indeed, that would be the case in the mind of a clear-eyed akratic agent. This point would then dovetail with the expanded concept of incomplete willing: If an agent can simultaneously possess contrary discretive judgments, then the clear-eyed incontinent agent does so, with one judgment directing her to act on her inordinate passion, and another (from reason-proper) directing her to refrain. However, the latter constitutes knowledge she merely has, but does not attend to through practice, leaving this willing incomplete because she does not choose it wholeheartedly enough to enforce an effective command for use. So her discretive judgment from reason-as-passion's-tool inclines her will's effective choice and use, instead. Thus, a Thomistic account could accurately describe the inner conflict occurring in the weak-willed agent, even to describing how she might act incontinently in the face of an opposing discretive judgment.

Aquinas could then fully employ the alternative Aristotelian characterization of the incontinent agent as someone who has knowledge—even particular knowledge—of how to act, but who does not attend to that knowledge by giving it complete actualization and confirmation in action. The agent *knows* what she should do, in the sense of having a fully particularized, rational directive for action—a discretive judgment; but she *lacks knowledge*, in the sense that she has not fully activated what she knows, by acting and conforming her character to it. That lack of knowledge-incorporation allows her to experience inordinate passions, which can usurp the guidance of her actively considered—but not fully, practically known—

rational deliberations. The agent remains clear-eyed in her *consideration* of the action, but she *acts* from passion. In this way, Aquinas could avoid having to saddle the incontinent agent with that implausible ignorance concerning reason's particular directives for action.

Fourth, and finally, Aquinas may well be better able to accommodate the alternative interpretation than Aristotle himself could. In giving the preferred interpretation, Dahl admits that it leaves Aristotle with a number of questions concerning the seeming brokenness of the human faculties for action that are difficult for him to answer. For instance, given that voluntary action should proceed from reason, why or how can passions arise so strongly that they can overcome actively considered rational deliberation? Or again, why or how do humans come to have this liability, this susceptibility of reason to passion? In other words, why should the human action-faculties have these kinds of flaws and vulnerabilities (Dahl, 214)? Honestly, I do not know whether Aristotle could satisfactorily answer those queries. In contrast, with the doctrine of original sin already integral to his view, Aquinas can deal easily with those questions. In fact, we have already seen such answers in our brief discussion on the instability of rational deliberation and the disordering effects of sin (sections 5.3.1–5.3.3). Aquinas's theory of human action describes a system operating under *damaged* conditions. Aquinas does not need to adduce auxiliary explanations for the vulnerabilities of the human faculties for action; those justifications emerge as natural implications of his central tenets that human beings have been disordered by original sin, and that we further damage ourselves through our own active sins. I think, therefore, that Aquinas may well be better able to accommodate the alternative interpretation than Aristotle himself could. Indeed, this point of comparison will figure in the next chapter's conclusions in the defense of a Thomistic rational-action model in the face of competitors like Aristotle's. For now, though, let me simply propose Aquinas's superiority as a final reason to think he can incorporate the alternative interpretation of Aristotle on "having" versus "using" practical knowledge.

In summary, then, we have seen that Aquinas's conception of practical reason suits the fruitful, alternative interpretation of having versus using practical knowledge, that he can expand the concept of velleity to include willings that constitute full intentions (in our sense), that his psychology can allow such occurrences in incontinent actions, and that his overall view is better able than Aristotle's, in certain respects, to account for the implications of the alternative interpretation. While this section has not definitively demonstrated that Aquinas's system can interpolate the alternative interpretation of

Aristotle, the argument gives us reason to believe that a successful interpolation can be achieved.

With the alternative Aristotle interpretation incorporated, Aquinas can finally account for the phenomenon of clear-eyed incontinence. The new model shows how an agent need not be ignorant of relevant, obvious particulars of her action, how she might hold an intention (in our sense) to act on reason's ends and yet simultaneously act in an opposing way, and of how she might experience the characteristically intense mental conflict that results from doing what one, even then, discretively judges—and perhaps chooses and commands—ought not to be done. Thus, this modified Thomistic model possesses superior explanatory power and is more experientially adequate.

6.5 EXPLAINING THE PHENOMENON OF SELF-DIVISION

The new model employs the notion of less-than-wholehearted choices, which result in ineffective commands. The nature and causes of such choices still need explication, and to that task we shall now turn, because it figures prominently in the account of the most distressing phenomenon of weakness of will—the sense of self-division experienced by the agent.

6.5.1 Aquinas's Initial Explanation

The key to explaining the incontinent agent's feeling of self-division lies in the account of *habit*—especially of habits in the will itself. Habit's effects also provide vital elements in explaining the possibility of ineffective commands. Aquinas's present view of habit can do some of this work, but not all. As we saw in our exposition of Aquinas's view (section 5.3.3), he does not think habits reach necessitating force in general, but only under certain circumstances. Aquinas writes that a habit "does not, of necessity, produce its operation, but is used by [the agent] when [she] wills" (*ST* I–II q.71, a.4). He often describes habit almost as a tool, something that makes acting easier and that the agent can use (or not) when desired. Thus, Aquinas says, a person "while possessing a habit, may either fail to use the habit, or produce a contrary act" (I–II q.71, a.4). Only when the agent does not attentively deliberate, then, does the habitual disposition—because of the ease and naturalness of satisfying it—determine which action is performed (Aquinas, *OE* q.6, rep.24; *ST* I–II q.109, a.8, resp.).

On the other hand, Aquinas does admit that a person falling into an evil habit may retain free will, but lose her capacity for free *action* (*OE* q.6, rep.22). That is, such a person remains free in her choice of which action to perform at a given moment, but the *scope* of her choices may narrow in a way that makes satisfying the habit unavoidable. In Aquinas's words, "In specific cases we are able to avoid this or that movement of lust or anger, but we cannot avoid all movements of anger or lust in general" (*EG* chp.5, lec.4). The sinful motivation is always present and arises at every opportunity, whether consciously noticed or not (Aquinas, *ST* I–II q.109, a.8, resp.). Satisfying the habit emerges as a choice-option so easily and repeatedly that a person cannot help but choose it eventually. Thus, a habituated agent may not feel *compelled* at any one point to act on the habit, but she may find that she cannot *never* act on the habit (Aquinas, *OE* q.6, rep. 23). Indeed, such habitual lapses may be quite frequent; for Aquinas says of the person in the grip of sinful habits that "it cannot be that [she] remains for a long time without . . . [committing] sin" (*ST* I–II q.109, a.8, resp.). So while Aquinas does not commit to the notion that some habitual actions cannot be refrained from, he does accept that agents cannot refrain from *sometime* acting habitually.

Moreover, Aquinas also admits that the bondage of sinful habits, which he calls "the law of sin," can deleteriously affect a person's rational control over her own actions. The law of sin makes us like "the beasts that are led by the impulse of sensuality," "depriving [us of our] . . . proper dignity" of rationally controlling our actions; and the deprivation worsens "the more [one] deviates from the path of reason"—that is, the more one hardens the sinful habit (Aquinas, *TL* q.91, a.6. resp.). The law of sin's "accomplished effects" includes that it "resists reason," and that it "reduces the [agent] to a state of slavery" (Aquinas, *ER* chp.7, lec.4). Commenting on the biblical passage in Rom. 7 where the apostle Paul describes the experience of the divided-self phenomenon, Aquinas explains that once an agent becomes "a slave to sin" through habituation, she may affirm the directive of the divine law in her intellect—she may even propose that directive to her will; but she now continues to act contrary to the law "in as much as sin works in [her] as if possessing dominion" (chp.7, lec.3). In this way, Aquinas apparently does recognize a kind of helplessness on the agent's part in the face of the opposition her sinful habits present her reason (chp.7, lec.4; *EG* chp.5, lec.4).

Presumably, he must mean this helplessness to refer to the overall unavoidability of habitual actions, which we noted above. Unfortunately, while representing a step in the right direction, that kind of in-the-long-run inevitability of satisfying a habit does not seem to provide any sense in which habit could overpower rational deliberation *in a given action*, to bring about clear-eyed incontinence. Further, I'm not sure the helplessness to avoid *never* lapsing into habitual action could offer a galling enough source of frustration to prompt the dissociative perceptions of divided-self phenomena. An "ex-smoker" might know she will still lapse and have a cigarette in times of extreme stress; but because of the relative rarity of such resurgences of old habit, she might not be much bothered by them.

Unfortunately, then, Aquinas's construal cannot explain the full range of phenomena. Since on Aquinas's view, "however much a person is habituated [she] can nonetheless by deliberation act contrary to custom," that undercuts his explanation for the occurrence of clear-eyed incontinence (*OE* q.6, rep.24). For in such a case, the agent *does* deliberate and *actively consider* deliberation's result; therefore, Aquinas's psychology of habit does not help us understand why the agent would act against those deliberations. Or again, if an agent remains free to act in opposition to her habit when she wills to do so, the agent should not experience the helpless frustration and shame that could lead her to dissociate herself from the habitual inclination. That is, Aquinas's present picture of habit does not seem conducive to explaining the divided-self phenomena. In short, the Thomistic account needs augmentation by interpolating a more Augustinian psychology of habit.

6.5.2 Augustinian Psychology of Habit

Aquinas takes much of his view on the formation and impact of habits from Augustine's ideas, and his explanation of incontinent actions can be strengthened by adopting an even more Augustinian conception of the psychology of habits. So let us first briefly survey Augustine's position, and then we can examine and augment Aquinas's use of Augustine.

Augustine maintains that habits are powerful indeed; they can so seriously interfere with normal human agency that they can compromise or even remove our free will regarding action (*Conf* IX.i (1)). He accepts the same general picture of the formation of sinful habits that we have already seen with Aquinas. First, because of our sinful state, our disordered appetites produce inordinate passions. Then when we repeatedly act upon such passions, we form habits, or lasting dispositions, to continue those actions. Augustine further stipulates that if we do not resist that formation—or worse, if we act until the habit hardens—then satisfying the habit "becomes necessity" (VIII.v (10)). Unlike Aquinas, he denies that careful deliberation can always override habit. He maintains that sinful habits can "fetter" an agent's mind, even if she considers matters clearly (IX.xii (32)). Augustine also follows Paul by calling this fetter "the law of sin," or "carnal custom," and he holds that it resists a person's rational directives, thereby "capturing [her] under the law of sin" (*Augustine on Romans: Propositions from the Epistle to the Romans* props. 45–6). As Alasdair MacIntyre puts it,

> [I]t is . . . inescapable, so Augustine took himself to have discovered both in his own life as recorded in the *Confessions* and in the lives of others, that the full intellectual apprehension of [what is right to do] . . . is not by itself sufficient to generate right action. (*WJWR* 154)

Thus, an agent under the law of sin can rationally direct herself to refrain from her habitual action, yet she may no longer have the freedom actually to refrain; she does "not have free will so as not to sin, but only so much that [she does] not want to sin" (Augustine, *AR:PER* props. 13–18).

However, Augustine stresses that the agent still bears moral responsibility for these habitually necessary actions, even if they occur in spite of her resistance (*On Free Choice of the Will* bk.3, XVIII, 172). For while abstaining may lie beyond her power *now*, that helpless condition results from her *voluntary past performances* in acquiring the habit; the necessity she suffers has emerged as a penalty from her prior voluntary sin (*FCW* bk.3, XVIII, 178–9). Indeed, since the will works in the "direction and ordering of [one's] desires," evil habitual states that hinder the will's choices are the *will's own product*; the very habitual state itself is a *voluntary condition* (MacIntyre, *WJWR* 154). Therefore, Augustine writes that "the violence of habit" holds "even the unwilling mind," and deservedly so, "since by [the agent's] own choice [she] slipped into the habit" (*Conf* VIII.v (II)). So when she acts on the habit against her wishes, her habit effectively renders her the *passive* sufferer of a punishment (VII.iii (5)). Yet she may still "be blamed" for these actions, since she voluntarily assumed that condition of passivity (Augustine, *FCW* bk.3, XVIII, 172–5).

6.5.3 Augustine on the Phenomenon of Self-Division

Furthermore, Augustine's account of habit at last offers us a means to make sense of the most serious conflict-phenomenon, that of the agent's perception of a division in her very self. Augustine explains that when an agent rationally directs herself contrary to a habit, her willing ability—the appetitive force—itself divides between the opposing inclinations (*Conf* VIII.x (22)). But that leaves her rational directive engaging the will only in a qualified, partial way which cannot effectively bring about action; she wills ineffectually, because she wills *incompletely* (VIII.viii (19–20)). However, the habitual inclination—while not approved by reason—has been imprinted on the will strongly enough that it engages appetitive force sufficient to bring about action. So action proceeds from the habit rather than the rational directive (VIII.v (10–12)).

Yet the agent *identifies* herself with what she *now* wants to will, with her rational directive. Here we recall Aquinas's statement that we often identify ourselves and our agency with our intellects. Augustine would agree, for he describes the agent as seeing herself as "passive and unwilling rather than active and willing" in the habituated actions (VIII.v (10–12)). Moreover, the agent's shame and frustration over her inability to change her behavior lead her to *dissociate* herself from the habitual inclination (VIII.x (22)). In this way, she begins to see the habitual behavior as being caused by an "alien nature" or an "unidentifiable power"; her *pride* prompts these dissociative fantasies, so that she can *avoid blaming herself* for continuing to perform actions of which she does not approve (V.x (8)). Again, Augustine supports his analysis with a detailed example from his own life; he describes how his mind felt torn when he tried to quit his sexual habit. He was willing himself to reject his habitual actions, but it was ineffective. Then he began commanding his will itself, as if it were somehow not himself, but the ineffectiveness continued (VIII.ix (21)). In the face of his unrelieved failure to change, Augustine began identifying himself only with his reason, which supported the change; he saw himself as separate and divided from that recalcitrant part of his will that clung to habit.

Thus, Augustine's psychology of habit explains a second crucial aspect of incontinent actions—the phenomenon of the agent experiencing division in her own mind. Coupled with the explanations of clear-eyed incontinence and the voluntariness of habitually necessary actions, this point makes Augustine's construal of habit exceptionally valuable in accounting for incontinence. But can this psychology fit into Aquinas's theory? To that question we will now turn.

6.5.4 Adapting Aquinas to Fit Augustine on Habits

I think our prospects for a successful interpolation are good, for Aquinas says a number of things that cohere with Augustine's position. Indeed, I believe Aquinas's conceptions of limited unavoidability and helplessness represent an attempt to align his view with Augustine's. What holds Aquinas back from complete agreement is his commitment to the traditional Aristotelian picture of practical reason. Now, the adoption of the alternative Aristotelian conception of practical reason and of the broadened range for the idea of incomplete willing or velleity (sections 6.4.1 and 6.4.2), presents an opportunity to bridge the gap to Augustine's view on the effects of habit. Thus, I believe the Thomistic system can easily accept the change to the stronger Augustinian notions.

First, to apply the modified conception of velleity, recall that Aquinas believes an incomplete willing can occur when reason fluctuates between opposing motives regarding what action to command, and so "does not command perfectly" (*TH* q.17, a.5, rep.1). Now, since *command* constitutes reason's follow-through activity after the will chooses an action, and since the problem in command occurs because of fluctuation between opposed motives, then something must already have gone wrong in *choice*, in which the will inclines to one determinate action.

Aquinas proposes that incomplete willings arise because reason directs the will toward an *impossibility*, toward something that reason has no expectation of achieving (q.13, a.5, rep.1). For the will cannot effectively choose an action that the agent understands cannot be done. I can tell myself to fly, but my will cannot truly choose to do so, because I know I *cannot* fly. And the failure of choice during incontinence is similar. The will can only "half-heartedly" choose an action it *cannot want to execute through use*, since it also has powerful opposing motives. Then because the choice is motivationally undercut, reason cannot effectively command that it be acted upon, and command fails too. But what makes the object of reason's discretive judgment an impossibility for the will to carry out?

The answer is: a hardened, opposing habit *in the will itself*. In our discussions so far, we have focused on habit as it occurs in the sense appetite—on how habituation strengthens passions and makes them constant and abiding. However, the will, as the rational appetite, can also be habituated and itself can be the subject of virtues and vices (Aquinas, *DQV* q.2, a.1, resp.). So when an agent forms a habit regarding an inordinate desire, she not only strengthens the desire so that it is more difficult to avoid or resist, she also accustoms her will to choosing to act on the desire. Aquinas writes, "by repeated external actions, the inward movement of the will . . . [is] most effectually declared" (*TL* q.97, a.3, resp.). That is, habitual action shows what the will itself is most inclined to choose.

The will's habits then emerge as crucial for explaining clear-eyed incontinence. We recall that Aquinas labels the distinguisher of the incontinent agent as the state of her will (section 5.3.5). The incontinent and continent agents are similar with respect to reason; they both correctly understand the ends for action. Further, the incontinent shares the state of her concupiscible sense appetite with the continent agent; they both experience strongly inordinate desires (Aquinas, *ST* II–II q.155, a.3, resp.). The difference between the two agents is found in their wills; the continent chooses to follow reason, and the incontinent to follow desire. So continence and incontinence reside most properly in the will (q.155, a.3, resp.; rep.2). Aquinas originally describes incontinence in which reason-proper's deliberations and discretive judgment are obscured by passion—because will allows reason's attentions to be diverted—so that the subsequent choice collapses. Now, I propose that what distinguishes this kind of incontinence from clear-eyed incontinence (and particularly from that involving the sense of self-division), is the *will's habitual inclination* for the incontinent action. No diversion of attention is needed when will itself already contains a decisive inclination toward the incontinent action.

Aquinas explains that reason-proper may incline the will to a certain end on the *universal* level, but may have the viability of that inclination "destroyed in the eligible particular, by means of the inclination of a habit" (*ER* chp.7, lec.3). That gives us the key to choice's and command's failures in incomplete willing: reason-proper cannot successfully command the will to use the faculties to perform a *particular* action, because that command would conflict with a habit; and the agent cannot, in the particular, *not* want to act on her habit. So she cannot effectively choose not to satisfy the habit.

The phrase "satisfy the habit" especially applies here, since part of habit's power lies in making habitual actions "lovable" and "connatural" to the agent (Aquinas, *ST* I–II q.78, a.2, resp.). The habit literally forms "a kind of nature" for the agent that "makes the activity proper to it . . . natural and, consequently, delightful" (Aquinas, *DQV* q.1, a.1, resp.). In other words, the agent *always enjoys* acting on her habit, if for no other reason than simply that the action is habitual. That is particularly important to remember with regard to will habits, since they do not, in themselves, have to be directed at something pleasant, the way concupiscible habits do. Thus, performing a habitual action feels right and normal to us; refraining causes tension and unease. After decades of habituation, my skin crawls at the mere thought of not brushing my teeth for a week, let alone what I would feel if I actually attempted such avoidance. Indeed, since the habitual disposition is always present, I always feel better as I brush my teeth—even if that conflicts with other desires, like getting quickly into bed and out of the cold bathroom—because while I am brushing, it "scratches" the habit's "itch." It quiets the habit's demand by satisfying its "need," Also, this satisfaction still obtains when I get no sensory pleasure from the action—say, when I brush because I know it's time to, even though I don't feel any food uncomfortably lodged in my teeth. That shows the habit's hold on my will.

Therefore, an agent with a habituated will "is always glad for what [she] does through habit" so that the agent can want to refrain, "not because . . . [the action] in itself is displeasing to [her], but [only] because of [her] reaping some disadvantage from [it]" (Aquinas, *ST* I–II q.78, a.2, rep.3). The habituated agent, then, can only desire in an *indirect* way to not act on her habit. She always has a desire directly for the habitual action, yet can desire to refrain only out of dissatisfaction with the consequences of the action, not out of dissatisfaction with the action itself.

However, that places her rational judgment to refrain at a "leverage" disadvantage against her habitual judgment to act, like lifting a weight at arm's length versus lifting it close to one's body. Or again, it is as if the judgment to refrain were a cog pushing to turn another, the will, that is also being pushed in the opposite direction by a third cog, the habit. Yet rational judgment's cog engages the will's only at the tips of the teeth, while habit's nestles fully into the gaps. Habit's cog would push more effectively, and reason's cog likely would slip and allow will's cog to turn habit's direction.

Aquinas also points out that a habit is a "quality" in the will produced by the will's being "wholly dominate[d]" in the direction of the habitual inclination, which requires many judgments and acts to generate:

> [O]bviously reason . . . cannot wholly dominate [the will] . . . in a single act [of judgment] that [a certain action] should be willed. . . . Consequently, the [will] . . . is not at once wholly controlled. (*TV* q.51, a.3, resp.)

In other words, habit elicits a "wholehearted" inclination of the will, but a discretive judgment not supporting a habit—and especially one working against a habitual disposition—does not. When reason's judgment opposes a habit, then, in attempting to incline the will, the former "beckons" with less than total dominance, while the latter does so in a wholly dominant fashion. Thus, in spite of discretively judging to refrain from her habitual action, an agent could find herself choosing and performing it anyway.

Here is an example of how a will-habit's control could work: in performing the actions that acquire a habit, the agent acts because she wills to do that *sort* of action—she approves of them at the universal level. Say, she becomes a habitual heavy drinker because she likes to "party hearty." Having gained the habit, though, she may later decide she no longer approves of such behavior—she hates the hangovers and the hurtful things she says while drunk. She then adopts a new universal end; reason-proper directs her to avoid heavy drinking. Because of the undesired consequences it brings her, the agent *can* want to rid herself of the heavy drinking habit; so her will *can* intend (in Aquinas's sense) that at the universal level, which prompts reason to deliberate about what particular actions to take. Those deliberations reach a discretive judgment to refrain from going to her friend's drinking party, currently in progress. However, because of her heavy-drinking habit, she finds that she *cannot* fully want not to "party hearty" on *this* occasion. Her will's habitual disposition narrows the range of particular actions that can appeal to her. So while her will can intend (in Aquinas's sense) the universal end of quitting the heavy drinking, she cannot successfully will the particular choice of skipping this drinking party.

It seems, then, that Aquinas's system, having absorbed the revisions regarding practical reason and velleities, can now accommodate the Augustinian psychology of habit. But that should not be surprising, since Aquinas has, all along, been attempting to characterize incontinence in a way that goes beyond Aristotle by incorporating Christianity's insights, particularly as they emerge in Augustine's views. As Alasdair MacIntyre puts it,

> [Aquinas's] treatment of the tendency to disobedience in human nature in terms of *mala voluntas* [that is, of evil will] separates it radically from Aristotle's treatment of *akrasia*. Thus Aquinas is committed in a very particular way to giving an account of practical rationality which, even if Aristotelian in its general structure, integrates into that account the central themes of Augustine's psychology. (*WJWR* 181)

Thus, while some changes from Aquinas's original position on habit do need to be made, they are clearly within the spirit of his overall view. As was the case with the revision concerning practical reason, the sheer breadth and complexity of Aquinas's system makes me hesitate to say that this Augustinian interpolation definitely will not cause Aquinas significant problems. But as far as I can see, that is the case. And perhaps my assertion can gain confirmation in the next sections, when we see how this new view of habit can help Aquinas in two ways: first, by how well it maps onto Aquinas's model of human action to provide a detailed explanation of clear-eyed *akrasia* and of the causes of the experience of self-division; and second, by how well it allows Aquinas to solve key problems, including ones that dogged Hare's and Davidson's views.

6.5.5 Modeling Clear-Eyed Akrasia *and Self-Division*

Three possibilities regarding the habituation of the will emerge to explain the action-process breakdown that generates clear-eyed incontinence and the feeling of self-division. With all three, we need to keep in mind that the effects of the will's habituation occur in conjunction with the rationally deleterious effects of inordinate desires, which themselves may well be habitual. In my descriptions, I shall focus on the interaction of will and reason, but we must remember that the sense appetite's inordinate desires for pleasure are active in these scenarios, too. Thus, the inclination to the habitual act is compounded because the agent is moved to it not only by the will, but also by the sensitive appetite (Lalor, 3,227). That said, here is the first possible construction: perhaps the agent's reason-proper discretively judges that she should stay home from the party, but her will, through its habit, is so thoroughly inclined toward attending that the discretive judgment cannot move the will to choose staying home—the will cannot *effectively choose* to do so. Further, since the agent's habit makes attending the party seem attractive, reason-as-tool (of the habit) judges that the party ought to be attended. That particular option *can* be chosen effectively, so choice and action follow. In this scenario, reason-proper's guidance stops at discretive judgment. The will's only choice is for attending.

Here we can see how the current account of habit augments the alternative interpretation of Aristotle regarding practical reason. The agent's practical knowledge was "operative"—to use Anthony Kenny's terms—up to the discretive judgment, which is merely "present." Reason-proper's prior acts, universal judgment and deliberation, had "thrusted toward action" and prompted the next steps in the action process; but discretive judgment does not, because the agent's dispositions—her habits—have not been integrated well enough with her practical knowledge. Also, the earlier explanation of clear-eyed *akrasia* is fleshed out. We now see how this agent can remain entirely clear-eyed in her judgment of what ought to be done, yet choose incontinently anyway, because of her drinking habit.

However, this possibility leaves the agent merely judging that she ought to stay home, not commanding herself to do so, or even choosing to do so. She never forms a full intention (in our sense) to stay home; she judges that she ought to, but never in her self agrees to that. She has a specific judgment about what to do, but never a specific *desire* to do it. Some sense of the agent's conflict and resistance to her habit may, therefore, be missing.

Yet a supplementary point about the interaction of reason and will may at least partially correct this shortcoming. Aquinas notes that reason and will interact not only in producing external actions, but also in that their executive acts can be directed at their own functioning. He writes, "the act of the will and of reason can be brought to bear on each other, inasmuch as reason reasons about willing and the will wills to reason" (*TH* q.17, a.1.

resp.). In other words, the normal interaction of will and intellect in generating a human action consists of "elicited" acts, where each act represents an "immediate exercise" of one faculty in response to a prior action-step by the other; those are different from "commanded" acts, in which reason enjoins will to use its executive power on itself or on reason (Donagan, "TAHA" 650). So not only are bodily motions commanded, but "there are also acts of mind and will that are commanded" (McInerny, 179). Indeed, even the activity of the sensitive appetite can be commanded, in limited ways. (Donagan, "TAHA" 650).

For example, suppose I am not hungry but am presented with the opportunity to eat a gourmet meal; I might command myself to dwell on the delicious food until I excite my sense appetite to hunger. Or again, I might command myself to stop thinking about a certain thing, like a catchy but annoying pop song. In this case, the act of reason is itself the ultimate object of the command. Or I might command will to make a choice. Suppose I judge that it would be good for me to will a certain thing—say, a commitment to an exercise program. I choose to so will and command myself to do it. But notice that the command aims at the will itself—it enjoins the will to use itself in a certain way (Donagan, "TAHA" 651). Further, what I do is *not* the same as choosing and thereby committing to the exercise program; I am *commanding myself to choose*. And for anyone who has attempted regular exercise, the difference between the two is painfully obvious, particularly with respect to how effectively the latter can motivate actual exercise.

The agent in the grip of her drinking habit could well find herself commanding herself to choose not to attend the drinking party. She discretively judges she ought not go, but prepares to leave anyway, and starts mentally berating herself with "No, don't do that!" or perhaps with "Stop wanting to go!" She has this indirect ability to want not to satisfy her habit; she can want to not want to go drinking. She can even choose and command not wanting to drink tonight. But of course, her will, imprinted with the drinking habit, simply cannot in this way get rid of its inclination to drink. Moreover, her will may attempt to exercise use on her reason, when reason presents it with unappealing discretive judgments. When she rationally judges she should stay home, her will, which is habituated to the opposite inclination, effectively tells reason, "Think again!" Thus, the will's habitual inclination makes reason-as-tool consider the good of attending the party. She may even come back around by commanding herself to stop thinking about how much fun it would be to go drinking; again, she can oppose the habit in this indirect fashion.

This ability to indirectly command one's own will and reason could help to explain why the incontinent agent, even though she does not reach a choice to stay home, feels as if she has. After all, she is commanding her-self to (choose to) stay home. Thus, she experiences a heightened level of inner conflict. Also, and crucially, we can see the agent beginning to *dissoci-ate herself from her choice to go*. When she issues commands to her own reason and will, she treats them as if they were not under her direct control, as if they were not her very self. She does not simply change her choice, she commands that the choice be changed; she does not change her train of thought, she commands that the thoughts be changed. She treats the com-ponents of her own self as if they were some recalcitrant "other."

With this supplemental point about commanded acts of reason and will, the first possible construction, in which the agent's habit prevents her from choosing based on reason-proper's discretive judgment, gains new strength. It augments its explanation of the more intense, internal struggle that is characteristic of clear-eyed incontinence. Moreover, it uncovers some of the sources of the divided-self phenomenon. However, since commanded acts of will and reason also fit with the other two possible constructions, which already include some sense of the agent's desiring to perform her dis-cretively judged action, the latter possibilities may yet be explanatorily stronger construals.

The second possible construction, then, is this: perhaps the habit may stop the will at *consent* with regard to reason-proper's discretive judgment. We recall from the breakdown of a human action (section 5.1.3), that Aquinas ac-tually distinguishes two will-acts that follow discretive judgment. One was choice; the other was consent. The two frequently merge into one will-act, but not always. When discretive judgment yields *more than one option as appro-priate for immediate action*, the will *consents to all of them*, and expresses a prefer-ence by *choosing—and acting on—only one* (Aquinas, *TH* q.14, a.1, rep.1; q.15, a.3, rep.3). However, even though choice alone engenders action, consent does create desire to perform the specific actions that have been discretively judged. As Aquinas puts it, "Hence, the application of appetitive movement to a determination of the deliberation is consent proper" (q.15, a.3, resp.). More-over, of the options consented to, the one chosen is a determination of will alone; choice gets no more input from reason beyond what consent had, but merely expresses a preference by the will (Stump and Kretzmann, 361). And in the case of an agent with a hardened habit, the will's preference would al-most certainly accord with its habitual disposition, with its "totally dominant" inclination. Yet that agent would still have a *desire* to perform the action di-rected by her consented-to, habit-opposing discretive judgment. She would possess both components of an intention (in our sense): a rational directive to perform a specific action, coupled with a desire to do so.

In this construction, the habitual drinker's discretive judgment from reason-proper is operative; it does thrust toward action by prompting the next step, consent. The agent judges that she should stay home from the party tonight, and her will consents to that. But her attention is continually being drawn to the pleasures of drinking, both by her sense appetite and by her will—the latter due to its habitual inclination to drinking, and the former due to the prospect of satisfying its inordinate desire for drink (which, presumably, is also habituated). From that favorable attention, habit can rush reason right past deliberation to discretive judgment (Aquinas, *DQV* q.1, a.1, resp.). So her reason-as-tool discretively judges that she should go to the party, to which her will also consents. So both attending and staying home have enough appeal to her to receive consent. However, attending suits her will's habit, its dominant inclination, and therefore her will's choice is to attend. Now, like the agent in the first construction, this agent does not *choose* to stay home, but unlike the first agent, this one does have a *desire*, by her *consent*, *specifically* to stay home. As was noted above, she has both needed components for having an intention (in our sense) to stay. Thus, she may feel like she has made the choice to stay, and somehow has been thwarted from it.

Adding in the supplemental possibility of the agent's commanding herself to choose to stay home, this construction portrays intense internal struggle, with an increased motive toward dissociation. The agent may now feel like she is being "dragged away" from (what she thinks was) her choice not to go the party. She (thinks she) chooses to stay, but the "choice" fails, somehow; she tries to reinforce the "choice" by commanding it, but that fails too. What can she conclude but that something not under her control overpowers her?

However, even with this second construction, it remains true that the agent never commands herself to stay home. She does not fully exemplify Aquinas's comment about command failing when it is issued from conflicting motives. The command she does issue, to her will to choose staying home, may well be wholehearted, but simply made impossible by the will's hardened habit—as the habit prohibited choice, in the first construction. To see how the agent could reach the point of commanding herself to stay home, and yet attending anyway, we need to explore one more possibility.

The third possible construction, then, is this: perhaps reason-proper's discretive judgment *can* incline the will to choose, but only *partially*. The agent's will not only consents, but also does choose staying home, but not wholeheartedly—exemplifying Augustine's notion that the will's motivational force is divided when reason attempts to override habit. This scenario exploits Aquinas's recognition that the will can make more than one choice simultaneously. The agent here resembles one doing two actions at once; she makes *two simultaneous choices*, one from reason-proper's discretive judgment, and one rooted in the habitual inclination. Since she cannot enact both choices at once, however, the one that engages more of the will's motive force drives her action. Of course, the habit, representing many past choices and a (nearly) wholehearted inclination, engenders more motivation than reason-proper's discretive judgment. Yet the discretive judgment *is operative*, and in a more robust sense than in the last construction; this time, it brings on choice. And the choice may engage enough motive force to allow reason-proper to command staying home. Unfortunately, because the choice behind it is so much less than wholehearted, that command simply is not empowered enough to prompt use. Reason-proper's command is merely present, not operative.

In our example of the heavy drinker, the agent does choose to stay home, and commands herself to do so. But her choice is halfhearted at best, since she also very much wants to go to the drinking party. So through her habit, she makes a choice to attend, too. Of course, both choices cannot be enacted at once, since their actions oppose each other. Her will wavers between the two choices. At this point, her command to stay home is undercut; it lacks solid motivation and cannot elicit use. Reason-as-tool's command to go is also undercut, but not nearly as badly; the agent feels conflict, but the more wholehearted habitual inclination that backs the command still can elicit use. So she begins to leave for the party. Then, as we saw in the supplemental point, she begins commanding herself to reaffirm reason-proper's directed choice, with the same failing results as in the previous constructions. The agent in this construal now feels even more thoroughly dissociated from her attendance at the party. She chose not to go—she had a full-bodied intention (in our sense) to stay home and commanded herself to do so; and when that failed she even tried to fix it by commanding herself to remain firm in her choice, but she still went to the party. How, she wonders, can that be her fault? How can it even be *her* action, anymore? What could be holding her back from her own intentional guidance? But of course, no one outside herself forced her to go to the party. Thus, she forms notions of divisions in her very self. There is "something bad" in her, which prevents her from acting as she judges she ought.

At last, then, this third construction yields a model that can account for incontinent acts performed in the face of a presently held, opposing intention (in our sense). It also provides a basis for the dissociative experiences of a divided self. Moreover, we have a new, more accurate way of understanding Aquinas's earlier assertion that the agent, in the midst of her incontinent action, is merely "pretending" and "saying these words" that she should not act so, while "in [her] heart [she] does not think this way" (*CNE* VII.L.3: C1344). Before, we were forced to interpret that as meaning the agent acted in ignorance, that her discretive judgment against the action had collapsed, leaving only words of admonition that the agent no longer understood or believed. Now we can see that she does still recognize what she should do, and still even believes it—she commands herself to do it; but her heart just is not in it—that is where her pretense lies, in commanding herself to do (and to choose) reason's action, as if she wholeheartedly desired to do it, which she does not. It is not in her reason-proper's discretive judgment that she is merely saying the words, but in her command. Finally we have a rational-action model that shows how an agent can fail to do what reason directs, without having some cognitive defect concerning those directives. In this model, as often as her will-habit dominates her inclinations regarding particular actions, an agent finds reason-proper's discretive judgments and commands ineffectual in guiding her behavior.

6.5.6 Classifying Clear-Eyed and Self-Divisive Incontinence

The newly modified psychology of habit also allows Aquinas to answer objections raised against his characterizing clear-eyed rational failure and self-division as aspects of incontinence. Firstly, it assuages Norman Kretzmann's concerns that clear-eyed and self-divisive acts must represent an unnamed category—hitherto unnoticed by Aquinas—between incontinence and the vice of intemperance. Secondly, it diverts charges raised by Kretzmann and Gareth Matthews that self-division is primarily a self-deceptive, rather than an incontinent, phenomenon.

We recall that Kretzmann relegated the experiences of clear-eyed rational failure and self-division to

> a stage of immorality *between* Aristotle's and Aquinas's recognized stages of incontinence and intemperance. For there seems to be a kind of despair in which the agent consciously wills against [her] reason *without* having earlier willed in keeping with it, as in the case of a self-loathing, unrepentant alcoholic. Since such a person loathes [her] sin, [she] is not intemperate; and since the on-again, off-again feature is excluded, it is not a case of weakness of will. [Emphasis in original] (191 n.24)

In other words, because the agent follows her inordinate appetites without having interventions of successful, *complete* willings to resist those appetites, she cannot count as incontinent. The agent cannot muster a complete willing for her rational directive. So the lament from Rom. 7, with its references to a self divided, must characterize the new intermediate stage, since the "I" of the passage wills only incompletely and ineffectively (188–9). But that interpretation conflicts with Aquinas's account, which does attempt to capture the Rom. 7 scenario under the heading of incontinence (as we saw in section 6.1.2).

Now, we have already dispensed with Kretzmann's claim that incontinence cannot involve incomplete willings (again, in section 6.1.2), and our new understanding of the role of will-habits provides the basis for characterizing clear-eyed and self-divisive actions as properly incontinent. For we can see that such actions result from the condition of the agent's will. We saw in the last section that the distinguisher of the incontinent person was her will. *Temperate* agents possess both correct rational judgment about what to do and correctly moderated appetites in line with reason's judgment. *Intemperate* agents—as a kind of reverse image of the temperate ones—wrongly judge what to do, which aligns with their inordinate desires. Neither of those agents feels internal conflict, since each wills according to her harmonious intellect and appetites. So, as Kretzmann noted, clear-eyed and self-divided agents are not intemperate, because they experience inner conflict—indeed, the highest levels of it. Next, *continent* agents correctly, rationally judge what to do, but experience conflicting, inordinate appetites, to which they then correctly will in opposition. *Incontinent* agents have the same correct rational judgments and inordinate appetites, but incorrectly will to follow the appetites. Obviously, the clear-eyed and self-divided agents fit the incontinent description. For the root of their actions lies in their wills. They *do* possess correct rational judgment about how to act; they *do* have inordinate appetites; and they follow their appetites because of *bad choices by their wills*. Even though the bad choices now come from habits, those habits reside in the agents' wills.

Moreover, while the habits prevent reason-proper's guidance from generating complete willings, that prevention still stems from choices by the agent; for as habits in the will, the obstructing inclinations represent the weight of the agent's past choices. The necessity of the habituated choice does not violate the conditions of incontinence, which Kretzmann pointed out as requiring that the inordinate passions be resistible (176). For Aquinas says,

> Yet these [inordinate] passions, however vehement they may be, are not the sufficient cause of incontinence, but are merely the occasion thereof, since, so long as the *use of reason* remains, [a person] is always able to resist [her] *passions*. [Emphasis added.] (*ST* II–II q.156, a.1, resp.)

And the *will's habits are not "passions."* Irresistible passions would "take away the use of reason altogether" but the clear-eyed or self-divided agent does "retain the judgment of reason, which . . . [as an] incontinent [she] forsakes" (q.156, a.1. resp.). Further, as the rational appetite, the will effectively counts as *part of reason*, broadly characterized—which we have seen Aquinas affirm, repeatedly. To borrow a phrase from Kant, "the will is nothing but practical reason" (412). Therefore, the will's activity counts as the "use of reason." So the effect of will-habits is not under the same constraints to be resistible as passions' effects are, because passions obscure and even obliterate reason, but the will's habitual action actually "seems to proceed from a deliberate judgment of reason" (Aquinas, *TL* q.97, a.3, resp.). Clear-eyed and self-divisive actions, then, still represent a *voluntary, rational failure* by their agents. Thus, contrary to Kretzmann, these agents may differ enough from the standard cases to qualify as different subspecies of incontinence, but they do not differ so much as to be a different species of action, between incontinence and intemperance. In this way, then, the new characterization of will-habits vindicates Aquinas's view that the divided-self scenario of Rom. 7 is referable to incontinence.

However, another objection has been raised, by Gareth Matthews, that agents feeling self-division are not incontinent, but self-deceived and even hypocritical. Matthews argues that Rom. 7 employs a

> picture of oneself as a self-transparent agent . . . [so that] strictly speaking, one has performed only those actions whose motivation one can recognize as having been one's own; the rest are done by "sin, which dwells within me." (48)

But that picture ignores the fact that motivations are often hidden to the agent, especially in the case of sinful motives that are "at odds with one's better self" (45). And even shadowed motives are, of course, still part of the agent, of the "I" that acts. Therefore, when an agent attempts to distinguish herself from her sinful motives, just because they are opaque to her, her distinction is "profoundly self-deceptive" (49). More than that,

> the motivation for some of [an agent's] actions may be opaque to [her] because [she] ha[s] repressed those dark impulses. If that is so, then the righteousness of [her] conscious self may be, so to speak, in ransom to that repression, and to the deeds it produces. In a certain way, then, [her] sinful self may make [her] righteous self possible. If that is so, disowning the actions of [her] sinful self is hypocrisy twice over. It is hypocrisy in that the sinful deeds are also [her] own. It is also hypocrisy in that [she],

as the righteous judge, owe[s] [her] distinct identity to having repressed
the impulses [she] now assign[s] to [her] dissociated self. (48)

In short, according to Matthews, a self-divided agent deceives herself
in repressing some motivations and then hypocritically saying they are not
hers; then she hypocritically maintains her own righteousness by denying
responsibility for her subsequent sinful deeds based on those repressed motives. Indeed, Kretzmann would agree with that, since one of the reasons he
denies that Rom. 7 could refer to incontinence is that he thinks any agent
who sincerely says she is unable to do what she thinks she ought, is "suffering not from weakness of will at all, but from *self-deception*" (177). If these
charges are correct, then, self-division will not be an aspect of incontinence,
but an example of hypocritical self-deception. And again, Aquinas would be
mistaken in interpreting Rom. 7 as describing incontinence.

However, while I grant the truth of Matthews's claim that hypocrisy
and self-deception are *involved* in divided-self experiences, I deny that they
are what, principally, *produce* such experiences. Indeed, Aquinas, himself, already recognizes the self-deceptive elements of self-divisive, incontinent actions. With regard to such an incontinent agent, he writes, "this [that not I,
but 'sin' does the action] cannot properly be understood, because [her] reason consents to the sin; and on that account, [she] [her]self does [it]" (*ER*
bk.7, lec.3). So Aquinas notes that this agent fools herself. And he further
debunks her notion that the alien power of "sin" controls her. He argues,

It is said, moreover, that sin dwells in a [person]—not as if sin were another thing, since it is a privation of good; but the permanence, of such
a defect in [the person], is designated. (bk.7, lec.3)

Not only, then, does Aquinas deny the reality of the self-divided agent's
"other," but also, with his references to the *permanence* of her disordered inclinations and the *consent* of her reason, he locates the true problem in the
agent's *will-habits*. Nevertheless, he does see an element of truth in the
agent's claim of self-division, since she does not act according to her reason-
proper, but rather her "reason . . . is overcome by . . . a habit from which reason is inclined toward evil" (bk.7, lec.3). Therefore, Aquinas still regards the
self-divided agent as incontinent. And we can see why, by examining the
root causes of the self-divisive phenomenon.

Matthews's erroneous causal ascription is exposed through the action-
models and the heavy-drinking example from the last section. Notice that
in all three constructions, the agent's sense of dissociation is not created by

self-deception; rather, its roots lie in her *frustration at her inability* and in the *phenomenology of commanded will- and reason-acts.* That is, the heavy drinker does not begin by telling herself that her drinking urges are not "her," and therefore are not her responsibility. She begins with the assumption that her actions and motivations are hers, and with the logical implication that they should be subject to her control—that may be a view of "self-transparent agency," but if it is psychologically naïve, it is hardly self-deceptive. In any case, the agent finds she cannot control her actions; she cannot effectively choose or command staying home from the drinking party. Crucially, this inability is real, even if indirectly voluntary (we shall see more about this in the next two sections). The agent reacts to this failure by commanding her will and reason to follow through with her discretive judgment to stay home; but those commands fail, too. She feels not only the inner conflict (which itself is real and not illusory) of opposing motivations, but also frustration, confusion, and shame at her failure of self-control. Now, notice that the experiential quality, the phenomenology, of commanded will- and reason-acts necessarily involves treating components of oneself as a subject—will and reason—as if they were objects for oneself to manipulate. The nature of the experience, completely apart from weakness of will, is already dissociative. When those dissociative qualities are placed in a context of the agent's failing to control her own actions, a feeling of self-division can result.

Of course, the *extent* of that feeling is self-deceptive; the agent takes her dissociative feelings to an extreme not rationally justified. But it is the dissociative experience of the incontinence that spurs her self-deception, not the other way around. As Amelie Rorty puts it, "Often akrasia works as a strategy *toward* self-deception" [emphasis added] (*MA* 237). Rorty also illuminates that causal connection with respect to the self-divided agent's situation:

> Akratic actions are often unsettling because their occurrence gives the agent a sense of vertigo about [her] qualifications as an agent; that is one reason why *self-deception often rides on the back of akrasia*, to steady the vertigo of a voluntary agent who seems unable to command [her]self. [Emphasis added.] (260)

So Rorty sees the fundamental problem as an akratic one; the self-deception is the agent's (admittedly poor) attempt at damage control.

Moreover, Augustine also examined the self-deceptive and hypocritical activities of a self-divided agent, and his insights align with Rorty's. He says the agent's misplaced pride in her own righteousness and self-control prompts her to self-deceptively cling to her conclusion of a division in her self; that also allows her to hypocritically distance herself from responsibility for continuing to act in a manner of which she disapproves (*Conf* V.x (8)). But Augustine also stresses the reality of the agent's inability to control her own actions, or even to regain that control by mental effort (VIII.v (10–12)). Furthermore, including references to personal experience, he affirms the dissociative nature of commanded reason- and will-acts (VIII.ix (21)). And he concludes that frustration and shame over her inability then fuel the agent's expansion of that dissociative experience into a full-blown division in her self (VIII.x (22)). Augustine, too, then, shows by experiential example that a self-deceptive attempt to save face may prompt an agent to hold on to her notion that her self is divided, but that the origin of that notion is not self-deception, but honest anguish over her helplessness in the face of her incontinence.

Thus, Matthews's and Kretzmann's accusations of self-deception and hypocrisy do help us see those factors at work in a self-divided agent; but they miss the fundamentally akratic nature of the actions that generate the feeling of self-division. Aquinas classifies clear-eyed and self-divisive rational failures as incontinent, and our new model, involving will-habits, helps vindicate his classification.

6.6 MECHANISTIC AND HOMUNCULARISTIC OBSTACLES

In the next sections, we will see how the Augustinian view of habit can aid Aquinas in navigating a "Scylla and Charybdis" that damaged both Hare and Davidson: the tension between homuncularistic and mechanistic explanations of weakness of will.

6.6.1 Avoiding Mechanism

The first, most immediate challenge is the threat of mechanism looming over the new model of clear-eyed and self-divisive incontinence. If the will chooses between discretive judgments because of a habit that necessitates a particular choice, then the resultant action appears mechanistic, with the final outcome not determined by the agent, but by a determining force in the inclination to one of the judged actions. Yet we have seen cogent objections to this sort of account. Indeed, Davidson—although he altogether misses the role of the will in producing action—rejects Aquinas's view, partly from the charge that it suffers from mechanistic problems (*EAE* 35–6). Davidson correctly asserts that when action is mechanistically produced, "it is not clear how we can ever blame the agent for what [she] does: [her] action merely reflects the outcome of a struggle within [her]. What could [she] do about it?" (35). Despite Davidson's bungled interpretation, then, if Aquinas's model of clear-eyed incontinent action should turn out to be mechanistic, Davidson's accusation would still hold: such actions would no longer count as voluntary—or even as intentional or human—and the agent would not bear moral responsibility for them.

However, Aquinas has the resources to explain such habitual actions as voluntary; indeed, this explanation dovetails with the Thomistic position on intentionality proposed earlier (section 5.4.1), that of attributing voluntariness and intentionality *by degrees*. Moreover, it is Augustine's insights regarding habit that give us the means to explain how habitually necessary actions could count as voluntary. In our new model of clear-eyed weakness of will, the will's choice—between two discretive judgments to act—is determined by the will's habitual inclination toward one or the other. Yet in Augustine's account (section 6.5.2), we saw that these habitual actions can still bear moral weight because of the *voluntary acquisition* of the habit (*FCW* bk.3, XVIII, 172–5).

This situation resembles the moral responsibility of a drunk driver: she may not control her actions as she runs down a pedestrian; she may even have "blacked out" and so drive as if sleepwalking. But we hold her responsible for her hit-and-run accident, because she *voluntarily* got drunk and did not provide for a "designated driver." Her accident followed consequently upon her voluntarily entered condition, so she bears responsibility. Her reckless driving counts as a moral action, for it is voluntary *indirectly*. The agent does not possess full voluntariness in her performance of the action; but her full voluntariness in entering the drunken state carries over to her driving while drunk, to make that action voluntary, at least to some degree. Extended generally, the implication of cases like the above is that in order for us to classify someone's action as voluntary, and to hold her morally responsible for it: either (a) she had to be able to do something other than the action, *or* (b) *if performing this action was unavoidable,* she had to be able to do some *prior thing that would have made the action avoidable*—or at least voided her responsibility for it (Wyma, 59–60).

Moreover, we might hold the drunk driver less responsible than if she had soberly run down a pedestrian. We might say the action's voluntariness decreases, because she could not foresee with certainty that she would drive, once drunk. Yet that presents no problem to the proposed Thomistic, sliding-scale model of voluntariness and intentionality and rationality. The agent's drunken driving counts as voluntary and intentional to some degree—depending on her familiarity with drunkenness, her knowledge of her own drinking patterns and behaviors, and so on (69, n.2). The central claim stands: her action does possess voluntariness and moral weight, even if she could not have refrained from it at the time.

Moreover, the same holds for actions necessarily generated from voluntarily acquired habits. No, the heavy-drinking agent could not have refrained, at the time, from her action of going to the drinking party; but yes, she could earlier have done something—namely, not "partying hearty" so much—that would have allowed her to refrain. And Aquinas agrees wholly with this Augustinian stance on voluntariness. In fact, he responds to an objection that since character determines our actions, we must not be free (*ST* I q.83, a.1, obj.5), with this claim,

> [E]ven these [habitual] inclinations are subject to the judgment of reason. Such qualities . . . are subject to reason, as it is *in our power either to acquire them*, whether by causing them or by disposing ourselves to them, *or to reject [acquiring] them*. And so there is nothing in this that is repugnant to free-will. [Emphasis added] (*ST* I q.83, a.1, rep.5)

That is why Aquinas says that habituated action "seems to proceed from a deliberate judgment of reason" (*TL* q.97, a.3, resp.). For even if the current action should be necessitated, it shows what the agent has judged and chosen all along. Aquinas concludes, then, that "[one] who does what [she] does not will does not have free action, but [she] can have free will" (*OE* q.6, rep.22). For she "has lost free will so far as concerns freedom from fault and misery, but not so far as concerns freedom from compulsion" (q.6, rep.23). In short, the agent cannot avoid doing what she does, but it is not by compulsion; her action is still voluntary because it proceeds from her will and her will's (originally free) choices.

Now, perhaps we would assign such habituated actions an attenuated or indirect voluntariness, a lesser degree of voluntariness than a nonhabituated act would receive, for the agent might not have foreseen that she was forming a habit, and certainly might not have realized when she was nearing and crossing habit's threshold. Yet we could justifiably assign some degree of voluntariness, nonetheless. Indeed, such a "degreed" ascription would allow us to recognize that these habituated actions *do* possess less intentionality and voluntariness than human actions should ideally possess. And that seems right, for this admission then deals with a problem of agency that has been following us since the analysis of Hare's view—namely, that self-divisive incontinent actions do not seem fully voluntary (section 2.2.3). Thus, the degreed conception allows us to continue characterizing habitually necessitated actions as "intentional" or "human," while at the same time permitting us to acknowledge that human agency does seem hampered or compromised in such actions.

Therefore, Augustine's psychology of habits presents us with a valuable aid in incorporating the alternative interpretation of Aristotle (with its acceptance of action in the face of opposed discretive judgments) into a Thomistic model for action, without making such actions appear mechanistic. And in doing so, the new, more Augustinian model rebuts Davidson's objection of mechanism.

Moreover, this Augustinian conception of habit offers Aquinas additional explanatory aid on a few related issues. First, Augustine's view of the chain of habitual necessity helps account for the incontinent agent's difficulties in fully integrating her practical knowledge. Dahl and the other Aristotelian commentators had explained the need for integrating one's practical knowledge into one's character—for fully realizing that knowledge by using it to mold one's dispositions and to guide one's actions. Now we can see that the presence of opposing habits would constitute a serious stumbling block to such integration. Not only does the existence of a contrary, habitual disposition demonstrate that character integration has *not* occurred, but also the habit's opposing inclination could *prevent* the agent from performing the sort of actions that would lead to integration of the practical knowledge. Further, when those obstructive habits reside in the will—the rational appetite, the practical executor of the intellect—it becomes even more appropriate to call them defects in the agent's practical knowledge.

Indeed, Augustine describes an example from his own life to show habit's hindrance to practical knowledge. In a mystical experience, Augustine gains knowledge of the divine plan and his place in it; he becomes completely intellectually convinced of how he ought to act, and why (*Conf* VII.x (16)). Yet despite his conviction, he finds himself acting in accord with his "sexual habit," his "customary condition" (VII.xvii (23)). Moreover, he cannot escape this condition, since his intellectual efforts to redirect his actions remain ineffectual in the face of the opposing habit (VIII.vii (18)). So from his own life, Augustine identifies the occurrence of clear-eyed incontinence, and he offers "the resistance of carnal habit" against his practical knowledge as an explanation of how this phenomenon can happen (*FCW* bk.3, XVIII, 177; *AR:PER* props. 13–18). Thus, the Augustinian view of habits aids Aquinas in fleshing out what it means to not have one's practical knowledge integrated into one's dispositions.

Second, this psychology of habit helps account for the perceptual habits that can have so much impact on akratic action, and which pressed the problem of mechanism so mercilessly on Davidson (section 4.5.3). That is, as Amelie Rorty has noted, the elements of our perceptions have varying degrees of importance to our practical reason; for example, practical reason regards it as more important that a perceived piece of cake is on someone else's plate, than that the cake tastes sweet. Yet the *salience*—the noticeableness and apparent relevance—of those two elements may be quite disproportionate to their rational importance (Rorty, *MA* 221). And what makes some elements overly salient, what draws the agent's attention inordinately to them, is a habit in the agent's perception itself.

Marcia Cavell calls such habits the "transitive" parts of the stream of experience in acting, that is, the "things like feelings of activity or the process of reflecting or drawing a conclusion" (305). Cavell points out that while these experiences are not part of the content of what is thought or reasoned, they *do* affect what an agent concludes or does. Cavell seems to picture something like this: *how* an agent perceives her possible actions, the *manner* in which she reflects on her competing ends for action—such things affect what the agent decides to do. An agent's habits of perception, say, may result in her focusing on the pleasure associated with eating her friend's piece of cake, rather than on the action's weightier negative social consequences. Virtually automatically, that might connect the agent's practical reasoning with the end supplied by a gluttonous, inordinate passion. Then with an end and a matching belief about perceptual particulars, the agent's will-habit (assuming she has one concerning gluttonous eating) does not require deliberation to reach a "judgment" and choice that can bring about her swiping and eating the cake.

Now, Aquinas already acknowledges the existence and importance of perceptual habits, so their impact is allowable in his model. He writes, "the sense powers do have an innate aptitude to obey the command of reason, and hence there can be habits in them" (*TV* q.50, a.3, rep.1). Now, Aquinas does not mean that the sense organs themselves can be habituated to take in only certain information; the sense organs function completely naturally and beyond the control of reason. Rather, reason can inculcate habits "in the powers commanding [the sense organs'] movement" (q.50, a.3, rep.3). That is, in consciously directing our attention, time and again, to certain perceptual elements—say, to sweet-tasting items seen—the power of focusing attention itself becomes "disposed" to noticing and concentrating on sweets (q.50, a.3, resp.). In the end, then, Aquinas remarks,

> activities which are from the soul by means of the body [like perception] belong principally to the soul and secondarily to the body. . . . For this reason, the dispositions to such activities are found principally in the soul. (q.50, a.1, resp.)

So perceptual habits reside mostly in the cognitive powers of focusing and directing attention. Nevertheless, they do have a bodily element, too. Aquinas writes, "But secondarily, [perceptual habits] can be in the body insofar as the body is disposed and conditioned to be readily subject to these activities of the soul" (q.50, a.1, resp.). In some ways, then, the body itself may change to make the perceptual habits' operations easier. Thus, Aquinas has a ready account for this crucial dimension of habituation.

Initially, then, the upshot of perceptual habits is that their effect may make an action performed through a necessitating will–habit seem less mechanistic. It is not the will–habit alone that determines the agent's action; but rather, the agent does the determining, by means of the way she has perceived her action, and so on. On that account, the will–habit is not the sole cause of the action, but is only an inclination ready to have its motive force "activated" by the agent's transitive experiences.

Unfortunately, perceptual habits also increase the threat of mechanism in a new way, argued by Mark Johnston (also in section 4.5.3). Johnston thinks that weak-willed actions are brought about under the influence of mental processes "that are purposive but not initiated for and from a reason" (65). Johnston calls such processes "mental tropisms," and describes them as "nonaccidental, purpose-serving mental regularities," or as "characteristic pattern[s] of causation between types of mental states" (66, 86). He gives as an example this perceptual tropism: "an automatic filtering process that is ordinarily inaccessible to introspection and which determines that what is salient in perception will be what answers to one's interests" (87). In other words, this tropism would ensure that what the agent notices about her prospective actions would correspond to the aspects singled out in appetitive inclinations. So Johnston's described perceptual tropism seems very much like the perceptual habit that influenced the agent to focus on her action in ways that fit her akratic habitual inclination. The problem, Johnston points out, is that mentally tropistic behavior has an important similarity to the tropistic behavior of plants in leaning toward the sun: *neither kind of behavior is intentional.* Mentally tropistic processes have purposiveness; but if they are normally below the threshold of introspection and not the sort of activity that the agent consciously intends to do, at best we might call them subintentional. That would mean that incontinent actions are brought about subintentionally, a consequence Johnston affirms (65).

It seems that an agent's transitive experiences are *exactly* the kinds of mental processes that are going to be shaped—or at least greatly influenced—by mental tropisms. How a person perceives or reflects or considers is very much affected by that person's perceptual habits, by the degree of reflexivity in her mind-set, and so on. Those are the sorts of mental traits that are normally unobserved by the person, and that are not normally intentionally invoked. Our akratic cake eater does not intentionally focus on the deliciousness of the devil's food and frosting. Instead, as a cake lover, that is simply where her perceptions automatically gravitate. The tropism picks out action-aspects that only then lead to the formation of beliefs about what actions fit her situation. That is, the tropism does its work before the agent has enough information to make judgments about what she is doing. And since the agent's perceptions connect to her habitual inclinations so that judgment, choice, and action align with them, the agent's action again appears mechanistic; the action is driven by factors outside her control, and perhaps even beneath her notice.

However, given the Augustinian insights regarding habit and voluntariness, Aquinas can avoid that mechanistic conclusion. Indeed, this constitutes one of Aquinas's significant advantages over Davidson. We recall, from the earlier treatment of this issue in analyzing Davidson's view (again, section 4.5.3), that Davidson had no defense against the charge that the effect of perceptual habits was both significant in producing incontinent actions and beneath the level of voluntariness and intentionality. But that helplessness resulted from Davidson's psychology of desire; he had only one category of psychological motivations—pro attitudes. He did not differentiate passing fancies from lifelong habits, but lumped them together and considered all their functions as more or less the same. Therefore, when it was recognized that perceptual habits do their work before an agent forms beliefs about her situation, Davidson had no way to construe such effects as intentional. For in his view that required both a pro attitude (for which the perceptual habits did count) *and* a belief about the appropriateness of presently acting on that pro attitude (which was not present, since such beliefs were the results of the perceptual habits). Aquinas's view, however, *does* distinguish between the nature and operation of merely presently occurrent inclinations and habitual inclinations. Moreover, strengthened by Augustine's insights regarding habits, Aquinas possesses the resources to explain how even the effects of perceptual habits, normally beneath the agent's notice, can still be construed as voluntary.

As we have seen throughout this section, Augustine—and through him, Aquinas—can give a cogent account of how habitual effects are voluntary *indirectly*. And that holds for perceptual habits and their effects on action, as well. Again, the habits are formed by the repeated, fully voluntary judgments, choices, and actions of the agent. Once the habits are in place, they may distort the agent's judgments with their unnoticed emphasis on the salience of certain perceptions; but that emphasis only emerges from the agent's repeatedly judging—in a completely unhindered way—that those are the key perceptual elements, and from her focusing attention on them. Certainly, the fact that perceptual habits' effects are normally beneath the agent's awareness may decrease the degree of voluntariness of actions that those effects help produce. Yet that also fits with the degreed conception of voluntariness/intentionality that Aquinas's view utilizes for human actions. And in any case, the indirect voluntariness that characterizes even the perceptual habits' effects, given their voluntary acquisition, guarantees that voluntariness will not be totally absent from subsequent incontinent actions.

Therefore, the Thomistic view, modified with the Augustinian conception of habits, can characterize habituated actions—even necessitated ones or those affected by unnoticed perceptual habits—as voluntary, *at least to some degree*. Not only does that allow Aquinas sweepingly to rebut charges of mechanism, it also makes his theory more accurate to the phenomena. For, as nearly every account of self-divisive akratic actions has affirmed, such actions seem to compromise a person's agency. Now we can see how that occurs, without having to drop those actions entirely from the category of human, intentional action; Aquinas's modified view can "save the phenomena" of self-divisive and other habituated actions, while still capturing them under his conception of rational action.

But can this new model avoid swinging to the opposing pole of homuncularism? To that question we shall now turn.

6.6.2 Avoiding Homuncularism

The second challenge for the new psychological model is the charge of homuncularism, explaining agency by postulating "little men" inside the agent. By saying the will determines which judgment prompts action, perhaps we commit Aquinas to an implausible homuncularism. The will seems to have enough powers of its own to count as an agent. Not only is it an executive faculty that makes choices and motivates action, but it also has inclinations and habits of its own. It can generate discretive judgments without proceeding through rational deliberation. It seems able to resist and control reason, forcing reason to make certain judgments or think about certain objects and ends.

In fact, Davidson objects to views like Aquinas's that postulate faculties of reason, desire, and will, on the grounds of homuncularism—although, oddly, Davidson does not recognize that Aquinas's view actually employs those three faculties, and although, ironically, Davidson's own account, suffers from homuncularist problems (as we saw in section 4.5.3). In any case, Davidson writes,

> Here there are three actors on the stage: reason, desire [in Aquinas's case, the sensitive appetite], and the one who lets desire get the upper hand. The third actor is perhaps named "The Will." It is up to The Will to decide who wins the battle [between reason and desire]. If The Will is strong, he gives the palm to reason; if he is weak he may allow pleasure or passion the upper hand. (*EAE* 35)

Davidson admits this model avoids problems of mechanism, since "The Will . . . can judge the strength of the arguments on both sides, can execute the decision, and take the rap" (35). However, he charges that "we seem back where we started. For how can The Will judge one course of action better and yet choose the other?" (36). In other words, this model is "absurd" because it simply moves the problem of incontinence back from the agent into the will itself—it makes the will into its own incontinent agent (35–6).

Furthermore, Davidson is not alone in making this accusation against Aquinas's view. Alan Donagan notes that a common objection is that

> Aquinas's theory of action is a "faculty psychology" in which human beings are resolved into a collection of faculties, or powers, each of which is then treated as a quasi-agent. ("TAHA" 654)

So the threat of homuncularism already loomed over Aquinas's theory. And with all the functions that the will can have in our newly modified Thomistic model, this objection seems increasingly pressing.

However, Aquinas certainly does not intend his view to be homuncularistic—rather, quite the reverse. As has been noted several times, Aquinas regards "the intellectual part" as "principle" in a person, and he realizes that we frequently identify it with the person (*ST* I q.75, a.4, rep.1). Yet he writes, "it is necessary to say that the intellect is a power of the soul, and *not the very essence of the soul*" [emphasis added] (q.79, a.1, resp.). In fact, he does not even think the intellect is truly a "part" of the soul, in the sense of existing as its own little piece; for he claims, "We must . . . conclude that in [a human being] the sensitive soul, [and] the intellectual soul . . . are *numerically one soul*" [emphasis added] (q.76, a.3, resp.). In other words, the sensitive appetite and the intellect are not separate pieces of a soul, but only *distinct abilities* of one soul. And more than that, "it is clear that [a person] is *not a soul only*, but something composed of soul and body" [emphasis added] (q.75, a.4, resp.). So Aquinas obviously does *not* think that the intellect equals the person, that in itself it is an agent. And since the intellect is the faculty that chiefly tempts us to make that identification, Aquinas definitely would deny that any other faculty, by itself, could constitute an agent.

Indeed, Donagan argues that the homuncularist objection is "vulgar," because it merely latches on to Aquinas's verbal descriptions of faculties and misses his real characterization of agency. Thus,

> For convenience, Aquinas often speaks of what a power such as the intellect does or can do. But such statements, if they are indispensable to his theory of action, can readily, if sometimes cumbrously, be reformulated as statements . . . about what human beings, as possessing that power, do or can do. (Donagan, "TAHA" 654)

That is, Aquinas regards *persons* as agents, and agency requires certain abilities, for instance, to conceive of courses of action and to motivate oneself into action. Aquinas simply organizes related abilities under labels like "reason" or "will" or "sensitive appetite" and, for ease of discussion, describes the activities of those "faculties."

Of course, mere denial of homuncularism does not guarantee a vindication from it—as we saw with Davidson's view (yet again, section 4.5.3). Aquinas's ability truly to defend against this objection depends on his answer to this question: do any of the faculties have, within the powers "collected" under their "labels," all—or even nearly all—the requisite abilities for agency? Happily for Aquinas, his answer is "no!" Given the model of the principles of human action—the faculties of reason, will, and sensitive appetite (divided into the concupiscible and the irascible)—that was presented in setting out Aquinas's system (section 5.1.1), we can see that no single faculty includes enough range of abilities to allow it to function as an agent.

To recap briefly the earlier discussion, here are the basic abilities under each faculty-label: Reason is the capacity primarily responsible for the *guidance* of action. Included within reason are the *cognitive* abilities to *apprehend* possible objects of action, and to *consider* and *compare* those objects in order to *judge* and *direct* the best course of action (Aquinas, *ST* I q.82, a.4, rep.3; *TH* q.14, a.6, resp.; q.17, a.1, resp.; Kretzmann, 174).

Will is the capacity primarily responsible for the *motive force* that produces action (174). Will includes the abilities to *form preferences* and *make choices*, and to *move the body into action* (Aquinas, *TH* q.14, a.1, rep.1; q.15, a.3. resp.; q.16, a.2, resp.). However, the will possesses *no cognitive abilities*, no thinking or understanding. Through its choices it simply provides motive force to ends and means presented to it as good by reason (q.8, a.1, resp.). As John Driscoll puts it in commenting on Aquinas, "The will is a blind power. It tends towards objects as they are known by the intellect" (3204).

The sensitive appetite is the capacity to be affected by objects we perceive. The sensitive appetite is activated by, and provides *motive force* toward (or away from) goods (or evils) *apprehended by the senses* (Kretzmann, 174). That appetitive movement is experienced as a passion, which, in addition to the motive force, creates a *physical change* in the body itself (Lalor, 3225). Those motivations are represented in reason as goods or evils, which can then, indirectly, guide the will; and the physical changes may make it difficult for reason to attend to any other aspects of action than those corresponding to the passions (Kretzmann, 175).

As we have seen, all these faculties can be habituated: reason in its powers of attending—which seem the true home of perceptual habits; will in its preferential inclinations; and the sense appetite in its passional inclinations—and in the body's disposition to the passional transformation. In reason and the sense appetite, habituation does not add any new abilities, but only provides an automatic focus or augmentation to the already present ones. But in the will, again as we have seen, habit enables will to eliminate the reason-acts of deliberation and possibly even discretive judgment in producing action; so some new ability is gained.

Given the abilities grouped, it is obvious that the sense appetite cannot function as an agent. The sense appetite includes no cognitive abilities; the separate power of sense-perception must activate it. Nor are the inclinations and bodily changes produced by the sense appetite sufficient, in themselves, to cause action. The inclinations must be apprehended and construed by reason as goods, and even then they do not necessarily move the will to choice and use. Thus, the sense appetite lacks critical aspects of agency, both cognitively and motivationally.

Reason, too, clearly seems inadequate for agency. Reason does, of course, include all the cognitive abilities agency requires—awareness, action-judgment, and so on. But reason entirely lacks motivational power. Discretive judgment may identify an action to be done, but it cannot, without the will, cause the action. Nor can it necessarily move the will to cause the action, as evidenced by the will's ability to choose from among discretive judgments consented to. For the will effectively disregards the judgments not chosen, and nothing in any one judgment forces the will to choose it (Stump and Kretzmann, 361). Indeed, reason's very "movement" of the will is not by means of motivational force from reason, but only by conceiving of a good—serving as "eyes" so that the "blind" will can have a goal to move itself toward (361–2). Even command, reason's "Do it!" executive activity, only conveys motive force that has already been created by the will's prior choice. Therefore, reason is insufficient for agency; it includes the requisite cognitive abilities but lacks the motivational ones.

The will's status, however, seems more questionable, especially when the habituated will's powers are recognized. Obviously, the will includes the motivational powers agency needs. The will can produce motivation, causing bodily movements to generate exterior action, as well as prompting the exercise of cognitive powers within reason. Now, if the habituated will can dispense with deliberation and perhaps even with discretive judgment, has it gained cognitive abilities in its own right? If it has, then the will does seem to be a homunculus, a "little agent."

Fortunately for Aquinas, it is not necessary to grant the will any cognitive ability to perform even its habituated activities. If habits are merely lasting inclinations in the will, those trained, imprinted inclinations could explain how the will might choose without recourse to deliberation and discretive judgment. For Aquinas, in discussing the will act of choice, writes, "when a [discretive] judgment or decision is evident without inquiry, there is no need for the inquiry of deliberation" (*TH* q.14, a.4, rep.1). That is, given a certain intention (in Aquinas's sense) of a desired end for action, if the appropriate action is immediately obvious, deliberation can be skipped. Indeed, even the separate act of discretive judgment can be skipped, because reason's *general judgment functions as discretive judgment*. With the general judgment in mind, mere recognition of the current situation leads to choice, because the indicated action is so obvious as to be specified effectively already. Similarly, the will's habits function by *making choice obvious* from general judgment and perception of the situational particulars.

Thus, in the example of the heavy drinker, as soon as reason (as tool of the inordinate passion and habit) proposes that a certain end—say, partying hearty—is good and recognizes that a drinking party is occurring, the will takes that as a discretive judgment to go to the party. The will's habitual inclination is so focused that reason's presentation, of a possible goal and a possibility for satisfaction of that goal effectively counts as judgment to pursue that goal in that satisfaction. Therefore, the will still chooses in response to a judgment of reason (even if it is a subverted one). In this way, the will can skip deliberation and discretive judgment to reach choice, without possessing cognitive powers.

Moreover, it is not the case that reason is a mere cognitive extension of will, that reason is under such tight control by will that reason's powers are effectively will's. This point emerged from the earlier discussion, when I argued against the interpretation of Stump and Kretzmann (section 5.1.1). To briefly recap: Given that Aquinas clearly supposes will to have the power to *cause* reason's acts (q.82, a.4, resp.), Stump and Kretzmann characterize this causal control as extensive; they speak of "the will's occasional *coercion* of the intellect" [emphasis added] and its capacity "to direct the intellect's attention" (362). That implies that reason's considerations are determined by the will in both their direction and outcome. Reason becomes a mere tool under the will's control, and the will becomes effectively "self-directed" (360, 362). Now if Stump and Kretzmann's interpretation were correct, Aquinas's psychology would perilously veer into homuncularism.

However, as I argued earlier, that interpretation does not fit Aquinas's description of reason's operation. For one thing, Aquinas asserts that every movement of the will occurs under some kind of guiding apprehension from reason (*ST* I q.84, a.4, rep.3). For another, he repeatedly proposes that the freedom of will and choice are dependent on reason. That is, he portrays the will's freedom as, to some extent, emerging from reason's ability to consider opposing possibilities with regard to courses of action (q.83, a.1, resp.). For example, he claims, "[A person] does not choose with necessity. . . . The reason for this lies in the very power of reason" (*TH* q.13, a.6, resp.). He also writes that because "reason is a power that compares several things together," the will "may be moved; but not of necessity from one thing" (*ST* I q.82, a.2, rep.3). Moreover, he claims we are free in our actions because we "can deliberate about them, for when deliberating reason is related to opposite alternatives, and the will can tend to either" (*TH* q.6, a.2, rep.2). He even calls reason "the regulative power of all the internal affections [that is, appetites]" (*OE* q.3, a.9, resp.).

In fact, Donagan argues that a crucial point in "Aquinas's theory of action [is] the priority it affirms of intellect over will" ("TAHA" 652). For, Donagan claims, Aquinas makes the will's freedom "wholly a matter of the non-necessity of any [rational] judgement a [person] can arrive at . . . as to the goodness of an end or the suitability of a means" (652–3). So the source of freedom is *external* to the will, and not a power of the will itself (653). Unfortunately, while Donagan rightly sees Aquinas's affirmation of reason's independence from will, he goes too far in assessing reason's powers. He has missed will's ability to choose between discretive judgments, which shows an internal locus of the will's freedom. Moreover, Donagan's construal would rotate the possibility of homuncularism back to reason; reason possesses both cognitive powers and control over free choice, and thereby seems like an agent on its own.

For that reason, my own interpretation of Aquinas's psychology now revises not only Stump and Kretzmann's position, but Donagan's as well. Here, then, is how I see the relation of will and reason: It is undeniable that the will *can* prompt reason to act. However, it is also clear that not all acts of reason—particularly reason's initial apprehensions—occur because of the will's bidding. Further, I argue that reason possesses some spontaneity, or indeterminacy, and self-guidance in what it apprehends in its consideration of both ends and means. As Ralph McInerny says, "The will can command us to think but this bears on the exercise and not the specification of thinking" (179). For the power of attending to an idea is cognitive, belonging not to will but to reason. Moreover, that helps make sense of the diminished voluntariness present in habituated actions; when the will's choice occurs without reason's deliberations, the will's freedom is reduced because it is no longer aided by reason's ability to consider present alternatives.

Yet reason is not the sole controller of action. The will has influence over reason's considerations. For instance, having thought of some object of action appealing (or repellent) to the will, reason may be prompted to consider it more (or less). Again, though, if additional consideration is called for, the will does not control the thought path consideration follows; rather, reason does. But it certainly is the will that controls when reason stops considering and deliberating, and full action begins. As Driscoll observes, "The last practical judgment of reason which decides that this particular good should be chosen, *is* the last only because the will wishes it to be so" (3,206).

This interpretation preserves aspects of freedom and independence in both reason and the will, and thereby harmonizes Aquinas's descriptions of those faculties. Since it leaves their functions connected, it also fits with Aquinas's statement that will and reason "include one another in their acts" (*ST* I q.82, a.4, rep.1). Moreover, this construal also helps to make sense of a distinction that critically relates to Aquinas's account of incontinence.

Aquinas differentiates "the *inward* man" from "the *outward* man"; the former refers to "the intellectual part," the latter to "the sensitive part with the body" (q.75, a.4, rep.1). The terminology obviously recalls Paul's language from Rom. 7, and Aquinas's characterization of reason–proper and reason–as–tool; so we may well expect his analysis here to pertain to those other issues. Aquinas connects the inward–outward distinction to the tendency for identifying a thing with what is principle in it, and he says the intellectual part is identified with the person "in accordance with truth" (q.75, a.4, rep.1). We know, of course, that Aquinas cannot mean that a person simply *is* her intellect, since he explicitly denies that, as we saw above.

Happily, now that we grasp the capabilities of the psychological faculties, we can see what Aquinas does mean: the "intellectual part" uses the broader sense, which includes both reason and will. And between them, *will and reason cover the abilities necessary for agency*; they include both the requisite cognitive and motivational powers. Reason and will could constitute an agent—as, presumably, they do for noncorporeal beings like angels. That is why we are tempted to identify ourselves with our (broadly considered) intellects, and why an agent beset with passions from the sensitive appetite can easily regard herself as under attack from outside her person. That is why we begin with a naïve assumption that our agency should be "self-transparent." That is why Aquinas regards the temperate person's "It is not I" denial as importantly true—she feels the inordinate appetites, but in the tightest boundary of her agency does not affirm them; and why Aquinas regards the self-divided person's denial as true, but only in a "perverse" way—although the inclination of her will-habit truly is not subject to her direct control, it comes from within those minimal boundaries for agency.

Most crucially of all, though, we can now see why Aquinas ultimately denies that the intellect really is the human being: while some kind of agency may be possible with only the faculties of reason and will, human agency is not. Human agency requires the sensitive faculties, the perceptions and appetites, too. Human will and reason cannot function without "the sensitive part with the body"; the "outward man" is still the man, and not something extraneous. Humans are essentially embodied—even in heaven we need, in the end, to have bodies (Aquinas, *TH* q.4, a.5, reps.4, 5). "The use of reason requires the due use of the . . . sensitive powers, which are exercised through a bodily organ" (Aquinas, *ST* I–II q.33, a.3, rep.3). Our wills execute action by moving our bodies; the appetites of our bodies inform what our reason sees as good, and on and on. That is why incontinent actions, no matter how inordinate the passions' roles become, remain human actions; such actions still occur through the normal abilities of human agency. In this way, then, Aquinas maintains his position that *all* of the principles of action—reason, will, and the sensitive appetites—are necessary for human action.

Therefore, will and reason—the potential targets of the homuncularist charge—both retain enough powers and distinctiveness that neither functions in itself as a "little agent." Rather, each includes abilities that make it a component of a functioning agent. Reason possesses guidance-ability that is independent of the will; the will possesses sole powers of choice and action-motivation; and even together they lack powers that allow a human agent to function, namely, those appetitive and perceptive abilities associated with the sensitive faculties. Thus, my interpretation of Aquinas's psychology stakes out ground that safely avoids homuncularist territory. In addition, when augmented with the Augustinian view of habit, the nonhomuncularist model is still able to save the most troublesome incontinent phenomenon, regarding self-division. Finally, then, we successfully preserve Aquinas's essential insight and characterization "of human beings themselves, and not only of events occurring within them, as genuine causes of their actions—'*agent* causes'" [emphasis added] (Donagan, "TAHA" 654).

6.7 THE MODIFIED MODEL'S EXPERIENTIAL ADEQUACY

To quickly sum up the results of the last several sections: we have seen that, with the addition of an alternative interpretation of Aristotelian practical reasoning and of a more Augustinian psychology of habits, our Thomistic model of incontinent action gains the explanatory power to better account not only for clear-eyed incontinence, but also for the phenomenon of perceiving divisions in the self. Jointly the two changes allow the Thomistic view to do an excellent job of "saving the phenomena" of akratic actions. Moreover, the problems that hindered the experiential adequacy of Hare's and Davidson's theories are solvable in the Thomistic model; in particular, Aquinas's modified theory successfully avoids both mechanistic and homuncularistic explanations. Our remaining concern, then, revolves around the rational-action requirement used by the modified Thomistic system. So let us at last turn our full attention to this notion of intentionality and rationality *by degree*.

6.8 RATIONALITY/INTENTIONALITY BY DEGREE

First, a brief review of how we arrived at this conception of rational action: initially, in examining Hare's view, we noted his observation that what we call intentional action in fact forms a continuum of rationality—both in the extent of conscious rational deliberation, and in the degree of rationality displayed (section 1.1.3). That is, some intentional actions—such as thoroughly deliberated career moves—seem fully rational; they occur from, and because of, well-reasoned, fully considered prescriptions to act. However, other intentional actions—such as absentminded attempts to swat away a pesky fly—seem far less rationally directed; we just react, and the actions occur without much reasoning at all. And other actions—like weak-willed ones—fail to display what we rationally think we ought to do. Next, in assessing Davidson's view, we saw that he required intentional action to be caused and rationalized by a primary reason in the mind of the agent (section 3.1.7). But this requirement collapsed into acting for *a* reason, instead of acting *according to* reason; therefore, it did not constitute a demanding enough standard to qualify as a model for rational action. Yet even with that loose requirement, Davidson was not able to construe incontinent actions (accurately described) as meeting that rational "standard." Worse, all the attempts to solve Davidson's problems revolved around eliminating any essential connection between acting intentionally and acting rationally, because that seemed the only way to account for incontinent actions as intentional (section 4.7.2).

That brings us to our present position. I reject the Davidsonian "solutions" that disconnect rationality from intentionality. Having recognized that "intentional" actions not only vary in their rationality, but also include acts with little rationality at all, I do not suppose that intentionality must *not* require rationality, that intentional action need not conform to a rational standard. Rather, I propose that intentionality does essentially involve rationality, and that our actions become intentional only to the degree that they conform to the regulative norm of the rational standard. Yes, weak-willed actions fail to satisfy that rational standard; and, yes, such actions do count as intentional. But the degree of their intentionality corresponds to the *extent* to which they measure up to the rational norm. I do recognize a broad continuum of degrees of rationality present in our actions; I simply propose that we ascribe intentionality based on a proportionally corresponding continuum.

Amelie O. Rorty—who has, during our investigation, shed light on crucial aspects of incontinent action—also acknowledges the need for such a continuum of intentionality. Having surveyed actions ranging from "preconscious [perceptual] discrimination" to "self-consciously and systematically justif[ying] clusters of propositionalized beliefs," she concludes that "intentionality can be a matter of degree" (*MA* 222).

Rorty further concurs that the canons of rationality serve as an *essential norm* for what constitutes intentional activity. She writes,

> If the effective normative power of the capacities central to critical rationality had no independent status, the justificatory strength of any rational

argument could only be a function of the effective causal strength of the [belief and desire] subsystems that formed it. . . . [T]he power of the capacities for rational integration [of desires] cannot merely be a function of their causal (psychological) strength in relation to other subsystems that compose the self. . . . [C]ritical rationality cannot just be one component of the system of subsystems. Its power must be a direct function of its rational authority, rather than of the vicissitudes of its psychological and physical history. . . . Nor can [critical rationality be merely] . . . a regulative ideal for rational inquirers and responsible agents . . . [rather than a] descriptive account of the self. The rational have, by definition, actualized that ideal: it *is* the way they function. [Emphasis in original] (227)

That is, actions cannot be produced by psychological motivations that are effective merely because of their causal strength; the agent's rational capacities must possess presumptive control, in order for what she does to be understandable as intentional, at all. The mere capacity for rationality demands that reason have this kind of control. For,

Responsible agents . . . must be able to carry out a rationally structured complex plan of action, [thus necessarily] giving the capacities for critical rationality not only the authority but also the effective force that reflect the normative power of their rational justification. The strength of the cause must be a function of the strength of the reason. The requirements of responsibility and rationality are not satisfied by assigning the subsystem of critical rationality the weight it would have on a principle of "One subsystem, one vote," or even "Weight each subsystem according to its psychological strength." (225)

So even though our actions may not always fully satisfy the rational norm, it functions as more than an ideal to strive for in acting intentionally; it measures the success of the striving itself by assigning relative degrees of intentionality corresponding to the degree of rationality displayed (227).

Moreover, Rorty notes an important condition for the assignment of intentionality by degrees: it requires the possibility of failing to integrate what one holds rationally desirable into one's dispositions and motivations. That is, only someone who interprets her behavior "through the lenses" of a rational standard, while at the same time not actually possessing psychological motivations that have been fully conformed to that standard, could find her actions partially—but not completely—meeting the rational norm. For "only a *presumptively integrated* person," whose self contains "relatively autonomous [motivational] sub-systems" not entirely under her rational control, but who nevertheless "treats the independence of her constituent sub-systems as *failures* of integration," could act so as to *partially* fulfill the demands of rationality [emphasis added] (228). To the extent, then, that such a person could integrate her rational goals into her psychological motivations—could conform the motivating dispositions to what reason directs—she could begin to define her resulting activities as intentional. This agent would work increasingly to define her behavior as intentional, by bringing her appetites and pleasures (and other motivations) into accord with her rational appraisals and descriptions of her actions (Rorty, "Akrasia and Pleasure: *Nicomachean Ethics* Bk. 7" 276). Thus, the *need* for such a conforming process presents a condition for assigning intentionality by degrees.

And the presence of the need indicates that an agent's psychological faculties *should be, but are not*, fully under her reason's control. Rorty states,

> Explaining the phenomena of systematic, discriminative, entrenched irrationality [like akrasia] requires postulating interfering [psychological] systems that, while falling outside the system of . . . [critical rationality], nevertheless also function within the system of rational beliefs and attitudes. (*MA* 216)

That is, explicating the psychology of the kind of agent susceptible to incontinence must utilize distinct subsystems; some of those have to *operate at least partially independently from the agent's reason*, while at the same time *falling under reason's normative control*. The unintegrated subsystems create the possibility of acting other than according to reason, but that must be conjoined with an assumption of reason's control, or such actions would not count as rational failures. For, "Where there is no presumption of, or capacity for, rationality, there are no failures of rationality" (219).

6.8.1 Aquinas's Theoretical "Fit"

We can see the relevance of this condition when we examine the "fit" of this degreed rational standard to the Thomistic model of human action. For Aquinas does indeed present us with a model of the human action-faculties that includes *faulty integration* of rational direction into the motivating appetites. As we saw earlier, extant humanity suffers from the loss of its original state of order and innocence (section 5.3.2).

Aquinas describes the original human condition thusly: "reason had perfect hold over the lower parts of the soul [that is, the appetites], while reason itself was perfected by God in being subject to Him" (*ST* I–II q.85,

a.3, resp.). This original order Aquinas calls "the law of [humanity] . . . al-
lotted to [us] . . . by the Divine ordinance . . . according to [our] proper natural condition . . . [namely,] that [we] should act in accordance with reason"
(*TL* q.91, a.6, resp.). And in short, "Properly speaking, [a human being] is
that which is according to reason" (*ST* II–II q.155, a.1, rep.2).

After the Fall, however, humanity forfeited that rational control and
our appetites became disordered. We suffered a "destruction of the commensuration of [our] desires" (Aquinas, *CNE* VII.L.1: C1295). We "are naturally directed to virtue" and charity only in a *diminished* way (Aquinas, *ST*
I–II q.85, a.3, resp.). Instead, our appetites can arise "not from reason"; that
is, fear, anger, malice, and so on, can move us without reason's direction—
even in spite of rational urgings (Aquinas, *ER* chp.7, lec.3). And when rationally directed, our sense appetite still is "hindered from wholly following
the command of reason" (Aquinas, *TH* q.17, a.7, rep.1). Sinful actions
worsen this disorder, in that "through sin the reason is obscured . . . the will
hardened against the good . . . and concupiscence [that is, inordinate pas-
sion] more inflamed" (*ST* I–II q.85, a.3, resp.). As a result, extant humanity
operates not under the law proper to its nature, but under "the law of sin,"
which first "resists reason" and eventually "reduces the [person] to a state of
slavery" (*ER* bk.7, lec.4).

Now, we must work to bring our appetites into line with reason's directives. The actions we perform through the motivation of those appetites
reflect how much or how little of that rational control we have achieved.

Obviously, then, Aquinas offers just the sort of picture of humanity that
would place us in the class of agents who can fail to integrate their rational
directives into their motivational dispositions. Human agents, in Aquinas's
view, fulfill Rorty's condition for the possibility of assigning intentionality
by degree. Moreover, the originally innocent state of humanity provides a
model for how human, intentional action *should* work—for what it *should*
be. The action-production of originally innocent humans would meet the
norm of full, deliberate, rational control according to God's law. The actions
of fallen humanity would meet that norm to a certain extent, determined
by how thoroughly the given agent's appetites had been conformed to reason's assessment of the divine law. Therefore, we could quite plausibly attribute intentionality and "human-ness" in various degrees to the actions of
fallen humanity. We can see, then, that Aquinas's model of the human agent
easily lends itself to a conception of rational action that assigns intentionality by degrees.

Furthermore, Aquinas recognizes that voluntariness can attach to an
action in different ways, including by degrees. First, he says, an act may be

voluntary *"in itself,"* when the agent wills it directly. Second, an act may be voluntary *"in its cause,"* when the agent directly wills something that then results in the second action, which may not in itself be voluntarily performed—Aquinas specifically mentions the example of drunken behavior, here, and would apply the point to habituated *akrasia* (*ST* I–II q.77, a.7, resp.). Or again, a person may voluntarily perform an action by *directly* inclining her will toward it. But she may also *indirectly* allow her will not to prevent an action's occurrence—as in the kind of incontinent scenario where resistible passion influences action (q.77, a.7, resp.). More importantly, though, Aquinas sees that in some cases of indirectly willed or voluntary-in-cause actions, voluntariness can diminish. For instance, if a person had no general acquaintance either with alcohol or with drunks, and so could not foresee her likely behavior if she became drunk, her bad behavior while drunk would be less voluntary than if she were an experienced drinker with a history of "drunk and disorderly" citations. Indeed, factors like ignorance not only diminish voluntariness, they also reduce the moral *weight* of the less-voluntary actions (q.76, a.4, resp.). Thus, the novice drinker's subsequent rudeness is also less sinful than the experienced drinker's. In short, the extent that factors like ignorance or passion "influence the activity of the intellect and will determines the effect they have on the voluntariness of what we do" (Driscoll, 3,217).

In addition, Aquinas recognizes that some human actions involve more conscious deliberation than others, and that some utilize little or none at all. He points out, for example, that although we still act for an end, we do not actively deliberate in making small choices—say, whether to pick up the blue or the red pencil in order to write a report—that do not affect the achievement of the end (Aquinas, *TH* q.14, a.4, resp.). And, of course, we have seen, at length, how actions emerging from habit may occur without reason's deliberation. Aquinas's view, then, allows that some human actions are more consciously deliberate than others, more voluntary than others, and more morally "weighty" than others.

On that account, given that actions can possess higher and lower degrees of the qualities that qualify them as "human" (and "intentional" in our sense), it seems only a small and logical step to admit that actions can thereby possess higher and lower degrees of humanness (or intentionality) itself. For our actions' "degree of imputability" to us—that is, how much they characterize us *as human*—is "dependent upon the extent that knowledge and will are [properly] involved [in their production]" (Driscoll, 3211). Now, I have not seen any passages in which Aquinas explicitly refers to humanness as subject to degrees, so I cannot say that he saw it in this light.

However, the Thomistic theory of action certainly could easily accommodate this degreed conception of humanness, and we can now see why.

6.8.2 Intentionality-by-Degree and Akratic Action

Let us take a moment, then, to review the way in which the degreed standard of humanness and intentionality would explain incontinent actions. An incontinent action does not occur from the deliberation of reason-proper. Rather, a passion or will-habit interferes with the operations of reason-proper, and inclines the will through the guise of reason-as-tool. In cases prompted by passion, reason and will do not operate "of their own accord," but under passion's influence; the incontinent action is not completely under the agent's control, and so is less than optimally voluntary and less than fully sinful, but does retain some degree of sinfulness and voluntariness (Aquinas, *ST* I–II q.77, a.6, resp.; a.7, resp.). Moreover, the agent does have *a* reason for her action—she satisfies some passion, such as the appetite for pleasure. Yet she recognizes that this motive does not accord with reason, since she understands the unlawfulness of the incontinent action. Therefore, she acts in a less-than-optimally-rational manner, as well. Further, since humanness emerges in actions voluntarily performed from, and in accord with, reason, an incontinent action is less than fully human. The action qualifies as human to the extent that it remains under the agent's control, as measured by the degree to which it approximates the normative process of acting according to reason-proper's assessment of what (lawfully) should be done.

In addition, this explanation based on diminished voluntariness and rationality also applies to habitually necessitated incontinent actions. For such deeds remain voluntary in cause, as the agent acted voluntarily in acquiring the necessitating habit. That voluntariness then "carries over" to the habituated action, but perhaps only in a partial or qualified way. The agent may have only imperfectly understood that she was forming a habit, what that formation implied, and so on. These factors would diminish the voluntariness of the actions later necessitated by the habit. To the extent, then, that the habituated actions could count as voluntary, they could be measured in their approximation to the course of action directed by reason. From that measurement, a rough degree of humanness could be assigned, corresponding to the action's voluntariness.

This Thomistic conception of rational action casts both passionate and habituated incontinent actions as failures of reason. The actions do not come from reason-proper, nor do they accord with reason-proper's assessments of what should be done. And in conjunction with that fault, "the proper movement of the rational appetite or will must, of necessity, become ... impeded" (Aquinas, *ST* I–II q.77, a.1, resp.). Reason, whose practical job is guiding the will according to God's law, fails in allowing such actions to occur as they do. Moreover, this view recognizes that habitually necessary incontinent actions may well compromise their author's agency. For example, Aquinas admits that in an agent experiencing self-division, "sin works in [her] as if possessing dominion" (*ER* bk.7, lec.3). However, all of these actions do come about through—by means of—the agent's reason (albeit as tool); even the habituated actions retain some form and degree of voluntariness proportionate to their semblance of proper rationality.

From that approximation of rational control, then, our Thomistic theory assigns the incontinent actions a degree of humanness and intentionality. Precisely described these actions fall short of being properly or fully human or intentional. But commonly or loosely described, they are human and intentional, because they fit into the continuum of degrees of rationality and intentionality. On that account, the Thomistic model of rational action which I have proposed does not deny the rational failure inherent in weak-willed actions. Yet the theory still explains such actions within the framework of its construal of intentional action as action from, and according to, *reason*. That, I believe, constitutes the solution we have sought.

6.9 SUMMARY CONCLUSIONS ON AQUINAS'S VIEW

It has been a long analysis, so let me present a quick recap of our findings regarding Aquinas. With respect to practical rationality: First, Aquinas's view provides a clear and practically usable standard of rationality in action. Second, this standard applies to the entire range of intentional actions. Third, Aquinas's view essentially connects acting intentionally with acting from, and according to, reason. Therefore, Aquinas offers a workable standard of practical rationality that meets the needs of a rational-action theory.

Further, Aquinas's theory adequately accounts for incontinent actions. It construes akratic actions as resulting from failures of reason. Moreover, when augmented by an interpretation of Aristotle different from that used by Aquinas, and by an Augustinian alteration in its psychology, the modified Thomistic model gains the ability to explain all the important phenomena we have seen associated with akratic actions. The theory can account for the akratic agent's inner conflict, including the struggles involved in acting against discretive judgments and even commands. It explains the possibility of clear-eyed *akrasia*. In addition, it shows how the agent could experience

such a serious and intractable conflict during habitually necessary incontinent actions, that she might come to see her very self as divided. Thus, the
modified Thomistic model deals with a robustly characterized portrayal of
weak-willed action.

Moreover, by adopting a degreed conception of the rational, regulative
norm for intentionality, the modified Thomistic theory can account for incontinent actions within its framework of rational action. The theory admits the rational failure and compromised agency that incontinence may involve. Yet the Thomistic account places such "damaged" actions into a
continuum of rationality and intentionality in which those acts still count
as intentional and human. In this way, the modified Thomistic view provides
the solution we have sought: it offers a standard for practical rationality
strong enough to differentiate between acting for *a* reason and acting *according to* reason—that is, it requires a sufficiently rigorous link between intentionality and rationality. However, by construing the satisfaction of that
requirement as a matter of degree, the theory also can accommodate rationally faulty incontinent actions within its rational-action model. At last
we have a rational-action theory that can both admit that weak-willed actions, in all their complexity and messiness, *do* occur and show how those
actions still qualify as rational and intentional.

CONCLUSION

Finally, by way of conclusion, let me note proposed possibilities for further investigation into theories of rational action.

First, I realize that Aquinas's model of rational, human action comes with a great deal of baggage. Davidson's view at least possessed the virtue of not requiring extraneous metaphysical assumptions about the nature of the human soul, about that soul's role in the world, and so on. Not so with Aquinas's theory, which requires belief in God, belief in the correctness of Christian interpretation of divine law, belief regarding the proper fulfillment of human nature, and more. Such prerequisite assumptions may make Aquinas's theory unattractive. Perhaps it offers a working model of rational action, but not the best one. I believe a critic such as Amelie Rorty would level just that kind of charge against the proposed Thomistic view. That possible attack calls for work on two fronts: on one, to see whether at least some of the speculative aspects of Aquinas's teleological view can be streamlined out; on the other, to investigate speculatively light rival models of rational action that do not depend on teleology at all.

7.1 STREAMLINING THE SPECULATIVE WEIGHT

On the first front, the defense of my Thomistic view demands investigation of whether some of the external metaphysical supports can be streamlined out of the Thomistic, teleological theory of human action. For example, this position's standard of practical rationality demands that human action have one ultimate end so that progress toward or away from that end can be measured by assigning degrees of rationality to various options for action. But must that end be constituted by a communion with God? We might question whether some less metaphysically speculative conception of human fulfillment also could play this role, or whether that would still be able to supply the needed kind of usable, accessible, rational standard.

Now, Aristotle's system presents an obvious possibility for a more streamlined, yet still workable, teleological, rational-action theory. Obviously, though, a full and in-depth comparison of Aristotle's and Aquinas's positions would require a book of its own, so I'm not going to attempt it here in my conclusion. However, I will offer a sketched comparison—emphasizing that it is a mere sketch. Nonetheless, I think the quick comparison shows, in a bare-bones way, why Aquinas's model of rational action is likely to be superior to Aristotle's.

7.1.1 Streamlined Aspects of Aristotle's View

In this comparison, we first see several ways in which Aristotle's system is more streamlined. After all, much of Aquinas's view is based on Aristotle's, yet Aristotle's position is not wedded to Christian theology and so is free from commitments to belief in the God, afterlife, and revelation of Christianity. That unloads much of the speculative baggage from Aquinas's system.

Also, Aristotle's psychology itself seems more parsimonious. He makes do without proposing a distinct faculty of will; he speaks of reason, desire, and habitual dispositions and of their interactions, but he never discusses a faculty for the power of choosing. To illustrate, Aristotle writes, "decision [that is, what Aquinas calls 'choice'] will be deliberative desire to do an action that is up to us" (*NE* 1113a11–12). And, "decision involves reason and thought" (1112a16). Or again, "the origin of decision is desire together with reason that aims at some goal" (1139a32–33). Hence, for Aristotle, Aquinas's will-act of choice seems reduced to an interaction of reason and desire. If the other will-acts are also eliminated as such, as I believe they are, then Aristotle's psychology need not include will at all. As Anthony Kenny writes in the rather incongruously titled *Aristotle's Theory of the Will*:

> Volition [supposedly] is a mental event which precedes and causes . . . human actions. . . . The freedom of the will is to be located in the indeterminacy of these internal volitions. . . . It is true that this account of the will is not to be found in Aristotle. This is not to Aristotle's discredit. (vii)

For Aristotle's psychology thereby possesses greater simplicity than Aquinas's.

Further, Aristotle's action-model appears simpler than Aquinas's. Aristotle describes reason-acts, like deliberation, prior to decision, but none posterior to it. And of course, given the last point, no will-acts could follow decision. Aristotle writes, "Now the origin of an action—the source of the movement, not the action's goal—is decision" (*NE* 1139a31–32). Indeed, this is the passage that underlay Aquinas's comment that choice was the efficient cause of action (*CNE* VI.L.2: C1133), which made it seem that Aquinas's model stopped at choice (section 6.4.2). For in Aristotle's view, decision does present the last step in action-production. With decision made, "it is necessary . . . to act at once on what has been concluded. . . . [I]t is necessary . . . for someone who is able and unhindered to act on this [decision] at the time" (*NE* 1147a25–31). That is, the agent acts straightway upon, and because of, decision. In Terence Irwin's words, the agent "must immediately act" once a decision is made ("Notes" 352). Thus, Aristotle's rational-action model, itself, streamlines out some of Aquinas's.

7.1.2 Explanatory Losses from the Streamlining

Considering points like the ones above (and there surely are others too), it may well seem that Aristotle's rational-action theory is less speculatively weighted, and therefore more plausible, than Aquinas's. However, that increased plausibility is illusory, and the collapse of that illusion traces directly to the streamlined aspects of Aristotle's theory.

First, notice what Aristotle loses by making decision the last step of action-production. Aquinas's "order of execution" vanishes; Aristotle only has is what Aquinas called the "order of intention." But it was the executive order, and the opportunities for reason and will failures within it, that made it possible for Aquinas's view to account for the phenomena of *akrasia* in the face of presently held intentions—that is, of clear-eyed *akrasia* in its starkest occurrence. Aristotle, then, must push back the akratic rational failure to decision or some prior stage. Yet, that means that the akratic agent must fail in her intention to do the rationally approved act. For we saw, in Aquinas's view, that an agent does not truly form an intention (in our sense) until she chooses an action; only then does she have a judgment directing, and a desire to perform, a specific action. Since Aquinas's "choice" is the same stage as Aristotle's "decision," the upshot is that if the akratic agent must fail either to make or maintain her decision—as is the case in Aristotle's construction—then the agent cannot act against a presently held intention. Either she does not successfully form an intention for the rational action, or she must lose the intention during her weakness. Thus, in spite of the contemporary interpretations of Norman Dahl and the others, Aristotle's account of *akrasia* must rely on some cognitive rational failure, and not on an executive rational failure. However, as we have seen, the latter sort of failure is the key to explaining clear-eyed *akrasia*.

Moreover, Aristotle's difficulty is compounded by uncertainty concerning whether he effectively distinguishes reason's (discretive) judgment from decision and even from acting. That is, it is not clear whether Aristotle sees the conclusion of a practical syllogism as a rational judgment (like Aquinas's discretive judgment), as decision, as the outward action, itself, or as some necessarily linked combination. Irwin, for instance, thinks Aristotle regards the conclusion as a judgment inextricable from decision and its resultant action. Irwin writes that if someone has "drawn the right conclusion ... [she has] hence formed the right decision" ("Notes" 352) and that "the formation of the conclusion ... at once leads to action" (351). In contrast, Anthony Kenny claims that, "the conclusion of a piece of practical reasoning ... is a decision to act (*ATW* 142). Normally, Kenny says, decision and the resultant action are so closely linked that it is pointless to distinguish them; yet, in certain circumstances—like incontinence—they can be separated, so that decision alone is the conclusion, or perhaps so that the decision itself becomes or counts as the action (142). Dahl, however, thinks Aristotle sees the conclusion as the outward action; he also distinguishes the conclusion from a rational judgment—which would correspond to Aquinas's discretive judgment—that precedes the conclusion but can be severed from it (*PRAWW* 206). Or again, David Charles thinks the conclusion must be a judgment, not the action, but that it is so tied to the action that it could not fail to produce the action unless the agent held it in an "off colour" or defective manner (*APA* 120). And advocating yet another perspective, Sarah Broadie writes, "for Aristotle there is *no* sort of practical knowledge [and hence no rational judgment in the action-process] that necessarily gives rise to the corresponding action" (*EA* 285). So, in her view Aristotle repudiates any strict connection between judgment and decision and action.

The upshot of this confusion is that Aristotle may or may not have to cut off the akratic agent's practical reasoning prior to the conclusion of reason's syllogism. That is, we saw above that the akratic agent cannot reach, or at least maintain, a decision for reason's action during her *akrasia*; thus, she does not have, or loses, the intention—in the full sense including a desire to perform a specific action—for the rational action. Now, though, we can see that depending on what Aristotle thinks the practical syllogism's conclusion is, he may have to deny that the akratic agent even reaches the judgment-stage immediately preceding decision. For if the judgment and decision and action are bound together, then an agent could not possess a rational directive for a specific action and yet fail to act on it. On this interpretation, during the akratic agent's weakness, she could have neither the desire nor even the rational judgment to perform a specific action; she no longer would have either of the critical elements of an intention. That lack would place explanation of clear-eyed *akrasia* completely out of reach.

Of course, if Dahl's interpretation is correct, then an akratic agent could not conclude reason's practical syllogism while acting out of passion. But the agent could retain the judgment directing reason's approved action, so she would still possess a semblance of an intention in that she would recognize what, specifically, she should do. Therefore, some explanation of clear-eyed *akrasia* remains possible. The same is true for Broadie's and Charles' constructions. And that is, after all, the intent of their interpretations of Aristotle's "have" versus "use" distinction regarding practical knowledge (section 6.4.1). But even their interpretations cannot allow Aristotle to account for *akrasia* in the face of a robust intention—including both the directive and the desire for a specific action. Aristotle's truncated action-model cannot accommodate that. Moreover, these contemporary interpretations cannot evade the difficulties arising from Aristotle's reduction of the will, as we shall now see.

Second, then, by eliminating the faculty of will, Aristotle falls into significant problems. The absence of the faculty of will hinders Aristotle's ability to construe akratic actions as voluntary. In Aquinas's view, even though incontinent actions do not proceed from reason-proper, they are still chosen. The will's failure to hold to reason-proper's discretive judgment is voluntary—it is free and an activity within the will's functional parameters. Even in the extreme cases involving the feeling of self-division, the habits that pull the will are of its own generation and thus retain an indirect voluntariness. For Aquinas, fortified by Augustine's psychology,

> [I]t is possible for someone to know unqualifiedly what it is best to do in
> a particular situation and for there to be no defect in the passions as such,
> except that they are misdirected by the will. (MacIntyre, *WJWR* 156)

So incontinence stems directly from the will's activity, from voluntary choice. Moreover, as part of reason, broadly characterized, the will's weakness counts as a kind of rational failure. However, these things are no longer true in Aristotle's model.

For Aristotle, the efforts under the akratic agent's conscious control lack nothing; the problem lies in a failure or malfunction of the "*non-rational* part of the soul" [emphasis added] (Broadie, *EA* 290). That is, the agent's passions are ill shaped enough that they can arise inappropriately. Now, the inappropriate passions represent a kind of rational failing in the agent's possessing them since their presence implies that reason's ends have not been fully integrated into the agent's dispositions. Yet, in the akratic action, itself, the agent does not voluntarily, rationally falter. Rather, in spite of the agent's resistance, her rational judgment is "dragged about by passion" (Dahl, *PRAWW* 210–11). So the akratic agent experiences "a genuine state of conflict" in which she *would act* on her rational judgment, but "is *prevented* from doing so . . . [by a] strong conflicting desire" [emphasis added] (215). In this picture, the akratic action does not represent the agent's rational— and therefore voluntarily controllable—decision; it occurs counter to it. Indeed, the akratic action seems not even to proceed from a decision at all. As Alan Donagan has observed, "Aristotle was reluctant to acknowledge that . . . [an agent] acting out of character or on impulse genuinely chooses at all" ("TAHA" 643). The akratic falls into the latter category, for an impulse of passion drives her action. Thus, Aristotle writes that "the intemperate person decides [to act on her appetites] . . . but the incontinent person does not" (*NE* 1148a18). And also, "of those who do not [act on] decision [the incontinent] is led on because of pleasure" (1150a25). This lack of decision, though, seems to remove the akratic action from the agent's voluntary control. Even if we consider an agent's character to be subject to her voluntary formation, thereby making the aberrant state of the akratic's passions—and perhaps the resultant action—blameworthy to some extent, that still does not make her akratic failure voluntary. In Aquinas's view, even when the agent's choices are restricted by habits, she still chooses. Not so, in Aristotle's model. Aristotle can trace *akrasia* to only two possibilities: one, "some imperfection in that particular person's knowledge at that particular time of what is good and best," or two, "some imperfection in the education and disciplining of the passions" (MacIntyre, *WJWR* 156). Neither of those expresses a choice at that time by the agent. The voluntary choosing of the action is gone; only the conscious recognition of what is done and why remains. Aristotle attempts to assign voluntariness to the action merely because the agent "acts in knowledge both of what [she] is doing and of the end [she] is doing it for" (*NE* 1152a16).

Yet his position remains squarely in the sights of Davidson's objection of mechanistic action (which we earlier saw Aquinas successfully avoid; section 6.6.1). We recall that Donald Davidson attacks models of action that pit reason against passion with no inclusion of choice by the agent:

> The image we get of incontinence from Aristotle . . . is of a battle or struggle between two contestants. Each contestant is armed with his argument or principle. One side may be labeled "passion" and the other "reason"; they fight; one side wins, the wrong side, the side called "passion." . . . On [this] story . . . it is not clear how we can ever blame the agent for what [she] does: [her] action merely reflects the outcome of a struggle within [her]. What could [she] do about it? And more important, the . . . image does not allow us to make sense of a conflict in one person's soul, for it leaves no room for the all important process of weighing considerations. (*EAE* 35)

In short, in Aristotle's view, the agent makes no choice between reason and passion; there is no way for her to consider the relative merits of each "principle" and make her choice, either well or badly. Her action occurs mechanistically, with the outcome depending simply on which "side" within her possesses more motivational strength.

And again, Aristotle's problem here stems directly from his reduced psychology. Given Aquinas's psychology, including the faculty of will, the agent "can judge the strength of the arguments on both sides, can execute the decision, and take the rap," as even Davidson admits (35–36). Given Aristotle's psychology, with only reason, desire, and habitual dispositions, the agent simply cannot do those things. That leaves Aristotle—whether interpreted in the traditional or alternative ways concerning practical reason—with a large hole in his explanation of *akrasia*.

Third, and lastly, Aristotle's lack of Christianity's explanatory resources leaves him with some very difficult questions to answer. One of those is, Can the teleology of human nature be adequately grounded and specified? Both Aquinas's and Aristotle's views crucially depend on certain functions and goals embedded in the very essence of being human. Because human nature is directed to a certain goal, we can gather reasons about why and how we should try to reach it. With a specified goal, we can rationally measure our actions against it—are we progressing toward it or not? Now, in Aquinas's case, Christianity provides the grounding and specification of that teleology. God creates according to His purposes, so that human nature has functions and purposes as part of that larger plan. The upshot is that human life has a goal, namely to praise God and enjoy Him forever, as the Heidelberg Catechism puts it. Christian revelation supplies the grounding for that teleology by telling us about God and His purposes. Moreover, that revelation also provides the specification for how to reach our essential goal; scripture gives us directions about what God wants from us. Thus, given the access to the divine perspective granted by the Christian worldview, Aquinas explains both why our essential functions and purposes are what they are and why certain courses of action are suitable while others are not. However, lacking those resources, Aristotle cannot answer those questions as definitively as Aquinas can.

Because Aristotle operates solely from the human perspective, his ability to ground and specify his teleology is limited and shaky. It is not that Aristotle's empiricist techniques are useless—far from it!—but we recognize that they reach, or even exceed, their limits right in the area where Aristotle needs them on this issue. As Descartes remarks in his *Meditations on First Philosophy*,

> [There are] innumerable things whose causes escape me. For this reason alone the whole class of causes, which people customarily derive from a thing's "purpose," I judge to be useless. . . . It is not without rashness that I think myself competent to inquire into . . . purposes [of natural things]. (55)

With that Aristotle's ability to determine the purposes of human nature is casually dismissed as obviously inadequate. We may not have Descartes' antipathy to Aristotle, but we do, I think, share his skepticism, and rightly so. We unaided humans simply do not have the capability to reliably discover what human beings—or any other animals—are "for." Moreover, our prejudices and agendas make our teleological pronouncements even more suspect—Aristotle's exaltation of metaphysical contemplation, as the true heart of human excellence (*NE* 1177a15–1179a30) leaps to mind, here. But in that case, Aristotle cannot successfully ground his claims about the functions and goals of human nature. And if he cannot give sufficient grounding to what those functions are in the first place, he has no hope of ultimate justification for any specifics he might offer as to how to realize those goals. In short, given the tools his theory and worldview provide, Aristotle cannot offer the grounding and specification needed by his teleology.

Furthermore, that builds into a problem in answering a second question: how does reason provide a comparative measure for all our intentional-action possibilities? Again, Aquinas's Christianity provides him a ready answer. God's laws give us a basis from which to judge every human action. We know that we are designed to be in loving relationship with God, to become more Christlike and thereby more in tune with God. In Christ's example and the various revealed divine commands, we have a standard sufficiently clear and comprehensive to allow reason to comparatively rank actions in all aspects of our lives, according to how well the acts do (or do not) lead towards God. Not so, for Aristotle.

Because Aristotle cannot successfully establish the foundations of his teleology, reason cannot adequately compare actions. That is, if he cannot justify the specifics about what the good for human life is, he cannot show that action *x* is more rational than action *y*. For how can we tell which are the most rational acts to perform if we do not know which ones best contribute to our good? Unfortunately, since we do not have a sufficiently clear and justified picture of the human ends, we simply cannot know which acts would lead towards or away from our good, let alone know which acts would better contribute to that good. As an analogous illustration, if we do not know whether we are going to Seattle or Minneapolis, it is impossible to pick the road to take out of Spokane. Even if we had our destination narrowed to Seattle or Portland, we would still be hard-pressed to identify the best route. Just so, with respect to Aristotle's view and the rational measure for action. Given the point, above, reason cannot reliably identify the more and less rational actions.

Lastly, as we saw in the previous chapter (section 6.4.2), Aquinas's Christian worldview lets him answer a third question: why would humans suffer from incontinence in the first place? But Aristotle would find answering difficult. For Aquinas, the possibility of incontinence lies crucially in the destructive effects of sin. Aquinas's theory of human action describes a system operating under damaged conditions, which view is a natural implication of his Christian tenets that human beings have been disordered by original sin and that we further damage ourselves through our own active sins. However, as Dahl noted, it is not at all obvious why, in Aristotle's metaphysical biology, the human action-faculties should have the kinds of flaws and vulnerabilities that make incontinence possible in the first place (*PRAWW* 214).

As an illustration of Aristotle's difficulty, consider this assessment by Sarah Broadie: human beings need to be raised from "first nature" by training so that they will not follow every physical impulse, "for otherwise the capacities for distinctively human ends, innate though they must be, get no chance to be regularly actualised" (*EA* 269). That observation may be true, but how? It seems decidedly odd, in Aristotle's teleological view of biology, to have a species such that its members, if left alone and given the opportunity to do what their nature points them towards, would not develop into the fulfillment of that nature. Given, too, that the problem is specieswide, it looks as if the very nature of human beings is damaged or defective in some way. But how could that be? Frankly, I do not see how Aristotle can successfully distinguish a "first nature" that has to be transcended from a truly human nature and its fulfillment without recourse to the kind of explanation Aquinas offers concerning original sin. As Alasdair MacIntyre notes, using Christianity's "strong thesis about the inadequacies and flaws of the natural human order," Aquinas applies "this understanding of fallen human nature . . . to explain the limitations of Aristotle's arguments" (*WJWR* 205). Unfortunately for Aristotle, that explanation cannot be had without the surrounding Christian framework (or at least something quite similar with respect to a fallen humanity), which he lacks.

Now, let me be clear, here: I am not attempting a plausibility-comparison between Christian theology and Aristotelian metaphysics. Nor am I asserting that Aquinas's Christian worldview has no aspects that might draw skepticism. Rather, I am pointing out illustrations of this claim: if the "operating parameters" of Aquinas's view are accepted, he can answer the questions regarding human teleology, practical rationality's measure, and human brokenness; yet if Aristotle's operating parameters are adopted, he still cannot answer those questions. Once the basic systems are accepted, Aquinas's can do more explanatory work than Aristotle's. And as we have just seen, crucial elements of that explanatory superiority rest on Aquinas's Christian worldview.

To conclude this comparative sketch—and I reemphasize that it is a mere sketch, and a quick one—I think we can now see that although Aristotle's system definitely does streamline out sizable portions of Aquinas's, that streamlining also results in unacceptable losses in explanatory power. Such losses give us reason to believe that Aquinas's view may offer a better rational-action theory than Aristotle's can. And again, Aquinas's superior power seems closely tied to the Christian framework of his system.

7.1.3 Additional Streamlining Possibilities

With the above argument, I do not mean to imply that no significant streamlining from Aquinas's view is possible without seriously damaging the position. I do think that is the case with respect to the presence of the Christian worldview in Aquinas's system; we just saw one reason why Christianity is so critical to Aquinas's explanatory success. However, Aquinas's theory incorporates the whole system of Aristotelian physics and metaphysics, too. And while the present investigation may have made me into a neo-Thomist (somewhat to my surprise), I remain a complete non-believer in Aristotelian physics, and I have many problems with Aristotelian metaphysics. So, I, for one, certainly hope that Thomistic ethics and action theory do not crucially depend on broad acceptance of those Aristotelian views. As far as I can see, the physics can be dropped without any losses to ethics or action theory. Further, while the metaphysics does have significant impact through supplying teleological parameters for human nature—which, as we have seen, are vital to Thomistic ethics and action theory—I am not at all convinced that Aquinas needs Aristotelian metaphysics, generally, to maintain that teleology. Rather, much of that could be supported from Aquinas's Christian resources. Making good on these claims, however, would once again take a new book. For now, I simply want to note that there are significant, speculative aspects of Aquinas's view that likely can be streamlined out in order to make the Thomistic rational-action model even more appealing.

We shall return to the explanatory power of Aquinas's Christianity, but first let us conclude the preview of further work by looking at possible challenges from rival rational-action theories that are speculatively light in completely eschewing the kind of teleology utilized by Aristotle and Aquinas.

7.2 NONTELEOLOGICAL RIVAL CONCEPTIONS

On the second front, then, critics like Amelie Rorty might argue that metaphysical or religious teleology is, itself, unnecessary for a rational-action theory. Yet, to make such assertions plausible, those critics need to propose a working model of rational action that does not require such teleological underpinnings. For instance, as we saw, Rorty also advocates the correct sort of degreed conception of rational action (section 6.8). But is a functional, nonteleological model available?

Part of teleology's role is to explain the necessary connection between rationality and intentional action. For Rorty, that role would seem to be played by her analysis's demonstrating that normative rationality is necessarily constituent to intentionality. That is, it is no longer requisite that we act rationally so as to fulfill our natures by obeying God's rational law, but rather we must act rationally in order to be able to perform any kind of intentional behavior.

For Aquinas, though, another part of teleology's role is giving us the content of the rational standard. Reference to the ultimate end of all action—namely, knowing and loving God—allows us to assess which actions would aid or hinder reaching that goal because it provides a measure for possible actions. That, in turn, allows us to see which specific actions are rational and even makes possible our assignment of gradations of rationality. I can tell that, upon entering a cathedral, "cursing God" would be an irrational act, "admiring the architecture" would be a rational one (since it causes me to consider beauty, which may indirectly lead me to contemplating how that is ultimately, perfectly exemplified in God), and "singing a hymn of praise" would be a more rational one (since it directly improves my attitude towards God).

It is in replacing this teleological role, of supplying guidance for the specific assessments of practical rationality, that, I believe, Rorty's analysis of intentionality would fail her. The questions for Rorty are these: can you tell us clearly what would constitute your rational requirement—what, in your view, is the goal of practical rationality? And further, how could an agent identify actions as more or less rational? Surely practical rationality's goal cannot be merely procedural, requiring only the complete integration of motivations with ideals. Are we to say that a fully integrated, unconflicted torturer is as rational as a fully integrated philanthropist? To answer yes would destroy any possibility of moral objectivism, the support of which, we recall from section 1.5, was one of the principal hopes of a successful rational-action theory. Suppose, then, that Rorty would answer no. She would need to supply a substantive goal for practical rationality, a particular value both paramount over others and realizable to some commensurate extent in any possible action.

We saw earlier (section 5.1.6) that for a person to be capable both of rationally comparing her action-options and of having some reason even for actions she deems irrational (like incontinent ones), there must be a "weak commensurability" of those options. That is, while the different actions might realize a plurality of incommensurate values, the agent needs one value that has application to all the options, so that they would all be measurable in terms of it (Wiggins, "WWCODD" 255–56). Thus, while a given action might realize a certain value and thereby have some reason for its performance, it could lack the special, commensurate value (which is presumed to be of paramount importance), so that the action would yet be irrational (256–57). Rorty would need, then, to supply an account of such a paramount, weakly commensurate value in order to give practical rationality a substantive goal, an adequate measure, for action. In short, she needs a description of a certain kind of life as ideal. But apart from a teleology of humanity (or of rational beings in general), what could justify that kind of substantive goal?

But perhaps Rorty could propose rationality itself as the paramount value. Every action has some degree of value to practical rationality, and obviously actions are rational to perform just so far as practical rationality values them. However, that is an unsuccessful dodge, for it brings on the second question, from above, with inexorable force: how could an agent identify actions as more or less rational? Davidson's view, we recall, apparently utilized just this evasion, and his failure, in the face of the second question, is instructive.

7.2.1 Davidson's Nonteleological Position and Failure

Davidson proposes that prima facie judgments assess actions in terms of a single value, rather than in terms of their overall desirability, as "unconditional" judgments do. And his "all things considered" (ATC) judgment, which represents the verdict of practical reason, is itself prima facie. We saw that the only plausible way for the ATC judgment to work is for it to be a prima facie judgment on the particular value of rationality (section 4.2.4). Thus, Davidson utilizes rationality, itself, as a weakly commensurate value present to some extent in all possible actions, whose calculation—obviously!—determines which actions are rational to perform.

Moreover, Davidson's overall action-theory is nonteleological. He resists proposing some overall goal for human life or even categorically identifying some values (other than rationality) as more important than others. As a result, Davidson provides no explicit, practical, evaluative measure to compare prima facie judgments' rational weights. Indeed, he claims that in practical reasoning we lack

> a general formula for computing how far or whether a conjunction of [prima facie judgments] . . . supports a conclusion [about what to do] from how far or whether each conjunct supports it. (*EAE* 39)

That is, to the question, how can an agent identify which action is most rational to perform? Davidson's first reply is, "We have no clue how to arrive at [the ATC judgment] from the [prima facie judgments'] reasons" (39).

However, Davidson recognizes that he needs a comparative, evaluative measure on which to base actions' rational values. The agent must be able to make use of such a measure, given that she needs to evaluatively compare and rank her competing prima facie reasons in order to reach an ATC judgment. Davidson admits,

> Shoulds, oughts, goods, and evils compete for our final approval or choice of a course of action; therefore we need to be able to construct [prima facie] sentences [like the ATC judgment] that combine considerations. . . . Now we will need a principle of inference corresponding to each evaluative word which says that if something is a reason for holding something to be obligatory, or good, or desirable, etc., then it is a [comparable] reason for holding the thing . . . to be intention-worthy. ("RE I–IX" 210–11)

Or, in short, "It is not enough to know the reasons on each side [of the question of what to do]: [the agent] must know how they add up" (*EAE* 36).

Therefore, Davidson attempts to provide a nonteleological answer to the question of how an agent can rationally evaluate her competing prima facie reasons. This answer involves the principle of charity in interpretation (as we saw in section 4.6.1). This principle directs us to assume that others are largely rationally coherent in the frameworks of their thoughts and actions because that is a requirement for interpreting their behavior in terms of intentional and rational content. This policy of rational accommodation

> necessarily requires us to see others as much like ourselves in point of overall coherence and correctness—that we see them as more or less rational creatures mentally inhabiting a world much like our own. . . . [I]n so far as people think, reason, and act at all, there must be enough rationality in the complete pattern [of their thoughts and actions] for us to judge particular beliefs as foolish or false, or particular acts as confused or misguided. (Davidson, "EE" 18)

However, that merely describes a rational procedure of aligning and integrating values and motivations and actions. And as we just saw, that seems insufficient for a theory of rational action.

Davidson, though, adds to the procedural requirement one designed to yield a standard for rational evaluation: in interpreting your behavior, I must assume that you are largely correct in your evaluations, the rational rankings you give your pro attitudes. To do that,

> I must also match up your values with mine; not, of course, in all matters, but in enough to give point to our differences. This is not, I must stress, to pretend or assume we agree. Rather, since the objects of your beliefs and values are what cause them, the only way for me to determine what those objects are is to identify objects common to us both, and take what you are caused to think and want as basically similar to what I am caused to think and want by the same objects. . . . There is no room left for relativizing values, or for asking whether interpersonal comparisons of value are possible. The only way we have of knowing what someone else's values are is one that . . . builds on a common framework. (19)

Thus, Davidson here asserts that charity requires us to assume large-scale agreement between our evaluations and that we must take that agreement as the standard that determines—or at least offers a basis for determining—the correctness of evaluations.

In other words, according to Davidson, the measure of how evaluations are to be made, of how prima facie reasons are to be rationally ranked, is constituted intersubjectively, that is, in the agreement between us. We must be guided by "the ineluctably objective and intersubjective elements . . . in evaluation" (3). Or again,

> [E]verything depends on our ability to find common ground. Given enough common ground, we can understand and explain differences, we can criticize, compare and persuade. The central point is that finding the common ground is not subsequent to understanding [how to rank and compare prima facie judgments], but a condition of it. (20)

So by starting from points of intersubjective agreement, we have a basis for assessing how evaluative judgments like prima facie reasons should be ranked and compared. At points of disagreement, our common ground provides a starting point for determining which of our evaluations are deviant—that is, which ones are anomalous and depart from the shared rational pattern of evaluative ranking and comparison. We will then be in a position to label deviant evaluations or comparative rankings as irrational because they depart from the intersubjective standard.

The intersubjective agreement, then, is Davidson's nonteleological measure for rationality in action; conforming to that common standard becomes reason's substantive goal, by which it can rank and compare the rational weights of prima facie judgments. Rather than establishing and justifying some measure of value for reason, we simply assume the correctness of what is commonly agreed upon in evaluative ranking. Then, by appealing to points of intersubjective agreement, an individual could determine whether her judgment-rankings and subsequent intentions were in line with the shared standard. If they were, then she could affirm that she acted rationally; if not, she would have to investigate the possibility that she is being irrational in acting against the shared standard of better reason.

However, this intersubjective agreement does not effectively meet Davidson's theoretical need. Two serious problems plague this standard. First, the evaluative measure's intersubjective nature indicates that incontinence would often be apparent to the agent only after the fact. That the agent has violated her own rational standard might well be visible only when her action is considered in the communal judgment, when she can see whether it fits into the rational pattern of the intersubjective agreement. It would be as if the agent were a member of a club. She agrees to the club's rules, but exactly what those rules require is a matter interpreted by the club as a whole. She might find for an individual action that she alone cannot tell whether or not it breaks the rules. That is only clear when the action is considered in the club's communal judgment. Even if the club ruled that her action broke a rule she had agreed to, that would not be like incontinence. In an akratic action, the agent needs to be able to tell on her own at, or before, the time of action whether her intention is in line with her better reason, whether her evaluation is in accord with her rational standard. But that might often not be the case with Davidson's proposed intersubjective evaluative standard. So use of this standard would not stay true to the common experience of weakness of will.

The second problem stems from the same root as the first. The need to appeal to intersubjective agreement—in order to assess whether prima facie judgments are being correctly compared, ranked, and combined—ensures that this evaluative measure is going to be unusable in daily practice. That is, this intersubjective standard will not be helpful to the agent in trying on her own to decide what to do now in reaching her own ATC judgment now. It would be a practical impossibility for an agent to discover and reason from intersubjective agreement in making everyday decisions about what she rationally ought to do. On that account, Davidson has not provided anything like the concrete, practically workable measure of evaluative rank and comparison, which he, himself, requires of an adequate theory of practical rationality and rational action. Davidson offers no practically useful method for an agent to sift her prima facie reasons in reaching an ATC judgment, or in establishing a better reason to act for or even against. Thus, Davidson's theoretical ship runs aground on the rocks of this problem. He simply cannot satisfactorily answer the question of how an agent could identify which actions were rational to perform.

7.2.2 Implications for Nonteleological Rational-Action

In the end, Davidson's problems resemble Aristotle's, only worsened. Where Aristotle could not sufficiently justify his teleology and so could not adequately specify which actions are more and less rational, Davidson has no teleology and cannot even begin (in any practically useful way) to specify which actions are more and less rational. The broader lesson yielded from Davidson's failure is that teleology is crucial to a successful theory of rational action. Practical reason must have a substantive, and not merely procedural, goal in order to be able to comparatively evaluate different actions. Rationality must have some value, aside from itself, that is both supreme in importance and weakly commensurate across actions, on which to base its

practical assessments. Rationality cannot be the value reason bases its judgments on because actions simply will not be judgeable as more or less rational without reference to the kind of external value just described. And a
metaphysical or religious teleology of human nature seems to be the only
candidate for supplying such a value because that value must, in effect, distinguish the ideal, or at least good or desirable, human life. In short, rational
action, in which reason identifies what ought to be done, is only possible
when reason has as its goal the kind of human life that ought to be sought.

Teleologies of a nonmetaphysical/nonreligious sort could be proposed
on a more limited level. A theory could, for example, describe the ideal for
a certain profession, similar to Alasdair MacIntyre's account of practices in
After Virtue (187ff.). With the goal of excellence in the profession as a given,
reason could work from this *telos* and identify actions as more or less rational
for that pursuit of excellence. However, all too quickly, it becomes clear that
such a limited *telos* cannot be sufficient for practical reason. What happens
when the agent wants to decide whether to spend more time at home with
family or at work? Practical reason has no means to compare work values
with home values. As MacIntyre himself sees, practical reason's needs force
the boundaries of its teleology wider and wider, until it encompasses what
"constitut[es] the good of a whole human life" (203). At that point, practical reason must have recourse to just the sort of metaphysically or religiously
based teleology that was originally to be avoided.

Therefore, any theory that attempts to provide a rational-action standard without reference to a religiously or metaphysically speculative teleology seems doomed to failure. That is why I think Rorty's nonteleological
analysis of intentionality cannot allow her, or other similarly minded critics
of teleology, to successfully model intentional action as rational action.
Nonteleological theorists will, like Davidson, find themselves unable to provide a pragmatically usable measure for practical reason and, subsequently,
unable to comparatively evaluate specific actions according to their rational
values. And a rational-action theory that includes no way for an agent to
identify her most rational options clearly fails in general, and, more particularly, in our project of analyzing incontinence. For,

> it will only, of course, be in the light afforded by an account of what it
> is to be successfully and adequately practically rational that the nature
> and significance of failure and inadequacy can emerge. (*WJWR* 128)

Or again, as Rorty herself admits, "Where there is no presumption of,
or capacity for, rationality, there are no failures of rationality" (*MA* 219).

That is, if a theory cannot explain the rationality in a normal intentional action, it has no hope of explaining the irrationality in weak-willed actions. Therefore, if explaining weakness of will is the crucible of testing for rational-action theories of practical rationality and intentional action, non-teleological theories seem likely to be burned up as dross.

Frankly, I believe something like the Thomistic view's Christian, metaphysical underpinnings is necessary in generating a successful model of rational action. In any event, with the Thomistic case made, the onus now lies on the critics to propose a workable, rival rational-action theory—be it of less speculative teleology or of no teleology at all.

7.3 THE CHRISTIAN
WORLDVIEW'S EXPLANATORY POWER

Now, at last, we are finally in a position to appreciate the claim I made in the introduction, that this book's comparative analysis of rival conceptions of practical rationality also becomes the start of an inductive defense of Christianity. So near the close of the book, I do not want to rehash the full argument completely, so for evidence let me simply point out several critical, theoretical aspects in which Aquinas's view is superior to Hare's and Davidson's, and in which that superiority is owed to Aquinas's Christian worldview.

First, the comparison with Hare: His theory was of particular interest because he connected his model of rational action to a theory of objective morality. Considering him as a rational-action theorist, Hare's worst problems were (1) that he could not apply his standard of practical rationality and so could not explain weakness of will as a rational failing, except within the narrow bounds of moral actions, characterized as involving the interests of other people; (2) that he had to attribute weakness of will to faults in the agent's cognitive grasp of what ought to be done; and (3) that his measure of practical rationality, critical thinking, was effectively impossible in practice.

Aquinas also connected his rational-action model to a theory of objective morality. But by contrast, Aquinas did offer a practically workable measure of rationality in action, was able to characterize the weak-willed agent's cognition of what to do as complete, did apply his rational and moral measures to every intentional action, and was able to characterize any instance of incontinence as some kind of rational failure. Why? What made the crucial difference for Aquinas?

To my mind, the clear answer is that Aquinas utilized the explanatory resources of the Christian worldview, and Hare did not. Hare attempted to build his model of practical rationality and objective morality with no reference to anything speculative; he appealed to no metaphysical or religious perspectives on human nature. But it is exactly the Christian teleology and metaphysical psychology that allowed Aquinas to solve Hare's problems. Only from the ideas that our whole lives are owed to, and fulfilled, in God and therefore ought to be directed towards relationship with God does a truly comprehensive, combined rational and moral action-standard emerge. What other measure could possibly characterize every intentional action— even tiny, sheerly personal ones, like pausing to admire the lawnmowers in Sears—as possessing both moral and rational value, comparable to other action-options? None known to me. Moreover, the Christian conception of God's character, combined with God's commands from Christian revelation, yields a suitably practical standard for assessing rationality in action. To use that standard, we do not have to be critical thinking archangels, but only acquainted with God's character and His commands—and children can do that. Furthermore, it is Christianity's psychology of the will and the broken workings of fallen humanity that allow Aquinas to explain how incontinence is possible even when the agent's rational understanding is complete. As we saw in several instances, the view of humanity as, by nature, damaged, crucially aids the ability to explain the incontinent agent's psychology. Thus, over and over again, in accounting for incontinence—in this crucible of practical reason—Aquinas's model's ability to endure the fires that burned Hare's comes from Aquinas's Christian worldview.

Second, the comparison with Davidson: His view had the putative virtues of casting the whole spectrum of intentional action as essentially rational action and of characterizing incontinent actions, in any area, as rational failings with a common nature. Davidson also eschewed any metaphysically or religiously speculative elements from his system. Yet, as a rational-action theorist, Davidson suffered several catastrophic failures, the most foundational of them being (1) that his rational-action requirement collapsed into merely acting for a reason, rather than according to reason; and (2) that his theory still could not successfully account for robustly characterized incontinent actions as exemplifying intentional action.

We just saw, in the last section, that Davidson's failures stem largely from his lack of teleology. He could not move beyond merely acting for a reason because he had no substantive goal, no *telos* of human life, to appeal to in sifting the various reasons to act, in order to reach reason's verdict of what rationally ought to be done. Moreover, Davidson's nonteleological view construed intentionality as an all-or-nothing quality, the rigidity of which prevented him from being able to stretch the concept to cover incontinent actions with their faulty rationality. He had no room to conceive of intentionality as something human thought and action possessed in degrees. If, as several of his critics urged him to, Davidson had cast his rationality-requirement as an ideal for intentionality—something for human action to strive towards—he would have been able to describe the varying degrees of rationality exhibited in intentional acts, but would have severed rationality from being an essential element of intentional action. For in that case, an agent's motivation to perform an action and her rational evaluation of that action would no longer have any necessary connection; intentional action would no longer be, by nature, rational action, since less rational ones would be just as intentional as more rational ones, only not as ideal. That is, Davidson's nonteleological view forced him into a dilemma: on the one horn (his choice), he could cast the intentionality-rationality connection as essential and all-or-nothing, but fail to be able to account for incontinence as intentional; on the other horn (his critics' choice), he could cast the intentionality-rationality connection as an ideal to work towards by degrees, but have to allow that intentionality and rationality were no longer necessarily linked.

Again, the difference for Aquinas is the teleology drawn from his Christianity. Aquinas's understanding of fully rational action was not merely an ideal but a regulative norm for human, or intentional, action. Aquinas's norm came from his understanding of humanity-as-it-was-created-to-be, exemplified by Adam and Eve, pre-Fall, and by Christ. That teleological understanding allowed him to characterize defectively rational actions as also, and thereby, defectively human, or intentional. Our less-than-perfectly rational actions are truly human, or intentional, only to a degree. It is not that we act intentionally and have a goal of full rationality to aim at (as a Davidsonian ideal would have made it), but rather that we act humanly, and intentionally, only to the extent that we approach full rationality. The teleology of human nature allowed Aquinas to link the degree of rationality we exhibit to a degree of humanness and intentionality because the teleology posited rationality as essential to distinctively human and intentional action. Moreover, the Christian conception of fallen humanity once again helped to explain why we do not operate at optimal levels of rationality. And the degreed-conception of itentionality subsequently made it possible to stretch intentionality (in some degree) to cover even badly irrational, incontinent actions. In this way, yet again, Aquinas's Christian resources enabled his view of practical rationality to survive the fires that charred Davidson's.

Of course, this shows only that Aquinas's Christian position is explanatorily superior to Hare's and Davidson's theories, not that it is superior generally. But given the previous sections' sketches of comparisons to other possible, rival conceptions of practical rationality, we have reason to believe that the Thomistic superiority would still stand, and again attribute much of its success to its Christian components.

Now, let me stress that even if future comparisons work out as projected, I do not think that would prove that (something like) Aquinas's Christian view must be true. In all honesty, even as a Christian I do not regard Christianity (or any systematically comprehensive view) as capable of definitive proof (or disproof). However, I do think Christianity (and other comprehensive systems) can be made more (or less) plausible. And one factor very important to plausibility is a system's ability to account for significant elements and phenomena of human life. Intentional action and practical rationality are two such elements, and incontinence is one such phenomenon. Moreover those three intersect in a very puzzling way. As I have argued throughout this book, explaining incontinence serves as a trial by fire, as a crucible, for theories about practical rationality and intentional action.

When subjected to that trial, theories can emerge either as dross or as refined metal, perhaps golden, even. In the former case, the theory's plausibility is badly damaged by its inability to give a satisfactory explanation for these important aspects of human life; in the latter, the theory's plausibility may increase in two ways, first by virtue of the successful explanation it offers, and second, by virtue of its ability to adapt to initial explanatory failures so as to turn them into successes. The first virtue shows the view's present explanatory power, the second how much hope should be placed on the possibility of extending that explanatory power in the face of future problems.

Obviously, the crucible has badly charred both Hare's and Davidson's theories of rational action. Just as clearly, Aquinas's distinctively Christian rational-action theory has emerged intact and, I believe, stronger for the trial. Moreover, the ability that Aquinas's view displayed in adapting to changes—the alternative conceptions of practical knowledge and habit—demonstrates just the kind of flexible strength that would justifiably allow adherents to be optimistic about the theory's ability to survive future explanatory challenges, future crucibles.

That combination of explanatory power and flexibility gives Christianity, as spelled out in a Thomistic system, a sizeable boost in its plausibility, compared to rival systematic views. Certainly that is the case in comparison to Davidson's and Hare's views, and, quite frankly, I am confident it will continue to be the case in contests with other rivals; hence my claim that this book's analysis forms the start of an inductive argument for Christianity. However, the further defense of Aquinas's Christian worldview is for other books' investigations; this one's is done.

7.4 CLOSING PRACTICAL REMARKS

Before I close, though, I want to make a few remarks about the practical impact of weakness of will. After all, the reason I was initially drawn to this subject was not fascination with action theory, but frustration over my own mystifying, akratic actions. So aside from enlightenment concerning the how of incontinence, I desperately wanted helpful information concerning what to do about it.

On that second matter, Aquinas is actually quite useful, and even seems prescient, given the findings of our modern recovery industry. With his picture of habituation's effects in the passions, the body, the will and even reason, Aquinas offers an account of incontinence that links closely with our contemporary understanding of addiction—which is, after all, the paradigm of loss of self-control, of *akrasia*. Moreover, like twelve-step recovery programs, Aquinas holds that the incontinent agent needs outside help, and that ultimately none will do but God's.

It is true that, as a person who truly believes in and wants, to some extent, to follow reason's guidance, the weak-willed agent feels remorse and immediately "repents at once" of her action (Aquinas, *ST* II-II q.156, a.3, resp.). But her internal desire to change will not enable her to do so. That becomes particularly clear, given what we have seen of the power of will-habits, which incontinence frequently involves. Nor can education do the trick, for "knowledge does not suffice to cure the incontinent"—indeed, understanding what she ought to do was never the akratic's problem (q.156, a.3, rep.2). Further, outside advice will be of no real help since that cannot curb her passions (*DQV* q.1, a.6, rep.2).

Since she cannot recover alone, the incontinent agent needs physical and spiritual aid from others, the "application of the external remedy of admonishment and correction, which induce [her] to begin to resist [her] desires, so that concupiscence is weakened" (*ST* II-II q.156, a.3, rep.2). Further, while that helps, what she truly must have is "the inward assistance of [God's] grace which quenches concupiscence" (q.156, a.3, rep.2). For, "human reason cannot stand perfectly except to the extent that it is governed by [the Holy Spirit, who] . . . stirs up and turns the affections to right willing" (*EG* chp.5, lec.4). So although the encouragement and efforts of others can help the incontinent begin to change, only God's assistance can make that change stick, make it stable. Hundreds of years, then, before the existence of twelve-step groups, Aquinas prefigured their basic principles, writing, "We admitted we were powerless," and "Made a decision to turn our will and our lives over to the care of God." Chalk up another explanatory success for Aquinas.

Let me finish with one last Thomistic insight truly useful to me, personally. As a Christian, and therefore (supposedly) infused with God's grace, I found my weakness of will doubly confusing and frustrating. Why and how could that still be happening? People told me that if I were truly a Christian, things would not be that way (which was both unhelpful and depressing to me). Aquinas, on the other hand, writes,

> [O]ne who repents receives by grace charity and all the other virtues, but because of the *lingering dispositions* of [her] prior sins [she] *experiences difficulty in the performance of the virtues* which [she] has received. (Emphasis added; *DQV* q.2, a.2, rep.2)

That is, gaining the virtues through practice has the concomitant effect of breaking opposed habits and generally decreasing opposed passions; but gaining the virtues by entering Christ's grace "does *not* . . . at the same time remove contrary dispositions" (emphasis added; q.2, a.2, rep.2). Therefore, while grace initially may break the hopeless stranglehold of opposed habits, it still leaves behind "a certain disposition" that is only just shy of a full-strength habit (q.1, a.10, rep.16). Given that, obviously it is possible for Christians to suffer from *akrasia*, even seriously so. Knowing that could have spared me a lot a destructive self-doubt about my own Christianity! Such experiences also mean, though, that the incontinent Christian needs to seek further grace from, and accept further correction by, the Holy Spirit. And that definitely has been how it has worked for me.

However, the nature and pursuit of such correction are questions for another book, even a different kind of book. Indeed, at this point, all further questions and analyses I leave for another time. I believe I have given our investigation here as full a treatment as the parameters of this work will allow. For once, as far as I can tell, I have followed through and done what I believed I ought.

BIBLIOGRAPHY

Aristotle. *Nicomachean Ethics*. Translated by Terence Irwin. Cambridge, MA: Hackett, 1985.

Aquinas, St. Thomas. *Commentary on the Nicomachean Ethics*. Translated by C. I. Litzinger. Chicago: Regnery, 1964.

———. *Disputed Questions on Virtue*. Translated by Ralph McInerny. South Bend, IN.: St. Augustine's Press, 1999.

———. *Opera Omnia*. Vol. 20, *In Epistolam ad Romanos*. Paris: Vives, 1876, 377–602.

———. *On Evil*. Translated by Jean Oesterle. Notre Dame, IN: University of Notre Dame Press, 1995.

———. *On the Epistle to the Galatians*. Translated by F. R. Larcher, O.P. Aquinas Scripture Series 1. Albany, NY: Magi Books, 1995. CD ROM.

———. *Summa Theologica. Complete English Edition in Three Volumes*. Translated by the Fathers of the English Dominican Province. San Francisco: Benziger Brothers, Inc., 1947–1948.

———. *Treatise on Happiness (ST I–II qq.1–21)*. Translated by John A. Oesterle. Notre Dame, IN: University of Notre Dame Press, 1983.

———. *Treatise on Law (ST I–II qq.90–7)*. Washington, D.C.: Regnery Gateway, 1991.

———. *Treatise on the Virtues (ST I–II qq.49–67)*. Translated by John A. Oesterle. Notre Dame, IN: University of Notre Dame Press, 1984.

Audi, Robert. "Weakness of Will and Practical Judgment." *Nous* 13, no. 2 (1979): 173–96.

Augustine, St. *Augustine on Romans: Propositions from the Epistle to the Romans, Unfinished Commentary on the Epistle to the Romans*. Translated by Paula Fredriksen Landes. Chico, CA: Scholars Press, 1982.

———. *City of God*. Edited by Vernon J. Bourke. Translated by Gerald G. Walsh, S.J., et al. New York: Image Books, 1958.

———. *Confessions*. Translated by Henry Chadwick. New York: Oxford University Press, 1991.

————. *On Free Choice of the Will*. Translated by A. S. Benjamin and L. H. Hackstaff. New York: Macmillan, 1964.

Brandt, R. B. "Act-Utilitarianism and Metaethics." In *Hare and Critics: Essays on Moral Thinking*, edited by Douglas Seanor and N. Fotion, 27–41. New York : Oxford University Press, 1988.

Bratman, Michael. "Practical Reasoning and Weakness of the Will." *Nous* 13, no. 2 (1979): 153–71.

Broadie, Sarah. *Ethics with Aristotle*. New York: Oxford University Press, 1991.

Cavell, Marcia. "Dividing the Self." In *Language, Mind, and Epistemology: On Donald Davidson's Philosophy*, edited by G. Preyer et al., 299–311. Boston: Kluwer Academic Publishers, 1994.

Charles, David. *Aristotle's Philosophy of Action*. Ithaca, NY: Cornell University Press, 1984.

Dahl, Norman O. *Practical Reason, Aristotle, and Weakness of the Will*. Minneapolis: University of Minnesota Press, 1984.

Davidson, Donald. "Deception and Division." In *The Multiple Self*, edited by Jon Elster, 79–92. New York: Cambridge University Press, 1986.

————. *Essays on Actions and Events*. New York: Oxford University Press, 1980.

————. "Expressing Evaluations." The Lindley Lecture, University of Kansas, Lawrence, KS, April 22, 1982.

————. *Inquiries into Truth and Interpretation*. New York: Oxford University Press, 1984.

————. "Paradoxes of Irrationality." In *Philosophical Essays on Freud*, edited by Richard Wollheim and James Hopkins, 289–305. New York: Cambridge University Press, 1982.

————. "Replies to Essays I–IX." In *Essays on Davidson: Actions and Events*, edited by B. Vermazen and M. B. Hintikka, 195–229. New York: Oxford University Press, 1985.

————. "Reply to Peter Lanz." In *Reflecting Davidson*, edited by Ralf Stoecker, 302–3. New York: de Gruyter, 1993.

————. "Reply to Ralf Stoecker." In *Reflecting Davidson*, edited by Ralf Stoecker, 287–90. New York: de Gruyter, 1993.

————. "Reply to Thomas Spitzley." In *Reflecting Davidson*, edited by Ralf Stoecker, 330–32. New York: de Gruyter, 1993.

Descartes, René. *Meditations on First Philosophy*. Translated by Donald A. Cress. Cambridge, MA: Hackett, 1979.

Donagan, Alan. "Consistency in Rationalist Moral Systems." *Journal of Philosophy* 81 (1984): 291–309.

————. "Thomas Aquinas on Human Action." In *The Cambridge History of Later Medieval Philosophy: From the Rediscovery of Aristotle to the Disintegration of Scholasticism, 1100–1600,* edited by Norman Kretzmann et al., 642–54. Cambridge: Cambridge University Press, 1982.

Driscoll, Rev. John A., O.P. "On Human Acts." *Summa Theologica*. Vol. 3. San Francisco: Benziger Brothers, Inc., 1948, 3,201–19.

Evnine, Simon. *Donald Davidson*. Palo Alto, CA: Stanford University Press, 1991.

Frankfurt, Harry G. *The Importance of What We Care About*. New York: Cambridge University Press, 1988.

Grice, Paul, and Judith Baker. "Davidson on Weakness of the Will." In *Essays on Davidson: Actions and Events*, edited by B. Vermazen and M. B. Hintikka, 27–49. New York: Oxford University Press, 1985.

Hare, R. M. "Comments." In *Hare and Critics: Essays on Moral Thinking*, edited by Douglas Seanor and N. Fotion, 199–293. New York: Oxford University Press, 1988.

———. *Essays in Ethical Theory*. New York: Oxford University Press, 1989.

———. *Freedom and Reason*. New York: Oxford University Press, 1963.

———. *Moral Thinking*. New York: Oxford University Press, 1981.

———. "Weakness of Will." In *Encyclopedia of Ethics*, edited by Lawrence C. Becker and Charlotte B. Becker, 1304–7. Vol. 2. New York: Garland, 1992.

Johnston, Mark. "Self-Deception and the Nature of the Mind." In *Perspectives on Self-Deception*. Edited by B. P. McLaughlin and A. O. Rorty, 63–91. Berkeley and Los Angeles: University of California Press, 1988.

Kant, Immanuel. *Grounding for the Metaphysics of Morals*. Translated by James W. Ellington. 3rd ed. Cambridge, MA: Hackett, 1993.

Kenny, Anthony. *Aristotle's Theory of the Will*. New Haven: Yale University Press, 1979.

Kretzmann, Norman. "Warring against the Law of My Mind: Aquinas on Romans 7." In *Philosophy and the Christian Faith*, edited by Thomas V. Morris, 172–95. Notre Dame, IN: University of Notre Dame Press, 1988.

Lalor, Rev. Juvenal, O.F.M. "The Passions." *Summa Theologica*. Vol. 3. San Francisco: Benziger Brothers, Inc., 1948, 3,220–35.

Lanz, Peter. "The Explanatory Force of Action Explanations." In *Reflecting Davidson*, edited by Ralf Stoecker, 291–301. New York: de Gruyter, 1993.

MacIntyre, Alasdair. *After Virtue*. 2nd ed. Notre Dame, IN: University of Notre Dame Press, 1984.

———. *Whose Justice? Which Rationality?* Notre Dame, IN: University of Notre Dame Press, 1988.

Mathews, Gareth B. "It Is No Longer I That Do It." *Faith and Philosophy* 1, no. 1 (January 1984): 44–49.

McInerny, Ralph. *Aquinas on Human Action: A Theory of Practice*. Washington, D.C.: Catholic University of America Press, 1992.

McLaughlin, Brian P., and A. O. Rorty, eds. *Perspectives on Self-Deception*. Berkeley and Los Angeles: University of California Press, 1988.

Mele, Alfred. *Irrationality: An Essay on Akrasia, Self-Deception, and Self-Control*. New York: Oxford University Press, 1987.

Nagel, Thomas. "The Foundations of Impartiality." In *Hare and Critics: Essays on Moral Thinking*, edited by Douglas Seanor and N. Fotion, 101–12. New York : Oxford University Press, 1988.

Peacocke, Christopher. "Intention and *Akrasia*." In *Essays on Davidson: Actions and Events*, edited by B. Vermazen and M. B. Hintikka, 51–73. New York: Oxford University Press, 1985.

Pears, David. "The Goals and Strategies of Self-Deception." In *The Multiple Self*, edited by Jon Elster, 59–77. New York: Cambridge University Press, 1986.

———. *Motivated Irrationality*. New York: Oxford University Press, 1984.

———. "Motivated Irrationality, Freudian Theory, and Cognitive Dissonance." In *Philosophical Essays on Freud*, edited by Richard Wollheim and James Hopkins, 264–88. New York: Cambridge University Press, 1982.

Plato. *Republic*. Translated by G. M. A. Grube and C. D. C. Reeve. Rev. ed. Cambridge, MA: Hackett, 1992.

Robinson, Richard. "Aristotle and *Akrasia*." In *Articles on Aristotle*, edited by J. Barnes, M. Schofield, and R. Sorabji, 79–91. Vol. 2. London: Duckworth, 1977.

Rorty, Amelie O. "*Akrasia* and Pleasure: *Nicomachean Ethics* Book 7." In *Essays on Aristotle's Ethics*, edited by A. O. Rorty, 267–84. Berkeley and Los Angeles: University of California Press, 1980.

———. *Mind in Action: Essays in the Philosophy of Mind*. Boston: Beacon Press, 1988.

Seanor, Douglas, and N. Fotion, eds. *Hare and Critics: Essays on Moral Thinking*. New York: Oxford University Press, 1988.

Spitzley, Thomas. "Evaluative Judgements." In *Reflecting Davidson*, edited by Ralf Stoecker, 315–29. New York: de Gruyter, 1993.

Stoecker, Ralf. "Reasons, Actions, and Their Relationship." In *Reflecting Davidson*, edited by Ralf Stoecker, 265–86. New York: de Gruyter, 1993.

———, ed. *Reflecting Davidson*. New York: de Gruyter, 1993.

Stump, Eleonore, and Norman Kretzmann. "Absolute Simplicity." *Faith and Philosophy* 2, no. 4 (October 1985): 353–82.

Taylor, C. C. W. "Plato, Hare, and Davidson on *Akrasia*." *Mind* 89 (1980): 499–518.

Urmson, J. O. "Hare on Intuitive Moral Thinking." In *Hare and Critics: Essays on Moral Thinking,* edited by Douglas Seanor and N. Fotion, 161–69. New York : Oxford University Press, 1988.

Vendler, Zeno. "Changing Places?" In *Hare and Critics: Essays on Moral Thinking,* edited by Douglas Seanor and N. Fotion, 171–83. New York: Oxford University Press, 1988.

Watson, Gary. "Skepticism about Weakness of Will." *Philosophical Review* 86 (1977): 316–39.

Wiggins, David. "Weakness of Will, Commensurability, and the Objects of Deliberation and Desire." In *Essays on Aristotle's Ethics*, edited by A. O. Rorty, 241–65. Berkeley and Los Angeles: University of California Press, 1980.

Williams, Bernard. "The Structure of Hare's Theory." In *Hare and Critics: Essays on Moral Thinking,* edited by Douglas Seanor and N. Fotion, 185–96. New York: Oxford University Press, 1988.

Wyma, Keith D. "Moral Responsibility and Leeway for Action." *American Philosophical Quarterly* 34, no. 1 (1997): 57–70.

INDEX

ABOUT THE AUTHOR

Keith Wyma is associate professor of philosophy at Whitworth College in Spokane, Washington. Specializing in ethics and action theory, he earned his Ph.D. in philosophy from the University of Notre Dame in 1997. His research areas include virtue ethics and moral responsibility. Prior publications include articles in *American Philosophical Quarterly* and a book, edited by Peter van Inwagen, on the problem of evil (forthcoming). He is currently working on a book on virtue ethics in the Wall Street professions (Rowman & Littlefield, forthcoming). In addition to teaching ethics for the philosophy and religion departments at Whitworth, he cochairs a campus-wide required interdisciplinary course on applied ethics and public policy.